OLD TESTAMENT
Chapter By Chapter

VOLUME ONE
Genesis - Esther

DANIEL GOEPFRICH

Copyright © 2022, Daniel F. Goepfrich

Old Testament Chapter by Chapter, Volume One
by Daniel Goepfrich

www.DanielGoepfrich.com

www.TheologyIsForEveryone.com

Printed in the United States of America

All rights reserved solely by the author. The author guarantees all contents are original and do not infringe upon the legal rights of any other person or work. No part of this book may be reproduced in any form without the permission of the author.

Scripture quoted by permission. Unless otherwise designated, all Scripture quotations are from the NET Bible® copyright © 1996, 2019 by Biblical Studies Press, L. L. C. http://netbible.com All rights reserved. All italic and bold-type emphasis has been added by the author.

ISBN: 978-1-945774-78-2

Trust House Publishers
P.O.Box 3181
Taos, NM 87571

www.trusthousepublishers.com

Ordering Information: Special discounts are available on quantity purchases by churches, associations, and retailers. For details, contact the publisher at the address above or call toll-free 1-844-321-4202.

1   2 3 4 5 6 7 8 9

For all who love the Scriptures
and desire a faithful and accurate interpretation
so they can know the Savior better and love Him more.

Table of Contents

Preface 1

Introduction to the Old Testament 5

Genesis 9

Exodus 81

Leviticus 127

Numbers 155

Deuteronomy 185

Joshua 219

Judges 241

Ruth 261

1 Samuel 267

2 Samuel 297

1 Kings 321

2 Kings 345

1 Chronicles 371

2 Chronicles 391

Ezra 417

Nehemiah 427

Esther 439

Preface

These books (volumes one and two) and their companion book on the New Testament (published in 2017) were born out of the desire to help Christians build confidence in their knowledge of the Bible. The best way to use them is to read the Bible passage first, followed by the corresponding chapter in this book. I hope to give benefit to the most people possible by writing with several types of readers in mind.

Four types of readers

Some readers may want an overview of the entire Old Testament, so each book begins with an introduction which may include information on the author, the recipients, or the historical situation surrounding the book which prompted its writing. Together these introductions provide a brief survey of the entire Old Testament.

Other readers want a short, simple summary of an individual chapter to supplement their Bible reading or study. They will find the notes to be succinct yet full of principles and applications.

Certain readers may desire insight on some of the more difficult passages without going into as much detail as a full exegetical commentary does. I have attempted to address these passages by at least mentioning, if not explaining, some of the more prominent views offered by other scholars. The footnotes often contain more information for those who want to study further.

Finally, although this is not a technical commentary, some readers will appreciate where I have included advanced terminology and information. This is often related to passages where the Hebrew language of the Old Testament is indispensable for proper interpretation. Again, the footnotes often contain additional information to assist with this type of study.

Basic theological positions

The notes and interpretation come from a worldview that embraces these key foundational truths:

1. God meant the Bible to be understood and interpreted in its plain, natural sense within the original languages and context in which he gave it. The Bible is a unique work that, as God's very Word, has final authority over every area of faith and life.

2. God has worked with his creation in various ways with various people groups over the centuries and has given his revelation cumulatively, so we must carefully interpret every passage of Scripture considering those differences.

3. God has two chosen people groups—Israel and the Church—which are distinct in every way, including their beginning, present relationship with God, and their future. The two are not to be conflated or confused in any way.

4. Just as past prophecy was fulfilled literally, future prophecy will also be fulfilled literally, including a seven-year Tribulation on the earth, which will be preceded by Jesus removing the Church to be with him in Heaven and followed by Jesus' literal, physical reign on the earth from Jerusalem.

5. Jesus' death and resurrection are the only terms by which any man, woman, or child can be made right with God. Any individual who attempts to earn God's free gift of salvation or utterly refuses it will be separated from God for eternity. Those who embrace God's terms for the forgiveness of their sin will spend eternity with him.

Special notes about this book

God's name

There is an ongoing debate about how to write/pronounce God's name. Most of the time (but not always), the Hebrew text contains only the four letters YHVH (or YHWH). Converting the "Y" to a "J" in English (neither Hebrew nor Greek have the letter "j") and using the vowels for the Hebrew word for "lord" (*'adonai*), most people have come to know God's name as "Jehovah." To more accurately reflect the Hebrew name, throughout this book I have transliterated God's name "Yehovah," using the "Y" rather than the traditional "J." Other Hebrew names (such as Joshua, Josiah, etc.) have retained their traditional spelling.

Constable's Notes

The commentary quoted most often throughout the book is by Dr. Thomas Constable. There are two reasons for this. First, his *Notes* contain the depth and breadth of a long-time scholar. He is well-read and quotes liberally from many others to explain, support, or negate a point. Second, Dr. Constable has made his *Notes* on every book of the Bible available online for free, updating them every year. At the time of this book's publication, you can access them at https://planobiblechapel.org/constable-notes-html/.

"Digging Deeper"

There are three standalone articles entitled "Digging Deeper" included in this book. These articles address the following topics in a little more detail than the chapter notes: "The Abrahamic Covenant" (found in Genesis 12), "The Mosaic Covenant" (Exodus 19), and "Is God a Genocidal Murderer?" (Deuteronomy 7). More articles like these plus a different look at the Old Testament books are available in a free ebook from Theology is for Everyone (theologyisforeveryone.com).

Date abbreviations

It is common in modern works to refer to dates by BCE (Before Common Era) and CE (Common Era). Since this book is inherently related to the Bible, it seemed best to keep the traditional abbreviations BC (Before Christ) and AD (*Anno Domini*, Latin for "the year of our Lord"). There is no difference to the dates regardless of whether a person uses BC/AD or BCE/CE.

Charles Ryrie once wrote, "Everyone is a theologian—of one sort or another." No matter what type or level of theologian you think you are, I hope you will find this book beneficial in your Bible study and spiritual growth. For further discussion or to ask specific questions about a passage or topic, please join our Facebook group, "Theology is For Everyone" (facebook.com/theologyisforeveryone), or visit theologyisforeveryone.com for additional resources.

Acknowledgements

Many people contributed to this book with their questions and suggestions, but I owe a great deal of gratitude to my wife, Saralynn, for her involvement in helping prepare this book. She read the entire manuscript at least twice and some sections multiple times. Her input is always invaluable in bringing clarity and corrections that I would have otherwise missed. Any errors or confusing statements are solely mine.

Introduction to the Old Testament

The Old Testament is a fascinating collection of 39 individual writings—narrative books, poetry, wisdom, and prophecy. Many of them have two or more of these styles throughout.

Categories and Order

Some of the original Hebrew books were combined, resulting in only 24 listed in the Jews' table of contents. The combinations were 1–2 Samuel, 1–2 Kings, 1–2 Chronicles, Ezra–Nehemiah, and "The Twelve" minor prophets. By the time of Jesus, these 24 books were categorized into three sections and in a different order than they are in our Bibles today. (This is still true in modern printed editions of the Hebrew Bible.)

The first section is the *Torah* (Hebrew for "law") which contained the five books of Moses in their still-common order: Genesis, Exodus, Leviticus, Numbers, and Deuteronomy. The second section is the *Nevi'im* (Hebrew for "prophets"). These are subdivided into the "Former Prophets" (Joshua, Judges, 1–2 Samuel, and 1–2 Kings) and the "Later Prophets" (Isaiah, Jeremiah, Ezekiel, and The Twelve). The third section, the *Ketuvim* (Hebrew for "writings") contained the final eleven books: Psalms, Job, Proverbs, Ruth, Song of Songs, Ecclesiastes, Lamentations, Esther, Daniel, Ezra–Nehemiah, and 1–2 Chronicles. There are at least three interesting observations we can make about these sections.

1. The first three letters of the names of these three sections provide the abbreviation T-N-K, pronounced *tanak*, which is commonly used as the "name" of the Hebrew Bible (often spelled *Tanakh*).

2. Although Daniel is considered by church scholars (and Jesus, Matthew 24:15) to be one of the great Hebrew prophets, the ancient rabbis did not. They recognized that his visions came through God's Spirit but did not think they rose to the level of prophecy, so his book is listed with the "writings" rather than the "prophets" as in Christian Bibles.

3. These three sections go by different names in the New Testament. The *Torah* is sometimes called "the book(s) of Moses" (Mark 12:26) or "the law of Moses" (Luke 24:44). The entire *Nevi'im* may be categorized under "Isaiah," even when another prophet spoke or wrote the words (Mark 1:2). The *Ketuvim* was referred to by its first and prominent writing: the Psalms (Luke 24:44). In fact, in Luke 24:44, Jesus referred to the entire *Tanakh* when he told the apostles, "EVERYTHING WRITTEN ABOUT ME IN THE LAW OF MOSES AND THE PROPHETS AND THE PSALMS MUST BE FULFILLED." This is significant because many additional books had been written in the intervening 400 years since Nehemiah and Malachi were completed, but the Jewish people never considered them to be part of Scripture, and Jesus authorized only the 24 books of the *Tanakh* (all 39 modern divisions) as God's inspired text.

Old Testament Chronology

While most of the Old Testament books contain history, only eleven truly advance the Old Testament story's chronological timeline. These are Genesis, Exodus, Numbers, Joshua, Judges, 1–2 Samuel, 1–2 Kings, Ezra, and Nehemiah.

The other 28 books can be divided into two main groups. Six provide "color commentary" to the main eleven, i.e., they give additional detail about the story without advancing it (Leviticus, Deuteronomy, Ruth, 1–2 Chronicles, and Esther). The other 22 books give incidental information that fits within the overarching story. Six of these are primarily poetic (Job, Psalms, Proverbs, Ecclesiastes, Song of Solomon, and Lamentations); the rest are prophetic (Isaiah, Jeremiah, Ezekiel, Daniel, and the Twelve). More detail about Old Testament chronology is available in the ebook, "The Story of the Old Testament" from Theology is for Everyone (theologyisforeveryone.com).

Languages and Locations

Most of the Old Testament was written in Ancient (or "Biblical") Hebrew. However, two major sections (and a few other verses) were composed in Aramaic (sometimes called "Chaldean"). During the 7th and 8th centuries BC, Aramaic was the diplomatic and scholarly language in Babylon and Persia, so it is not surprising that we would find Aramaic in two books written during that time. The book of Daniel begins and ends in Hebrew, but 2:4b–7:28, the section that focuses on Gentile world history, was written in the language of the Gentiles. The second major passages in Aramaic are Ezra 4:8–6:18 and 7:12–26 which contain the transcription of letters and memos to and from Gentile world leaders.

Most of the Old Testament was written within the borders of ancient Israel, but other locations include the Arabian desert and modern-day Iraq and Iran (ancient Babylonia and Persia, respectively).

Although we do not know exactly how many people God used to compose the Old Testament, we can name at least 30 different men who contributed to these Scriptures, spanning approximately 1,000 years (*c.* 1400–400 BC).

However, no matter the style, language, category, or immediate subject matter, we can say that the Old Testament is primarily the story of God and people—not just any or all people, but a special people: Israel, the people of God.

Genesis

Genesis has the privilege of being the first book of the Bible. Its first word is also its title in Hebrew (בְּרֵאשִׁית, b^ereshith) and means "in the beginning." The English title is from the Septuagint[1] (γενεσις, genesis), which also means "beginning" or "generation." In Genesis, we find the story of the beginning of all things. Among these things, Genesis specifically records the beginning of the created universe, humanity, sin, nations and languages, and the nation of Israel. In Genesis, we also find the introduction to how God would deal with sin, the beginning and end of the first dispensation, and the commencement of three more dispensations that are still influencing the world today.[2]

Although there is no name attached to this book to identify the writer, Jewish history has consistently assigned Genesis through Deuteronomy[3] to

---

[1] The Greek translation of the Old Testament produced around 150 BC and often abbreviated "LXX."

[2] Charles Ryrie defined a dispensation as "a distinguishable economy in the outworking of God's purpose." In other words, a dispensation is just how God rules this world in different ways at different times. A new dispensation begins whenever God adjusts His dealings with mankind, often by way of providing new revelation. (Quote from Charles C. Ryrie, *Dispensationalism, Revised and Expanded* [Moody Publishers, 2007], 33.)

I have written at length on the various dispensations in chapter three of the book *What is Dispensationalism?* (Grace Abroad Ministries, 2019).

[3] These five are often called the *Pentateuch* (which means "five scrolls" in Greek) or the *Torah* ("law" in Hebrew) and stand together as the first five books of the Hebrew Scriptures.

Moses, who probably wrote during the 40 years of Israel's desert wandering.[4] Jesus repeatedly agreed with this understanding, often quoting Moses by name, most significantly in Luke 24:44 when he invoked the three traditional divisions of the Hebrew Scriptures—"THE LAW OF MOSES AND THE PROPHETS AND THE PSALMS"—which refer to the 39 books (and only those books) commonly called the "Old Testament."[5]

The first eleven chapters of Genesis have been attacked for centuries by those who reject a normal, literal interpretation of the Bible. Because at least 2,000 years of history are packed into these few pages, the detail is naturally limited, which bothers people because of the impact of the major events in this section—creation, the Flood, and the tower of Babel. In reality, these chapters refute every evolutionary view concerning beginnings, geological findings, and human development. Unfortunately, even many Christians have chosen to pit "science against Scripture" and consider the sacred text as inferior to personal experience, rejecting the Bible as God's inerrant Word and absolute truth. This has caused an immeasurably destructive impact against both true science and Christianity in all civilized nations.

Genesis can be outlined easily using two sets of natural divisions in the text. One outline follows the six key persons—Adam (ch. 1–5), Noah (ch. 6–11), Abraham (ch. 12–24), Isaac (ch. 25–27), Jacob (ch. 28–36), and Joseph (ch. 37–50). The second comes from the Hebrew word תוֹלְדוֹת (*toledoth*), which means "generations." Whereas the "key person outline" focuses primarily on the human race as it narrowed down to Israel (the main focus of the Old Testament), the "*toledoth* outline" is much broader, telling the story of creation and all families of humanity—creation (2:4); Adam (5:1); Noah (6:9); Noah's sons—Shem, Ham, Japheth (10:1, 32); Shem (11:10); Terah, Abraham's father (11:27); Ishmael (25:12); Isaac (25:19); Esau (36:1, 9); and

---

[4] Although Moses could have written Genesis during his previous 40 years as a desert shepherd, the events of the other books did not occur until after that time.

[5] The Roman Catholic Church adds several other writings to their Old Testament which have never been included in the Hebrew Scriptures or recognized as inspired Scripture outside of the Catholic Church.

Jacob (37:2).[6] The best study of Genesis probably includes both outlines, acknowledging their respective emphases.

Chapter one tells of the beginning of all created things. Even a casual reading of this chapter leaves the reader with the impression that an uncreated God made everything in the earth and universe out of nothing and within a timeframe of six days (as understood in the modern experience of a literal day). Nothing in the text brings this into question; on the contrary, the repeated phrase "EVENING AND MORNING" confirms it. Additionally, as the reader continues into Exodus and reaches Exodus 20:8–11, this interpretation is substantiated and strengthened.

Unfortunately, this approach has been rejected, not only by secular, evolutionary scientists but also by believers who otherwise claim to uphold the authority of the Scriptures. Three other theories are usually offered to contradict the "original, 24-hour day creation" teaching. The first attacks the concept of "original," insisting that there must have been a gap between Genesis 1:1 and 1:2. Thus, it is called the "Gap Theory." Depending on which view is being considered, this gap could have been any length of time (even billions of years) that took place after the "original" creation (including angels or even a pre-Adamic race of people). This gap is usually thought to contain disastrous events like Satan's fall and a first (unrecorded) judgment on the earth, which brought it to the "chaotic" state found in 1:2. The majority of Genesis 1, then, records the "recreation" of the earth as we observe it now.

The second view attacks the concept of the days as being literal, 24-hour days. Often called the "Day-Age Theory," its proponents attempt to fit the evolutionary ages into the creation account by reading each of the six "days" as geological ages, each one lasting for millions or billions of years. This would allow the time necessary for the evolutionary timeline, which begins in the water and culminates in the most recent age with humans.

The third view is based on the "Day-Age Theory" but attempts to minimize its obvious flaw: Genesis clearly says that God declared himself to be

---

[6] These ten "generations" are the only occurrences of *toledoth* in Genesis.

the Creator. This has led to a hybrid of evolution and creation called "Theistic Evolution,"[7] which maintains all of the tenants of the "Day-Age Theory" with one small change—Theistic Evolution teaches that God guided the evolutionary process. This allows God to be the Creator while bowing to the secular "science" that claims billions of years of adaptation as the source of creation.[8]

Against these theories, there is much to commend the natural reading of the text. In 1:1–2, God created an expanse of space containing a formless, watery mass that he would proceed to turn into the perfect environment for his prize creation—humanity. Over the first three days, he <u>prepared</u> this space—first creating energy and light (vs. 3–5), then providing a protective atmosphere around the planet (vs. 6–8), and finally creating dry ground and vegetation for future land creatures (vs. 9–13). During the second set of three days, he <u>populated</u> the three areas previously mentioned—celestial bodies in the universe (vs. 14–19), creatures designed for water and air (vs. 20–23), and, finally, creatures designed for land (vs. 24–25), culminating with humans (vs. 26–30). Except for the land animals, birds, and humans, God's method of creation was simply to speak things into immediate existence. The humans were commissioned to rule God's creation with God's authority by reproducing and filling it up with their descendants. At the end of this creative week, God surveyed "ALL THAT HE HAD MADE" and declared it to be exceedingly good (vs. 31).

Chapter two is often charged with containing a second creation account that conflicts with chapter one. However, the first three verses conclude

---

[7] Theistic Evolution should not be confused with "Intelligent Design" (ID). Whereas Theistic Evolution requires God to use evolution to create all things, ID does not require God at all. Many atheists agree with ID teachings and believe that Nature is the "intelligence" behind its own creation. ID is <u>not</u> the same as Biblical Creationism.

[8] However, it still ignores the specific phrase "after its kind," which is repeated throughout the account. This phrase refutes any kind of evolution (whether by God or random adaptation) that requires one kind to change into another.

chapter one's account, declaring that "EVERYTHING" in heaven and earth was complete. The Hebrew text uses the phrase "and all their host" in verse one. When used of heaven, "host" often means angels as well as celestial bodies, signifying that the angels were created during this time as well.[9] Rather than introducing a new creation account, the *toledoth*[10] in verse four emphasizes that this one account includes all the "generations" of creation; there is nothing in creation that is not a part of this record.

Beginning with verse five, Moses recorded a more detailed explanation about what happened on the sixth day, especially regarding the creation of humanity. Whereas 1:26–27 states only that God created humans as male and female in the image of God,[11] chapter two explains how that took place. Although God prepared everything during the creation week, it was not until the man was created to cultivate it that the growth of the plant world took off (vs. 5–6). Rather than creating humans with just his word, God formed the first man out of the earth. The name "Adam" (*'adam*, Hebrew for "man") is just a shortened form of the Hebrew word for "ground" (*'adamah*). This "man" was an inanimate object (like a statue) until God breathed into him "THE BREATH OF LIFE,"[12] causing him to live (vs. 7).

---

[9] Since "THE SONS OF GOD" were present and rejoicing when God "LAID THE FOUNDATION OF THE EARTH" (Job 38:4–7), there is credibility to recognizing they were created before Genesis 1:2. This, however, does not require a "gap," if 1:1 is viewed as a summary statement of the whole story rather than a chronological event that occurred before 1:2.

[10] See the introduction for the explanation of the *toledoth* structure of Genesis.

[11] Interestingly, the Old Testament almost completely ignores the image of God concept (except in Genesis 9:6). It is not until the New Testament, where we find that the full image can begin to be restored in Christians and that we discover just how far-reaching the effects of sin are, especially in relation to the image of God in humanity.

[12] There is some significance to the fact that the word translated "life" is plural in Hebrew ("breath of lives"). Some have taken this to indicate both the animating life (that animals have) and the spiritual life / image of God (that separates man from animal). This spiritual life is what was damaged by sin and can be restored only through Christ (1 Corinthians 2:14; 15:46; Ephesians 4:24; Colossians 3:10).

To this man, God gave a garden or orchard as a special place to fellowship with God while he worked with his hands in God's creation (vs. 8–15). In this environment of perfect fellowship and productivity, God issued only one command: the man was not to eat from a specific tree in that orchard (vs. 16–17). The result would be instantaneous death, defined as the separation of the man from God, broken fellowship. Sometimes this is called the "Edenic Covenant," as if it were a covenant that God made with Adam.[13] However, nothing in the text leads to that conclusion. There is no covenantal language here; it was simply a law that God placed over man.

The primary reason some give for considering this to be a conflicting creation account with chapter one is that it looks as if animals were created after the man in chapter two, whereas God created them before the man in chapter one. The best explanation is to read "FORMED" in verse 19 to refer to the previous act ("had formed") rather than a new creative act. This is common in Hebrew and signifies that, even though God had already made them, he was now officially placing them under Adam's authority. The mention of the animals at this point is a minor note in the overall story of man's creation.

In bringing the animals to Adam for naming, God accomplished two things (vs. 18–20). First, he promoted Adam's authority over creation. Rather than naming them himself and presenting them to Adam (as he had named the major parts of creation in chapter one), God gave Adam both the privilege and responsibility to name them as he desired. Second, to foster a loneliness that could be solved only through human relationships, this display revealed to Adam that there was nothing like him yet in creation to pair with like the animals were. Thus, when God created and presented the woman to him, she filled the gap he had already felt, and he received her as God's gift.[14]

God created the woman from Adam's flesh and bone, part of the same kind of flesh so they could procreate "after their kind" just like the rest of creation

---

[13] Those who hold to a Reformed or Covenant Theological system would call this a "covenant of works."

[14] There is a great principle here that loneliness is not a sin. It is a God-designed emotional response to our human need for companionship. How we attempt to relieve that loneliness can be sinful, but the feeling itself is not.

(vs. 20–23). The last two verses contain Moses' notes explaining that this creative event set the tone for two things (vs. 24–25). First, one man and one woman was the God-designed pattern for human marriage. Both Jesus (Matthew 19:4–6) and Paul (1 Timothy 2:13; 1 Corinthians 11:8–9) quoted this passage to support this as the biblical pattern for marriage and the ongoing relationship between men and women, even after sin. Second, the fact that they were "NAKED, BUT...NOT ASHAMED" again indicates the perfect relationship and environment that God had designed for humanity.

Chapter three records the account of sin's entrance into humanity and its consequences. The fourth main character in this story—after God, the man, and the woman—is now introduced. The Hebrew word נָחָשׁ (*nachash*) does not strictly mean "snake," although it often refers to snakes. It more broadly refers to any kind of "serpent," including dragons, sea serpents, and sea monsters (see Isaiah 27:1 and Amos 9:3).[15]

The identity of this serpent has caused a great deal of debate and speculation. Although Genesis does not give much detail here, centuries later, the Apostle John would identify this "ancient serpent" as Satan, also calling him "the dragon" (Revelation 12:9; 20:2). If one holds to Ezekiel 28:11–19 as a description of Satan the cherub before and at his fall and one realizes that cherubim can look like animals (Ezekiel 1; 10:15; possibly Revelation 4:6–8), then it may be possible to understand the "serpent" as Satan's natural form. This may also help explain why Adam and Eve showed no concern about talking with the *nachash* or that it could talk with them.[16] What we do know is that they knew it and talked with it and that it looked like the other serpents God made.

There are three main sections to this chapter. In the first section, the serpent and the woman discussed God's law (vs. 1–7). He questioned the law itself, causing her to become confused. Then he denied what God had said ("YOU

---

[15] Interestingly, the companion verb means "to see by divination," a usage from ancient sorcery (Genesis 30:27; 44:5, 15; Leviticus 19:26, *et al.*).

[16] There is a great deal of speculation surrounding this, but most scholars have more questions than answers.

WILL SURELY DIE," 2:17; **"SURELY YOU WILL NOT DIE,"** 3:4). Finally, he added false information, slandering God's reputation and fully deceiving her into thinking that it was acceptable to disobey God (see 1 Timothy 2:14). Taking some of the fruit, she ate it and **"GAVE SOME OF IT TO HER HUSBAND WHO WAS WITH HER, AND HE ATE IT"** (vs. 6).[17]

The second section reveals the outcome of their decision to eat, namely the resulting curses and consequences (vs. 8–19). The immediate change was that **"THE EYES OF BOTH OF THEM OPENED,"** revealing their nakedness, both physical and spiritual, which brought a new sense of shame (vs. 7). They tried to cover that with leaves, but hearing God coming after them through the orchard, they hid in terror.[18] His interrogation lasted only a few minutes, but it revealed the guilt of both the humans and the *nachash*. In response, God announced consequences for each of them. Serpents would be confined to the ground,[19] and the Serpent Cherub would fight a losing war with a specific, future Man (vs. 14–15).[20] Women would see an increase in pregnancy and labor pains, and there would be a new conflict with their husbands for control in the home, with some men choosing to rule their women harshly (vs. 16). Men would be

---

[17] There is a common misconception that Adam knew nothing about this until Eve came up and handed him the fruit. The fact that he **"WAS WITH HER"** is both practically and theologically significant.

[18] Although the traditional understanding is that God had come to meet with them for a regular evening walk, some scholars have noted that the sound of God moving in this passage may refer to his coming in a thunderous judgment scene. See Jeffery Niehaus' explanation of this theory in *God at Sinai: Covenant and Theophany in the Bible and Ancient Near East* (Grand Rapids: Zondervan, 1995) and Douglas Stuart's review of this position in *Bibliotheca Sacra* 171:683 (July 2014), "'The Cool of the Day' (Gen. 3:8) and 'the Way He Should Go' (Prov. 22:6)".

[19] This is often used to explain why snakes do not have legs, but it could include a loss of flying capability as well.

[20] That this Human is called "her offspring" (or "seed of the woman") is often seen as a foreshadowing (not a direct prophecy) of Mary's virgin conception of Jesus. He was from a woman only, not a man and a woman.

required to do hard work to provide food because the ground has been cursed.[21] Physical death would now also affect all people (vs. 17–19).

The third section concludes the judgment of the humans (vs. 20–24). Exerting his authority again, the man named the woman "Eve," from the Hebrew verb "to live."[22] God killed an animal to provide a better covering for the humans than fig leaves, then expelled them from the orchard. The reason for this was that the orchard (which housed the tree of life) was their meeting place with God. Now that they had sinned and broken fellowship, they were no longer allowed in his presence. God secured the entrance to the orchard with other cherubim, so that no human could access it again. Nothing more is recorded at this time about what happened to the Serpent Cherub.

Chapter four records how humans began to populate the earth and how sin exponentially grew along with them. With the entrance of sin into humanity, a second dispensation[23] commenced. No longer were people innocent; now, they were controlled by their newly enlightened (but corrupted) consciences. We know nothing about specific laws God may have given during this time, but at the very least, there was an awareness of God and sin.

Probably shortly after settling in their new home outside the orchard, Adam and Eve conceived and gave birth to a son, Cain. It seems that Abel followed soon after that (vs. 1–2).[24] Moses gave very little detail of this first family, except that Cain was a farmer and Abel a rancher. At some point, they both brought

---

[21] The statement, "BECAUSE YOU OBEYED YOUR WIFE," gives insight into the relationship between husband and wife even before the Fall. Although they were equal in worth and value, there was still a hierarchy of authority, even before sin.

[22] In the Septuagint (LXX, the Greek translation of the Old Testament), her name is *Zoe*, which also means "life."

[23] The method by which God works with mankind, usually based on specific revelation or instructions. See the footnote in the "Introduction to Genesis" for more information.

[24] There has been some attempt over the years to portray Cain and Abel as twins, but the text does not give any indication that this was the case.

"AN OFFERING TO THE LORD" from their respective fields (vs. 3–5). It seems Cain's attitude about the offering is what made it unacceptable to God, while Abel's was accepted.[25] Although God warned Cain about the sin in his heart, he was unreceptive (vs. 6–8). Instead, he took out his rage and hatred against God by slaughtering his brother.[26] After allowing Cain to confess and repent, God approached him about Abel's disappearance, but he claimed to know nothing about it, so God banished him from the rest of humanity (vs. 9–12). No longer would he be able to work the ground, instead he would be a "HOMELESS WANDERER." Fearing that his family may take his life in revenge, Cain begged God for mercy, which he granted (vs. 13–16). Graciously, God would not allow anyone to murder Cain.

Founding a city named after his son, Enoch, Cain's family expanded (vs. 17–18).[27] Five generations later, Cain's descendant, Lamech, was the first recorded polygamist (vs. 19–22). He also fathered the men who would contribute to the domestication of animals,[28] the invention of musical instruments, and the making of metal tools. Capitalizing on God's mercy toward Cain, when Lamech killed a young man, he justified himself because he believed the young man had injured him (though he did not say how), and he invoked God's name to create an even greater curse on someone who killed him than if they had killed Cain. This is a good example of people who can contribute great things to their society without having the proper attitude toward God.

---

[25] There is nothing in the text that demands that this should have been a blood sacrifice. In fact, the word "sacrifice" is not even used. An "offering" under the Mosaic Law could be almost anything clean, and there is nothing to suggest that this pre-Law time was different.

[26] This may be the strongest case for those who believe the offering should have included blood. In this interpretation, Cain would have been saying to God, "If you want blood, here it is!" as he slaughtered Abel like an animal.

[27] The text does not say that Enoch was Cain's first son, only that he named the city after his son was born.

[28] Abel was a shepherd, so the word "livestock" in 4:20 probably refers to larger animals, e.g., oxen for plowing.

"Who was Cain afraid of?" is a common question about this story asked only slightly less often than "Where did Cain get his wife?" We find the answer at the end of the chapter. Returning to the Cain/Abel story, Moses recorded that Eve had another son in place of Abel, named Seth (vs. 25–26). According to 5:3, Adam was 130 years old when Seth was born, meaning that Cain and Abel were possibly in their late–120s when the murder took place. This would have given more than enough time for Adam and Eve to have many other children (and possibly grandchildren), including the woman Cain had married. Adam had "OTHER SONS AND DAUGHTERS" after Seth was born, and there is no good reason to assume that there were not others between Abel as Seth as well. Although Abel's family is never mentioned, there is nothing to say that he did not have one by this time as well. If Abel did have a family, this would have given Cain great reason to fear revenge from his extended family.

Without any laws against marrying close family relatives and without any long-term genetic mutation or disease present at that time, there was no physical, cultural, or moral reason for Adam and Eve's children to not marry or procreate with each other. In fact, there is no command anywhere in Scripture that prohibits these close relationships except for the Mosaic Law, which God gave strictly to the ancient nation of Israel nearly 3,000 years after Genesis 4. It is our growing knowledge of genetics and modern cultural prohibitions that make these relationships taboo today.

Chapter five introduces the second *toledoth* or genealogy in Genesis. It provides a short history of the first eleven generations of humans after Creation. There are at least four significant points made here.

First, all these people were made after the "LIKENESS" of Adam (vs. 1–3). Although Adam had been made "IN THE LIKENESS OF GOD," sin had somehow changed that likeness in Adam, and the new likeness was now being passed down via biological procreation.[29]

---

[29] There is also much to say, in conjunction with Romans 5:12, that this sinful likeness is passed down from the father alone, not the father and mother. This truth is essential to understanding how Jesus' virgin conception in a sinful woman allowed him to remain sinless. Jesus had a fully human nature, but without a biological human

Second, each of the men named is said to have lived for many hundreds of years, far longer than we live today. A normal, literal interpretation understands these to be standard earth-years, the same way chapter one describes a standard earth-day. If the days of chapter one do not reflect literal earth time, there is no reason to interpret this chapter in literal earth time either, requiring that at least three of the first five chapters of the Bible be explained away as figurative or fiction.

Third, understanding these to be standard earth-years, this chapter covers 1,556 years of world history, from Adam's creation through the first 500 years of Noah's life. Although many believe that there are gaps in this genealogy, which would create a longer timeframe, the text does not allow this interpretation. Even if people were missing from the list, the years remain the same because the men's ages relate to their descendants' birth dates. For instance, even if Seth were Adam's grandson or great-grandson instead of his son, that would not change the fact that Adam was 130 years old when Seth was born. Gaps in the list of names would not affect the number of years recorded. Thus, the genealogies listed here and in chapter 11 give strong support for the Young earth Creation interpretation of the Bible and this universe.

Fourth, this is a chapter of death. Except for Enoch (Jared's son, not Cain's son) in verse 24, where it says, "HE DISAPPEARED," the story of every man listed ends with "AND THEN HE DIED." The physical consequence of sin from 3:19 is shown to have been lived out almost without exception. Consequently, the first major section of Genesis begins with life and ends with death.

Chapters six through nine contain the story of a global Flood that destroyed all inhabitants of the earth, except for those rescued with Noah. Verses 1–4 set up the reason for the Flood, yet it is one of the most debated sections of the Bible. The debate surrounds the meaning of "THE SONS OF GOD"

---

father, he did not receive a sinful nature. Instead, his eternal divine nature became fused with his new human nature (the theological term is the "hypostatic union"), and he became the "only begotten" or "unique" God-Man, carrying 100% of both natures.

and "DAUGHTERS OF HUMANKIND" in verse two. There are three primary interpretations, depending on whether the "sons of God" are understood to be humans or angels. Those who see them as humans interpret them to be either 1) tyrannical (or even demonic) human rulers who married common, peasant women or 2) godly men from Seth's family line who married ungodly women from Cain's family line. The second seems to be the easiest to refute as the passage mentions neither Seth nor Cain, and it requires the assumption that the Sethites were generally godly while the Cainites were not. The fact that the Flood had to occur seems to reject that view.

The belief that these were unions of rulers and peasants does not adequately explain the emergence of the Nephilim, nor does it fully account for the wickedness that made global judgment necessary.

The third option is based on the view that the "sons of God" were fallen angels, not humans. While it does require a biological union and procreation between angels and humans, it seems to resolve the issues of the other interpretations. 1) The contrast is not between "sons" and "daughters" but between "God" and "humankind." Thus, the passage may legitimately read "divine sons" and "human daughters." These had a different nature than the human women. 2) The other clear usage of "sons of God" in Scripture is a reference to angels (Job 1:6; 2:1; 38:7). 3) This gives an added dimension to the description that Noah was "BLAMELESS" (vs. 9). While this can certainly mean "godly" in the context, the same Hebrew word is used to describe animal sacrifices as "unblemished," which could refer to the fact that his genetics had not been contaminated. 4) This was the ancient understanding of this passage, as shown in the LXX, where the Nephilim are called "giants" or "titans," and in 1 Enoch, which views the sons of God as fallen angels.[30] It also seems to best fit Peter's and Jude's understanding, both of whom linked the sin of these angels to the sin of Sodom and Gomorrah (2 Peter 2:4; Jude 6–7).

---

[30] While this is certainly not the strongest argument, we should not ignore this understanding of the ancient Jews. Additionally, every civilization has a "myth" or story of divine beings coming down to human women. It is possible that this event is the true story behind the ancient myths. (This is a good explanation of the various creation and flood myths found throughout ancient civilizations as well.)

No matter the identity of the "sons of God," the population of the earth had become so corrupted over the 1,500+ years since creation that God decided it was necessary to wipe out most of humanity and start over (vs. 5–8).[31] God described that ancient world as full of "WICKEDNESS…ONLY EVIL ALL THE TIME…FILLED WITH VIOLENCE." His solution was a global flood that would destroy all land creatures (humans and animals) and most air creatures. The rest would have to be intentionally protected to be saved.

Because of his faithfulness to God in the middle of that depravity, God chose Noah to rescue and repopulate the planet (vs. 8–21). Since we know so little about the pre-Flood environment, it is foolish to be dogmatic over incidentals like whether or not it had ever rained to that point.[32] Regardless, God told Noah to build a barge and gave him the specific dimensions and a materials list. Into that ark/box Noah would take his family of eight people and a male/female pair of every kind of land animal and bird to "KEEP THEM ALIVE." He was also supposed to take enough food to sustain the humans and animals during their wait. Noah obeyed God's instructions immediately and precisely (vs. 22; again in 7:5).

God's comment in 6:3, that "HUMANKIND… WILL REMAIN FOR 120 MORE YEARS," is often understood to mean that the lifespan of humans would no longer pass 120 years. While that seems like a good interpretation today, most people do not get anywhere near that age, and it was 1,000 years or more after the Flood before the lifespans settled that low. In this context, it seems better to understand that 120 years was God's date for the Flood. We cannot know how many of those 120 years Noah took to build the ark.

Chapter seven records the details of the Flood. The simple addition of the birth years from chapter five, along with the note in 7:11 that Noah was 600

---

[31] He could not destroy humanity and start over completely because of his promise to the serpent that a "seed of the woman" would defeat him. The human race cannot be eradicated without that prophecy being left unfulfilled and making God a liar.

[32] The comment in 2:6 about God causing mist to rise from the ground is not helpful because it speaks of the environment before man had begun cultivating the ground. It does not say that it had never rained even after man's creation.

years old when the Flood began, gives us a date of 1,656 years after Creation (1656 AM[33]) during which at least ten generations of sinful beings (humans and angels) had corrupted God's creation to the point of ruin.

After Noah built the ark, God told him to finish the instructions from chapter six, namely, to collect the animals and his family and enter the ark (vs. 1–5). One new instruction was to take seven pairs[34] of clean animals, one pair of unclean animals, and seven pairs of birds.[35] This was seven days before the Flood began. Once again "NOAH DID ALL THAT THE LORD COMMANDED HIM."

The amount of detail given in the rest of this chapter should not be ignored. None of the flood stories from other civilizations give this much detail, supporting the fact that this is the source material for their accounts. Notice:

- The Flood began "IN THE SIX HUNDREDTH YEAR OF NOAH'S LIFE, IN THE SECOND MONTH, ON THE SEVENTEENTH DAY" (vs. 6, 11)
- "THE RAIN FELL ON THE EARTH 40 DAYS AND 40 NIGHTS" (vs. 12)
- "THE ARK FLOATED ON THE SURFACE OF THE WATERS" (vs. 18). It was not meant to sail or for Noah to navigate; it just floated.

---

[33] The abbreviation AM stands for *Anno Mundi*, which is Latin for "In the Year of the World." Unlike BC (Before Christ) and AD (*Anno Domini*, "In the Year of our Lord"), which count "backward" toward creation and forward to today (based, inaccurately, on the year of Jesus' birth), AM counts the year of creation as Year 1 and continually increases. Using only the dates given in Scripture, the modern year 2000 would be approximately 6173 AM or 6,173 years since the Genesis 1 creation, meaning that Creation was about 4173 BC. (This is not the same AM that signifies morning instead of PM for afternoon. Those are also Latin but stand for *ante meridiem* and *post meridiem*, e.g., before and after midday, respectively.)

[34] Bibles and commentaries variously interpret this to be "seven animals" (three pairs plus one individual) or "seven pairs" (14 animals). Either is possible in the Hebrew text, which does not clarify for us. The ark had more than enough room no matter which God commanded.

[35] No information about clean and unclean animals has been given in the text so far, so it is impossible to determine which animals fell into each category. Using the categories found in the Mosaic Law, given more than one thousand years later, has some merit but should not be considered definitive.

- "ALL THE HIGH MOUNTAINS UNDER THE ENTIRE SKY WERE COVERED…MORE THAN 20 FEET" (vs. 19–20)[36]
- Everything "ON THE SURFACE OF THE GROUND" was destroyed, but only on the ground (vs. 21–23). There is no mention of water creatures anywhere in this account. Air creatures would also not have survived because both the land and air were uninhabitable during this time.
- The planet was submerged "FOR 150 DAYS" (vs. 24)

Although evolutionists reject the catastrophism of a global flood, the biblical Flood is the strongest argument against the uniformitarian view which evolution requires. Uniformitarianism states that "processes that operated in the remote geological past are not different from those observed now."[37] In other words, things have always worked in the same way that we see them working now. However, the Scriptures indicate that the Flood completely changed the nature of the environment and creation, including the geography of the earth, so that we cannot know what it was like before the Flood. Thus, the Flood and its effects are essential factors in the Young earth Creation understanding.

Chapter eight records the clean-up from the Flood. After covering the planet for 150 days, the water had receded enough for the ark to get stuck on a mountain top (vs. 1–5). However, it took more than two-and-a-half months before those mountains could even be seen. To gain information about their new environment, Noah sent out a raven and a dove at various intervals (vs. 6–12). It seems the raven did not come back (it easily could have survived by

---

[36] Due to the cataclysmic changes to the earth at this time, it is best to understand that mountains like Everest was probably formed during this event instead of thinking that the water needed to reach that height. We have no way to know how high the mountains were that the flood waters had to reach. Creation Ministries (creation.com), Answers in Genesis (answersingenesis.org), and the Institute for Creation Research (icr.org) all have many resources for further study of the Creation and the Flood.

[37] Dictionary.com, s.v. "uniformitarianism," http://www.dictionary.com/browse/uniformitarianism?s=t (accessed May 18, 2016).

scavenging), but the dove did. The first time it had nothing. The second time it had found an olive leaf. The third time it did not return. By the "TWENTY-SEVENTH DAY OF THE SECOND MONTH...IN NOAH'S SIX HUNDRED AND FIRST YEAR" the ground was ready to support life again, one year and ten days after the Flood began (vs. 13–14).

God invited Noah and all the animals out of the ark to take over the land and repopulate it (vs. 15–19). In response to God's deliverance, Noah "TOOK SOME OF EVERY KIND OF CLEAN ANIMAL AND CLEAN BIRD" and sacrificed them to God in praise and thanksgiving (vs. 20–22). At this time, God promised to "NEVER AGAIN CURSE THE GROUND BECAUSE OF HUMANKIND...[OR] DESTROY EVERYTHING THAT LIVES, AS I HAVE JUST DONE." Instead, he would institute at this time a kind of uniformitarianism (see notes on chapter seven) so that everything would run the same after the Flood. It is important to note, however, that man's sinful nature was not removed and would continue to propagate throughout succeeding generations.

Chapter nine concludes the story of the Flood and gives insight into the new environment humans and animals had before them. In the first section (vs. 1–7), God restated his command that Noah's family was to repopulate the planet. According to the genealogy in chapter ten, Noah had no more children, so this task was left to his three sons: Shem, Ham, and Japheth.

However, God also introduced a change in the environment and a change in government. To this point, humans and animals had a good relationship.[38] God changed the relationship after the Flood so that animals are now terrified of humans. The reason is that, although humans were vegetarian pre-Flood, God now allows us to "EAT ANY MOVING THING THAT LIVES" in addition to "THE GREEN PLANTS." The one restriction was that blood must be drained from the animal first, implying a verifiable slaughter process.

In this new relationship, where humans can kill and eat animals, animals now fight back and kill humans. God's new law was that any animal that killed

---

[38] What exactly that looked like is unknown, but it may at least partially explain how Noah was able to collect the animals and live with them in the ark for a year.

a human must die. Additionally, if any human murders another human, that person must also be put to death "BY OTHER HUMANS."[39] This began the third dispensation, Human Government. No longer were people ruled by their moral consciences; they would now be ruled by societal laws as well. The reason for this new law was to continually remind us that humans still carry the image of God.[40]

After giving these instructions, God made a covenant with Noah, all his descendants, and all living creatures (vs. 9–17). Contrary to what many scholars teach, this is the first covenant recorded in Scripture.[41] He promised that he would never again destroy all living things "BY THE WATERS OF A FLOOD." To reinforce the point: "NEVER AGAIN WILL A FLOOD DESTROY THE EARTH."[42] The visible sign of this covenant is the rainbow, which is created naturally by light shining through water. Even in a torrential downpour, the rainbow reminds us that whatever flooding may occur and whatever destruction it may bring, God will not allow it to destroy everything.

The chapter concludes with an account illustrating human depravity, even at this point in history, and setting the stage for the future conflict between Israel and the Canaanites. When this event took place is unknown, but it was

---

[39] This was more than just personal revenge. By instituting and commanding capital punishment, God implied a process by which society could determine genuine guilt and execute the perpetrator at the hand of the group. It is society's responsibility to purge evil from its midst and government's job to enforce that purging for the benefit, welfare, and protection of its citizens.

[40] It seems that there was no sanctity of life in the years leading up to the Flood. Notice that the concept of violence appears as a normal trait of the environment in 6:11, 13.

[41] Some believe and teach that God made covenants both before and after creation, including one before and one after Adam sinned. The word for "covenant" first appears in 6:18 and could refer to God's promise to keep Noah and his family safe through the Flood, or it could point to a future covenant that he would make with them after the Flood (which still promises that they would remain safe). This "Noahic Covenant" is the first clearly defined covenant in Scripture.

[42] The fact that he specified "a flood" three times in verses 11 and 15 means that his promise to destroy everything in the future with fire is fully within his rights and does not violate this covenant (see 2 Peter 3:7, 10–12 and Revelation 21:1).

long enough after the Flood that Noah could harvest from a thriving vineyard, and Ham had at least one child (vs. 20–28). At some point, Noah became completely drunk and passed out in his tent. What happened next is debated. Some people think Ham only saw his father naked and joked about it to his brothers. Others think that something sexual happened (not unlike Lot and his daughters in Genesis 19). The reason for this perspective is that the phrase "to see one's nakedness" is used later in the Mosaic Law for sexual relations (Leviticus 18:6–8, 10, 14, 16; 20:11, 17–21) and sexual perversion was a major sin of the Canaanites, Ham's descendants (Leviticus 18:24–30). No matter the extent of his actions, Ham did not just see Noah's nakedness, but somehow delighted in it.[43]

When Noah learned what had happened, he prophetically placed a curse on Ham's son, Canaan. The Canaanites would become "THE LOWEST OF SLAVES" to his family members, which indeed happened, especially for the Israelites (some later descendants of Shem).

Some older teachers and writers believed that, since most of Ham's family moved south into Africa (see chapter 10), this became a curse on all Africans, and they used it to support the slavery of dark-skinned peoples. They were sorely mistaken. Noah's curse was on Canaan, not Ham, and the Canaanites did not move into Africa. This abuse of Scripture to justify human slavery is just one example of why it is important to interpret the text carefully and not let our experiences and biases influence our interpretation.

Japheth's "TERRITORY AND NUMBERS" were expanded as his family set out north and became the ancestors of those from Europe and Asia. Although nothing in the passage gives any indication of other spiritual conditions, it seems that Shem already worshiped Yehovah, and Noah praised God for that and prophesied that the Shemites (or Semites[44]) would eventually overshadow the others.

---

[43] Thomas Constable (whom we quote throughout this book) does an exemplary job on this passage. His commentary can be downloaded for free at https://planobiblechapel.org/constable-notes.

[44] In Hebrew, the letter shin / sin (שׁ/שׂ) can be pronounced with an "sh" or just an "s." When used as an "s" it is the source of our words "Semitic" and the negative

Chapters ten and eleven explain where all humanity came from (Noah's three sons), and how we became dispersed over the planet in various tribes, nations, and languages. It is not meant to be a complete genealogy but simply highlight specific persons, tribes, or locations that were or would become prominent in ancient history.

Japheth's family moved north from Mesopotamia, the furthest away from what would become Israel (vs. 2–5). These tribes settled along "THE COASTLANDS" of the Mediterranean across southern Europe, the Mediterranean islands, Turkey, and into southern Asia.

Most of Ham's family moved south and west into the Arabian Peninsula and Africa (vs. 6–7). The names Cush, Mizraim, and Put are usually associated with Ethiopia, Egypt, and Libya, respectively. Cush had a prominent son (or descendant) named Nimrod. He expanded "HIS KINGDOM" to found Babylon and Assyria, covering areas east of the Jordan River. Mizraim's descendants covered northern Africa,[45] but Canaan's family stayed west of the Jordan and north of Egypt. This land was eventually named after him and included the region south of the Dead Sea. These Canaanite tribes were exceptionally wicked and would be the bane of the Israelites centuries later.

Shem's family stayed in Mesopotamia, primarily north of Canaan. This is modern Lebanon and Syria, along the great Tigris and Euphrates Rivers (modern Iraq), and deep into southern Arabia. It was part of these lands that Nimrod took over during his kingdom expansion.

Chapter eleven contains two sections: the division of languages and the key genealogy from Shem to Abram. Shortly after the Flood, after God had told the people to scatter across the earth, they determined to stay together and not disperse. Whereas chapter ten explains the divisions of humanity by language, there was a time that was not the case. Instead of spreading out, they intended to build a monument to themselves, "A CITY AND A TOWER" that would

---

"antisemitic." See the story in Judges 12 where the two pronunciations of this letter in the word *shibboleth* / *sibboleth* caused a fatal tragedy in Israel.

[45] *Mitsraim* is the Hebrew word for Egypt.

keep them together under their government and power (vs. 1–4). Knowing that they would revert to the same level of wickedness as before the Flood, God miraculously confused their languages by tribe, effectively forcing them apart from each other (vs. 5–9).[46]

When this event took place is unknown. Genesis 10:25 indicates that there was a type of division or separation on the earth during the time of Peleg. Whether this refers to the division of languages or physical divisions in the earth itself (separation of continents, etc.) is debated. If it refers to the event at Babel, and Peleg was born 101 years after the Flood, this defiance against God happened very quickly.

This event is also important because it explains how the various people groups came into being. As the tribes separated from each other, the dominant genetic traits would consolidate and present themselves in physical characteristics like size, shape, and color—all the things that make us feel different from other humans. However, it is essential to remember that all these differences within humanity came from Noah's three sons. Strictly speaking, there are no "races"; there are only ethnicities within one "human race."

Shem's genealogy is outlined here, much like Adam's in chapter five. Rather than just a list of names and places (as in chapter ten), Shem's line gives specific years. As noted in chapter five, whether there are gaps between people or not does not affect the actual dating because the age of the father when the son/descendant was born does not change, even if the next name is not a direct son. Therefore, Abram was born 352 years after the Flood.[47] Since Noah lived for 350 years after the Flood (9:28), we can see the proximity of time between these two patriarchs. This was due to the dramatic decrease in lifespans and how soon these men fathered these specific descendants.[48]

---

[46] God's statement, "COME, LET'S GO DOWN" has always been funny to me. They thought they were building something so big, into the heavens, yet God treated it as a dad getting on the floor to look at his child's Lego® town.

[47] Although Terah's age is not given at Abram's birth, we can date Abram's call in 12:1 to 2090 BC, when he was 75 years old according to 12:4.

[48] The average age of the father at the time of birth of the next listed generation in chapter five is 117 years. (Noah is not included, because he would skew the average

At the end of chapter eleven, the story shifts from the entire human race to a very specific family—Terah's—and even further to just one of his sons: Abram. The story of this family will be the emphasis of the remainder of the Old Testament. According to Joshua 24:2, both Terah and Abram were idol worshipers (probably the Akkadian moon god, Sin). They were from the city of Ur, a major worship center in southern Mesopotamia (probably near the modern Iraq/Kuwait border on the Euphrates River). Abram's brother, Haran, had a son and two daughters, but Abram's wife, Sarai, was barren. (Moses ignored Nahor at this point, but he will reemerge later in Genesis.)

Although Genesis tells of only one time that God called Abram, Stephen mentioned an earlier calling in Acts 7:2, "WHEN HE WAS IN MESOPOTAMIA, BEFORE HE SETTLED IN HARAN." This explains why Abram and Sarai moved from Ur to Haran, although his father and nephew, Lot, moved with him (11:31–32). However, it was not until after Terah died that God called Abram again, and he finally moved to Canaan.

Chapter twelve opens with God's second call to Abram after his father had died in Haran. Although we do not have the full content of the first call, this one contains what has come to be known as the "Abrahamic Covenant" (vs. 1–3). In this covenant, God promised to bless Abram and his descendants (who did not yet exist), by placing a blessing on those who would bless him and a curse on those who disdained him. His name would become so great in the world that many peoples would even bless one another using his name. Most importantly, God promised to make Abram into "A GREAT NATION." [49]

There was nothing Abram had to do to gain any of these things (except possibly leave Haran and move to Canaan[50]), and there is nothing that he could

---

at 500 years when he began to have Shem, Ham, and Japheth.) In chapter eleven, the average age is 31 years (excluding both Shem, 100, and Terah, 70).

[49] I have written at length on the specific details that Abram would have expected from the phrase "a great nation" in my chapter "How do Covenants Relate to the Kingdom" in *What is Dispensationalism?* (Grace Abroad Ministries, 2019).

[50] Since the covenant was not officially made until chapter fifteen, after Abram had moved, it was not technically in force until after his obedience. Thus, it was not

have done to breach this covenant, so it is called an "unconditional covenant." At 75 years old, Abram moved away from his family and religion in Haran, although his nephew, Lot, followed him (vs. 4–9). Once in Canaan, Abram traveled the entire length of the country, from north to south, scoping it out and building altars to worship Yehovah, who promised to give the entire region to Abram's descendants.

At some point after his arrival, a famine struck Canaan, and Abram decided to move south into Egypt to find food for his substantial employee base and flocks (see the notes on chapter 14), rather than trusting God to take care of him in Canaan (vs. 10–20). Because his wife was beautiful, he thought the Egyptians might kill him and take her for themselves if they knew she was his wife. However, if they thought that she was only his sister, he may have anticipated that someone might ask to marry her, and he would have time to leave Egypt during negotiations. It seems he never considered that Pharaoh would not ask permission for anything. Instead, the king just took her for himself, assuming she was not married. Although he did pay Abram very well for her, the king was not about to negotiate with a foreigner seeking food. This brought God's direct curse on the king's house (as promised in verse three). When he discovered the truth, Pharaoh expelled Abram and his company from Egypt, back to the famine of Canaan.

Chapter thirteen opens with a dejected (but enormously wealthy) Abram returning to Canaan from Egypt. His little detour had gotten him into trouble, but he made his way back to the last place he had met with God, Bethel, which means "house of God" (vs. 1–4). During this time of moving, Lot had also become very wealthy.[51] Between Abram and Lot, they had so many employees and animals that their ranches were literally causing the ground (which had already suffered from the famine) to become unsustainable, so their ranch

---

conditioned on anything except God's promise. However, one could argue that, had Abram never moved from Ur or Haran, the covenant would have never been put into force.

[51] It seems he was the sole heir of his father, Haran (11:27–28), and would have received Haran's part of the family estate when Terah died as well (11:32).

hands began fighting with each other whenever they found grazing lands and water (vs. 5–7).

In an impressive act of generosity and humility, Abram gave his nephew the first pick of anywhere in the area to settle and build his ranch; Abram promised to move away and find something else (vs. 8–12). After scouting the area, Lot discovered the valley south of the Dead Sea to be lush and populated, so he claimed the entire southeast region as his share and settled there. As he promised, Abram moved northwest deeper into Canaan toward Hebron, but not so far away that he could not keep an eye on Lot. God again promised Abram not only the entire land but also innumerable descendants, "LIKE THE DUST OF THE EARTH" (vs. 14–18).

The short statements in vs. 12, where Lot "PITCHED HIS TENTS NEXT TO SODOM," and vs. 13, describing "THE PEOPLE OF SODOM [AS] EXTREMELY WICKED REBELS AGAINST THE LORD," set up two storylines for later chapters. This description is emphatic because of the compounding adjectives. These people were not simply rebellious; they were "EXTREMELY WICKED...AGAINST THE LORD." Ultimately, Abram's family had no business being there.

Chapter fourteen presents a classic case of being in the wrong place at the wrong time. It opens with the story of a local skirmish between regional kings on the east side of the Jordan River and the Dead Sea (vs. 1–11). Four kings were terrorizing the countryside which they had already oppressed for more than a decade. Five of the subject kings had finally had enough and fought back: the kings of Sodom, Gomorrah, Admah, Zeboiim, and Bela/Zoar. This coalition was no match for the dominant four kings and ran away from them. The four chased them down and killed most of their armies then entered the cities of Sodom and Gomorrah (and presumably the others), looting them and taking all the civilians captive as well. The reason this story matters is revealed in verse twelve: "THEY ALSO TOOK ABRAM'S NEPHEW LOT AND HIS POSSESSIONS WHEN THEY LEFT, FOR LOT WAS LIVING IN SODOM."[52]

---

[52] This shift from "NEXT TO SODOM" (13:12) to "IN SODOM" (14:12) will become significant in chapter 19.

The beginning of chapter thirteen described Abram as "very wealthy," but it is not until here that we discover just how wealthy he was. A fugitive escaped from the carnage and ran to tell Abram what had happened (vs. 13–14). Abram immediately "MOBILIZED HIS 318 TRAINED MEN WHO HAD BEEN BORN IN HIS HOUSEHOLD." If none of these men were brothers, we could multiply this number by three (to account for each man having a father and mother), meaning that Abram potentially had up to 900 employees. This may or may not have included the ranch hands who took care of his vast herds, which could have numbered into the tens of thousands.[53] Suffice it to say, Abram owned a massive company of potentially more than one thousand employees and tens or hundreds of thousands of material assets, both in the ranching and agricultural industries!

With this 318-man security force (plus some local allies), Abram took off after the invaders (vs. 13–16). He chased them almost two hundred miles north, past Damascus, where he soundly defeated them. He rescued all the captives, including Lot, and all the stolen loot. On the way back home, Abram met Melchizedek, the king of Salem,[54] who was also a genuine priest of Yehovah (vs. 17–20).[55] He blessed Abram and blessed God for his work in Abram's life. In response, "ABRAM GAVE MELCHIZEDEK A TENTH OF EVERYTHING." Abram was also met by the king of Sodom, who offered Abram all the recovered loot if he returned the people to Sodom instead of keeping them as his slaves/servants (vs. 21–24). However, Abram refused to take anything, except what his men had eaten along the way. His reason for rejecting the reward was his trust in God: "THAT WAY YOU CAN NEVER SAY, 'IT IS I WHO MADE

---

[53] Historically, one shepherd could handle 100 sheep by himself, and Abram had "SHEEP AND CATTLE, MALE DONKEYS, MALE SERVANTS, FEMALE SERVANTS, FEMALE DONKEYS, AND CAMELS" (12:16).

[54] Salem is an older (or at least shortened) name for Jerusalem. The only other places that Melchizedek appears in Scripture are Psalm 110 and Hebrews 5–7.

[55] Much like Job and his friends, it is impossible to know how Melchizedek had come to know and worship Yehovah. Since we know that God spoke directly to Abram, one theory is that he spoke directly to others during this dispensation as well.

ABRAM RICH.'" However, Abram did not refuse his allies any reward the king offered.

Chapter fifteen is vital to Abram's story because it is here that God formally made his covenant with Abram. Abram was aware that becoming a great nation (12:2) was impossible without children, so we see our first hint that he intended to help God along with the plan whenever he did not understand it. As was normal at that time, Abram suggested promoting his trusted servant, Eliezer, to be his sole heir (vs. 1–5). However, that would not have accomplished God's goal; rather, Abram was indeed to have his own biological children. In 13:16, God promised that Abram's descendants would be like the dust of the earth; now he compared them to the stars in the sky as well.

Verse six seems to be a passing comment in Genesis, but it became the cornerstone of Paul's theology of salvation through faith alone. In Romans 4:3, 9, 22 and Galatians 3:6 Paul referred to this verse both directly and indirectly, showing faith as the only way by which a person can gain God's righteousness. Even James, who is often excoriated for promoting a "faith plus works" message, quoted verse six right in the middle of his contested passage (James 2:23). The truth is simple: Abram believed God, and that was enough to make him eternally right with God.[56]

Yet even faith does not remove all questions and doubts (as is evident throughout Abram's story). Immediately after fully believing God's promise, Abram asked how he could be sure that this would take place (vs. 7–8). It is at this point that God officially made his covenant with Abram. Using a standard ancient method for establishing certain contracts, God had Abram slaughter specific animals, cut them in half, and create a pathway between the carcass pieces (vs. 9–20). Normally, the two parties would walk together between them, symbolizing the severity of any breach of contract. However, this time, God walked through alone.

---

[56] For more explanation on the passages referenced above, see the appropriate chapters in *New Testament Chapter by Chapter* (Trust House Publishers, 2017).

After putting him into a deep sleep (compare this with Adam in 2:21), God made three unchangeable promises to Abram. First, his descendants would be enslaved in a foreign country for 400 years, but God would personally rescue them, bringing judgment on the oppressive nation, and they would return to Canaan with great wealth. Second, Abram himself would die in peace at an old age. Third, God reserved a specific tract of land for Abram's descendants that he will one day deliver to them.[57] The fact that God alone walked the path between the animals shows that neither Abram nor his descendants had any obligation to fulfill or breach the contract. We call this an "unconditional covenant" because it is based solely on God and his unchanging promises.

Digging Deeper: The Abrahamic Covenant

It is impossible to understand the story of the Old Testament without a grasp of the great promises that God made to Abraham.

If the Old Testament were a puzzle (which is how many people think of it!), God's covenant with Abraham, or the "Abrahamic Covenant," would serve as the corner and edge pieces within which all the other stories and teachings fit perfectly.

God's covenant with Abraham is unique in two ways. First, it is unconditional. In most covenants or contracts, both parties have obligations to uphold. If one party does not fulfill its part (condition), the covenant is breached, and all the pay-outs are no longer owed. In God's unconditional covenant, only God is obligated to act, and Abraham is guaranteed to receive the full pay-out because of God's faithfulness.

Second, this covenant is eternal. Over and over, God used words like *eternal*, *everlasting*, and *forever* to remind Abraham and his descendants that they never had to worry about losing out on the promises.

---

[57] Although Solomon was very close to seeing this fulfilled during his reign (1 Kings 4:21, 24–25), it will ultimately be fulfilled only under Jesus' reign in the Millennial Kingdom.

And what is this expected pay-out that they are still so interested in receiving? Only everything a person could wish for. First, Abraham's family would become a great nation. Now a nation not only needs a lot of people (Genesis 15:5), but also land to live in (Genesis 15:18–21; Deuteronomy 30:1–4), a government to rule and lead it (2 Samuel 7:8–16), and (in ancient times) a national religion (Jeremiah 31:31–34). Ultimately, all these promises will be fulfilled during Jesus' earthly reign in the Millennium (see Luke 1:31–33 and 22:20).[58]

Additionally, God promised great spiritual blessing to all people, not just Israel, through a specific Jewish descendant—Jesus of Nazareth (Galatians 3:16).

Chapter sixteen contains another example of Abram's attempt to further God's plan without seeking guidance from God. Because of Sarai's infertility, Abram had already offered his servant, Eliezer, as his heir, but God refused (15:2–3). This time, Sarai offered a solution. Since the promised heir had to be Abram's biological son (15:4), she offered another cultural option, that he should conceive through her Egyptian maidservant, Hagar, who would act as a surrogate for Sarai (vs. 1–2). Hagar probably joined Sarai as a gift from the Pharaoh in chapter twelve. It seems that the Holy Spirit intentionally had Moses repeat the verbiage from 3:17. The Hebrew text reads that Abram "listened to the voice of" his wife and violated God's plan, just as Adam did. In both cases, the men were held responsible for the outcome.

So, after ten years in Canaan without children to fulfill God's promise, Hagar conceived Abram's child. This led Hagar to look down on Sarai's infertility, causing reciprocal hatred (vs. 3–6).[59] Sarai did not think Abram was doing enough to stop Hagar's newfound insolence against her mistress, so Sarai complained to him. Shrugging off his responsibility, he told Sarai to do with

---

[58] For a more detailed discussion about these Jewish covenants and their connection to the coming kingdom, see my chapter "How do Covenants Relate to the Kingdom" in *What is Dispensationalism?* (Paul Miles, ed., Grace Abroad Ministries, 2019).

[59] This is a recurring theme in the Old Testament, whenever a man had multiple wives and one could not bear children (Leah and Rachel; Penninah and Hannah).

Hagar what she wanted, so she treated the pregnant woman badly enough that Hagar ran away into the desert.

There the supernatural messenger of Yehovah (probably the preincarnate Christ[60]) found her and quizzed her on what had happened (vs. 7–14). He told her to return to Sarai and left her with a promise and blessing that even Sarai could not take from her. Hagar would have a son who would become a strong, wild nomad, and who would eventually father a family too numerous to count.[61] Because God heard her "PAINFUL GROANS," she was to name the baby *Ishmael*, meaning "God hears." Hagar obeyed God and returned to Abram's home. Since he did name the boy Ishmael, she must have told him everything that God had said to her. To reinforce the timing in verse three and keep an accurate record of the chronology, Moses wrote that Abram's ten years of living in Canaan brought him to 86 years old (see 12:4) when Ishmael was born.

Chapter seventeen institutes what seems to be a condition in God's covenant with Abram: "WALK BEFORE ME AND BE BLAMELESS. THEN I WILL CONFIRM MY COVENANT BETWEEN ME AND YOU" (vs. 1–2). As God explained later in the chapter, the point was not that he had threatened to pull his covenant away from Abram. Rather, he was extending his promises, but each person in Abram's family would be required to appropriate it personally, and this necessitated their obedience to God.[62] God's blessings upon the family could never be removed, but those who rebelled against God would not participate in them.

---

[60] Some may see this as just an angelic messenger speaking on God's behalf, but Hagar believed that she saw God himself (vs. 13–14).

[61] Although the Ishmaelites are not included in the covenant promises which God gave strictly to Israel, they certainly are included in God's promise to make Abram's descendants numerous like the dust of the ground and the stars of the sky.

[62] This is a great foreshadowing of God's provision of salvation, which he made available to all people through Jesus' death. However, it is up to each person individually to obey the gospel's command to believe in order to receive it.

In chapter twelve, God promised to make Abram into "a great nation." Chapter fifteen followed that with a promise of innumerable descendants. Here God extended that to become "A MULTITUDE OF NATIONS," which is what *Abraham*, his new name, means ("father of nations"; vs. 3–8). Additionally, this unconditional, unchangeable covenant also became "PERPETUAL" or eternal at this point. It would be passed down to his descendants, and the spiritual aspect established a spiritual bond with Yehovah forever.

The one condition to participate in these blessings was male circumcision, which would act as a sign of their faith and obedience (vs. 9–14). Although God required all males in Abram's family and household to be circumcised, it is important to note that failure to do so would result in loss only for the rebel, not for all the nations that would come from Abram. Thus, this was still an unconditional covenant in that God guaranteed its fulfillment. However, rebels would opt themselves out of it if they chose to disobey him.

In addition to changing Abram's name to Abraham, God also changed Sarai's name to Sarah. Even though their new names were similar to their previous names, this event became a turning point in their lives as God added the last piece to their puzzle. In chapter twelve, God promised numerous descendants. In chapter fifteen, he said they would come through Abram's biological son. Now God added that this son 1) would come from both Abraham and Sarah, 2) would be born one year later, 3) would be named *Isaac*, and 4) would be the only one of Abraham's children through whom the covenant would proceed (vs. 15–19). Still not convinced, Abraham asked if Ishmael could fulfill it. Ishmael would certainly become numerous, as God had promised Hagar, but Isaac was God's choice (vs. 20–22).

So, Abraham did exactly what God had said (vs. 23–27). At the time he and every male in his household were circumcised, Abraham was 99 years old, and Ishmael was 13.

Chapter eighteen must have happened shortly after chapter seventeen, because Sarah was either not yet pregnant or not far along enough to know it.[63] The LORD (Yehovah, preincarnate Jesus) and two angels came to meet with Abraham, who welcomed them with shelter and a meal (vs. 1–8).[64] The conversation that took place while the meal was being prepared and eaten is not recorded (unless it included the conversation from chapter seventeen). Eventually, God asked where Sarah was, and Abraham said that she was in the tent.[65] God promised that he would "RETURN" the next year, and they would have a son (vs. 9–15). Sarah heard this and laughed to herself in response because of their advanced age and her lack of physical ability to conceive, but she denied it when he caught her. "IS ANYTHING IMPOSSIBLE FOR THE LORD?" was his assuring yet chiding response.

The rest of the chapter records a private conversation between God and Abraham (vs. 16–21). It is a wonderful picture of intimate fellowship with God. He looked at the two angels and asked whether he should let Abraham in on his plans, answering his own question by doing so. Allowing Abraham to give input into his decision to destroy Sodom and Gomorrah should not be surprising when we realize that this is exactly the fellowship and relationship that God always intended to have with humanity beginning with Adam. He had bestowed authority on humanity and now expected Abraham to exercise that authority with justice. God would not destroy them without everyone knowing all the facts, so he sent the two angels into Sodom to look for themselves.[66]

---

[63] The details of chapters 16–17 make it possible that they occurred at this same time.

[64] Although it is debated whether Abraham knew this was indeed God himself, I believe he did. He had walked with God for almost 25 years at this point and had talked with him face-to-face on many occasions. It seems improbable that he did not recognize the one who had come to be his friend (James 2:23; Isaiah 41:8).

[65] Constable notes that this may have been a nod to his questions centuries before when he inquired after Adam (3:9) and Abel (4:9).

[66] Although events like this can make it sound as if God is not omniscient, there are many times that Scriptures reveal that he makes decisions and acts in conjunction with information given him by his creatures, both angelic and human. This does not reject or diminish his omniscience but rather allows angels and people to join him in his work, as he has always intended.

Once they had gone, Abraham questioned God intently about this plan (vs. 22–33). While he certainly was concerned about Lot and his family in Sodom, Abraham's question in verse 25 unveils his main concern: "FAR BE IT FROM YOU TO DO SUCH A THING—TO KILL THE GODLY WITH THE WICKED, TREATING THE GODLY AND THE WICKED ALIKE! FAR BE IT FROM YOU! WILL NOT THE JUDGE OF THE WHOLE EARTH DO WHAT IS RIGHT?" Abraham was not bartering to save Sodom; he was wrestling with his finite understanding of the tension between God's mercy and justice. God would certainly not condemn the godly along with the wicked, but where was his line in this situation? Would he let the wicked live even if as few as ten godly people were among them? God's mercy was revealed; even ten righteous people would save the entire region. That satisfied Abraham and they both went on their way. Abraham must have thought that things in Sodom, under Lot's influence, were better than they were.

Chapter nineteen records how depraved humanity can become without any influence of godliness. It reveals just a fraction of what earth had become leading up to the Flood. The angels had left God and Abraham in chapter eighteen and went down to Sodom, where they found Lot "SITTING IN THE CITY'S GATEWAY" (vs. 1). This likely indicates that he had risen to a position of leadership in the city government in the years since Uncle Abraham had rescued him (chapter thirteen). Rather than turning people away from the wicked place, he was welcoming them into it! When the angels showed their intent to spend the night in the city square, he feared for them, begging them to stay in his home (vs. 2–3). The reason for his insistence is quickly revealed. "ALL THE MEN—BOTH YOUNG AND OLD, FROM EVERY PART OF THE CITY OF SODOM—SURROUNDED THE HOUSE," demanding that Lot hand the angels (no one, of course, knew they were angels yet) over to them so they could sexually abuse them (vs. 3–9).[67] Displaying a lack of basic morality, Lot valued his guests more

---

[67] "All" must be hyperbolic here, because Lot was certainly not part of this mob, and it seems his sons-in-law were not either (vs. 14).

than even his virgin daughters, whom he offered to the mob instead.[68] Lot insisted that what the men proposed to do was wicked. This caused them to flare up against him as well, accusing him of acting like a judge over them and threatening to molest him as well.[69]

The angels temporarily diffused the situation by causing their attackers to become blind and unable to find the house (vs. 10–14). Since it was obvious that there were not even the ten righteous people that Abraham had asked for, destruction was imminent, so they instructed Lot to collect any other family in the city before they destroyed it, but Lot's sons-in-law[70] found this concept to be ridiculous. Even still, the angels had to drag Lot and his wife and two daughters out of the city (vs. 15–22). When they told him to escape to the mountains, he hesitated again, arguing that he needed to be with people, and asked to be able to move to Zoar, which they permitted him to do. Once the family was clear, God began to destroy Sodom and Gomorrah with burning sulfur (vs. 23–29). Lot's wife kept looking back, longing for her home, and was caught in the judgment. Still, God honored Abraham's request to not judge the godly with the ungodly.[71]

Eventually, Lot felt it was not safe in Zoar either, so he went to live in the mountains anyway (vs. 30–38). There his daughters each got him drunk so they could become pregnant by him and preserve their family line. Since no family is mentioned for Lot until this chapter, it seems likely that his wife was from Sodom and his daughters were born there, meaning that Sodom's debauched lifestyle was all they had ever known, and Lot did little or nothing to train them against it. Thus, like Noah, Lot ended up drunk and naked in

---

[68] Many scholars attribute this to common Middle Eastern hospitality (where a guest can be valued more than family). However, even in that culture, this was inexcusable.

[69] It seems that they were not impressed with his role in the city government, because he was a foreigner.

[70] Unless Lot had older daughters married to these men, these were probably his sons-in-law "to-be." Given the actions of Lot's virgin daughters later in this chapter, it is possible that the girls had lost hope when their fiancés died in the judgment.

[71] In 2 Peter 2:7–8, Lot is described as a "RIGHTEOUS MAN...TORMENTED IN HIS RIGHTEOUS SOUL BY THE LAWLESS DEEDS HE SAW AND HEARD" in Sodom.

front of his children, who fathered children from whom eventually would come nations hostile to Israel.

Chapter twenty presents another of Abraham's failures to trust God. After the destruction of Sodom (and presumably hearing of Lot's safety), Abraham moved southwest to Gerar, where Abimelech was king (vs. 1–2). In a repeat of the incident in Egypt (12:10–20), Abraham and Sarah told Abimelech that they were siblings instead of spouses, so Abimelech took Sarah into his harem. It seems this was Abraham's standard plan everywhere they went (vs. 13), assuming no one feared Yehovah or would respect his marriage. Additionally, since Sarah was legitimately his half-sister, he reasoned that his life was in less danger by telling this story (vs. 11–12).

Abimelech, however, did know and fear Yehovah and was a righteous man who led his people righteously as well (vs. 3–7).[72] When God confronted him about taking Sarah (whom he had not even touched yet) and pronounced judgment, Abimelech remained firm in his innocence and said essentially the exact thing Abraham had done about Sodom: "You would not condemn both the righteous and wicked alike, would you?" Of course, he would not, so God told Abimelech to send Sarah home or he would die.

"EARLY IN THE MORNING," Abimelech did exactly what God had commanded (vs. 8–16). After telling his people what had happened, he interrogated Abraham on his deception, learning of his plan to do this everywhere he went. Abimelech chided Abraham, but returned Sarah, along with "SHEEP, CATTLE, AND MALE AND FEMALE SERVANTS" and silver to make things right, even though he was completely innocent. He also allowed Abraham to stay in his land as long as he wanted, an amazing act of generosity due to God's promise to bless anyone who blessed Abraham (12:3). In return, Abraham interceded for

---

[72] It is an interesting topic to consider how Abimelech and Melchizedek, along with possibly many others (including Job), knew and worshiped Yehovah during this time. Those who charge God with injustice for revealing himself to only a few people (like Abraham) miss God's gracious nature. Five hundred years after the Flood, people were worshiping and serving Yehovah even before Abraham moved to Canaan.

Abimelech, and God lifted the curse of infertility he had placed on his household (vs. 17–18).[73]

Chapter twenty-one opens as if it were going to be about Isaac, but Ishmael becomes the focus instead. As promised, God caused Sarah to become pregnant, and she gave birth to Isaac when Abraham was 100 years old (vs. 1–7). The name *Isaac* means "laughter" because they had laughed when God promised them this son a year earlier. Now that he had come, the laughter would be in joy rather than mockery.

When Isaac was finally weaned (probably 2–3 years later), Abraham celebrated with a great feast (vs. 8–13). However, during the feast, Ishmael did something with Isaac that Sarah did not like. Exactly what Ishmael did is not recorded, only that he was "MOCKING" Isaac. Sarah took this as a threat against her son, Abraham's rightful heir, and demanded that Abraham divorce Hagar and send her away. He was, naturally, reluctant to do this; however, God told him to do so and that it would not affect God's promise to make Ishmael into a great nation.

Abraham gave Hagar and Ishmael a few provisions and sent them away into the southern Canaanite desert, possibly sending them back to Egypt (vs. 14–19). Soon their provisions were gone, and they began to grow weary and dehydrated. Hagar left Ishmael under a scrub brush to die while she went a little further and cried out to God. It seems that Ishmael was crying out as well because God responded to his cry. God reaffirmed his promise to make Ishmael great and pointed Hagar to a well that would refresh them both. Ishmael did grow up as God promised and married an Egyptian woman like his mother (vs. 20–21).

The chapter ends with another brief encounter between Abraham and Abimelech (vs. 22–34). It was clear to Abimelech that God was with Abraham, so he asked Abraham for a treaty. He requested that Abraham treat him and

---

[73] In verse seven, God called Abraham a "prophet." This is the first use of this word in the Bible and its only occurrence in Genesis. Thus, even though Noah gave a prophecy regarding his descendants in chapter nine, Abraham was the first to formally be called a prophet.

his entire nation fairly, with no deception, and Abraham agreed. Abraham paid the price of the covenant by supplying the animals used in the legal ritual. Additionally, Abraham gave Abimelech "SEVEN EWE LAMBS." In the spirit of openness and honesty, Abraham brought up a concern that Abimelech's servants had claimed ownership over one of Abraham's wells. The lambs were Abraham's way of proving that he rightfully owned the well. They made the covenant, then Abimelech went back home, and Abraham planted a tree, worshiping God and planning to live there for a long time.

Chapter twenty-two is undated, but Josephus wrote that Isaac was twenty-five years old at this time, a gap of more than twenty years from the previous chapter.[74] If true, then Abraham had been walking with God for about 50 years. Moses prefaces this event with the explanation that what God asked Abraham was intended to test his faith and obedience (vs. 1–2). Abraham's love for Isaac had grown tremendously, perhaps too much, so God told Abraham to slaughter and sacrifice Isaac. God refused to give any further details until they arrived at a specific mountain in "THE LAND OF MORIAH," about a two-day journey from home.[75]

Abraham took Isaac and two servants without telling them anything other than it was a trip to worship God (vs. 3–5). When they reached the site, Abraham allowed only Isaac to accompany him. In a display of tremendous faith, Abraham declared, "THE BOY AND I...WILL WORSHIP AND THEN RETURN TO YOU." According to Hebrews 11:17–19, Abraham fully expected God to resurrect Isaac right there, after the sacrifice. As they ascended the mountainside, Isaac questioned the fact that they had no animal to offer (vs. 6–8). Again, Abraham responded in faith: "GOD WILL PROVIDE FOR HIMSELF THE LAMB FOR THE BURNT OFFERING."

---

[74] Flavius Josephus, translated by William Whiston, *Antiquities of the Jews*, 1.13.2. Other commentators have suggested ages from 18 to 33.

[75] Second Chronicles 3:1 identifies the Temple Mount in Jerusalem as the same region—and possibly the same mountain—where Abraham offered Isaac, very close to the place where God would put Jesus on the cross as the ultimate sacrifice for all people.

Arriving at the location, they built the altar, then Abraham prepared to slaughter Isaac and offer him as a whole burnt offering (vs. 9–14).[76] At the last possible second, before Abraham's knife slit Isaac's throat, the angel of Yehovah (preincarnate Jesus) stopped him and revealed that this was just a test. Specifically, it seems that Abraham's love had shifted from Yehovah to Isaac (vs. 2), so God put him in the position where he had to decide who was more important to him.[77] In his providence, God did not let the altar go to waste but miraculously provided a ram so the father and son could sacrifice and worship together.

The chapter ends with God once again confirming his covenant with Abraham, this time in Isaac's presence (vs. 15–19). They both needed to learn undivided devotion to Yehovah. After this encounter with God, they both returned to the servants, as Abraham had promised, and returned home. The mention of Abraham's brother, Nahor, and his family (vs. 20–24) sets up the upcoming marriage between Isaac and Rebekah.

Chapter twenty-three records the account of Sarah's death and Abraham's arrangements for her burial. The most significant part of the story may be the fact that, although God had promised the entire land of Canaan to Abraham's descendants, Abraham himself was still a "TEMPORARY SETTLER AMONG" (vs. 4) the citizens of the land and had to purchase a piece of property even to bury his wife. Ultimately, Abraham died owning no other land but that one parcel.

There are a few other significant points, as well. First, when Abraham asked to purchase land, the locals honored and respected him greatly ("YOU ARE A MIGHTY PRINCE AMONG US," vs. 6) and claimed that no one would think twice about giving him their tombs. Second, Abraham refused to accept a gift (see 14:22–23) and insisted on paying full price for whatever land they would sell him, specifically a cave at the end of a field (vs. 7–10; see David's similar response in 2 Samuel 24:21–24). Third, when the owner of the cave insisted

---

[76] Nothing is said about Isaac at this time, but he was obviously going along with it. One wonders if this extreme situation was the foundation of Isaac's spiritual apathy toward God in his later years.

[77] Interestingly, verse two contains the first occurrence of "love" in the Scriptures.

that Abraham have the entire field surrounding the cave, Abraham appreciated the generosity and paid full price for everything.[78] So he buried his wife in a cave at the end of a field on the only piece of Canaan he ever owned.

> "THESE ALL DIED IN FAITH WITHOUT RECEIVING THE THINGS PROMISED, BUT THEY SAW THEM IN THE DISTANCE AND WELCOMED THEM AND ACKNOWLEDGED THAT THEY WERE STRANGERS AND FOREIGNERS ON THE EARTH. ... AND THESE ALL WERE COMMENDED FOR THEIR FAITH, YET THEY DID NOT RECEIVE WHAT WAS PROMISED" (Hebrews 11:13, 39).

Chapter twenty-four is the longest in Genesis and explains what Abraham did to secure a wife for Isaac. Since Isaac was forty when he married (25:20), and Sarah was ninety when he was born (17:17), this chapter took place about three years after chapter twenty-three. At 140 years old, Abraham was concerned to make final preparations for Isaac to inherit everything and find fulfillment in God's promises, but Isaac was still unmarried. Abraham's greatest concern was that Isaac should not marry a Canaanite woman, so he sent his most trusted servant back to Haran to find someone from his extended family (vs. 1–9; see 11:31–32). Probably thinking he may die before he saw Isaac married, Abraham made his servant swear that, no matter what happened, Isaac was not to marry a Canaanite. The only exception was if no woman accepted the offer to move from her family to join Isaac in Canaan, then the servant was freed from his oath to Abraham.

The faith of this servant was incredible (vs. 10–21). After making the 500-mile journey north, he finally stopped at a well near the city where Abraham's brother lived. Not knowing anyone, he believed that God had personally chosen a woman for Isaac, so he asked God to show him plainly who she was. Since it was the time of day for the women to draw water, and since he had ten thirsty camels, he asked God to have the chosen woman offer to do the

---

[78] The conversation between Abraham and Ephron is humorous. "How much? Well, it's only worth 400 pieces of silver, but what is that among friends? [hint, hint]" "OK, here is 400 pieces of silver, then." "Wow, you are so kind. Thank you!"

hard work of watering them. Providentially, the first woman he asked did so, which he then considered might have been too easy of a test.

However, upon asking her of her family, he discovered that she was the granddaughter of Abraham's brother, Nahor—exactly who Abraham wanted him to find (vs. 22–33). He was welcomed into their home by her brother, Laban, where they took care of his camels and prepared to feed him as well. However, he insisted on not imposing on their hospitality if they did not intend to fulfill his mission, so he did not eat until he had told his story.

It was obvious from his initial conversation with Laban that Rebekah's brother was impressed with wealth, so the servant made sure to tell of Abraham's great prosperity and that Isaac (and thus Rebekah and her children) would be the sole heir (vs. 34–54). He also told of his request that God would point out the woman who should be Isaac's wife. Together, these things impressed Laban and his father, Bethuel, and they agreed that this was from God and that they would not stand in the way.

The following morning, however, as the servant prepared to return to Abraham, Laban and his mother asked if Rebekah could stay for another ten days (vs. 54–61). When he balked, they suggested that he let Rebekah make the decision, assuming she would not want to leave right away. However, she was ready to move on, so they loaded the animals and began the long journey home.

The Hebrew text includes a disjunctive[79] at the beginning of verse 62 to show a shift in the story. Much like in a movie, the scene fades from Rebekah in Haran to Isaac in Canaan, resting in "THE FIELD" that they owned, possibly remembering his mother and thinking about his future wife (vs. 62–67). At that moment, the caravan came into view, and he got up to greet them. Discovering he was her fiancé, Rebekah dismounted and went to meet him. He took her as his wife, and she helped comfort him in the loss of his mother.

---

[79] The opposite of a conjunctive (or conjunction), a disjunctive disconnects sentences rather than connecting them. While they do occur regularly, they are sometimes very important in the flow and interpretation of a passage.

Chapter twenty-five tells the story of three men. To move forward in the story, Moses needed to conclude both Abraham and Ishmael, then continue what happened with Isaac and Rebekah, so he wrote three distinct sections.

The first section finishes Abraham's story (vs. 1–11). Sometime after Sarah died, Abraham remarried and fathered six more sons. Constable notes that some scholars identify Keturah as Hagar,[80] but the plural "CONCUBINES" in verse six seems to reject that. How many concubines Abraham had is never revealed, but two are mentioned (including Hagar), and the plural may indicate at least a third.[81] He did not want these sons encroaching on Isaac and the covenantal promises, so he gave them gifts (instead of any substantial inheritance) "AND SENT THEM OFF TO THE EAST, AWAY FROM HIS SON ISAAC." After Abraham's death, Isaac and Ishmael came together one last time to bury him alongside Sarah.

The second section concludes Ishmael's story as well (vs. 12–18). He had twelve sons, who became chieftains of their own family tribes. Thus, God's promise that both Abraham and Ishmael would be the fathers of many nations came true. Abraham had eight sons who each had many descendants. Ishmael's family moved south and settled in the desert areas between Egypt and Arabia. Ishmael lived 49 years following Abraham's death and died surrounded by his family. There is no mention that he ever pursued Yehovah during his life.

The third section suggests that it will tell more of Isaac's story, but instead, Moses moved quickly to Jacob and Esau (vs. 19–34).[82] It is here we learn that Isaac was 40 years old when he married Rebekah. The story of her pregnancy comes quickly, so we might assume that it was shortly after their marriage,

---

[80] Constable, *Notes on Genesis, 2016 Edition*, 201.

[81] While we cannot get into much detail about this, polygamy was widespread in ancient Middle Eastern culture, as it often still is today. The fact that God never condemned these men for their polygamy, even though his established pattern for marriage is one man and one woman, is difficult to understand. Historically, there have been at least six different explanations ranging from polygamy being completely acceptable, acceptable in certain circumstances, and not acceptable at all. The overwhelming silence on this topic in both the Old and New Testaments is curious.

[82] Compared to the other patriarchs, Isaac gets less space than anyone else, and the one major story we do see in chapter 26 is devastating. This may be due to his general apathy toward God, which left very little of his story to tell.

when, in reality, they prayed for children for 20 years before God granted them. When she finally did become pregnant, it was a difficult time, and she asked God why. In a key prophecy, he revealed that she was carrying twin boys who would each become great nations, although the older would serve the younger.[83] When they were born, the first one came out red and was named *Esau*, which sounds like the Hebrew word for "red." The younger was named *Jacob*, which sounds like the Hebrew word for "heel," because he was holding onto Esau's heel in the womb.

The chapter skips a couple of decades as the boys grew, and their personalities developed. Esau was much like Isaac, a wild outdoorsman who loved to hunt and eat game. Jacob was more like Rebekah, calmer and more at home in the tents. Moses did not portray either of these traits negatively; however, each son would use them to his advantage.

In one remarkable instance, Esau came home famished after a long day of hunting, and Jacob set a trap for the hunter. Jacob offered some of his lentil stew in trade for Esau's birthright. The birthright customarily entitled Esau, as the firstborn, to a double portion of the inheritance and the leadership over the entire estate when Isaac died. Esau's comment, "WHAT USE IS THE BIRTHRIGHT TO ME?" reveals a general apathetic attitude and that he "DESPISED HIS BIRTHRIGHT," meaning that he cared more about his immediate gratification than anything else, especially the future. This would arise multiple times throughout his life. It was a con that Jacob had considered for some time, and he found the right time to execute it. This scheming would characterize most of his life as well.

Chapter twenty-six reveals a sad repetition of Abraham's life in Isaac's. The saying "like father, like son" is shown to be true in Isaac's decisions at this time. There is some debate (especially by those who do not take the text

---

[83] This is a classic example of a "near-far prophecy." Without ultrasound technology, there was no way for her to know that 1) there were twins and 2) they were both boys. Once the twin sons were born, proving the first part of the prophecy, they could be sure the second part would come true as well. This became a major point of contention within this family.

completely literally) as to whether this account is the same as Abraham's, retold for emphasis. However, the first line clarifies that this was "SUBSEQUENT TO...THE DAYS OF ABRAHAM."

The details are familiar. A famine struck the land of Canaan, and it seems that Isaac considered moving to Egypt for relief as Abraham had done in chapter 20 (vs. 1). This time, though, God intervened before he moved, meeting with Isaac and reaffirming his covenant with him (vs. 2–6). Everything that God had promised Abraham would be fulfilled through Isaac, so Isaac stayed in Canaan, but in the southern part near Gerar.

This region was where Isaac had grown up and where Abraham was on good terms with Abimelech, king of the Philistines. However, for some reason, when Isaac returned here, like Abraham, he thought his life was in danger if the local men decided to kill him to take Rebekah (vs. 7). Following his father's pattern, they perpetuated the story that Rebekah was his sister.[84] The first time, Abimelech took Sarah into his harem immediately, but God intervened before they could do anything. This time, Isaac and Rebekah lived "THERE A LONG TIME" when Abimelech happened to see them playing with each other one day as only a married couple should do (vs. 8–9).[85] Infuriated, he scolded Isaac for lying to him, saying that at any time one of the locals could have taken Rebekah. Abimelech put the word out throughout his realm, threatening anyone who touched Isaac or his wife (vs. 10–11). Whatever reputation Isaac previously had was ruined.

Although God continued to bless Isaac materially, Isaac had trouble with Abimelech's men (vs. 12–22). Repeatedly they filled the water wells that Abraham's men had dug and that Isaac was using. Rather than confronting them, Isaac moved further away and dug new wells, which they also filled. Finally, he was far enough away that they left him alone. He moved north once more, to Beer-Sheba, where he dug a well and built an altar to God

---

[84] Unlike Abraham's case, in which Sarah was really his half-sister, Rebekah was Isaac's first cousin, once removed.

[85] There is something to be commended about Abimelech's morality. Even though he had many wives, he still understood that certain activities were to be reserved for a husband and wife.

because God appeared to him there and again assured Isaac of his provision (vs. 23–25). As he did with Abraham years before, Abimelech came to Isaac to make a truce with him, which Isaac accepted (vs. 26–33).[86] Isaac then dug a well, close to his father's, and gave it a similar name—Shibah.

Because the focus of the narrative is about to shift to Jacob, the chapter concludes with a note about Esau (vs. 34). Unlike Abraham, it seems Isaac did nothing to make sure his sons married close to the family. As a result, Esau married, not one but two, Hittite women, who caused much grief for Isaac and Rebekah.

Chapter twenty-seven contains a major turning point in the life of Isaac's family and the story. Verse one indicates that Isaac was old enough that he had gone blind and was preparing to die (vs. 1–4).[87] Part of these preparations included disbursing the inheritance to his heirs, which required executing the birthright, normally given to the firstborn son. Over time Isaac and Rebekah had taken sides, each favoring one of the twins. Esau was the firstborn and an outdoorsman, making him Isaac's favorite, whereas Jacob was a quiet, deep thinker and preferred to stay at home. This favoritism, plus the prophecy that the younger son would eventually rule over the older son (25:23) caused Rebekah to groom Jacob for his leadership role in the family. It seems that Isaac either did not know about Esau selling his birthright (25:33–34) or he did not care, because he intended to give Esau his blessing anyway.

Rebekah moved into action right away, not willing to let "her son" lose the blessing she had prepared him for (vs. 5–17). Rebekah had been making Isaac's favorite meal long before Esau learned it, so she convinced Jacob to impersonate his brother and get the blessing from his father. Rebekah's intricate plan had a response to each of Jacob's hesitations, showing that she must have been thinking about this for some time (not unlike Jacob's previous

---

[86] Although some people see this as a different king (*Abimelech* simply means "my father is king" and may be a title rather than a name), his commanding officer was named Phicol, the same as the man who met with Abraham in 21:22.

[87] Isaac was only 137 years old at this point and lived to be 180 (35:28). Esau and Jacob were 77 years old.

scheme with the soup). It also means that she fully expected Isaac to move forward with Esau, revealing Isaac's public animosity to God's prophecy. Finally, Jacob gave into Rebekah's plan, disguised himself, and took the meal into Isaac (vs. 18–27). Although Isaac was initially suspicious, Jacob's disguise worked, and Isaac finally gave him the blessing, including the prophecy that his brother would serve him (vs. 28–29).[88]

Scarcely had Jacob left Isaac's tent when Esau entered with his father's favorite meal, ready to receive the blessing (vs. 30–38). Immediately, Isaac knew what Jacob had done and told Esau. When Esau asked if there was anything left, Isaac said that he had nothing left to give him. This may be the most tragic part of the story because all he had promised Jacob was material wealth. Nowhere in this chapter do we find Isaac passing down the blessing of Yehovah or repeating God's covenant with Abraham. These were not on Isaac's mind. With the material blessings having been promised to Jacob, all Isaac could do was reiterate that Esau would live in servitude to his brother (vs. 39–40). This caused Esau to hate Jacob and promise to kill him, so Rebekah tricked Isaac again (vs. 41–46). She had Jacob make plans to run away to her father's family to escape his brother, but she told Isaac that Esau's wives were horrible, so he should send Jacob back to her family to find a wife, as Abraham had done for Isaac.

There is much to be said about the fact that the prophecy would have come to pass even without the lying, scheming, and cheating we see in this chapter. God never commands or requires people to sin. While we cannot say how he would have made it happen, we can say that this family did not have to be ruined for God to have fulfilled his plan.

Chapter twenty-eight immediately continues the story from chapter twenty-seven. Jacob's life was in danger from his brother, Esau, so Rebekah intended to send him away to her brother, his Uncle Laban, 500 miles away.

---

[88] This part of the blessing is what Rebekah especially wanted Jacob to have, since that was what God promised before the boys were born. The birthright holder was responsible for taking care of the widowed and unmarried women of the family, and Rebekah knew that she would have an easy life with her favorite son at the helm.

With pseudo-piety, she told Isaac that she wanted Jacob (now 77 years old) to marry someone within the family instead of from the pagan tribes surrounding them (27:46). Finally, Isaac remembered the spiritual side of things, and he sent Jacob off with the blessings of Yehovah, first promised to Abraham (vs. 1–5). It seems that this may have been the first time that Esau heard that marrying the local women was a problem, so, attempting to win back his parents' favor, he married again—this time from the family of Ishmael (vs. 6–9).[89]

The rest of this chapter sets up the long story of God's dealings with Jacob. On the run for his life, Jacob stopped for the night about 50 miles north of home. Not knowing if his hunter-brother was on his trail, Jacob was now homeless, scared, and tired. Carrying only a few possessions, he fell asleep with his head on a rock (vs. 10–15). In a dream, he saw a stairway connecting earth and Heaven, with God sitting at the top and his angels traveling up and down. Here God introduced himself to Jacob (another indication of Isaac's lack of godly fathering) and reaffirmed the covenant that he had made with Abraham, promising to fulfill it through Jacob.

When Jacob awoke, he realized that he had met with God, fearfully recognizing that he did not truly know God, so he built an altar and named the place Beth-El, meaning "house of God" (vs. 16–22). However, Jacob—the master con artist—was unsure whether he could trust God, so he made this promise: if God fulfilled his end of the bargain (specifically, that he would successfully bring Jacob back to this spot), then Jacob would worship and follow him. What God eventually did with Jacob and his family is a wonderful picture of his trustworthiness, but it is sad to note that Jacob, son of Isaac and grandson of Abraham, was 77 years old before he met God personally and much older before he learned that he could trust him.

---

[89] The fact that Esau married multiple wives, both Canaanite and Ishmaelite, speaks to the lack of godly parenting from Isaac and Rebekah. Surprisingly, even with his lack of attention to spiritual matters, Isaac was the only one of the three major patriarchs—including Abraham and Jacob—to have only one wife and no mistresses recorded.

Chapters twenty-nine through thirty-one span the next twenty years of Jacob's life, the time spent in Haran with his mother's brother, Laban. Finishing his long journey to Haran, Jacob came across a well surrounded by a few shepherds and their flocks (vs. 1–8). He discovered that they knew of Laban and heard that his uncle was well. At just that moment, Laban's daughter (Jacob's first cousin), Rachel, approached the well with her flock (vs. 9–14). Even though the other shepherds said it was not yet time to uncover the well, Jacob did anyway and watered Rachel's sheep for her.[90] When he explained who he was, she ran to her father, who "RUSHED OUT TO MEET HIM" and brought him home, excited to hear Jacob's story. Because of the great distance, it is possible (and maybe likely) that Laban had not seen or heard from his sister, Rebekah, since she left to marry Isaac 97 years earlier.

After Jacob had stayed and worked for Laban for about a month, Laban approached him with an offer to stay on permanently (vs. 15–20). When he asked Jacob what wages would be fair, he responded that he had fallen in love with Rachel and wanted to marry her. Laban agreed, stating that she was worth seven years of Jacob's labor. However, at the end of the agreed time, Laban tricked Jacob, giving him Leah in marriage instead. Jacob did not realize the switch until the morning after the wedding night, when it was too late to do anything about it (vs. 21–30). Laban did offer him Rachel as well, under two conditions: 1) Jacob had to honor the full bridal week with Leah before taking Rachel, and 2) he had to work for Laban for seven more years. Jacob reluctantly agreed, but it was obvious that he loved Rachel far more than he did Leah.

Because of Jacob's disdain for Leah (especially compared to Rachel), God enabled Leah to have children but not Rachel (vs. 31–35). Jacob's first four children—Reuben, Simeon, Levi, and Judah—were all sons of Leah, while Rachel waited barren.

---

[90] It was 97 years earlier that his mother, Rebekah, watered the camels of Abraham's servant, possibly at this same well or nearby location. Abraham's servant and Jacob had come for the same reason—to find a wife for Abraham's descendant.

Chapter thirty has two distinct sections. The first tells the story of how Jacob fathered the rest of his children (except one). In the same way that Sarah gave Hagar to Abraham to bear a child in her place, Rachel gave Jacob her maid, Bilhah, as her surrogate (vs. 1–8). Bilhah gave him two sons, Dan and Naphtali, and Rachel believed that God had vindicated her and that she had won this battle with her sister. However, Leah was not about to let Rachel win, so she gave Jacob her maid as well (vs. 9–13). Zilpah also bore two sons to Jacob, Gad and Asher, so Leah once again had the "upper hand" in this sibling battle.

Jacob now had eight sons with three women, but none yet with his favorite wife. There was some overlap in the pregnancies of the women because all these and others were born during the second seven years that Jacob was with Laban. One day young Reuben (probably no more than 4–5 years old) found some mandrakes and brought them to Leah (vs. 14–21). Mandrakes were considered an aphrodisiac (see Song of Songs 7:12–13), so Rachel asked for some for herself, always looking for something to help her. Leah agreed but only if Rachel would let Jacob sleep with her that night; Rachel agreed. That night Leah conceived yet again, and over the next couple of years, she continued to have children—two more sons, Issachar and Zebulun, and a daughter, Dinah. Finally, God allowed Rachel to become pregnant, and she gave birth to a son, Joseph (vs. 22–24).

The second section of the chapter records an encounter between Jacob and Laban. After fourteen years and twelve children, Jacob was ready to move back home, so he asked Laban's blessing to send him on his way (vs. 25–30). Laban was not eager to do this because he knew that he had been blessed greatly by God on account of Jacob. However, Jacob had still been working for wages, not building his personal wealth, so he was ready to go. When Laban asked Jacob to name his price to stay, Jacob had a plan (vs. 31–43). Jacob promised to continue managing Laban's herds as long as he was able to keep the speckled and spotted animals (the rarer ones which were considered worth less than the others), which he would take at each birthing season. Laban quickly agreed and personally separated those from his herds and turned them over to his sons to manage three days away from his own flocks. Jacob must have known that the spotted animals would produce more spotted animals, but he also believed in a kind of superstitious magic that could cause pure animals to produce spotted ones at a higher rate than normal, so he used these tricks (only on Laban's strong, healthy animals) and kept adding more spotted lambs to his flock each season. "IN THIS WAY JACOB BECAME EXTREMELY PROSPEROUS" to the point that he went from owning nothing to having a great flock of his own in a matter of a few years.

Chapter thirty-one concludes the story of Jacob's attempt to leave Laban. For six years (after the promised fourteen), Jacob's flock had grown at Laban's expense, and he had come to view Jacob with suspicion and contempt (vs. 1–16). When Jacob realized this, he decided it was finally time to leave, which God confirmed for him in a vision. Although he had used superstitious methods to increase his flock in chapter thirty, here Jacob acknowledged that God was the one who had done it for him year after year. God had even told Jacob in a dream that he had been the one blessing him. In contrast, Laban had continually tried to change the deal for his benefit but continued losing his wealth to Jacob. When Jacob told all this to Rachel and Leah, they agreed and made plans to leave immediately.

Three days later, Laban learned that Jacob had left with his entire family, flocks, "AND ALL HIS MOVEABLE PROPERTY" (vs. 17–24). He also discovered that some of his "HOUSEHOLD IDOLS" were missing, so he gathered a posse and pursued Jacob, catching up with him after seven days. In what was probably a once-in-a-lifetime event for Laban, Yehovah came to him in a dream and warned him not to do anything to Jacob, not even bless him! He could not curse Jacob against God's blessing, and he could not bless Jacob beyond God's blessing, so God allowed him to do neither.

Laban stormed into Jacob's camp the next morning, full of questions and accusations (vs. 25–32). "Why did you sneak away? Why did you take my daughters and grandchildren from me? And why did you steal my household gods?" Jacob was ready for most of the questions. Given Laban's attitude toward him and his methods, he was genuinely afraid that he would lose everything if he told Laban he was leaving. However, he genuinely knew nothing about the missing idols and (foolishly) promised to execute whoever had stolen them. He challenged Laban to search everywhere and produce them, proving they had been stolen. After searching all the other tents, Laban finally came to Rachel's (vs. 33–37). She used the excuse that she was on her menstrual period to remain seated (on the hidden idols) instead of moving during his search. When Laban could not produce the idols, Jacob lashed out, accusing him of all his devious sins against him and his family (vs. 38–42). Humiliated, Laban (under God's warning to neither bless nor curse Jacob) offered a treaty with Jacob and promised that they would go their ways in peace (vs. 43–55). He managed to slip in a pseudo-threat by saying that, if Jacob were ever to hurt his wives or children or marry additional wives, God would know. Jacob agreed, swearing an oath to Yehovah, while Laban swore to his pagan gods. The next "MORNING LABAN KISSED HIS GRANDCHILDREN AND HIS DAUGHTERS GOODBYE AND BLESSED THEM" before returning home. Although he is referenced three more times in Genesis (32:4; 46:18, 25), Laban himself never comes back into the Scripture text.

Chapter thirty-two tells of Jacob's return to Canaan to encounter his brother, Esau. Even though it had been twenty years since Jacob left, his last memory of Canaan was Esau's threat to kill him (27:41), and he had no reason to believe that anything had changed, so he was afraid (vs. 1–12). The mention of "THE ANGELS OF GOD" in verse one is significant because Jacob saw angels in 28:12 as he left Canaan, and now he saw them again as he returned.[91] He named the place "MAHANAIM" (Hebrew for "two camps"), possibly a reference to his and the angels' camps.

Jacob sent messengers ahead to Esau to let him know that he was coming. When word came back that Esau was headed toward Jacob with 400 men, Jacob began to divide his possessions into two groups, hoping that, even if Esau captured one of them, the other would survive. Surprisingly and sadly, verses 9–12 contain Jacob's first recorded prayer. He had talked with God

---

[91] These are the only two places in the entire Old Testament this exact phrase occurs—"the angels of God."

multiple times in the past, but we have no record of Jacob initiating those meetings. Here he called out to God, asking him to fulfill his promise from 28:15 to allow Jacob to return unharmed.

That night Jacob put together a sizeable gift of animals and servants to send ahead in groups to his brother. Each group was to present itself to Esau, saying that Jacob was right behind them (vs. 13–23). Instead, it would be yet another gift of animals. Jacob hoped to buy Esau's peace. He also took his wives and children across the Jabbok River, sending them further ahead, so he was alone when he met Esau.

That night a man came to Jacob and wrestled with him (vs. 24–30). The text provides no details as to why the fight began except that the other man started it. Perhaps Jacob initially thought it was Esau or one of Esau's spies. As daybreak came, the man struck Jacob's hip, permanently dislocating it. Jacob finally recognized that this was God himself (probably the preincarnate Jesus), so he stopped fighting and just clung to him, refusing to let go without a blessing. Asking Jacob his name, God changed it to *Israel*, which means "God fights."[92] It was both an acknowledgment that Jacob had fought <u>with</u> God and that God would fight <u>for</u> him. Although he refused to tell Jacob his name, Jacob realized that he had seen God, and he named the location *Peniel* (or *Penuel*), meaning "the face of God." Over the centuries, teachers have suggested several potential spiritual applications of this event. Especially from a modern Christian perspective, the best may be that God had to bring Jacob to the end of himself before he finally began to rely on God. This was his "turning point," and his new name showed the spiritual change within him, of which the limp (like Paul's "thorn in the flesh," 2 Corinthians 12:7) was a constant reminder.

Early that morning, Jacob limped over to meet the rest of his family and await Esau's arrival (vs. 31). Moses added a note about the Israelites not eating from the part of an animal near where God disabled Jacob, but this seems to have been traditional, not a required commandment under the Law (vs. 32).

---

[92] Some people make this to mean something about Jacob, "God's Warrior," rather than about God himself.

Chapter thirty-three finally tells of Jacob's and Esau's reunion. When Esau arrived at Jacob's camp, Jacob had divided his wives and children into three groups, one behind the other (vs. 1–7). The order showed his obvious favoritism (in case any were to be captured or killed) with Bilhah and Zilpah in front with their children, followed by Leah with her children. Rachel and Joseph hid in the back. When Esau approached Jacob, they met each other and wept; it had been twenty years. Then Esau had two questions for Jacob.

First, "WHO ARE THESE PEOPLE WITH YOU?" There were sisters-in-law, eleven nephews, and a niece whom Esau had never met, so Jacob introduced them. As had Jacob, they all bowed low to Esau. Esau's second question was, "Why did you send me all those animals?" (vs. 8–11) Jacob explained that they were a gift, an obvious attempt to pay back what he had stolen in Esau's blessing. Esau refused, but Jacob insisted until Esau finally gave in and accepted the animals. Esau invited Jacob to Seir, where he could host his entire household, but Jacob was still skeptical of Esau's intentions, so he made a lot of excuses until Esau finally led the way home (vs. 12–20). Rather than traveling the 100 miles south to Edom, however, Jacob never followed. Instead, he moved a few miles west before stopping at Succoth. Finally, he made his way 20 miles west, across the Jordan River, and bought a piece of land near Shechem, where he settled and built an altar to God.

Chapter thirty-four takes place about 6–10 years after chapter thirty-three. Assuming Dinah was born about the same time as Joseph, during Jacob's second set of seven years working for Laban, they would have been six years old when Jacob finally left to return to Canaan (compare 30:25 with 31:41). After meeting with Esau, "JACOB TRAVELED TO SUKKOTH WHERE HE BUILT HIMSELF A HOUSE AND MADE SHELTERS FOR HIS LIVESTOCK" (33:17), and he subsequently "PURCHASED THE PORTION OF THE FIELD WHERE HE HAD PITCHED HIS TENT" near the city of Shechem (33:19). This probably allowed him a few years during which the youngest children (Dinah and Joseph) grew to be 12–16 years old.[93]

---

[93] Joseph was 17 years old in 37:2, so Dinah was probably not much older than that, if at all.

While living near Shechem (the city), Jacob's teenaged daughter, Dinah, went into town to play with her friends, when a man named Shechem (from whose father Jacob had purchased his land) saw her, seduced her, and raped her (vs. 1–5). Unlike many other instances of rape, Shechem honestly believed that he loved her (instead of hating her, 2 Samuel 13:14–15), so he asked his father to arrange for him to marry her (another indication of her approximate age). Although Jacob heard about the incident, he decided to wait until his sons returned from work before doing anything. The reason for this is unknown and widely debated.

When they heard about it, they were, naturally, furious (vs. 6–12). Shechem and his father tried to minimize the situation by making this a simple economic deal. Since they were already trading with each other, why not intermarry as well? Shechem was so love-struck that he promised to pay whatever the brothers demanded. Having learned all too well from both their father and Uncle Laban, these young men used their religion to deceive Shechem (vs. 13–24). They insisted that they could not intermarry while the men of Shechem were uncircumcised (the visible sign of the Abrahamic Covenant), but that ritual would change everything. They said that if every man in the city were circumcised, Jacob's family could become full economic and social partners with them. Planning their own deceitful scheme, the men thought they would be able to take over Jacob's wealth with this partnership, so they readily agreed. However, only three days into the healing process, Simeon and Levi[94] slaughtered every single Shechemite man in retribution for their sister's rape, and they brought her home (vs. 25–31). Although Jacob mourned the loss of his reputation and feared potential revenge from the surrounding tribes, the sons thought they were justified because of what Shechem had done to their sister, which the other men of the city did not condemn.

Chapter thirty-five tells of three great events at this point in Jacob's life. Immediately after the incident at Shechem, God told Jacob to move about 20

---

[94] They were Leah's second and third sons, two of Dinah's oldest brothers.

miles south to Bethel (vs. 1–8). This was where God had met with him when he first left Isaac and Rebekah and where Jacob had promised his allegiance to God if he brought him back (28:10–22). When his family looted Shechem, they must have taken the city idols as well because Jacob demanded that they all be destroyed before meeting God at Bethel. God protected them on this leg of their journey by making the surrounding tribes and nations afraid of them so they would not seek revenge for the slaughter at Shechem.

The first major event took place at Bethel, where God reaffirmed the covenant with Jacob that he had originally made to Abraham; he also reaffirmed Jacob's new name of "Israel" (vs. 9–15). As he had done nearly 30 years earlier, Jacob built an altar there, called the place Bethel ("house of God"), and worshiped God.

The second major event was after they left Bethel, during the 30-mile journey back to his parents' home in southern Canaan (vs. 16–20). Rachel had gone into heavy labor with her second child, but when they were between Bethel and Bethlehem, she died giving birth to a son. With her final breath, she named the boy Ben-Oni ("son of my suffering"), but Jacob named him Benjamin instead ("son of my right hand"). After only about twenty years of marriage, Jacob had to bury the woman he deeply loved and worked for fourteen years to earn the right to marry.

The third major event occurred shortly after Rachel's death (vs. 21–22). Reuben, Jacob's oldest son, slept with Bilhah, who was his mother's maid and father's concubine. This seems to have been a foolish challenge to his father's authority and an effort to begin living out his birthright as the leader of the family.[95] It backfired when it came time for Jacob's death (see 49:3–4).

Approximately thirty years after he left, Jacob finally returned to his father's home (vs. 27–29). Isaac was in his mid-160s by this point, so he was able to enjoy a reunion with his son and spend time with his daughters-in-law and his grandchildren for a few years until he died at 180 years old.

---

[95] See the account when Absalom slept with David's concubines in 2 Samuel 16:20–22.

Chapter thirty-six picks up on the mention of Esau in 35:29 and gives his genealogy (*toledoth*[96]) and the explanation of his tribal connections. Esau had married three women—two from Canaan and one from Ishmael's family—who gave him a total of five sons (vs. 1–5).[97] He had married the Canaanite women almost 40 years before Jacob originally left Canaan and married the Ishmaelite shortly afterward (26:34; 28:9). Additionally, he had moved to Seir because the land could not sustain both his ranch and Jacob's, whom he knew would certainly return as the legal birthright holder (25:33).

From Esau's five sons came ten grandsons, including Amalek, whose descendants would cause much grief for Israel centuries later (vs. 6–19). In partial fulfillment of God's promise that Abraham would be the ancestor of kings (17:6), Moses recorded the fourteen tribal chiefs or kings that came from Esau (much like the list he gave about Ishmael in 25:13–16). Because there were already people living in Seir, Moses also recorded the names of some of those tribal chiefs, with whom Esau's family had intermarried and finally overtook as rulers of the land (vs. 20–29).

Chapter thirty-seven begins with a verse that best fits at the end of the previous chapter. After explaining Esau's line and location, Moses noted, "BUT JACOB LIVED IN THE LAND WHERE HIS FATHER HAD STAYED, IN THE LAND OF CANAAN" (vs. 1). Verse two begins the final major section of the book, in which Joseph becomes the primary character of the story. Joseph was 17 years old, so this took place about eleven years after Jacob and his family left Laban (vs. 2). His oldest brothers were in their early 20s, and Benjamin was probably only one or two years old.

Joseph's story begins on the premise that "ISRAEL [JACOB] LOVED JOSEPH MORE THAN ALL HIS SONS" (vs. 3–4). Even though they worked together on Jacob's ranch, Joseph and his half-brothers (only Benjamin was his full brother) did not get along. It seems he regularly brought Jacob bad reports about them, and

---

[96] See the Introduction for explanation of the *toledoth* outline of Genesis.

[97] In their commentary on this passage, Keil and Delitszch give a lengthy explanation for why some names in this chapter differ from other passages in Genesis. (https://www.studylight.org/commentaries/kdo/genesis-36.html)

their hatred toward him was so bad that they "WERE NOT ABLE TO SPEAK TO HIM KINDLY." The "SPECIAL TUNIC" that Jacob gave Joseph served only to make it worse.[98]

At this time, God gave Joseph two different dreams that had the same meaning. In the first dream, the bales of grain that Joseph's brothers had bundled bowed down to his bale (vs. 5–8). In the second dream, the sun, moon, and eleven stars bowed to him directly (vs. 9–11). Everyone in the family, including Jacob, understood that Joseph believed they would all bow before him one day.

The defining event of the chapter, and the first one with a major impact on Joseph's life, took place when his brothers took the flock about 50 miles away (back to Shechem) to find adequate pasture (vs. 12–17). For some reason Joseph did not go on this trip; instead, Jacob sent him later to find out how they were doing and to report back. When he reached the place, he discovered they had moved on. As he came over the hill approaching their new camp, his brothers "SAW HIM FROM A DISTANCE" (vs. 18–24). Recognizing his coat, they were filled with rage and plotted to kill "the dreamer." Reuben tried to settle them down, but it was too late. They seized Joseph, stripped off his coat, and threw him into a dry well.

Shortly after that, a caravan of merchants came by, and Judah had an idea (vs. 25–28). Instead of killing Joseph, they could sell him, make a little money, and still tell Jacob that his son had been killed by a wild animal while wandering the countryside looking for them. The nine brothers agreed (Reuben found out about it later) and made the exchange, sending Joseph to Egypt. When they finally returned home, they showed a bloody tunic to Jacob, who

---

[98] Joseph's special robe has become so legendary that Andrew Lloyd Weber even named a musical after it ("Joseph and the Amazing Technicolor Dreamcoat"). Unfortunately, we do not know as much about this tunic as we might think. The NET Bible translators included this study note on verse three:

> "It is not clear what this tunic was like because the meaning of the Hebrew word that describes it is uncertain. The idea that it was a coat of many colors comes from the Greek translation of the OT. An examination of cognate terms in Semitic suggests it was either a coat or tunic with long sleeves (cf. NEB, NRSV), or a tunic that was richly embroidered (cf. NIV). It set Joseph apart as the favored one."

immediately recognized it as Joseph's and went into a deep, inconsolable depression (vs. 29–35). Meanwhile, hundreds of miles away, Joseph was sold as a slave to Pharaoh's "CAPTAIN OF THE GUARD" (vs. 36), possibly the head of royal security or the chief executioner.

Chapter thirty-eight takes a short break from Joseph's story to focus on Judah. The reason is implied in verse one: "AT THAT TIME JUDAH LEFT HIS BROTHERS" or "About this time, Judah left home" (NLT). Why did Judah leave home "AT THAT TIME"? It was his idea to sell Joseph and deceive Jacob (37:26). He certainly knew that Jacob would be devastated, but he probably did not know to what extent. When Jacob refused to be consoled, insisting that he would go to his grave in tears, Judah could no longer take what he had done, but instead of confessing it, he ran away, creating what is arguably the most embarrassing chapter in Genesis.

Moving about 30 miles away, he connected with the Canaanites and married a Canaanite woman who bore him three sons: Er, Onan, and Shelah (vs. 2–5). Fewer than 20 years later, Judah's sons were old enough to marry, so he chose another Canaanite woman, named Tamar, for his oldest son (vs. 6–11). The story is particularly brief over the next few verses because God kept the details to himself. For some unknown reason, God considered Er to be exceptionally evil and killed him. Onan, the second son, married Tamar and was to bear one child in Er's name,[99] but he refused to do so,ced God killed him as well.[100] Judah must have thought that Tamar was somehow responsible for his sons' deaths, so he refused to let Shelah marry her as well. Instead, he

---

[99] The purpose of "levirate marriage" was to produce a child as the deceased brother's heir so he would not be written out of the family tree forever. The most extreme example of this is found in a hypothetical situation that the Sadducees' concocted to confuse Jesus (Matthew 22:23–28). Onan's marriage was not the problem in this story.

[100] This judgment had nothing to do specifically with Onan's *coitus interruptus* as much as it was his attitude toward his dead brother. Onan was a selfish man, who accepted the "benefits" that came with the marriage but rejected the responsibility. This passage should not be used to condemn his sexual act apart from his attitude.

sent her back to her father's home (a grave insult to her and her family), justifying the decision by stating that Shelah was not old enough yet to marry.

"AFTER SOME TIME" (possibly no more than a few years[101]), Judah's wife died, and Tamar had realized that he would never let her marry Shelah. To clear her name and family shame, she needed a plan to prove that she was not at fault in Er's and Onan's deaths. Knowing that Judah would be traveling in the area for work, Tamar disguised herself as a shrine prostitute[102] (which included covering her face) and sat near the road where he would come by (vs. 12–23). When he did come by, it seems he thought that worshiping at her shrine may increase his wool harvest, so he used her services.[103] Since it was not a planned encounter, he did not have any money with him, so he left his identification seal with her as collateral until he sent back payment after the harvest. When he attempted to make the payment, she was nowhere to be found. He said, "LET HER KEEP THE THINGS FOR HERSELF," and forgot about it.

"AFTER THREE MONTHS," she was found to be pregnant (vs. 24–26). Judah knew that she had not married Shelah, but his "contract" with her was still intact, meaning that she had committed adultery. When he sent for her to have her killed, she secretly sent his identification back to him. Immediately, he realized what had happened, and concluded that, since he did not die after having sex with her, she was not at fault for his sons' deaths. Although he did not give her to Shelah, he also did not have sex with her again. She bore Judah two more sons, twins named Perez and Zerah (vs. 27–30). It was through

---

[101] It was only 22 years from the time that Joseph's brothers sold him into slavery and when they went to Egypt the first time to purchase food because of the famine. Because this trip included Judah, it seems he had reconnected with his family, which is not recorded in this chapter.

[102] Religious prostitution was a large part of the Canaanites' pagan worship, something that God repeatedly warned the Israelites to not engage in. The shrine prostitutes made themselves available at pagan worship centers to have sex with the "worshipers." In Israel, Eli's sons did this at the Tent of Meeting in front of Yehovah's altar (1 Samuel 2:22).

[103] It seems Judah became immersed in Canaanite culture much like Lot did in Sodom (see the notes on Genesis 19).

Perez that both Joseph and Mary descended, making this illegitimate son the ancestor of Jesus (Matthew 1:3; Luke 3:33).

The question of why Tamar did this is common. What did she hope to accomplish? She could not know that he would not be carrying money, so it seems unlikely that she planned to get his identification. Additionally, she could not know that she would become pregnant from this one encounter, so she would not necessarily have that to hold against him. The best explanation seems to be about the sexual act itself. If she could prove that she had sex with him and did not kill him, then she could be cleared of the deaths of the other men. This seems to account for both her actions and Judah's response.

Chapter thirty-nine resumes Joseph's story in Egypt, telling what was happening while Judah was away from home during the previous chapter. From the slave block in Egypt, Joseph was purchased by Potiphar, "THE CAPTAIN OF THE GUARD" or chief of Pharaoh's royal security (vs. 1–6).[104] During Joseph's time with Potiphar, God blessed them both as Joseph worked hard with integrity. Eventually, Potiphar put everything he owned into Joseph's control, making it so he did not have to deal with anything himself. The sole exception was Potiphar's wife; she, of course, was off-limits to Joseph (vs. 7–15). Yet he was young and handsome; she was rich and lonely. Like the seductress of Proverbs 7, she invited him into her bed, which he refused because it would be "A GREAT EVIL AND SIN AGAINST GOD" and his boss. This went on "DAY AFTER DAY" until she had had enough of his rejections.

One day when no one else was nearby, she grabbed his sleeve and dragged him toward herself (vs. 11–15). Fighting for everything, he ran away, leaving her screaming for "help" with his coat in her hand. She told the other servants in the house and her husband that "THAT HEBREW SLAVE" had tried to rape her and produced his coat on her bed as her primary evidence (vs. 16–20). (This is the second time someone had used his coat to lie about him and try to destroy him.) As expected, Potiphar was livid! How could Joseph have done

---

[104] Potiphar's high rank in the royal court would become a significant detail in Joseph's narrative.

that? Potiphar had trusted him! Without thinking, he threw Joseph into the palace dungeon.[105]

Again, God was gracious to Joseph. The royal warden had certainly come to know Joseph from Potiphar's house (and probably knew about Potiphar's wife as well) and knew that Joseph could be trusted (vs. 21–23). It was not long before Joseph had the same position in the prison that he had under Potiphar—in charge of the royal dungeon on behalf of the warden. How long Joseph served under Potiphar and how long he was in prison are unknown, but Joseph spent 13 years between the two of them (41:46).

Another explanation that some scholars have offered is that Potiphar knew of his wife's seductive ways but had not addressed them until now. Their marriage problems must have been the worst-kept secret in the palace. In this case, he would have known that Joseph was not lying and was furious at his wife for dragging Joseph down whom he trusted completely. However, the charge was public, and he had to do something, so he placed Joseph under the protection of his friend, the prison warden. A major reason for this interpretation is that, had Potiphar believed his wife, he would have had Joseph executed immediately rather than simply imprisoned in the best place for him to continue watching out for the young man.

Chapter forty records a story that seems moderately interesting on its own but becomes significant two years later (41:1). While Joseph was in prison, two of Pharaoh's most trusted officials were also sent to the dungeon: his "CUPBEARER...AND THE ROYAL BAKER." Together, these two men were responsible for everything the king ate and drank (vs. 1–4). One night in prison, they each had a dream, and Moses noted that each dream had its own meaning, and both were sickened because of them.

The following morning Joseph noticed that they both looked ill or depressed and asked about it (vs. 5–8). When they attributed it to their dreams, Joseph claimed that God would give him the interpretation for them. The cupbearer went first (vs. 9–15). He had seen a grapevine with three clusters of

---

[105] Where else would the captain of Pharaoh's personal security put a prisoner?

grapes. Noticing Pharaoh's cup in his hand, he squeezed the grape juice into the cup and gave it to Pharaoh. Joseph said that this indicated that in three days the cupbearer would be released back to his original position at Pharaoh's side. Joseph asked him to remember Joseph's kindness in prison and put in a good word for him with Pharaoh.

Feeling comfortable after the first interpretation, the baker told Joseph his dream as well. It was similar (vs. 16–19). Like the three grape clusters, the baker saw three baskets of baked goods on his head, but the birds were eating from them, not Pharaoh. Joseph said that the three baskets also represented three days, but the baker would be executed by impaling, and the birds would eat his flesh.

Three days later, as part of the king's birthday celebration, the two men were brought out of the prison to stand before Pharaoh and his court. Just as Joseph had prophesied, Pharaoh reinstated his cupbearer and executed his baker (vs. 20–23). However, the cupbearer completely forgot about Joseph, who remained in prison.

Chapter forty-one jumps ahead "TWO FULL YEARS" during which Joseph continued his faithful service in the royal dungeon. At that time, Pharaoh himself had two dreams in one night, similar but different (vs. 1–7).[106] In the first dream, he saw "SEVEN FINE-LOOKING, FAT COWS" walk up out of the Nile River, followed by seven thin, sickly cows. The thin cows ate the fat cows, but they remained thin. In the second dream, he saw "SEVEN HEADS OF GRAIN" on one stalk, also healthy. These were followed by seven sickly heads of grain, which "SWALLOWED UP" the healthy ones, again without any change. Knowing that these dreams must mean something, he immediately called together his spiritual counselors the next morning and told them the dreams (vs. 8–13). When none of them could come up with an explanation, the cupbearer finally remembered Joseph. He told Pharaoh what had happened two years earlier in prison and that Joseph's prophecies had come true exactly as he told them.

---

[106] Not unlike Joseph's two dreams so many years before. See chapter 37.

Encouraged with hope, Pharaoh called for Joseph, who came quickly, freshly bathed and shaven and in a new set of clothes to stand before the king (vs. 14–24).[107] Pharaoh told Joseph that he had heard that Joseph could interpret dreams. In an act of great boldness, Joseph declared, no, he could not, but God could—an insult to the gods the Pharaoh had trusted his wise men to consult. He told Joseph the detail of both dreams and listened intently to hear what Joseph would say. Unlike the dreams in the dungeon, which each had their own meaning, these two (like Joseph's) meant the same thing (vs. 25–32). Both the cows and the heads of grain represented years. The seven healthy cows and grain were seven years of extraordinary abundance for the herds and crops of Egypt. These would be followed by seven years of famine so great that they would not even remember the good years (no change in the lean cows or thin corn heads). The fact that God gave Pharaoh this dream twice in quick succession meant that this would start quickly, probably with the next harvest.

But Joseph was not content to give only the interpretation (vs. 33–45). Instead, he kept talking, giving his (God-inspired) opinion on what Pharaoh should do because of the dreams. He suggested that Pharaoh was looking at the man who should be in charge of storing excess food during the good years so that the kingdom would not be devastated during the famine.[108] Pharaoh was impressed and (rhetorically) asked his advisers if they could think of anyone better suited for this task than Joseph himself. (Since they could not even interpret the dream, they thought it best to agree with the king at this point.) So, Pharaoh appointed Joseph as Vizier over the entire nation of Egypt. As with Potiphar and the royal warden, Pharaoh did not even have to think about his kingdom, entrusting the entire government—including legislation—to Joseph.

---

[107] It is fun to consider that Potiphar may very well have been standing in Pharaoh's throne room as this happened and watched the whole thing unfold.

[108] The Hebrew text of verse 33 does not say, "Let Pharaoh look for a man..." The verb is not "look for" but "look at." Joseph was blatantly pointing to himself as the solution to Pharaoh's problem.

Thus, after 13 years of slavery and imprisonment, Joseph was finally given back his freedom at **"30 YEARS OLD"** (vs. 46–57). Pharaoh also gave him a wife, who bore him two sons—Manasseh and Ephraim. Joseph gave them Hebrew names, celebrating that God had helped him forget his troubles while still staying connected to his family heritage. He followed through with his advice to the king and collected so much food during the abundant years that he had to stop tracking it. When the famine finally came, he had more than enough to sell both to the Egyptians and the people elsewhere. The famine affected the entire surrounding regions, and Egypt was the only place to find food.

Chapters forty-two through forty-five record the climax of Joseph's story. The seven-year famine that Joseph foretold was so severe that even the first year brought visitors to Egypt to buy food. Jacob was no exception (vs. 1–5). Hearing there was food in Egypt, Jacob had his ten oldest sons[109] make the 150+ mile journey to purchase food for their family. Anticipating a simple exchange, they loaded up their donkeys with money and headed south.

After standing in line, they finally met Zaphenath-Paneah (the Egyptian name that Pharaoh had given to Joseph). Even after twenty years,[110] he recognized them immediately, but they did not recognize him (vs. 6–20).[111] Instead, they bowed down to him, just like he saw in the dreams they hated so much! Rather than initiating a reunion, Joseph chose to test them. Quizzing them, he learned that their father was still alive at home and that they had two younger brothers (but one of them had already died). Without warning, he charged them with espionage! Calling them spies from Canaan, he threw them all into prison for three days, saying that one of them could return home and bring back their younger brother to prove their story, but the rest would not

---

[109] This included Judah, who had returned home by this point (see chapter thirty-eight). However, Jacob was not willing to risk Benjamin's life by sending him on this trip.

[110] Thirteen years with Potiphar and in prison, plus the seven years of abundance.

[111] He would have changed physically from a 17-year-old to a middle-aged man. Additionally, between his wardrobe, make-up, language, and the fact that they did not expect to see him, it would have been more surprising if they <u>had</u> recognized him.

be released until then. After those three days, he reversed his decision, declaring that one brother would stay in prison and would not be released until the others returned with their younger brother.

Speaking amongst themselves in Hebrew, they agreed that God was finally punishing them for their treatment of Joseph two decades earlier (vs. 21–24). When Reuben reminded them that he was against their plan from the beginning, Joseph turned away and wept. (They did not realize that he could understand them.) When they agreed to his terms, Joseph had Simeon (the second oldest, possibly in private gratitude to Reuben) led away and the others released. Secretly, he also had all their money put back into their bags along with the grain he "sold" them and sent them on their way (vs. 25–28). At a rest stop on the way home, one of them found the money. Scared, they wondered what God was doing to them.

After returning home, they told Jacob everything that had happened, especially that Simeon was still there in prison and would not be released unless Benjamin went back with them (vs. 29–38). As expected, Jacob flatly refused, unwilling to lose the only remaining son from his beloved Rachel. Even when all of them found their money and Reuben swore on his own sons' lives to personally take care of Benjamin, Jacob still refused.

Chapter forty-three continues from the previous chapter, probably a year later. The famine was still in full force, and Jacob's family had run out of the food they had purchased in Egypt, so Jacob told his sons to return and buy more (vs. 1–10). Judah reminded him that they were not allowed to buy food in Egypt without bringing Benjamin with them. (No one brought up the fact that Simeon had been in prison the entire time awaiting their return.) As Reuben had done earlier, Judah promised Benjamin's safety but to the point of pledging his own life. (Reuben pledged the lives of his two sons.) The one who had sold Joseph now swore to protect Benjamin. After refusing again, Jacob finally relented (vs. 11–14). With the hope of seeing both Benjamin and Simeon again, he made his sons take enough money for the new food, the money that they had gotten back last time, and gifts to present to Zaphenath-Paneah (whom he still did not know was Joseph).

Upon their return to Egypt, Joseph saw that they had indeed brought Benjamin, so he arranged to have them all to his house for a banquet (vs. 15–25). Not knowing the language, they thought they were being taken away because they had not paid for their first food purchase. When they approached the subject with Joseph's chief of staff, he dismissed their concern, stating that he did indeed have the money. Instead, he had them freshen up and provided water for their donkeys. When they realized that they were supposed to have a meal with the Vizier, they prepared to give him their gifts when he arrived.

When Joseph entered the room, they bowed low again, presenting the gifts on behalf of their aged father (vs. 26–34). Joseph questioned them again about their father. When they introduced Benjamin, Joseph came to the point of tears and had to hide in another room to compose himself. Although they were guests at his banquet, the Hebrews had to eat at a separate table, because they were considered a lower class than the Egyptians. Astonishingly, the brothers noticed that they had been arranged in birth order, something they thought no one could have known. However, they were set at ease and ate and drank with Joseph, who showed an inordinate amount of preferential treatment toward Benjamin by giving him five times what the others received.

Chapter forty-four continues the unrelenting tests that Joseph put his brothers through. In addition to filling their sacks with more food than they requested, he ordered that their money be returned to them again (vs. 1–2). This time he also had his special goblet placed into Benjamin's sack. The next morning, shortly after the men took off for Canaan, Joseph had his servant go after them to accuse them of stealing his goblet (vs. 3–13). Of course, they were surprised at the accusation and denied everything. After all they had done, could the Vizier truly believe they were common thieves? Fully certain of their innocence, they declared that the one who had done this should die; Joseph's servant agreed. He looked carefully through each sack, beginning with Reuben's until he finally found it in Benjamin's, the last sack. They howled with grief and returned together to Joseph to plead their case.

The rest of the chapter records the speech Judah gave on behalf of his father and brother (vs. 14–34). He recounted every detail of their first meeting with the Vizier and the report they had to carry home to Jacob. He recalled how Jacob refused to let Benjamin go with them, fearing he would lose his only surviving connection with Rachel. Judah reminded him that they had returned the money they had found in their sacks along with gifts for him because of the mistake. Finally, he admitted that he had pledged his own life to Jacob should anything happen to Benjamin. Judah still carried the devastation that Jacob experienced when Joseph was lost, and he refused to let that happen again. The Vizier had demanded that the thief be imprisoned, but Judah begged that he be allowed to take Benjamin's place.

Chapter forty-five finally gives the big reveal. No longer able to hide his tears of joy, Joseph demanded that everyone but the eleven Hebrews leave the room (vs. 1–3). After sobbing so loudly that it rang through the hallways, he said one simple sentence in Hebrew, "I AM JOSEPH!", and the twelve sons of Jacob stood together as a family for the first time in 22 years.

Of course, his brothers could not believe it at first (vs. 4–15). After everything they had gone through (accusations, fear, imprisonment), they certainly thought this was another attempt to deceive them. Finally, Joseph convinced them by coming close, and they began to recognize him. He told them about the famine and that there were still five years left. Twice he attributed his presence in Egypt as an act of God, not just their jealousy, and insisted that he no longer held it against them, and they should not either. They spent some time talking with each other and getting reacquainted, but Joseph told them that the entire family needed to come to Egypt immediately because of the famine. He promised to take care of them and could not wait to see his father again.

Even Pharaoh himself participated in the celebration (vs. 16–24). He sent wagons with the men, so they could retrieve their families and move them to Egypt. He promised that he, too, would personally guarantee their safety and provision. Additionally, Joseph gave each of his brothers a set of fine Egyptian clothes and provisions for their journey, but Benjamin received silver and five sets of clothes. As Jacob had sent gifts for him, Joseph sent gifts back to his father. He sent his brothers home with a warning to not fear to return to Egypt with Jacob. So, they did as Joseph and the Pharaoh had instructed them (vs. 25–28). Returning home, they told Jacob everything that had happened and showed him the wagons and the gifts they brought with them, and he agreed to go with them.

Chapters forty-six through fifty conclude Joseph's story in three ways. First, they tell how Jacob's family was reunited, closing the story that began in chapter thirty-seven with Joseph's slavery. Second, they record the end of Jacob's life and his final words, which set the stage for the twelve sons becoming the fledgling nation named after their father, Israel. Third, they record Joseph's death and the prophecy that the family would one day return to Canaan.

Although Jacob began the journey, he had been deceived so many times over the years—even by his sons—that he was unsurprisingly suspicious (vs. 1–4). He stopped the caravan at the border of Canaan, at Beer-Sheba, where his father had dug a well decades before. There he built an altar and offered a sacrifice to Yehovah. That night God spoke to Jacob and assured him that this was the right decision. Not only would he see Joseph again, but Jacob would die in peace with Joseph standing right beside him. God also promised that Jacob's family would return to Canaan.

Verses 5–27 give the family lineage of all who left Canaan for Egypt. Jacob took a total of sixty-five descendants with him, plus his daughters-in-law (who were not included in the count). With the addition of Joseph and his wife and two sons, the family of Israel numbered approximately ninety people when they stood together in Egypt. Jacob sent Judah ahead to meet Joseph and let him know they were nearby (vs. 28–29). When Joseph saw Jacob, "HE HUGGED HIS NECK AND WEPT ON HIS NECK FOR QUITE SOME TIME."

Before they could get settled, Joseph stressed an important part of Jacob's upcoming interview with the Pharaoh (vs. 30–34). Since Egyptians considered shepherds "DISGUSTING," Joseph made sure that his family emphasized their occupation. He had already told Pharaoh the same thing. This would ensure that Pharaoh sent them out to the region of Goshen, away from the "civilized"

Egyptians, where the Hebrews could live with no interference, with as much pasture as they could want.

Chapter forty-seven contains three sections, spanning the remaining years of the famine. The first section has to do with the Hebrews settling into Goshen (vs. 1–12). Joseph introduced "FIVE OF HIS BROTHERS" to Pharaoh, who did exactly as Joseph had instructed them, saying that they were shepherds and herdsmen.[112] Pharaoh was so impressed that he even hired some of them to take care of his livestock (presumably so an Egyptian would not have to do so). When Jacob finally met Pharaoh, he "BLESSED" the king. Normally, this would have been unheard of. The lesser in rank never blessed those above him! However, Jacob was long past thinking about rank. He knew the living God and chose to display his gratitude by blessing the pagan king who had given his son back to him. What a wonderful picture of a man of God showing grace and gratitude in this situation!

The second section describes how Joseph managed the remainder of the famine (vs. 13–26). He had been selling food back to the Egyptians (who were extraordinarily wealthy because of the abundant years before the famine), but their money had finally run out; Pharaoh owned it all. With no money to exchange, Joseph accepted their livestock in trade. The following year, when Pharaoh owned all the livestock in Egypt, the people offered their very lives and land in exchange for food. Joseph found this acceptable and took control of every piece of land in Egypt (except Goshen and the priests' parcels) and made all the Egyptian people slaves of Pharaoh. Finally, at the end of the famine, Joseph gave the people seed to plant, but because they were Pharaoh's slaves, Joseph made a law that the people were to return 20% of every harvest into the king's storehouses (the same deal as during the years of abundance). Moses noted, when he wrote Genesis more than 400 years later, that Joseph's law was still in effect.

---

[112] The question of which brothers Joseph chose is never answered, but it seems plausible that Judah and Benjamin would have been in that group. It may have also included Reuben, his oldest brother, the one who tried to rescue him from death so many years earlier.

The third section briefly tells what happened in Goshen during that time (vs. 27–31). While the Egyptians were slowly becoming enslaved to Pharaoh (under Joseph's direction), Israel grew "FRUITFUL AND INCREASED RAPIDLY IN NUMBER." After seventeen years in that foreign land, Jacob came to the end of his life. In preparation for his death, he made Joseph swear that they would not bury him in Egypt but take his body back to Canaan and lay it with his family there.

Chapters forty-eight and forty-nine record Jacob's final blessings over his family. When Joseph heard that Jacob was about to die, he brought his two sons, Ephraim and Manasseh, to be blessed (vs. 1–7). Jacob reminded Joseph (who had certainly heard the story numerous times) that God had originally appeared to Jacob and confirmed with him the promises he had made to Abraham and Isaac. In an unusual act, Jacob adopted Ephraim and Manasseh as his own two sons, "JUST AS REUBEN AND SIMEON ARE." If Joseph had other children, they would carry his name and claim their Hebrew inheritance through their big brothers. In this way, Joseph received the double portion of the inheritance that was normally reserved for the birthright holder, one portion through each son.[113]

After he had announced his intentions, Jacob began the formal ceremony (vs. 8–20). He asked, "WHO ARE THESE?" and Joseph officially presented his two sons. Because Manasseh was the oldest, Joseph put him on Jacob's right side and Ephraim on the left. Yet, in a second unusual act, Jacob crossed "HIS HANDS...[AND] PUT HIS LEFT HAND ON MANASSEH'S HEAD." He then blessed Joseph and his sons. Joseph was naturally "DISPLEASED" and thought that Jacob had made a mistake because of his poor vision. However, when he tried to correct it, Jacob prophesied that (in a similar fashion to Jacob and Esau), Ephraim, the younger son, would indeed become greater than Manasseh, although Manasseh would become a great nation as well. His final blessing on Joseph

---

[113] Without special divine revelation, Jacob could not have known that Levi would receive no land when God parceled it out more than four hundred years later. In this way, Ephraim and Manasseh replaced Joseph and Levi in the inheritance, preserving twelve tribal lands.

was that he would retain the land of Shechem, which was where Joseph was finally buried (Joshua 24:32) within what would come to be the tribal land of Manasseh.

> The Hebrew word שְׁכֶם (sh\`khem) could be translated either as "mountain slope" or "shoulder, portion," or even taken as the proper name "Shechem." Jacob was giving Joseph either (1) one portion above his brothers, or (2) the mountain ridge he took from the Amorites, or (3) Shechem. The ambiguity actually allows for all three to be the referent. He could be referring to the land in Shechem he bought in Gen 33:18-19, but he mentions here that it was acquired by warfare, suggesting that the events of 34:25-29 are in view (even though at the time he denounced it, 34:30). Joseph was later buried in Shechem (Josh 24:32).[114]

Chapter forty-nine contains the longest prophecy in Genesis. With his final words over each of his sons, Jacob also made some prophecies regarding "WHAT WILL HAPPEN TO [THEM] IN FUTURE DAYS" (vs. 1–2).

Although *Reuben* was the firstborn, he lost his birthright by sleeping with one of Jacob's concubines (vs. 3–4; 35:22). He was strong, but he would not be a leader in the nation. *Simeon and Levi* were the close brothers who avenged their sister's rape at Shechem (vs. 5–7; Genesis 34). Like James and John in the Gospels, they were driven by their emotions, especially their anger, and Jacob said that they would end up scattered in Israel and not counselors in leadership.[115]

Judah was the first to get a primarily positive blessing, the oldest son who had repented after disqualifying himself (vs. 8–12). His three older brothers must have never restored their relationship with Jacob. The one who at one time sold his brother became the man who would lead the nation, through whom kings, and eventually, the eternal Messiah would come.

---

[114] The NET Study Bible note at Genesis 48:22.

[115] Levi was eventually "scattered," because the Levites had no land of their own, serving as priests in each of the other tribal regions. This also eliminated them from most governmental positions of leadership (although Moses and Aaron were Levites).

The use of the Hebrew word שִׁילֹה (*shiloh*) in verse ten has caused great difficulty for translators and commentators alike. However, all conservative scholars agree that it finds its ultimate meaning in the Messiah and his Kingdom. The promise that "THE SCEPTER WILL NOT DEPART FROM JUDAH...UNTIL HE COMES TO WHOM IT BELONGS" (NET, NIV, NLT)[116] reveals that the coming royal line will forever be through Judah; none of the others would successfully usurp it. In Messiah's Kingdom, the Judahites will be so wealthy that they can afford to tie their donkeys to their vines (and risk them eating everything) and still wash their clothes in the wine they will produce. Wine and milk will be as plentiful for them as water.

Zebulun was linked to the sea—both the Mediterranean and Galilee—and became involved in both land and sea trade routes (vs. 13). *Issachar* would be hard workers, willing to sacrifice their freedom and become slaves to their brothers in exchange for wealth (vs. 14–15). *Dan* (which means "judge") would become a judge over Israel and a powerful force as well (vs. 16–18). It seems this was fulfilled in Samson (Judges 13:2). However, Dan was one of the first tribes to embrace idolatry, and they fell the hardest. Jacob must have known that Dan would be in trouble, so he prayed for their ultimate deliverance.

Gad would also be a warring tribe, both the attacked and the attacker (vs. 19). *Asher* would become wealthy, providing riches to kings (vs. 20). Depending on the translation, *Naphtali* would be a "free spirit" tribe like a doe, until they settled down with their own little "fawns" (vs. 21; ESV, NIV, NLT). Another interpretation is that they would be good with words, possibly flattery or persuasion (NET, NASB, KJV). Deborah called Barak from Naphtali to help fight Sisera, the Canaanite general (Judges 4–5).

Joseph received the longest blessing of them all (vs. 22–26). Except for the prophecy that he would be attacked and yet defend himself, Joseph received no negative words from Jacob. He would be fruitful, powerful, and protected by Yehovah himself. Although God would fulfill his promises to Abraham through all twelve tribes as a nation, Joseph would receive a special blessing as

---

[116] "until Shiloh come" (KJV, NASB); "until tribute comes to him" (ESV, NRSV)

Jacob's favorite son and the leader of his brothers. Not coincidentally, it was the tribes of Ephraim and Judah that became the leaders of the two kingdoms when Israel divided.

Lastly, *Benjamin* also became a warring tribe, like "A RAVENOUS WOLF...DEVOURING THE PREY, AND...DIVIDING THE PLUNDER" (vs. 27). Moses reflected that each of these words was "APPROPRIATE" for the son who received them (vs. 28–33). Jacob instructed them to bury him along with Abraham, Sarah, Isaac, Rebekah, and Leah in the family cave, once they returned to Canaan, then he died.

Chapter fifty is bittersweet as it closes the first part of Israel's national history and the story of the patriarchs. Joseph had Jacob embalmed (probably to make the journey back to Canaan) and led the entire nation of Egypt in mourning for a full 70 days (vs. 1–14). Relaying his father's burial wishes to Pharaoh, Joseph requested that he and his brothers be allowed to take Jacob's body back to Canaan.[117] Not only did Pharaoh agree, but he also sent a full entourage with them in full regalia. When they reached the Jordan to cross into Canaan from the east, another week-long mourning ceremony became such a display that the news spreading across Canaan was that the whole nation of Egypt was in mourning; the deceased must have been someone of great importance. After the burial, the whole company returned to Egypt.

At this point, Joseph's brothers became afraid for their lives (vs. 15–21). Apparently, in their hearts, they never believed that Joseph had forgiven them for their crime against him. They assumed that it was Jacob who had held Joseph's revenge in check, but now that he was dead, Joseph would act in full force against them. Not even willing to face him personally, they sent a message that Jacob had given further final instructions for Joseph to not act

---

[117] It has been noted that, when Joseph was Grand Vizier, he would not have needed to request this permission from the Pharaoh. It is likely that he retired once the famine was over and his task was done. Joseph's request to "PHARAOH'S COURT" (not even Pharaoh directly) was met with some hesitancy, as shown by the army that was sent along with him and that the children and flocks were left behind, ensuring their return.

harshly against his brothers. This broke Joseph's heart. He had treated them so well for the past seventeen years. Did they truly believe it was a sham, and this was his true character?

People often quote verse twenty about God's sovereignty (especially in conjunction with Romans 8:28): "YOU MEANT TO HARM ME, BUT GOD INTENDED IT FOR A GOOD PURPOSE." Everything Joseph had seen and done had convinced him that God was at work, even to the point of using his brothers' hatred for divine purposes.

Joseph was 56 years old when Jacob died, and he spent another 54 years serving in Egypt until he died at 110 years old (vs. 22–26). As Jacob had adopted Ephraim and Manasseh from Joseph, Joseph adopted his grandsons back for himself. Joseph died as an ultimate example of growing faithfulness no matter his circumstances. From Potiphar's house to the royal dungeon to the palace, he served both his human masters and his God faithfully as it was within his ability, and his name became a favorite for centuries. Jesus' adoptive father was named after Joseph, rather than his great tribal ancestors, Judah or David. Joseph declared that, although he would be buried in Egypt as an officer of the state, he wanted his bones to be carried to his homeland when Israel finally returned, which they honored four centuries later (Joshua 24:32).

Exodus

Exodus is the second book of the Hebrew Bible and holds that position in every major translation as well. The Hebrew name of the book is וְאֵלֶּה שְׁמוֹת (ve'ēlleh shemoth, "these are the names") which are the first two words of the Hebrew text. The name *Exodus* comes from the Greek LXX[1] and the Latin Vulgate[2] translations. It is the second of five books written by Moses, the primary human character in the narrative.

Although the name *Exodus* suggests that Israel's exit from Egypt is the main theme, that is only one of several major events that point the reader to a greater overarching plan. Other key events in Exodus are Moses' commission, the introduction of Yehovah's name, God's power over the Egyptian gods and creation, the establishment of the Passover, the giving of the Law, and the establishment of the Levitical system and the Tabernacle. Most importantly, the exodus event itself was an act of gracious redemption by God, whose faithfulness required him to keep his promises to Abraham from six centuries earlier (see Genesis 15:13–14).

Thus, we see that the main theme of Exodus is not the exodus event itself but rather the faithful outworking of God's plan *for* Israel and *against* the spiritual forces who continually oppose him.

Chapter one spans approximately 280 years between Joseph's death and Moses' birth, both of which happened in Egypt. During this time, two key

---

[1] LXX is the standard abbreviation for the Septuagint, the Greek translation of the Hebrew Bible produced in the second century BC.

[2] The Vulgate was translated from Hebrew and Greek into Latin by Jerome in the fourth century A.D.

changes had taken place. First, Jacob's family had grown large, probably to more than one million people, which caused the Egyptians' concern toward this growing immigrant population (vs. 1–7). Second, Egypt had seen a power shift. A new nationalist dynasty was in control, which was unfriendly to the Hebrew people, especially considering their friendship with the previous dynasty (vs. 8–10).[3] Combined, these two situations looked to create a perfect storm against Israel.

The new king's solution was to hamstring Israel in two ways. First, he enslaved the nation, putting them to hard work doing building projects (vs. 11–14). This spread them out across the country and separated many families for long periods. However, "THE MORE THE EGYPTIANS OPPRESSED THEM, THE MORE THEY MULTIPLIED AND SPREAD." So, the Egyptians continued to add to their workload, causing them to do all kinds of labor.[4]

Second, the king ordered all midwives to kill Hebrew baby boys as they were being born (vs. 15–17).[5] This way, he thought, they could never grow into warriors against Egypt. Although it seems unlikely that there were only two midwives for so many people, only two were named. These women "FEARED GOD" and refused to obey the king's orders. When summoned to explain their actions, they lied, stating that the Hebrew women were not in labor long enough and delivered too quickly for the midwives to do anything (vs. 18–20). Because of this, God blessed them and their families (vs. 21).[6]

---

[3] Although they tend to ignore the Jewish connection, studies in ancient history record this animosity between the Hyksos and native Egyptians and the radical change in control over the empire at that time.

[4] Contrary to popular belief, it is unlikely that the Hebrews were involved in building the pyramids, which were probably already built when Israel arrived or at least before they were enslaved.

[5] This was the first attempted great holocaust against the Jewish people.

[6] Sunday School children are often taught that all lying is sin and that this story is no exception, but somehow God overlooked this lie. This unintentionally creates a duplicity in God's character in children's minds rather than enforcing that the midwives knew the same ancient principle that the apostles declared centuries later: "WE MUST OBEY GOD RATHER THAN PEOPLE" (Acts 5:29). Civil disobedience is proper and appropriate when human government demands its citizens to violate God's law.

Unable to accomplish his goals subtly, the king made it a public order that all his citizens were to throw Hebrew baby boys into the Nile River; only the girls could live (vs. 22).

Chapter two introduces the irony which upset the king's murderous plan from chapter one, proving that God was still in control of the situation. Clearly, Pharaoh did not see females as a threat because they would not serve as warriors should the Hebrews revolt against him. However, as these first two chapters reveal, the human heroes of the story were all female—the midwives, a princess, a sister, and a mother.

One specific boy was born to the tribe of Levi. Somehow his mother was able to hide for three months, at which time she entrusted him to God (vs. 1–4). Putting him into a watertight basket, she hid him among the reeds of the Nile River, probably hoping that another woman would find him there and rescue him. The boy's older sister was posted to watch and report back to their mother. In a surprising twist, the compassionate woman who found the baby was none other than the king's daughter (vs. 5–6). Even though she was able to recognize him as a Hebrew, she chose to adopt him anyway. Since the princess was unable to nurse him herself, the baby's sister offered to find a Hebrew woman who could do it for her (vs. 7–9). With permission from the princess, the girl wisely brought the boy's own mother, who nursed him through his weaning years (usually two to four years), all under the paid employment of the princess. When the boy was finally weaned, his mother presented him to the princess, who officially adopted him into the royal family, naming him *Moses* (vs. 10).[7]

Whether these women should have told the truth and faced execution can be debated. However, they saw themselves in a spiritual war and did what was necessary to deceive the enemy for the deliverance of their people. We see another example of this with Rahab in Jericho in Joshua 6 and Elisha in 2 Kings 8.

[7] There are several theories as to the meaning behind the name. From a Hebrew perspective, it sounds like the word for "to draw out." From an Egyptian perspective, *-mose* is found in many names (including *Thutmose*, the then-current Pharaoh), and means "son."

Stephen's account in Acts 7 gives a few details about Moses' early life between Exodus 2:10–11 that he himself did not include. Specifically, growing up as the princess' son, **"MOSES WAS TRAINED IN ALL THE WISDOM OF THE EGYPTIANS AND WAS POWERFUL IN HIS WORDS AND DEEDS"** (Acts 7:22). According to Stephen, the event in Exodus 2:11 took place when Moses **"WAS ABOUT FORTY YEARS OLD"** (Acts 7:23). It seems the princess had not kept the knowledge of his Hebrew heritage from him, so when Moses left the palace to observe the working conditions of his people and saw an Egyptian beating one of his kinsmen, he went into a rage and killed the Egyptian (vs. 11–15). The next day, when he tried to break up a fight between two Hebrews, they rebuffed him, asking if he would kill them, too. Discovering that his actions had become public, Moses ran for his life. The Pharaoh's fears had been confirmed: a Hebrew had taken up arms against Egypt.

According to Exodus 7:7, Moses was 80 years old when he returned to Egypt, so the events of the next few chapters span about forty years. Moses found himself **"IN THE LAND OF MIDIAN"** in southern Arabia (vs. 16–22). After defending a group of sisters from some rogue shepherds, he met their father—a godly priest named Reuel/Jethro[8]—and married one of the sisters, joining the family and eventually having a son. For forty years he tended his father-in-law's flocks while the people of Israel, whom he wanted to help, suffered at the hands of their oppressors (vs. 23–24). Finally, God began to act again on their behalf.

Chapter three opens with Moses in the desert with the family flock. According to Acts 7:23 and Exodus 7:7, this had been his life for about 40 years. Accustomed to the ways of the desert, witnessing a brush fire was nothing new until he realized that the bush was only on fire but not burning (vs. 1–3). Here on **"THE FAR [WEST] SIDE OF THE DESERT"** (probably near the Red Sea), God appeared to him, ready to deliver Israel from Egypt.

Calling Moses near, God introduced himself in the same way he had to the patriarchs so many years earlier— **"I AM...THE GOD OF ABRAHAM, THE GOD OF ISAAC,**

---

[8] Both names occur at different times throughout the Exodus account.

AND THE **GOD** OF **JACOB**" (vs. 5–10). God revealed to Moses that the oppression of the Israelites had continued—growing even worse under the new king—and that he was acutely aware of this and going to act on their behalf against the Egyptians. Then, in a similar fashion to Jesus' Great Commission (Matthew 28:18–20), God said essentially, "I am ready to go to work, so you go do this."

During his exile in the desert, Moses had lost all confidence in himself (vs. 11–13). The man who arrogantly thought he could stroll onto the scene and change things now doubted he could even stand before Pharaoh; he was just a shepherd after all. Besides, he thought the elders of Israel would likely not listen to him, due to either his Egyptian upbringing or his Midianite exile or both. How could he have possibly come to know the Israelite's God?

God responded by providing Moses with his personal name— "I AM" — a specific form of the Hebrew verb "to be" (vs. 14–17). God is "the one who is, the be-ing one." This is written using the tetragrammaton[9] YHVH/YHWH, which has come into English as *Yahweh* or *Jehovah*.[10] Unlike "God" or "Lord," this is not just a title but what God has revealed to be his actual name. God told Moses to gather the elders of Israel and tell them that he knew their plight and was ready to lead them back to the land he had promised them, using Moses as his spokesman and their leader.

He promised Moses that the elders would listen to him and support his request that the king would allow them to go three days into the wilderness to worship their God (vs. 18–22). In a more detailed repetition of his promise to Abraham (Genesis 15:14), God told Moses that Pharaoh would never willingly let the people go, so God would have to unleash his fury upon the Egyptians, and the Israelites would leave with clothes, silver, and gold—a victorious plundering of Egypt.

---

[9] "Tetragrammaton" means "four letters" and refers to the four consonants of God's name in Hebrew.

[10] See the Preface for more information about how God's name is translated and used in this book.

Chapter four begins with yet another question from Moses about his commission (vs. 1–9). God had already answered Moses' first question and promised that the people would listen to him (3:14–18), but Moses was not convinced. What if they did not believe him and asked for proof? God graciously gave him three miraculous signs: 1) his shepherd's staff would become a snake that, when picked up by the tail, would return to a staff; 2) his hand would become leprous or clean when he placed it into and removed it from his robe; and 3) water from the Nile, poured out on the dry ground, would become blood.

Even with these signs at his disposal, Moses still looked for an excuse to not go (vs. 10–12). The man who was at one time "POWERFUL IN HIS WORDS AND DEEDS" (Acts 7:22) because he had been "TRAINED IN ALL THE WISDOM OF THE EGYPTIANS" had spent half of his life conversing with nomads and animals instead of kings and no longer considered himself capable of that type of work. In a response like Jesus' encouragement for his new apostles (Matthew 10:19–20), God promised to put the right words into Moses' mouth, so that he did not need to worry about what to say. Finally, Moses blurted out, "Please just send anyone…else!" (vs. 13–17). God acquiesced, saying that Moses' brother, Aaron, would be the spokesman, but God would still work through Moses.

Unable to shake God's commission, Moses returned from the desert to his home to request permission from Jethro to leave (vs. 18–23; much like Jacob's request of Laban, Genesis 30:25–26). With Jethro's blessing and God's promise that his life was no longer in danger in Egypt, Moses packed up his little family and headed west. God told him that he was to perform the miraculous signs before Pharaoh, reminding him that the king would not listen. Moses' response was to declare that Pharaoh's rejection of Yehovah would cost him his firstborn son. God also had Aaron meet them along the road so Moses could fill him in on what was about to take place (vs. 27–31). Following God's orders, they met with the Israelite elders, performed the signs, and convinced everyone that this was God's plan and God's time.

The account in verses 24–26 is odd and has been explained in various ways but always without confidence. After threatening the Pharaoh's firstborn son, God came after Moses, threatening to kill him. Moses had not circumcised at least one of his sons.[11] Although circumcision was normal throughout the region, it was either only partially practiced (as in Egypt) or done just before marriage. It seems Israel was the only people to do it only on infants. However, as the *de facto* sign of God's covenant with Abraham (Genesis 17:9–14), Moses' neglect had brought God's judgment on his family. Why his wife did the ritual instead of Moses is unclear. Touching the boy's foreskin to Moses' feet ("feet" is often a euphemism for genitals), she called him "A BRIDEGROOM OF BLOOD." This may mean that, although he was already her groom, she had received him now a second time (back from the dead, in a sense) because of the bloody ritual.[12]

Chapter five records Moses' and Aaron's first meeting with Pharaoh, during which they did exactly as God told them to do (vs. 1–9). Instead of granting their request, however, Pharaoh believed he was bigger than Yehovah, so he made it harder on the people, giving them additional work to accomplish. They must have had too much time if they could plan an outing to the desert for a long weekend.

So they did not have to deal with the slaves, the Egyptians had elevated some of the Jews to foreman status (vs. 10–21). When these men received word that they had to keep up their quota <u>and</u> provide their own raw materials, they asked why the change and discovered that it was the result of Moses' meeting. Lashing out at Moses and Aaron, they blamed them for the worsening conditions. Essentially, they accused, "Our blood is on your hands."

Although God had told Moses that the king would not listen, it seems he had underestimated Pharaoh's rejection of God and thought he could reason with him (vs. 22–23). Ultimately, he blamed God for this trouble with a subtle, "I told you so!" "LORD, WHY HAVE <u>YOU</u> CAUSED TROUBLE FOR THIS PEOPLE? WHY DID

---

[11] Since the immediate context was about Pharaoh's firstborn son, many commentators assume that this was Gershom (the only son named to this point), though Moses had two (vs. 20; 18:1–6).

[12] The translations that say that she "threw" (NASB, CSB) or "cast" (KJV) the foreskin at Moses' feet unintentionally add an angry emotion to the story that is not necessarily there.

<u>YOU</u> EVER SEND ME? FROM THE TIME I WENT TO SPEAK TO PHARAOH <u>IN YOUR NAME</u>, HE HAS CAUSED TROUBLE FOR THIS PEOPLE, AND <u>YOU</u> HAVE CERTAINLY NOT RESCUED THEM!"

Chapter six is the final chapter of the story before God steps in and begins his process of rescuing Israel. Before then, God had to teach Moses a few more things. Responding to Moses' accusations in the last two verses of chapter five, God said, "NOW YOU WILL SEE WHAT I WILL DO TO PHARAOH" (vs. 1). Moses did not realize the privilege he had. Although they had certainly walked and talked with God, the early patriarchs had not known him by his name as Moses did (vs. 2–5). Additionally, God had made his covenants with them, but they did not get to see any of the fulfillment as Moses and this generation would. Thus, it was not just Moses' duty but his privilege to stand before the people and announce that God was about ready to work on their behalf, as he had promised their ancestors (vs. 6–8). Filled with renewed hope and courage, Moses told them the great news, but they immediately shot him down (vs. 9–13). Discouraged again, Moses complained that, if the people would not listen, how would the king ever listen to him? God charged him that, whatever happened, he had a job to do and he must complete it (vs. 28–30).

Verses 14–27 seem out of place for a couple of reasons. First, we would not expect a genealogy in the middle of this account of God getting ready to rescue Israel. Second, it is not a complete genealogy because it simply nods to Rueben and Simeon and ignores the other tribes except for Levi. Only verses 26–27 make it obvious why this list is here: "IT WAS THE SAME AARON AND MOSES... THEY WERE THE MEN WHO WERE SPEAKING TO PHARAOH KING OF EGYPT... IT WAS THE SAME MOSES AND AARON." This is not Levi's story; it's Moses' and Aaron's. Who were these guys? They were the third generation from Levi himself,[13] handpicked by God to lead his people, their family, back to Canaan.

---

[13] The ages of Levi, Kohath, and Amram show that this genealogy has no gaps. Together their final ages total 407 years, but there were only 386 years between Levi's and Moses' births. Thus, God fulfilled his promise to Abraham that "IN THE FOURTH GENERATION YOUR DESCENDANTS WILL RETURN" to Canaan (Genesis 15:16).

Some scholars have difficulty with this, though, taking these names to refer to broader clans within Levi's tribe. They point to 1 Chronicles 7:20–27, showing that

Chapter seven repeats God's commission to Moses and Aaron from chapter four, emphasizing that Moses would be "LIKE GOD" and Aaron would be his "PROPHET" or spokesman. Yehovah chose to deal with Pharaoh through Moses and Aaron only, so that Moses was, in a real sense, as God to Pharaoh, too (vs. 1–5). Once again, God said that Pharaoh would not listen to them (as had already been proven), so God would have to execute a series of judgments on him and his land. This would result in an even harder heart against God but a great deliverance of Israel as well. Moses noted that he was 80 and Aaron was 83 when this event took place, much older than the young, brash Amenhotep II (vs. 6–7).

God gave Moses and Aaron another "heads-up" at this time as well (vs. 8–13). Confident that he could humiliate these old men and their God, Pharaoh would ask for a sign. Aaron was to comply by throwing his staff on the ground, which he did, and it became a kind of serpent.[14] In response, the king's magicians worked their demonic dark arts and accomplished the same thing, except that Aaron's swallowed theirs! Rather than obeying God, Pharaoh's heart became hard against him, setting the scene for God's full onslaught attack against Pharaoh and his demon gods.

Verses 14–24 record the first of the ten plagues God brought against Egypt.[15] Because of Pharaoh's hard heart, God told Moses to meet the king by

---

Joshua came eleven generations after Joseph (Levi's brother), through Ephraim. They also point to 1 Chronicles 2:3–20, showing that Bezalel (a master craftsman for the Tabernacle) was six generations after Judah. (See the NET Bible study notes on Exodus 12:40 for more information.)

The best short answer is that not every family bore children at the same rate, and that does not change the fact that Moses and Aaron were the fourth generation, fulfilling God's promise.

[14] The Hebrew word is תַּנִּין (*tannin*), which is a broad term that includes any kind of reptilian monster (dragons, sea serpents), not just snakes. It is different than נָחָשׁ (*nachash*), the more specific term for serpent used in 4:3, when Moses threw down his staff. The LXX reflected the two meanings by translating the Hebrew word in 4:3 with ὄφις (*ophis*, "serpent, snake"), but here they used δράκων (*drakon*, "dragon, serpent").

[15] Many commentators have noticed a possible link between some of the plagues and the Egyptian gods, concluding that these were direct attacks from Yehovah against

the Nile River, which was considered a source of life for the Egyptians. At God's command and in plain sight of the king, Moses struck the river with his staff, and it turned to blood, killing all the life in it. Aaron raised his staff, pointing all around him, and any river water that had been diverted or collected also turned to blood. It seems that, once the fish died, the river became normal again. This is shown by the fact that Moses did not have to end this plague (as he did others) and that the king's magicians were able to duplicate the miracle, meaning that there was water again. However, the river was still contaminated by the dead fish, so the people had to dig wells around it to drink. Because of this, the king hardened his heart again.

Chapter eight could start with 7:25 to keep the next account together. After a week, Pharaoh had had enough time to consider Yehovah's demand, but he refused to accept again (7:25–8:4). God's second plague would be an invasion of frogs coming out of the river and swarming over Egypt. God said this would come against the king personally as well as all his people and servants. If God had to do this, he wanted the king to know that it was his fault.

Pharaoh refused to let Israel leave, so Aaron raised his staff again, calling the frogs out of the river onto land (vs. 5–7). Ironically, as before, the magicians were able to duplicate this miracle as well. Why would they want to add more frogs or blood? The answer is probably two-fold. First, they wanted to prove that their power was just as strong as Moses' God, so Pharaoh did not need to worry about him. Second, as much as they would have liked to undo the damage of the plagues, God certainly prevented them from doing that, so the best they could do was add to them, against themselves and their own people.

Egypt's demon gods. However, the biblical account never states this directly. God told Moses that he was punishing Pharaoh, not the gods, although Pharaoh considered himself to be deity. Since the gods were often linked to specific aspects of nature and natural events (river god, cow god, fertility god, etc.) and some counts have as many as 80 gods in Egypt, it should not surprise us to find that several gods might overlap with Yehovah's plagues.

Even so, this finally got Pharaoh's attention, so he summoned Moses and asked him to call off the frogs in exchange for the Hebrew weekend journey into the desert (vs. 8–15). In a bit of righteous condescension, Moses graciously allowed Pharaoh to pick the time that the plague would end, to prove that these miracles did not depend on certain times or places the way a magic trick would. The king said that "TOMORROW" would be the right time, so that's what Moses did. Unfortunately for the Egyptians, rather than hopping back into the river, the frogs just died, resulting in "COUNTLESS HEAPS" of rotting frog corpses. However, the end of the plague brought relief to Pharaoh and, possibly, a sense of control, assuming that he could end these as he pleased. So, he refused to honor his word, hardening his heart again.

The third plague was another swarm, this time of flying insects (vs. 16–19). Multiple commentators point out that these insects have been variously understood to be lice, ticks, mosquitos, or a kind of stinging gnat. Both animals and people were tortured by these things which were as numerous as dust and, it seems, were created from the dust. This time the Egyptian magicians had to admit defeat, stating that this was something supernatural, "THE FINGER OF GOD" (an unintentional admission that their tricks were not from God?), but even this did not sway Pharaoh, who hardened his heart again.

God judged Pharaoh again with a fourth plague, a swarm of flies (vs. 20–24). These were stinging or biting flies, because "THE LAND WAS RUINED" and they "DEVOURED" the people (Psalm 78:45, NASB).[16] This was the first time that God made a demarcation between the Egyptians and the Israelites; the land of Goshen was not affected by these flies. This caught Pharaoh's attention, and he relented to the point that the Hebrews would be allowed to sacrifice to God, but without leaving Egypt (vs. 25–32). Moses tactfully pointed out that God's curse was now on the land and that the Egyptians considered the Hebrew sacrifices abominable, both reasons that staying there would never work. Pharaoh grudgingly said they could go but insisted that Moses ask God to stop the plague. Moses did and Pharaoh reneged again.

---

[16] The word translated "devoured" in Psalm 78:45 is אָכַל ('akal), the standard Hebrew word for "eat." Whatever kind of flies these were, they damaged the land and gnawed on the people.

Chapter nine contains the fifth, sixth, and seventh plagues that God used to judge Pharaoh and Egypt. In the fifth judgment, God used a kind of pestilence or disease to kill off all the "LIVESTOCK IN THE FIELD," which affected both their wealth and their animal worship (vs. 1–7). It seems the specification "IN THE FIELD" is important because a few verses later there was still livestock that the Egyptians tried to protect. Moses made an interesting note that, because God promised that the Hebrews' livestock would not be killed, the king sent people to see if that indeed was true. Even though it was, he continued to harden his heart.

For the sixth judgment, God had Moses take a handful of soot from a furnace (possibly one of the very furnaces used to make the bricks of the Hebrews' slavery) and throw it into the air as Pharaoh watched (vs. 8–12). Across the entire land, both people and animals became covered with boils.[17] The fact that "THE MAGICIANS COULD NOT STAND BEFORE MOSES BECAUSE OF THE BOILS" indicates that they were still working to offset these plagues, but now they could not even show up. For the first time, Moses wrote that "THE LORD HARDENED PHARAOH'S HEART." This could have been either because of the continuing judgments or that Pharaoh had gone past the point of no return, where repentance was no longer an option, and nothing could prevent the rest of the judgments.

More than half of the chapter is devoted to the seventh plague (vs. 13–35). It has three main sections: God's warning (vs. 13–21), the judgment itself (vs. 22–26), and Pharaoh's response (vs. 27–35). For the first time, God had Moses tell the king more than just that he was going to act. This time God revealed the "why" behind the "what." God said that he could have struck Pharaoh multiple times over, but he had been gracious. Pharaoh thought he was

---

[17] The word for boils (שְׁחִין, *shichin*) is used only nine other times in the Old Testament outside of this passage. In Leviticus 13:18–23 it referred to a skin disease that required the priests' attention to determine whether the person was clean or unclean. In Deuteronomy 28:27, 35 God promised to afflict the Israelites with these same boils of Egypt if they disobeyed him in their new land. Both 2 Kings 20:7 and Isaiah 38:21 use this word to describe the sores that Hezekiah had, and Job 2:7 puts them on Job as well.

standing against Yehovah when instead he was being propped up by Yehovah so God could display both his power and grace. An unprecedented hailstorm with severe lightning would kill every person or animal not inside a building, so God told the king to send a warning message throughout the country. Some Egyptians believed the warning and took refuge, but others did not, so when the storm came, many people and animals died. Additionally, the hail destroyed the trees and the crops that had already started to grow, so there was no food until the later harvest.

Pharaoh's response looked like what God had been waiting for: "I HAVE SINNED THIS TIME! THE LORD IS RIGHTEOUS, AND I AND MY PEOPLE ARE GUILTY." Yet Moses did not believe this was true repentance (far different than believing the king would respond positively during his first meeting), and he was right. As soon as the storm ceased, Pharaoh hardened his heart again, refusing to release the Hebrews.

Chapter ten records the last two plagues before the final judgment during which Israel left Egypt, proving that the worst was yet to come. They had already seen swarms of frogs, gnats, and flies, but the eighth plague was debilitating locusts (vs. 1–20). Although the hail did an enormous amount of crop damage, there were still green shoots visible everywhere, and the locusts finished them. At this point, even Pharaoh's servants knew that this was not a bluff. They begged the king to not let Moses destroy their land, so Pharaoh made Moses an offer to let only the men go into the desert to sacrifice to God. When Moses said it would be all or none, the king ironically responded that it would take an act of God for him to let all of them leave. When the locusts came, it did not take long for them to realize the extent of what was about to happen, so "PHARAOH QUICKLY SUMMONED MOSES AND AARON," stating that he would allow Moses to forgive him "THIS TIME ONLY" if they would get rid of the locusts before they destroyed everything. Once again Moses prayed to have the plague stopped, and once again God hardened Pharaoh's heart.

Compared to the others, the penultimate judgment may seem mild (vs. 21–29). However, the psychological effects of three days of "ABSOLUTE DARKNESS" must have been terrifying, especially for the people who were not privy to the conversations between Moses and Pharaoh. After everything that had already happened, the heavy darkness was foreboding. Every sound made them wonder if their lives were in danger from an unseen enemy. More importantly, this dark calm caused many of the Egyptians to rethink their belief in Yehovah, intuitively knowing that the darkness meant something terrible was around the corner. When Pharaoh had had enough, he tried one more negotiation with Moses. All the people could go, but their animals had to remain in Egypt. Moses sarcastically asked if the king would send some of his own animals for the people to sacrifice since they were going to offer *animal* sacrifices. Not having their own would make the trip worthless. Angrily, the king sent them out, saying that they would die if they ever came back to him. Moses agreed; they would never see his face again.

Chapter eleven is short, just ten verses, yet it sets the stage for one of the greatest events in Israel's history. In verses one and two God told Moses that this was the end of the line. One final judgment would secure Israel's release from Egypt forever. God instructed that the Hebrews talk with their Egyptian neighbors, telling them that they were leaving and asking for jewelry and other provisions for their trip. Because of the plagues, the Egyptians feared and respected Moses, and they respected the Hebrews as well (vs. 3).

Standing before Pharaoh (apparently, before he left in 10:29), Moses announced the final judgment that would come that night (vs. 4–10). God promised that he would visit Egypt, killing the firstborn son of every family, both human and animal. Pharaoh was not too great nor was the lowest slave too unimportant to suffer this tragedy—everyone would be affected. However, Israel would again be spared, so much that not even a dog would bark at them as they left. This was God's final sign to Pharaoh that he was sovereign. Additionally, since Pharaoh would never again see Moses' face, it was his servants who came to Moses to beg the Hebrews to leave. As before, God promised that the king would not listen.

Chapter twelve is the greatest chapter in the book of Exodus. Not only was the nation finally released from centuries of slavery, but God established the Passover as well, foreshadowing the death of Christ and the ultimate salvation of both Jews and Gentiles.

Two weeks before Moses talked to Pharaoh in chapter eleven, God had established a new calendar with Moses that the Israelite nation was to follow from that day forward (vs. 1–11). They immediately had two recurring appointments on their new calendar. On the tenth day of the first month, each family was to choose a male lamb or kid from their flock and set it aside for four days. On the fourteenth day, they were to slaughter the animal, roast it over a fire, and eat it along with unleavened bread and bitter herbs. Anything leftover that they could not eat was to be burned completely. They were also to smear some of the blood from the animal on the exterior door frame of their houses as a visible sign that they were obeying God. The night of the fourteenth was the time God said he would pass through Egypt, killing the firstborn sons. This was the day that Moses stood before Pharaoh (11:4). When he sent the destroyer through Egypt, God himself would protect those with the sign of the blood from any harm (vs. 12–13).

This meal was not to be a one-time thing (vs. 14–20); it was to remain on their national calendar forever. In addition to the actual Passover meal on the 14th of the first month, the people were to celebrate a Feast of Unleavened Bread for seven additional days (the 15th through the 21st). Thus, the beginning of each new year would commemorate their miraculous deliverance from Egypt. As children and grandchildren were born, the story would be passed down of how God protected and delivered their people, crushing Egypt in the process. This was to be such a solemn memorial that anyone who ate yeast during this time was to be banished from Israel altogether.[18] When Moses and Aaron met with the elders of the people and relayed all of these commands, "THE ISRAELITES WENT AWAY AND DID EXACTLY AS THE LORD HAD COMMANDED" (vs. 21–28).

"IT HAPPENED AT MIDNIGHT" just as God had promised (vs. 29–39). Every firstborn male in Egypt—human and animal—was killed by God's destroying

---

[18] The lack of yeast commemorated their swift preparation and departure from Egypt. They did not have time to properly proof the bread. It needed to be mixed, baked, and eaten in a night.

angel, but God himself covered those who had smeared the blood on their door frames. Every non-Israelite household with a firstborn (which would have been most) found at least one person dead—grandfathers, husbands, fathers, and sons, along with many animals.[19] This included the heir to the throne—the Pharaoh's firstborn son.[20] As Egypt wailed, the Israelites prepared to leave, and the people shoved items at them—"WHATEVER THEY WANTED"—just to get them away.

Taking the count of 600,000 men[21] (vs. 37) to be a literal number means that the total number in Israel's group must have been two million or more (plus animals), a concept that is increasingly coming under attack in academia. Even conservative commentators like Constable think that large of a number causes "incongruities," though he holds to the literal number as the best option.[22] In addition to the Hebrews, Moses mentioned a "MIXED MULTITUDE" of others who left with Israel. These were probably other slaves and Egyptians who had come to believe in Yehovah as God or at least thought of him as the only one who could protect them against whatever Pharaoh would do next. Numbers 11:4 notes that some of these non-Hebrews instigated the complaining in the wilderness. Moses also noted that Jacob's family finally left Egypt after "430 YEARS, ON THE VERY DAY."[23]

The chapter closes with strict instructions about who could participate in the Passover celebration (vs. 43–51). Due to the non-Israelites who left Egypt

---

[19] In my home, both my oldest son and I would have died, since I am a firstborn son as well. My parents' home would have been skipped because there are no longer children at home and my father was not the oldest son in his family.

[20] Although no civilization would willingly admit this tragic event, many scholars have written on the archaeological evidence proving that Thutmose IV, Amenhotep II's successor, was not his firstborn son, who had died mysteriously.

[21] The official census taken at Mount Sinai a year after they left Egypt counted 603,550 men over the age of twenty who could serve in the army, plus the tribe of Levi, plus all the women and children (Numbers 1–2).

[22] Constable, *Notes on Exodus 2021 edition*, 118.

[23] They were not slaves this entire time, but it spans the time from when they left Canaan (c. 1875 BC) until they left Egypt (c. 1445 BC). They would not begin their re-entry to Canaan for another 40 years (c. 1405 BC).

with them, God made it clear that only Israelites could participate. Further, only those men who had been circumcised could participate, even if they were Hebrew. However, if a foreigner wanted to join the celebration, he could be circumcised first as a sign that he was voluntarily and officially joining the nation and placing himself under God's covenant with them, along with everything that would come to include.

Chapter thirteen tells the other side of the firstborn story (vs. 1–16). For those who rejected him, God killed the firstborn sons of their families. However, for those who believed him, God claimed the firstborn sons as his own, to be set apart for him. Again, as was true with the death toll in Egypt, this included both sons and animals. The animals were to be sacrificed,[24] but the sons would be redeemed via an animal sacrifice.

The purpose of this ritual was two-fold. First, the people needed to be told and constantly reminded that God was their sovereign ruler and that they were to swear their complete allegiance to him. Whereas many demon gods would demand the lives of children through sacrifice, Yehovah simply wanted them dedicated (set apart) to him. The animal sacrifices showed the cost of being set apart. Second, succeeding generations needed to be taught the significance of God's sovereignty and the Passover, so this would become the "talking point" for every generation. When the question came up about why they did this, the older generations were to point back to the original Passover and explain Yehovah's grace and power.

Verses 17–22 provide a sort of footnote, setting the stage for another major display of God's power over Egypt and Pharaoh. Rather than leading Israel back to Canaan via the normal travel highway (which was also much shorter), God took them through the Egyptian desert. Even though they had many men who could fight if necessary, God knew that facing Philistine warriors just days out of Egypt would cause a great deal of emotional and spiritual damage, so he

---

[24] The mention of the donkey (vs. 13) is significant because it was not going to be an acceptable animal for sacrifice when the law was established a few months later. They could buy out the donkey's life by sacrificing a sheep in its place (like they did for a son), or they could break the donkey's neck (no blood).

protected them by leading them the long way around. To affirm his continued presence with them, God used a "PILLAR OF CLOUD" during the day and a "PILLAR OF FIRE" during the night to stay in front of the people.

Chapter fourteen tells the great story of Israel's deliverance at the Red Sea. Not using the commercial highway between Egypt and Canaan kept them from facing the Philistines, to be sure (13:17–18), but it also meant that they no longer had a path to move eastward because the Red Sea was in the way. Of course, God knew this and planned it so that he could display his power over Egypt once again, and he told Moses to have Israel camp facing the sea (vs. 1–9). Essentially, they were boxed into a kind of ravine with only one visible option: go backward. Hearing about their situation and unable to believe that he let the people leave, Pharaoh saw his chance to capture them again, so he took all of his chariots and infantry and blocked their path from behind. Israel was now sandwiched between Pharaoh and the sea.

It did not take long for Israel to figure out what had happened, and they immediately began to complain to Moses about his inept leadership which seemed to guarantee their demise (vs. 10–14). Knowing that this was God's doing, Moses publicly encouraged them to stop complaining and watch God work on their behalf. Privately, though, he went back to God and asked what to do. God's response? "Keep moving forward!" (vs. 15–22) Rather than retreat, God's plan was for Israel to walk toward the obstacle in their path so that he could remove it. As a visual for the people, Moses was to stand with his hand stretched out over the water. God moved to the back of the camp, between Israel and Egypt, to prevent a night attack and to light the way so Israel could see, then used the wind to supernaturally create a path of dry ground through the water while the entire camp of Israel walked across safely.

After being released from God's cloud, Pharaoh saw what had happened (vs. 23–30). Unable to explain it, he thought he could use the same path, so he continued his chase through the sea. When the Egyptians were all off-shore, God had Moses raise his hand over the waters again, and they came crashing down on the army—whom God had stranded there—killing every single one of them. Thus, God used the Red Sea to provide both a safe path for his people and judgment on his enemies.

The final verse shows that God accomplished what he wanted with this event. The people of Israel (and those who had come with them) 1) "SAW THE GREAT POWER [OF] THE LORD," 2) "THEY FEARED THE LORD," and 3) "THEY BELIEVED IN THE LORD AND IN HIS SERVANT MOSES" (vs. 31). As much as they only saw God's power in the plagues of Egypt, this time they embraced Yehovah himself, and they looked at Moses with new respect.

Chapter fifteen is often called "the song of Moses" because Israel stayed on the eastern shore of the Red Sea to celebrate what God had just done for them. It seems that Moses composed and sang a song and the people responded in phrases (vs. 1, 20–21). The song can be divided into two parts. They praised God for what he did (vs. 1–10) and for who he is (vs. 11–18).

Verses 1–10 celebrate God's destruction of the Egyptian army. They recounted what had happened over the course of the previous night—how God had used wind and water to overthrow the chariots and drown the army. They praised him for shielding them and using his strength on their behalf. They recognized him as the God of their fathers and promised to worship him.

In verse eleven the song shifts to a celebration of God himself. Over the course of the previous weeks or months, Yehovah had shown his superiority over creation and the Egyptian gods. Though some would say that this phrase— "WHO IS LIKE YOU, O LORD, AMONG THE GODS?" —is hyperbolic, Moses knew that the Egyptian gods were real, though inferior to Yehovah. He wanted Israel to come to trust in Yehovah as the only true God in the face of the demon gods of the tribes and nations around them.[25] Because of who he is, they could trust that no matter who or what they faced between the Red Sea and Canaan, nothing would compare to him, and the nations would shake

---

[25] This is why their eventual idolatry was so offensive to God, because they essentially traded him in for the inferior demons of the pagan nations, rather than embracing him the way his chosen people should.

before him. In fact, forty years later, when they finally marched into Canaan, the Canaanites were still talking about the Red Sea (Joshua 2:10)!

After the celebration God had the people move into the Arabian wilderness (vs. 22–27). After three days, their celebratory high had been eclipsed by the lack of water, especially when the first water they found was undrinkable. In an act of grace, God purified the bitter water by having Moses throw a tree into it. This was yet another visible sign of God's power and grace; he would always take care of them. There he called on the people to trust him, promising that, if they would "DILIGENTLY OBEY" him, the diseases of the Egyptian plagues would never touch them. He would not only be their provider but also their healer. This was the three-day trip that God wanted Israel to take from Egypt to sacrifice to him, but after three days they were already complaining. Not far away was a full oasis, plenty for people and animals alike. God knew that he was taking them there, but they needed to learn to trust him along the way.

Chapter sixteen recounts the Israelites' third occasion of complaining and a series of three gracious gifts that God gave to them. After a short break at the Elim oasis, God had Israel move further into the Arabian wilderness. Only one month out from Egypt[26] they were complaining again, this time about food (vs. 1–3). The lesson that God wanted them to learn about his provision had not yet sunk in, so God told them about three gifts he was going to give them.

First, he would provide food for them every morning (vs. 4–23). Although some have tried to explain it with natural phenomena, this food did not exist before this time and stopped once they entered Canaan, forty years later (Joshua 5:12). It could be ground, baked, or boiled, so they could use it as a base for nearly every meal. Additionally, it was always just enough for their need. They were each to gather in the morning only what they could eat that

---

[26] They left on the fifteenth day of the first month of their new calendar (the day after the Passover on the fourteenth), and this story picks up on the fifteenth day of the second month.

day. If they tried to keep some for the next day, it would rot. This "manna"[27] was the very definition of "daily bread."[28]

Second, God would provide them with a large amount of meat. It was normal for quail to fly low enough to be caught in nets or be hit out of the air in this part of the world.[29] There is no reason to think less of this provision because it was a normal part of God's creation. However, it was still miraculous for God to provide enough for all the people. Though this was not a regular occurrence (Numbers 11 indicates it happened again the following year), the amount of meat was enormous! Moses wrote that *"THE ONE WHO GATHERED THE LEAST"* still *"GATHERED TEN HOMERS,"* approximately 2,000 liters, or more than 50 bushels! Dried properly, this meat could have lasted the people for a long time.

The third gift was not considered to be so at first. When giving instructions about the manna, God ordered that the people collect in the morning only what they could eat for that one day; anything leftover would spoil. The exception was on the sixth day when he specifically told them to collect twice the amount (vs. 19–30). The reason for this was because *"TOMORROW IS A TIME OF CESSATION FROM WORK, A HOLY SABBATH TO THE LORD."* The Hebrew word for "cessation" here, often translated as "rest" (KJV, ESV, NIV, et al.), is שַׁבָּת (*shabbath*) which means "cease, desist" from activity rather than "rest." The purpose behind this weekly observance was not a nap but an intentional cessation of their normal work which they set aside to acknowledge God's provision.[30] This was difficult for them to grasp because they were likely not given this time off during their slavery, and the surrounding nations in Canaan

---

[27] The people asked Moses, *"WHAT IS IT?"* (מַה־הוּא, *mah-hu'*), which led to the descriptive name מָן (*man*, "what?") from which "manna" derives.

[28] This is most certainly what immediately came to the mind of Jesus' listeners when he used this phrase centuries later (Matthew 6:11).

[29] Most major commentaries at least mention this as normal.

[30] It was also not designed for a weekly worship service or gathering. That started later during the Babylonian captivity and was embraced by the early church. The Sabbath as a rest from work is not a command or law for Christians, but regular gathering together is.

would not observe it either. Israel was going to have to continue to trust that God could provide for them while everyone around them seemed to get ahead.

The final verses of the chapter were added later (vs. 32–36). Sometime after the Meeting Tent and the Ark of the Covenant were built, God had Moses and Aaron scoop some manna into a pot and keep it in the Ark so that future generations could see it, not just hear about it. (Obviously, that part did not spoil after the first day.) Additionally, the note about the people eating manna for forty years was probably included at the end of the forty years of nomadic wandering, once they entered Canaan.

Chapter seventeen records two more challenges Israel had to face. Only two months out of Egypt—having been supplied with food and water, along with protection from the Egyptians at the Red Sea—the nation camped at Rephidim on their way to Mount Sinai (vs. 1–7; Numbers 33). Once again, they needed water, and, once again, they complained about it. This time they went so far as to slander God himself— **"IS THE LORD AMONG US OR NOT?"** The fact that God did not work on their timeframe led them to question his presence and goodness, even though they could see the cloud/fire pillar and were experiencing his provision every day (manna and quail). In this case, God chose to miraculously provide water again. He commanded Moses to strike a specific rock in the presence of **"THE ELDERS OF ISRAEL,"** who could verify to the nation what had happened. God caused water to come from the rock, enough to quench the thirst of everyone.

While they were there, the Amalekites attacked them (vs. 8–16). God had spared the Israelites from the Egyptians and had led them away from the Philistines, but he also had to prepare them for the battles that would come in Canaan and prove that he would lead and protect them even in battle. Although no numbers are given, Moses had Joshua take a select company from the overall army to fight while Moses stood above them with his staff (now a symbol of God's power). Hur and Aaron went with him for support (and possibly to pray with him). Interestingly, when Moses' arms got tired and drooped, the Israelites began to lose, but when he kept them raised, they won.

So, Aaron and Hur had Moses sit down, and they held up his arms until Amalek was completely defeated.[31] In celebration of the victory, Moses built a memorial altar which he named "THE LORD IS MY BANNER" (*Yehovah-nissi*). God had him record the events for posterity to make sure that Joshua knew what had happened because Amalek would one day be annihilated.

Chapter eighteen is often referenced in books on biblical leadership and pastoral ministry because of the practical wisdom presented here. In the first half of the chapter, Moses' father-in-law met up with the Israelites, bringing with him Moses' wife and two sons whom Moses had left behind a few months earlier when he returned to Egypt (vs. 1–12). It was a wonderful reunion as Moses shared with Jethro the things that God had done for them—the plagues, the Red Sea, the miraculous water and food, and the victory over the Amalekites. Jethro was in awe of Yehovah because of what Moses shared, and they sacrificed an offering together. Moses introduced Jethro to Aaron and the elders of Israel, who joined them in a fellowship meal.

The next day it was back to business, and Jethro sat with Moses as people came to him for instruction, guidance, and arbitration (vs. 13–27). Exactly what this entailed and how often Moses did this is not recorded, but it was long and hard enough that Jethro thought it would be disastrous for both Moses and Israel if it did not change. He recommended that Moses should focus on doing what only he could do—speaking with God, getting instructions from him, and relaying it to the people. Other capable leaders from among the tribal clans could do most of the other work. Jethro suggested that Moses set up a tiered system whereby people could take their issues to increasingly higher levels as necessary; Moses would be the last resort.[32] The wisdom was offered graciously and received humbly. In a method that the

---

[31] Many commentators and preachers over the years have likened this to intercessory prayer or group prayer, stating that it unleashes God's power in our life situations. It also illustrates the ongoing support that strong leadership requires.

[32] This is similar to the United States judicial system with various courts at local, state, and federal levels. Ultimately, the Supreme Court is the final arbiter, although legislators can change the laws that the courts interpret.

apostles imitated in Acts 6, Moses had the people nominate trusted leaders from within their clans from whom he chose his subordinates in this area (Deuteronomy 1:9–18). Jethro quietly went back home, although he almost certainly visited many times over the next 40 years until his death.

Chapter nineteen sets the stage for the covenant that God was going to make with national Israel. Two months to the day after leaving Egypt, they finally arrived at "THE MOUNTAIN OF GOD" (3:1; 18:5; 24:13), the same place Moses had met God a few months earlier at the burning bush (vs. 1–8). Mount Horeb (or Sinai) was going to become a special place for the Jewish people. Before presenting the specific covenant regulations, God had Moses deliver this ultimatum to the people: "IF YOU WILL DILIGENTLY LISTEN TO ME AND KEEP MY COVENANT, THEN YOU WILL BE MY SPECIAL POSSESSION OUT OF ALL THE NATIONS, FOR ALL THE EARTH IS MINE, AND YOU WILL BE TO ME A KINGDOM OF PRIESTS AND A HOLY NATION." In hindsight, although God is not a charlatan looking to deceive, the people should have asked to hear the requirements first, so they would have known they could not possibly live up to them. Instead, they quickly and naïvely agreed to do "ALL THAT THE LORD HAS COMMANDED." When Moses relayed their answer, God began to put it into action.

Before they could stand before God in this new covenant relationship, they had to be clean (vs. 9–15). The physical steps God had them take represented the spiritual cleansing he would expect: their clothes were to be washed; they were to abstain from sexual relations[33]; they were to recognize boundaries that would prevent them from coming directly to God. These restrictions were so stringent that anyone who crossed the boundary would be put to death, even animals. God's holiness would be on full display, and they could not violate it without punishment.

On the third day of the cleansing and fast, God descended to the mountain, visible only by thunderclouds, lightning, smoke, and booming sounds (vs. 16–

---

[33] Although he did not use the word "fasting," this is similar to what Paul told the Christians in 1 Corinthians 7:1–5, that sexual relations between a husband and wife could be set aside temporarily for prayer but must be resumed as a normal, regular part of married life.

25). He called Moses to come up the mountain to meet with him. Before their official meeting, God warned Moses to go back down the mountain to make sure the people did not cross the boundary, in case they were confused as to when they could approach. Moses somehow thought that the initial warning would have been enough, but God knew better and sent him back anyway. This time, when Moses returned to the mountain, Aaron was to come with him.

Digging Deeper: The Mosaic Covenant

One of the biggest areas of confusion regarding the Old Testament has to do with the laws given to Israel in the Mosaic Covenant, beginning with the Ten Commandments. There seems to be no end to the debate over whether people today (especially Christians) are required to follow the 600+ commandments given by Moses.

While many Bible-believers honestly want to do what is right to please God, they are often frustrated due to the mockery of unbelieving skeptics who love to point out their "favorite" ridiculous laws about shaving techniques and tattoos (Leviticus 19:27–28), wearing clothing of mixed fabrics (Leviticus 19:19), or not eating bacon (Leviticus 11:7).

The truth is simply this: Christians are not required to follow the Old Testament law. In fact, no one is. This is true for four reasons:

1. God gave that law to the nation of Israel only. God told Moses, "WITH THESE WORDS I HAVE MADE A COVENANT WITH YOU AND WITH ISRAEL." (Exodus 34:27). The Mosaic Law was never given to or reiterated in the New Testament for the church.
2. God gave that law to show humanity's need for a true Savior. The law was only to be a "GUARDIAN UNTIL CHRIST, SO THAT WE COULD BE DECLARED RIGHTEOUS BY FAITH" (Galatians 3:24).

> 3. When Jesus came, he fulfilled the law completely. Jesus said, "I HAVE NOT COME TO ABOLISH THESE THINGS BUT TO FULFILL THEM" (Matthew 5:17).
> 4. Once fulfilled, the command and need to follow the law ended with Jesus. "CHRIST IS THE END OF THE LAW" (Romans 10:4)
>
> Although the Old Testament Law was never given to the church, Christians are not free to do anything they want. Christians are commanded to obey a new law, sometimes called "the law of Christ" (Galatians 6:2) or "the law of liberty" (James 1:25). While it is true that the law of Christ does include most of the 10 Commandments (because God's holy character can never change), Jesus summed it up like this in Matthew 28:19–20: "MAKE DISCIPLES OF ALL NATIONS...TEACHING THEM TO OBEY EVERYTHING I HAVE COMMANDED YOU." So, we do have a law to obey, but you will not find it in the Mosaic Covenant of the Old Testament.

Chapter twenty begins God's set of instructions in what would come to be known as the Mosaic Law. These instructions are set forth and explained over the next several chapters of Exodus as well as in Leviticus and repeated in Deuteronomy. The "Ten Commandments" which God gave first in this chapter serve as a kind of overview of the entire Law. In a sense, they comprise the Constitution of the newly formed nation of Israel, broadly outlining what would become both the civil and moral law of the land.

After receiving Moses and Aaron back on the mountain (19:24), God began by stating why he had the authority to give these commands and why it was proper for Israel to receive them: "I, THE LORD, AM YOUR GOD, WHO BROUGHT YOU FROM THE LAND OF EGYPT, FROM THE HOUSE OF SLAVERY." This reveals two major points about the Mosaic Law. First, the Law was not given to bring them into covenant with God but because they were already in covenant with him. God had already redeemed them and expected them to live in a redeemed way.[34]

---

[34] Obedience to the Law did not put them into the covenant. God gave them the Law because they were already in.

Second, the Law was given to national Israel, no one else. None of the other surrounding nations were expected to live according to these laws. They were, in fact, specifically meant to set Israel apart from those nations.[35]

As has been noted by commentators for centuries, the Ten Commandments divide nicely into two sections: relation to God and relation to each other. The first four commandments detail Israel's relation to God (vs. 3–11).[36] They were to acknowledge Yehovah as the only true God, above the demonic gods of the other nations (vs. 3). They were not to minimize him by making idols that could never fully represent him (vs. 4–6).[37] They were not to misuse his name for their own purposes (vs. 7).[38] They were to consistently observe the Sabbath day that God had established a month earlier (chapter 16), so they would keep trusting him for their provision (vs. 8–11).[39]

The next six commandments detail Israel's relationships with their countrymen. These are primarily based on respect for each other: for their parents (vs. 12), their lives (vs. 13), their marriages (vs. 14), their possessions

---

[35] Disregarding for the moment the fact that the Law ended with Christ anyway (Galatians 3:24; Colossians 2:14), it is important to not fall to the deceptive teaching that the Law applies to anyone beside Israel, especially the New Testament church. The Mosaic Law was **never** given to or meant for the church.

[36] There is some debate among Catholic and Protestant teachings regarding the exact division of these commandments (partially because of some minor differences between the Exodus and Deuteronomy versions). More information is available in many commentaries, but the division explained here follows the standard Jewish understanding.

[37] Jesus is the only one who can fully represent God in a physical, tangible way (John 1:14, 18; Hebrews 1:1–3).

[38] This has less to do with cursing and more with the misappropriation of his name for mystical or "magical" incantations, oaths, or using it to authorize something that he did not and would not authorize. I have often compared this last type of misuse to identity theft—doing something in God's name that he would not do.

[39] The specific mention of the six days of creation as the pattern for six days of work provide a strong support for the interpretation of Genesis 1 as six literal days in the creation week.

(vs. 15), their reputations (vs. 16),[40] and their relationships (vs. 17).[41] Respect for parents is the only one to which a promise is attached, specifically a long, peaceful life.[42]

As Moses and God conversed, the people heard only thunderclaps, which terrified them (vs. 18–21). As much as Moses wanted them to hear from God, based on what they were seeing, they were content (for now) to let Moses talk to God, and they would receive it secondhand. Following the first ten laws, God repeated his prohibition of any kind of idols, even those meant to worship him (vs. 22–26). He also commanded that they build one altar that the whole nation would use for sacrifices. He did not allow them to sacrifice and worship when and where they wished—only the places where he designated by making his presence known. Any other permissible altars were to be simple, made of earth or stone, as long as the stone was natural and not carved. The altars were not to be so tall that steps were necessary so that the priests would not expose themselves beneath their robes as they climbed. Even under the Mosaic Law, Yehovah wanted his worship to be simple, modest, and not distracting, with the focus remaining on him.

Chapters twenty-one through twenty-three contain a series of judgments or "ORDINANCES"[43] that God laid out to further explain the first ten, broad commandments. These laws are grouped into seven sections, each one offering specific examples of how the Ten Commandments could be lived out.

---

[40] The ninth commandment was not "Do not lie" but "Do not perjure yourself under oath by slandering someone else."

[41] Covetousness goes beyond simple greed for more items. It is when a person wants what a neighbor/friend already has, thereby hurting their friendship. This is also the only one of the ten that is purely in the heart and cannot be observed by others.

[42] Somehow, I don't think the perennial parental threat— "I brought you into this world…"—is exactly what God had in mind here though it does fit.

[43] The Hebrew word is מִשְׁפָּט (*mishepat*), which refers to a legal decision.

Although many of these seem like they should be common sense, pagans and those who live outside of a godly worldview do not naturally follow them.[44]

The first grouping has to do with treating slaves well (vs. 2–11).[45] Slavery was often voluntary, either for the maximum allowed time of six years (if they were repaying a debt) or for life (if the slave chose this). All debts within Israel were forgiven every sixth year so that the people could "sabbath" together as a nation. With few restrictions, entire families were to be set free. If the slave was female and married into the owner's family, she was to be given full rights as a daughter or wife. These details display God's intention for the sanctity of all human life.

The second grouping has to do with respecting the lives of other people, the sixth commandment (vs. 12–26). God had already established capital punishment for all humanity in Genesis 9:5–6, which he continued under the Mosaic Law.[46] All premeditated murder was to be dealt with by execution. Accidental homicides, when the killer was not in control of the situation, were not held against the killer. Respect for life goes beyond killing. Kidnappers were to be executed, and those physically injured were to be paid restoration for time lost from work. Pregnant women were considered to be carrying a human with full rights. Even slaves were to be freed in case of criminal injury.

The third grouping addresses the actions and owners of animals (vs. 28–36). Animals that killed people were to be killed as well, and the responsibility for the person's death could be applied to the animal's owner in cases of negligent homicide. While it appears that slaves were not valued the same as free citizens (vs. 31–32), every person was part of a group with varying

---

[44] This is obvious within our own judicial system, which requires redundant laws to plug loopholes that people regularly exploit.

[45] The topic of slavery will always be controversial, especially since it was never banned or outright condemned in Scripture. However, passages like this should show that God demanded respect for all fellow humans, even though he allowed his people to live and work within the cultural system of the day.

[46] The reason that capital punishment should be continued today is because it was instituted before the Mosaic Law. The question of whether capital punishment acts as an effective deterrent for these crimes is moot. God commanded that we execute murderers, no matter if it ever stops someone else from committing the same crime.

monetary value based on age and gender as well as enslaved or free (Leviticus 27:1–8). This valuation did not reflect their inherent personal worth but rather their civil value within society. Owners were responsible for their actions and their animals' actions toward other people and animals.

Chapter twenty-two could begin with verse one (as in English Bibles) or verse two (as in the Hebrew text), depending on whether one places it in the previous animal section or the new section on theft. The fourth of the seven judicial groupings in these three chapters addresses reimbursement due to theft or negligence (vs. 1–15). Thieves were required to "MAKE FULL RESTITUTION" if they were caught alive, but if the owner killed them in the act, that killing was justified. "FULL RESTITUTION" was always more than the original loss, sometimes by up to five times. Even losses due to an out-of-control fire, theft, or damage while in someone else's possession needed to be reimbursed. Personal responsibility is a major theme of these laws.

The fifth grouping addresses human life in a few miscellaneous areas (vs. 16–31). Sexual promiscuity and "consensual relationships" were not taken lightly. God designed and intended sex only for marriage, so those who had premarital sex were required to get married.[47] Sex with animals was strictly forbidden. Sorcery was tied closely with drug use and demonism, all of which were forbidden. Offering sacrifices to other gods was forbidden. All these things demanded the death penalty. God required that all people were to be treated with respect, whether slave or free, widows or orphans. Lending to the poor was good and proper if interest was not charged against them. If the only collateral was the man's coat, the lender even had to return it before nightfall, so the borrower could cover himself while he slept! As he had already declared in chapter thirteen on the eve of the Passover, God repeated his ownership over the firstborn males of both people and animals. They were to be set apart for him, making the entire nation a holy people.

---

[47] Other laws would come later to explain situations of rape and adultery. This one simply addressed two unmarried, consenting adults.

Chapter twenty-three contains the last of God's basic judicial decisions which started in chapter twenty-one that set the precedent for the rest of the Mosaic Law. The sixth grouping elaborated on the ninth commandment, about not bearing false testimony in court (vs. 1–9). In addition to not allowing people to lie on the stand personally, God forbade conspiracy to commit perjury, even by passively following the lead of others they knew were going to lie in court, and he forbade bribery. The poor are often misrepresented in court, so God specifically commanded that they were to receive the same fair representation and full justice as those who were not poor. Even foreigners living under Israel's law were not to be oppressed by the judicial system.

The seventh and final grouping addresses some remaining details about worship (vs. 10–18). In addition to slaves being freed in the sabbath year (21:2–11), the entire land was to be given a rest every seventh year as well, as a part of Israel's recognition of God's provision. The poor and the animals could eat wild crops, but planting was not allowed. Also, as a part of their national worship, God required that the people gather crops three times throughout the year to make sacrifices and bring offerings—Passover/Feast of Unleavened Bread, the early harvest, and the late harvest. Bread/grain offerings could not be mixed with blood; fat must be burnt before morning; goat kids could not be boiled in their mothers' milk; and no god's name but Yehovah's was even allowed on the people's lips.

After laying out these commands, God promised that he would send his representative[48] ahead of them into the land of Canaan to destroy the wicked nations (vs. 20–33). So that the land would not grow wild before Israel could inhabit it, God would conquer the land slowly, giving Israel only as much as they could handle and control at a time. As time went on, the Israelites would be tempted to worship the pagan demon gods, but Yehovah insisted that they must not. If they did, or if they even made pacts with the Canaanites, God would remove his supernatural protection from them.

---

[48] Although the Hebrew term is מַלְאָךְ (*male'ak*, "messenger, angel"), the fact that God's "NAME IS IN HIM" and he had the authority to "PARDON...TRANSGRESSIONS" gives good reason to understand this as the second person of the Trinity—the visible Yehovah, the Eternal Son, the Preincarnate Jesus.

Chapter twenty-four records the binding covenant on the people of Israel. In chapter nineteen, the people had presumptuously declared, "ALL THAT THE LORD HAS COMMANDED WE WILL DO!" (19:8) God had not given them any commandments yet, so one could claim ignorance and eagerness to please God. At this point, however, God had just laid out more than one hundred judicial commands, including the overarching Ten Commandments, and had Moses write them into book form on a scroll (vs. 3–8). Not only that, he had read them all aloud to the people. This time when they said, "WE ARE WILLING TO DO AND OBEY ALL THAT THE LORD HAS SPOKEN," they had no excuse. Moses sealed their promise with blood, ratifying their covenant with God. They were now bound to obey it flawlessly.

With this in place, God invited Moses, Aaron, Nadab, Abihu, and the seventy elders from Israel (probably those Moses had installed upon the recommendation of his father-in-law, 18:25–26) to join him on the mountain (vs. 1–2, 9–11). Since they saw only God's feet and a kind of "PAVEMENT" under them, they were obviously on their faces.[49] The statement that "HE DID NOT LAY A HAND ON" them means that they did not fully "see" him, which would have required death. After this fellowship and meal with God and each other, God invited only Moses to join him further up the mountain within his glory cloud (probably the shekinah glory, vs. 12–18). The others were to handle the responsibility of administration over the people until Moses returned. This turned out to be forty days later, cut short because of the grievous sin described in chapter thirty-two. It was during this time that God gave Moses the commandments written in stone. The people already had the paper copy, so they had no excuse for what was about to take place.

Chapters twenty-five through thirty-one record in detail what Moses saw and heard during his forty days on the mountain and the instructions that God

---

[49] The reference to God's "feet" can be explained in one of three ways. It could be an anthropomorphism, where a human feature is attributed to God. It could have been a vision. Or it could have been the visible Yehovah, the second person of the Trinity, in his glory. I prefer this explanation, which could be compared to the apostles' experience on the Mount of Transfiguration (Matthew 17:1–8).

gave him for building the traveling place of worship for the Israelites. God asked the people for a freewill offering of precious metals and stones, fabrics, wood, oil, and spices with which they would build for him a "SANCTUARY" (vs. 1–9). It was in this place that God's presence would be among them when they were encamped, rather than just in front of them in the traveling cloud and fire. God gave Moses a specific blueprint—the "model home" and furniture that he wanted them to build—so that it could be done exactly.[50]

The first, and most important, piece in the new structure was to be an "ark" (vs. 10–22). It was a rather small wooden box[51] overlaid with gold. Since the people would be prohibited from touching it, it required rings on the corners in which gold-overlaid wooden poles could be inserted to carry it. The lid was made of solid gold, and it had two sculpted gold cherubim on top of it facing each other, with their wings spread out touching each other. Inside this box, Moses was to place the stone commandments that God gave him. The lid was called the "ATONEMENT LID" or "mercy seat" —more special than even the box itself—because it was there, with the cherubim "looking on," that the blood was applied to atone for sin. God said that this ark was the place that he would meet with Moses, the human mediator between God and the Israelites.

The second piece of furniture was a table, a little smaller than the ark (vs. 23–30). Like the ark, it was to be made of wood and covered in gold. It, too, would be carried on poles. There were to be golden "PLATES...LADLES...PITCHERS, AND...BOWLS" on it for use with the sacrificial offerings, and it would hold "THE BREAD OF THE PRESENCE," representing God's provision for his people.

The third piece of furniture in the sanctuary was a seven-pronged lampstand (the menorah), made from about 75 pounds of pure gold (vs. 31–40). Each of the seven prongs held a separate lamp so it could give plenty of light to the entire area in which it stood.

---

[50] Hebrews 8:5 states that what Moses built was a copy of what he saw while on the mountain.

[51] This is a different Hebrew word than what Moses used for Noah's "ark" in Genesis 6–9. This ark was only 45 inches (114 cm) long x 27 inches (68.5 cm) wide x 27 inches (68.5 cm) high.

Chapter twenty-six introduces the "TABERNACLE" structure itself. Although there are different explanations for exactly how it looked and what could be seen from the inside and outside, this was essentially a framed tent with embroidered fabric and goat skins which served as curtains for the walls and roof. The frames were wood overlaid with gold, and the multi-colored fabrics had pictures of cherubim sewn into them. The gold and colors made it a beautiful place to meet with God. Both the framed walls and the curtains were designed in sections so they could be taken down and moved to the next location as the nation traveled.

Inside this tent was a smaller, enclosed tent called the Holy Place, which held the table and the lampstand. It included a curtain to partition off a separate room in the back called the Most Holy Place.[52] This room was to remain distinct from the Holy Place because it would house "THE ARK OF THE TESTIMONY" and the atonement lid.

Chapter twenty-seven opens with a description of the next piece of furniture, the altar of sacrifice (vs. 1–8). The altar was a 7 ½-foot square box that stood 4 ½ feet high and was covered in bronze.[53] All the utensils used on it were also to be made of bronze. On the top of the four corners were sculpted horns that served a variety of purposes. On the bottom of the four corners were rings to hold the carrying poles.

Secondly, this chapter describes the courtyard that surrounded the tabernacle/sanctuary (vs. 9–19). Measuring 150 feet by 75 feet,[54] the curtained outside walls were shorter than the walls of the tabernacle structure inside, so people could see the tabernacle without having to go inside the courtyard. Like the altar, the bases of the wall frame, the tent pegs, and the curtain rods were all to be made from bronze. Thus, the precious metals started with gold and silver for the tabernacle—where God's presence was—and decreased in

---

[52] The way of stating this in Hebrew was "Holy of Holies." It is the same reason the Song of Solomon is sometimes called the "Song of Songs," meaning "the best of songs," from the first verse of the book.

[53] 229 cm x 229 cm x 137 cm

[54] 45.7 m x 22.8 m

value to bronze in the courtyard where the people came to offer their sacrifices, have the sins covered, and meet with God.[55]

The people were also to provide fresh-pressed olive oil for use in the lampstand in the tabernacle (vs. 20–21). Since this light was to stay lit, except for cleanings, they would have to continually bring olive oil as an offering to God.

Chapter twenty-eight describes in detail the priests' clothing, beginning with those of Aaron, the high priest. It consisted of six different parts, each with function and meaning: "A BREASTPIECE, AN EPHOD, A ROBE, A FITTED TUNIC, A TURBAN, AND A SASH." He was required to wear this outfit whenever he was in the tabernacle. The ephod was a sewn robe, with a stone on each shoulder engraved with the names of six of the tribes of Israel. The breastpiece contained twelve gems in four rows, each symbolizing one tribe, and a pocket in which he placed the "URIM AND THUMMIM" when they were not in use. Over these, the high priest wore a blue robe or tunic. Along the bottom hem hung an alternating pattern of pomegranate-shaped balls of yarn and golden bells. As Aaron walked around ministering, the bells would continually sound. The sash kept the robe closed. Over the turban was a golden headband engraved with the phrase "HOLINESS TO THE LORD." (In 29:6, this headband is called a "HOLY DIADEM.") The design of this outfit was both "FOR GLORY AND FOR BEAUTY."

The other priests were to wear special robes with sashes and headbands as well (vs. 40–43). Additionally, all the priests (including the high priest) were to wear a specific linen undergarment that covered him from his waist to his thighs. Anyone who did not wear these under his priestly robe would die.

Chapter twenty-nine details the very specific ritual that God had Moses perform to consecrate the priests and the new tabernacle so they could begin

---

[55] Bronze was regularly used in instances with sin or judgment (e.g., the bronze serpent in Numbers 21:9 and the bronze mountains in Zechariah 6:1).

to serve in God's presence.[56] First, the priestly outfits had to be washed, then Moses anointed the priests with oil and fastened their outfits on them. For seven days (vs. 35–37) Moses was to make a sacrifice of a young bull, two rams, and unleavened bread, cakes, and wafers (vs. 1–3). After the priests laid their hands on the heads of each of the animals, Moses killed and burned the animals, splashing the blood variously on and around the altar. The entrails of the bull and the first ram were burned on the altar, but the rest was burned completely outside the camp (vs. 10–18).

Some of the blood from the second ram was touched to the priests' right ear lobe, right thumb, and right big toe, along with being sprinkled on the altar (vs. 19–34).[57] The meat of this ram was divided into three parts. The entrails and right thigh were burnt completely, along with one each of the bread, cakes, and wafers, after the priests "WAVED" them before God. One breast was also waved before God then given to Moses for food. The other breast and thigh were reserved for the priests as their portion for food, along with the rest of the unleavened bread, but anything left over was to be burned completely the next morning.

Upon the completion of this ritual, the altar and its utensils and the priests with their outfits were considered to be purified and consecrated to God (vs. 35–37). After this, anything that happened to touch the altar would be considered holy.[58] Finally, God established a set of daily sacrifices that the priests were to offer every morning and evening: a one-year-old lamb (vs. 39–43). Upon completion of all these preparations, God promised that his

---

[56] Even though Moses explained this here, the consecration of the priests did not occur until Leviticus 8, where Moses went into further detail.

[57] The blood signified that the priests were completely cleansed and set apart to God before they could stand between God and the people.

[58] This is backward from the normal course of the Law. Usually, clean items became unclean when touched by anything unclean, not the other way around (see Haggai 2:10–13). In this case, the altar consecrated anything that came into contact with it, including people, meaning that the priests were required to remain at or near the altar as they served (see 1 Kings 2:28). This may give us the precedent to understand how Jesus could touch sick and dead people without becoming unclean under the Law. Rather than being defiled by them, he cleansed them.

presence would come to the tabernacle and he would meet with his people there.

Chapter thirty opens with a new piece of furniture not yet mentioned, the altar of incense (vs. 1–10). This small box and the poles to carry it were overlaid with gold, and it was placed directly in front of the curtain dividing the Holy Place from the Most Holy Place. The sole purpose of this smaller altar was for burning one specific incense, not "STRANGE INCENSE...NOR BURNT OFFERING, NOR MEAL OFFERING, AND...NOT...A DRINK OFFERING." The high priest was to burn this incense every morning and evening when the lamps were trimmed. The only exception was on the Day of Atonement (Yom Kippur) when blood was sprinkled on its horns before the high priest entered the Most Holy Place.

To pay for the construction (and probably the ongoing maintenance) of the tabernacle, God told Moses that every annual census would incur a tax of one-half-shekel (6 grams) of silver on each male aged 20 years and older (vs. 11–16). Since this first census counted more than 600,000 men (Numbers 1:46), this would raise millions of dollars annually. This eventually became the annual "temple tax" that even Jesus paid (Matthew 17:24).

This tax was called a *"RANSOM"* for the lives of the men. It seems that a census was not naturally a good thing (possibly revealing trust in military strength and population instead of God; see 2 Samuel 24:1–4, 10), so God mandated that the tax was to be set aside for his worship rather than the government's benefit. Because of this, it was the same for everyone; the rich could not give more or the poor less. Everyone's life was valued the same.

A second new piece of tabernacle furniture was a large bronze basin of water that sat in the courtyard, between the altar and the sanctuary itself (vs. 17–21).[59] Here the priests would wash their hands and feet before they could enter the tabernacle or burn incense to God. If they did not cleanse themselves in the basin first, they would die.

---

[59] When Solomon constructed his basin in the Temple, it was 15 feet (4.5 m) across (1 Kings 7:23).

The chapter closes with two recipes. The first was for the special anointing oil that Moses was to use on the new tabernacle, including the furniture, utensils, and the priests themselves (vs. 22–38). The second was for the incense that the priests were to use in the tabernacle worship. God gave a strong warning that no one else could manufacture these exact recipes or use them on anything else as an oil or a perfume. Anyone who did so would be banished from the nation.

Chapter thirty-one contains the first biblical mention of someone being "FILLED...WITH THE SPIRIT OF GOD" (vs. 1).[60] Bezalel, along with Oholiab, was commissioned by God himself to do (or possibly) oversee the crafting of all the furniture, fabric, clothing, and oil for the tabernacle (vs. 1–11). This was an enormous task and required God's supernatural enablement to accomplish it quickly and correctly.[61]

This is now the third time in Exodus that God has emphasized the importance of the Sabbath (vs. 12–17). In chapter sixteen God gave Israel the Sabbath as a gracious gift of rest after they came out of centuries of slavery. He then codified it into the Law as one of the Ten Commandments in chapter twenty. Now he repeated that the people "MUST KEEP MY SABBATHS" as a sign of the special relationship between them and God. None of the other nations had this.[62] The Sabbath was not only a day for physical rest; it was a day for the Israelites to remember Yehovah.

God gave Moses "TWO [STONE] TABLETS OF TESTIMONY" that Moses said were "WRITTEN BY THE FINGER OF GOD." Although God does not have physical fingers, this could mean that he created them as he did during the creation week (see

---

[60] Exodus 28:3 describes people being "FILLED WITH THE SPIRIT OF WISDOM," which could certainly mean the same thing, but the reference to the Holy Spirit here is unmistakable.

[61] Without knowing anything else at this point in the biblical record, we can see that Spirit-filling has always been necessary to accomplish God's work in God's way.

[62] This is a good reference for those who believe that the Sabbath is a required part of Christianity, whether on Saturday or Sunday.

32:16; Psalm 8:3). Some believe that it simply refers to the power and authority behind them.[63]

Chapter thirty-two describes the first event that would start 900 years of Israelite idolatry, the precise reason they would be taken into exile in the 7th and 8th centuries. After only a few weeks of waiting for Moses to return from his meeting with God (looking at the tabernacle model, getting the blueprints, and receiving God's law) and after promising twice to do everything that God commanded, they "broke" the first two of God's commandments.

Although some have tried to mitigate Aaron's actions, there were no excuses (vs. 1–6). He had gone with Moses and the other elders to meet with God. He knew what Moses was doing on the mountain, yet when the people demanded of him—the first high priest of Yehovah—to make them visible gods (not as scary as the God on the dark, fiery mountain), he gave in. With a bold declaration, he announced, "THESE ARE YOUR GODS, O ISRAEL, WHO BROUGHT YOU UP OUT OF EGYPT."[64] He followed this by building an altar and setting a feast day to worship Yehovah, using the very name of God.

When God told Moses what was going on at the base of the mountain and threatened to destroy the new nation, Moses interceded on behalf of the people, yet it was clear that his main priority was to maintain God's reputation among the pagan nations (vs. 7–14). When Moses came down from the mountain and saw exactly what was happening, he became furious and shattered the tablets on the ground, like the people had "broken" what was written on them (vs. 15–20). He ground down and burned the idol, dumped the ashes in the water, and made the people drink it.

---

[63] Pharaoh's magicians used the phrase "finger of God" in reference to the plagues as well (8:19). The only other place this concept occurs is when John noted, in the confrontation between Jesus and the Jewish leaders about the adulterous woman, that "JESUS BENT DOWN AND WROTE ON THE GROUND WITH HIS FINGER" (John 8:6).

[64] Although only the golden calf is described, the Hebrew text uses the plural "these…gods," implying that there was more than one. Verse 31 refers to plural "gods of gold" as well.

When Moses questioned him, Aaron tried to blame the people first, then suggested that it was a miraculous event (vs. 21–29). Moses asked who among the people had been faithful to God instead of worshiping the idol, and the Levites responded. At Moses' command, the Levites killed about 3,000 people for this heinous sin. Moses returned to the mountain to see if God would forgive the people for their sin (vs. 30–34). He told God that he would rather die than see all the people killed for this sin. Instead, God said that he would not forgive their sin, but he would defer their punishment until a later time. Until then, Moses was to continue leading them to where God had told him, probably Kadesh-Barnea, where they were to enter Canaan. However, he did send a plague on them (a reverse fulfillment of 15:26).

Chapter thirty-three describes the effects that the people's sin had on their fellowship with God. Although God told Moses to continue leading them to Canaan, the land he had promised to the patriarchs, he said that he would not personally accompany them because their rebellious hearts would lead him to destroy them (vs. 1–6). This was a horrific thought to the people—that God had abandoned them—so when God commanded them to remove the things they had used in their worship of the idols, they obeyed immediately and completely.

Because the tabernacle was not yet built, Moses erected a little tent where he could meet with God on behalf of the people (vs. 7–11). However, rather than being in the middle of the camp, as was the original plan, this tent was a distance away. God could not dwell with them in their sin. Instead, only Moses was allowed inside the tent, and it seems that Joshua stood guard there constantly.

Once while in the tent, Moses asked God for a special favor (vs. 12–23). The intimate fellowship he had enjoyed to this point could be eclipsed by only one thing: seeing God's full glory. This, God promised, could never happen, because it would kill Moses. However, God promised that he would allow Moses to get a glimpse of the "afterglow" of his glory after he had passed by.

Chapter thirty-four shows how God fulfilled his promise for Moses to briefly see his glory. Back on the mountain, God made the stone tablets again after Moses cut them out of the mountainside. Ascending the mountain, Moses was joined by both the Father (invisible) and the Son, the visible presence who announced the Father (vs. 1–7). Moses asked God not to abandon the nation and instead pardon them and lead them to Canaan (vs. 8–9). For much of the rest of the chapter, God reiterated his covenant with Israel, laying out his demands for undivided worship. He promised that he would clear the land of the pagan inhabitants, if the people remained committed to him, obeyed his laws, and did not develop friendly relationships with the pagans. Of all the commands already given, it was important that they remembered the Sabbath (the fourth time this is mentioned in Exodus) and the three holy feasts and that they redeemed all firstborn sons and animals before God. For another forty days and nights, Moses stayed on the mountain communing with God. The note that Moses "DID NOT EAT BREAD, AND HE DID NOT DRINK WATER" during this time points to God's sustaining power over all his creation, even humans.

The final verses of the chapter describe the effects of God's presence on Moses (vs. 29–35). Because of his time with God, Moses began to glow. One could say that he spent so much time with God that God began to "rub off" on Moses. It was such a drastic visible change that Moses wore a veil over his face after relaying to the people what God had told him. Centuries later, Paul referred to this phenomenon, comparing it to the "veil" that blinds the Jewish people from believing in Christ, whereas believers experience God's Holy Spirit personally indwelling each of us (2 Corinthians 3:12–18).

Chapters thirty-five through thirty-nine are essentially a repetition of chapters twenty-five to thirty-one. In the former section, Moses was on the mountain receiving detailed instructions from God about the design and furniture of the tabernacle they were to build. Chapter thirty-one introduced Bezalel and Oholiab as the two men that God commissioned to oversee the actual work. In this second section, the work is finally done under the supervision of those two men and according to God's instructions to Moses.

Before the work on the tabernacle began, Moses gave three sets of instructions. First, he reminded the people that they were not to work on the weekly Sabbath day, not even to kindle a fire (vs. 1–3). This is the fifth time in Exodus that Moses relayed God's command to observe the Sabbath. The people would naturally be excited about getting the work underway, and they would be tempted to skip the Sabbath to complete it more quickly. However, there were two problems with this. One problem is that, since the Sabbath was to be holy to God, even building the tabernacle would profane it. The other problem is that, if they began ignoring the Sabbath this soon, it would easily be forgotten once the work was done.

The second set of instructions had to do with funding the tabernacle project (vs. 4–29). This was not to be a tax or coercion on the people. Instead, everything that was necessary to craft the structure, the furniture, the curtains, the priests' garments, the anointing oil, and the incense were to be given freely from the people to God—as much or as little as they wanted. To emphasize this, the NET Bible uses the following translations: "OFFERING," "WILLING HEART," "HEART STIRRED HIM TO ACTION," "SPIRIT WAS WILLING," AND "FREEWILL OFFERING."

The third set of instructions was the public commissioning of Bezalel and Oholiab (vs. 30–35). Although God had already set them apart to oversee the construction project, Moses now presented them to the people as God's appointed supervisors. As part of their role, they were also to teach people who were skilled and willing to work how to follow God's blueprint.

Chapter thirty-six opens with a situation that nearly every ministry would love to experience. When Bezalel, Oholiab, and their team began taking inventory of the freewill offerings that the people were bringing, they were amazed (vs. 1–7). They discovered that they had received far more than the design called for, and the people were still standing in line with more! When they told Moses, he had them stop taking inventory and go throughout the camp telling the people to stop bringing items for the temple.

Following God's instructions meticulously, the craftsmen and women began with the tabernacle structure and curtains (vs. 8–38). Whereas before, they had promised, "Everything the Lord has said we will do," but then broke God's law, now they obeyed it to the letter with excited and willing hearts.

Chapter thirty-seven continues the work of building the tabernacle and its furnishings. After the tent, they built the ark of the testimony (vs. 1–9), followed by the table for the Bread of the Presence (vs. 10–16) and the gold lampstand (vs. 17–24). Following these was the smaller altar for burning incense before the Most Holy Place, along with "THE SACRED ANOINTING OIL AND THE PURE FRAGRANT INCENSE" (vs. 25–28). In each case, these were done exactly as God had laid out in chapters twenty-five through thirty-one.

Chapter thirty-eight continues the record of the actual construction of the tabernacle. Working from the Most Holy Place outward (just as Moses had been told), they built the altar for burnt offerings with all the detail as instructed by God (vs. 1–7). They also built the water basin for the priests to wash (vs. 8). Around the outside of the tabernacle itself, they erected framed walls and curtains to form a courtyard (vs. 9–20).

The inventory listed in verses 21–31 is given in talents and shekels, so an exact translation is not possible. However, based on several commentaries and various Bible translations, the estimates are nearly unfathomable. The tabernacle used approximately two tons of gold, almost four tons of silver, and nearly three tons of bronze. Of these, the only part that the people were commanded to give was some of the silver, based on the number of the men twenty years old and older—the rest was given freely. According to verse 26 and Numbers 1:46, there were 603,550 of these men who left Egypt, along with their families, flocks, servants, and many non-Israelites.[65]

Chapter thirty-nine finishes the record of the construction work, focusing on the priests' garments, especially the particular items that the high priest wore: the ephod (vs. 1–5), the onyx shoulder pieces (vs. 6–7), the jeweled

---

[65] Although most commentators and historians deny these as real numbers, 600,000 men easily multiplies to more than two million people having left Egypt.

breastplate (vs. 8–21), the outer robe (vs. 22–26), the turban (vs. 27–29), and the engraved golden headband (vs. 30–31).

Particularly significant in this chapter we find this phrase after the description of each of the pieces: "JUST AS THE LORD HAD COMMANDED MOSES" (vs. 1, 5, 7, 21, 26, 29, 31). This is not to imply that the tabernacle was not done properly. Three times Moses clearly stated that everything was done correctly (vs. 32, 42, 43). However, the high priest had a unique role in the life of the Israelite people, and the repetition of that phrase emphasized the importance that everything was completed to the perfection of God's standard.

Once everything was finally complete, the workers brought all the pieces for Moses to inspect (vs. 32–42). It is interesting to wonder if he was excited to see in real life what God had shown him on the mountain. After carefully examining everything, Moses declared that it was all done well, so he blessed the pieces and the people.

Chapter forty presents the first date mentioned since 19:1 when they had reached Sinai "IN THE THIRD MONTH AFTER THE ISRAELITES WENT OUT FROM THE LAND OF EGYPT." We know that Moses had been on the mountain for forty days twice—almost three months (24:18; 34:28) —plus some other time that had passed (24:15–16; 33:7–11; 34:29–35). Although there is no way to tell exactly how long it took the people to do all the work for the tabernacle, it was certainly less than six months.

So, just one year after leaving Egypt and only nine months after arriving at Sinai, everything was ready to assemble. God told Moses to use the pieces to build the tabernacle "ON THE FIRST DAY OF THE FIRST MONTH, IN THE SECOND YEAR" (vs. 1). Whether he had to do it by himself with no help, and whether it took him more than one day to accomplish is never stated, but the verbs translated with "YOU ARE TO" throughout this section are masculine singular in Hebrew, and it certainly implies that Moses did the work alone. As in the previous chapter, we find the repeated phrase "JUST AS THE LORD HAD COMMANDED" with a few variations (vs. 16, 19, 21, 23, 25, 27, 29, 32). "SO MOSES FINISHED THE WORK" (vs. 33).

Finally, it was completed, and "THE CLOUD COVERED THE TENT OF MEETING, AND THE GLORY OF THE LORD FILLED THE TABERNACLE" (vs. 34). As before, when the cloud or fire moved, the people followed. However, now, the cloud and fire stayed in the middle of the camp, hovering over the Most Holy Place where Moses would regularly meet with God.

Leviticus

The book of Leviticus spans only about 30 days while the Israelites were still camped at Mount Sinai but after they built the tabernacle as Exodus describes. As is common with many of the Hebrew books, the title is simply the first word, in this case, וַיִּקְרָא (vayyiqerah, "and he called"). The name *Leviticus* comes from the Septuagint, the Greek translation of the Hebrew text. Entitled Λευειτικον (*Leueitikon*), it deals with the newly formed Levitical system of sacrifices, purity, and holy days for the nation of Israel.

Leviticus is often used by unbelievers to charge Christians with hypocrisy, accusing them of selectively obeying only parts of the Scriptures while ignoring other sections. This comes from a lack of understanding of the Levitical system itself. As part of the Mosaic Covenant, this law code was given solely to the nation of Israel as both the moral and civil standard which was to set them apart from the pagan nations surrounding them when they moved into the land of Canaan. The weekly Sabbath forced them to rest while the nations around them continued their economic pursuits. The sacrifices emphasized that violations of the two great laws of love—for God and their neighbor—required a bloody substitute to atone for sin.

Most of all, the Mosaic Law was a constant reminder that—for the people of God—even the secular was sacred. In all things, they were to be holy, set apart to God. Christians are not bound to the laws in this book, yet it reinforces the truth that God and his standards never change. Because Jesus has fulfilled the entire law and its requirements for us, there is no excuse for a believer to not "BE HOLY BECAUSE I, THE LORD YOUR GOD, AM HOLY" (19:2).

Atonement

The concept of atonement is found predominantly in Leviticus. Nearly half (48%) of the uses of the word in the Bible occur in Leviticus. The Hebrew word is כפר (*kpr*), which means "to cover, smear, pitch; appease." It is the same root word that forms *kippah*—the Jewish head covering—and Yom Kippur—the Day of Covering/Atonement.

In the Old Testament, atonement is not the same as forgiveness. Strictly speaking, the words *atone* and *atonement* mean only that the sins of the people were covered by the sacrificial blood. Thus, the animal sacrifices looked forward to Jesus' death on the cross—the final sacrifice which removes sin—but could not remove them.

In the New Testament, there are two Greek words used only about Jesus' death (and each is used only twice) that try to bring out the concept of atonement. In 1 John 2:2; 4:10, we find ἱλασμός (*hilasmos*;), which means "an offering that appeases or satisfies" and refers to the offering itself. In Romans 3:25 and Hebrews 9:5 is ἱλαστήριον (*hilasterion*), which means "the means or place of appeasement" looking back to the atonement lid of the ark of the covenant. In some English Bibles, both words are translated as "propitiation," from the Latin *propitiare*, "to appease." Thus, Jesus' death is both the final sacrifice that God accepted for sin and the place where God's wrath against sin was finally satisfied.

Chapter one seems to pick up immediately from the end of Exodus. After Moses had finished assembling the pieces that the people had crafted, God's glory and presence filled the tabernacle (Exodus 40:33–34). From there, God called Moses to meet with him, and he gave Moses the rest of the law code that he had begun on the mountain (Exodus 20–23).

Whereas the previous laws dealt primarily with the interaction between the people, with the altar now functioning, God began to outline the exact sacrificial system that they were to follow. This chapter gives the regulations for burnt offerings. They were to be **"DOMESTICATED ANIMALS"** not wild animals, and they could be from either a herd or flock (vs. 2). If **"FROM THE HERD"** it must be **"A FLAWLESS MALE"** (vs. 3–9). If the offering was a young bull, God required that the animal must be presented at the tabernacle before the priests. If it was for atonement, the presenter was to place his hands on the animal's head, signifying the transference of sin from the person to the animal.[1] It was the presenter's responsibility to slaughter the animal, skin and quarter it, and wash the entrails. It was the priests' responsibility to arrange the parts on the altar and burn them. The ritual was the same if the animal was a sheep or goat (vs. 10–13).

Birds were also acceptable offerings if they were turtledoves or young pigeons (vs. 14–17). In this case, it was the priests' responsibility to remove the bird's head, drain its blood, and essentially butterfly it (while keeping it whole) and then burn it on the altar.

Chapter two introduces the "GRAIN OFFERING." Rather than coming from the herds, this came from the fields. Specifically, this grain was to be wheat, as opposed to barley, another common crop. It could be offered in three ways—raw, cooked, or toasted. If the people brought the grain raw, it was to be mixed with a little bit of olive oil and frankincense (vs. 1–3). The priests would put part of it on the altar to burn and would keep the rest.

If the people brought their offering cooked, it could be baked like a flatbread (vs. 4), grilled (vs. 5–6), or fried (vs. 7), but it was always to be accompanied by olive oil. Again, the priests would put part of it on the altar and keep the rest (vs. 8–10). It was especially important that yeast was never included in any kind of offering on the altar (vs. 11–13). (This was true of anything that would spoil quickly, like honey or milk). However, because this was a provision of food for the priests, the people were to make sure they salted it well.

Finally, the people could choose to toast the grain kernels for their offering (vs. 14–16). Again, it was to be mixed with olive oil and frankincense, and the priests would burn some and keep some. The sacrifices were God's primary method for the people to financially support the priests since they would not be allowed to own land or herds.

---

[1] As Leviticus will explain, not all burnt offerings were for sin.

Chapter three introduces the third type of sacrifice, the "PEACE-OFFERING." This was different from the others in that the one who offered the sacrifice also got to participate in eating from it, rather than leaving it for the priests alone. The peace-offering symbolized peace or fellowship between the presenter and Yehovah and became like a communion meal between them. After laying his hands on the animal's head, the presenter slaughtered it and cleaned out the fat and kidneys from its entrails (vs. 1–5). The priests splashed some of the blood on the altar and burnt the fat and kidneys before God. Whether it was a bull, a sheep or goat, male or female, it had to be flawless (vs. 6–17). The people were never to eat the fat nor the blood. This is why the kidneys were always burnt along with the fat: they filter impurities from the blood.

Chapter four introduces the "SIN OFFERING," the price required for any violation of the law that was done unintentionally.[2] The stipulations for the sin offering varied slightly depending on who sinned. If it was the high priest or the entire nation, the offering was to be a young bull (vs. 1–21), once the sin has come to their attention. The priest was to slaughter the bull, cleaning the fat and kidneys from the entrails and sprinkling blood on the altar of incense and before the curtain of the Most Holy Place. The fat and kidneys were burnt on the altar, but the rest of the carcass was burned outside the camp. God guaranteed atonement and forgiveness for unintentional sin by this method of sacrifice.

If the sinner was a leader of the people, he was required to offer a male goat for his sin offering (vs. 22–26). The priest would burn the fat and kidneys as before, but the rest of the animal was given to the priests as their portion, instead of being completely burned. If the sinner was "AN ORDINARY INDIVIDUAL," he could bring a female goat or sheep (vs. 27–35). After laying his hand on the head of the animal, he would slaughter it and clean out the fat and kidneys. As before, the priests would burn those parts and keep the rest for themselves. In

---

[2] Intentional sins are called "trespasses," and some willful sins had no sacrifice available (Numbers 15:30–31).

each of these instances of unintentional sin (violation of God's law), God promised atonement and forgiveness for those who made their sacrifice this way.

Chapter five continues instructions for individuals who had sinned, offering specific examples. Failing to testify as an eyewitness, touching anything unclean, and swearing a thoughtless oath—all these required a sin offering to God (vs. 1–6). The instructions for offerings are repeated from chapter four. For those who could not afford to offer a sheep or goat, two turtledoves or pigeons were acceptable (vs. 7–10). For those who could not afford even that, God allowed a grain offering to be substituted as a sin offering (vs. 11–13). Two things are important to note here. First, lack of wealth was no excuse to not seek atonement and forgiveness from God. God's law was not designed to bankrupt anyone. A second perspective reveals that God was ready to forgive anyone. He showed neither favoritism for the wealthy nor disdain for the poor.

Verses 14–16 address issues when a person has contaminated a holy item. Rather than simply making himself unclean, he had made something dedicated to God unclean. In this case, he was required to offer a ram or the price of the ram in silver. He also had to pay the cost of the holy item plus a 20% surcharge.

For violating certain laws, the price was a ram or its worth in silver (vs. 17–19). In the Hebrew text, the first seven verses of chapter six (English) are numbered as 5:20–26, which makes sense because it continues to deal with the offerings for these "trespasses." Again, a few examples of trespasses are given—extortion, theft, false testimony. These required the same sacrifice as contaminating a holy item: one ram (or its worth in silver) plus the value of whatever was stolen and a 20% surcharge.

Chapter six (in Hebrew) starts with English 6:8. In this chapter and the next, God laid out the instructions for how the priests were to deal with sacrifices that were brought to the tabernacle. Burnt offerings were done in two stages (vs. 8–13). After making the offering on the altar in the tabernacle and letting it burn overnight, the priest had to change his clothes and take the ashes outside the camp. God made a special note that the fire on the altar must never be allowed to go out. It was to burn constantly.

It is important to note that, once an offering was brought to the tabernacle, it was considered holy, which means that it must be eaten in a holy place, e.g., the tabernacle itself. Most of these offerings were required to have been eaten the same day they were offered, although some were allowed multiple days. Even after the grain offering was burned on the altar, the rest of it (the priests' portion) was not allowed to be leavened (vs. 14–18). There was a special grain offering required whenever a new high priest was appointed (vs. 19–23). This was offered in two phases in one day and was required to be burned completely. For sin offerings, a special note was made regarding the pot in which the offering may have been boiled (vs. 24–29). If it was a clay pot, it was required to be broken, because it had become unclean. If it was a bronze pot, then it could be scrubbed and considered clean again.

Chapter seven continues the regulations for sacrifices. Instructions for guilt offerings had already been given, but this section added the note that any of the priests could eat it, not just the officiating priest (vs. 1–7). Hides and grain offerings were to be considered the property of the officiating priest, not necessarily all the priests, like some of the offerings in chapter six (vs. 8–10).

The peace offering had a few different variations. One was the "thank offering" (vs. 11–15). This offering was to be accompanied by all three types of grain offerings (baked, grilled, and toasted), and it was given to the priest who presented it to God. A "votive or freewill sacrifice" could be eaten on the first or second day from its presentation, but not the third day (vs. 16–21).[3] If the meat of the offering was touched by something unclean, it would automatically become unclean and was required to be burnt completely. No one unclean could eat the meat of this offering.

The last kind of peace offering was the "wave offering," named so because the person "waved" part of the meat before God before it went on the altar

---

[3] "Votive" means "offered in fulfillment of a vow" rather than "freewill" or "voluntary."

(vs. 28–36). The breast and the right thigh of the animal were reserved for the priests, but the presenter could eat the rest.

Once again (see 3:17) God made it clear that the people were never to eat the fat or the blood of any animal, even those made clean for sacrifices (vs. 22–27). If the animal died from natural causes (not a sacrifice), the fat could be used for other purposes but not eaten.

Chapter eight begins a narrative section detailing the actions that Moses took in response to the instructions God had just given him. Chapters one through seven were God's instructions to Moses on the day that the tabernacle was finally assembled, but none of those instructions had been carried out yet. In the next few chapters, Moses recorded what happened when he began to obey God's commands.

Before any of the other sacrifices could be offered, Moses had to purify Aaron and his sons according to God's instructions in Exodus 29. Although he had assembled the tabernacle in Exodus 40, Moses had not yet officially instated the priests, so that was his first obligation. Bringing Aaron and his sons in front of the tabernacle and the people, Moses washed them, dressed them in their appropriate garments, and anointed them as God had instructed (vs. 1–13). He then took "THE SIN-OFFERING BULL, THE TWO RAMS, AND THE BASKET OF UNLEAVENED BREAD" and offered them on the altar (outside the camp for the bull) as God had instructed, splashing the blood and applying it to the priests where appropriate (vs. 14–29). Finally, Moses used the special anointing oil and some blood from the altar to anoint the priests, making them clean and able to stand between the people and Yehovah (vs. 30–36). For seven days they were to remain in the tabernacle until Moses returned for the next step in their inauguration.

Chapter nine picks up one week after chapter eight. Once the priests had fulfilled their consecration week in the tabernacle, it was time for them to take their role. Moses said that if they followed everything carefully, God's presence would appear for the people.

Before they could offer sacrifices for the people, they first needed their own atonement, so Moses had Aaron sacrifice a "SIN-OFFERING CALF...FOR HIMSELF" and a whole burnt offering, following the instructions God had given to Moses (vs. 1–14). Once this was complete, he was able to present "THE SIN-OFFERING...FOR THE PEOPLE" and "THE BURNT OFFERING...ACCORDING TO THE STANDARD REGULATION" (vs. 15–21). He followed this with a grain offering and multiple peace offerings. (One wonders if this was also just to give him practice with each kind of offering.)

After all this had been completed properly, Aaron blessed the people, and "MOSES AND AARON THEN ENTERED INTO THE MEETING TENT" (vs. 22–24). When they reappeared, God's presence did fill the place, and he sent fire upon the altar to consume the sacrifice. The people were naturally overcome with fear, and they fell with their faces to the ground in worship.

Chapter ten is a sad conclusion to the festivities of the day when God's presence took up residence in the tabernacle. For some reason, Aaron's two oldest sons, Nahab and Abihu, decided to offer incense to God (vs. 1). Exactly what was wrong with this is unknown, but several suggestions have been offered by various commentators: 1) it was the wrong incense; 2) it was the wrong time; 3) it was not their job; 4) they were unfit (see verse eight).

Regardless of their infraction, the same fire that had just accepted Aaron's offerings rejected his sons', and they were killed immediately (vs. 2). It seems that the Holy Spirit spoke through Moses at this time because he immediately knew what had happened and had God's message for Aaron (vs. 3–7). He said that God would not be dishonored, so Aaron and his other sons were not allowed to mourn for these two, because of their sin. The rest of Israel was allowed to mourn, though. Moses ordered two of Aaron's nephews to carry the bodies outside the camp and bury them.

God gave two new commands at this time, both directly to Aaron (vs. 8–11). First, the priests were not allowed to drink "WINE OR STRONG DRINK" while they were on duty. This specific prohibition has led some to think that this may have been Nadab's and Abihu's sin. Others have made the application that God's people should not drink alcohol at all, because we are always "on duty" in worship. Second, God insisted that all the people know the difference between clean and unclean, holy and profane. The next several chapters would delineate many of these items.

The death of those two men would not cause the day to stop, so Moses told the remaining priests to bring their families into the courtyard to eat their portion of the sacrifices (vs. 12–20). These had to be eaten at the tabernacle because they had been made holy. When Moses discovered that one of the goats had been allowed to burn completely, instead of the priests eating part of it, he became angry at them. Aaron, however, displayed the right attitude, asking, "Given what took place today, do you think God would have been pleased if we had done that?" Constable rightly notes, "God is more gracious with those who fear Him—and yet make mistakes—than He is with those who do not fear Him as they should."[4]

Chapters eleven through fifteen contain the lists of clean and unclean items and practices for the Israelite nation, beginning with their oft-referenced foods. God had just commanded Aaron "TO DISTINGUISH BETWEEN THE HOLY AND THE COMMON, AND BETWEEN THE UNCLEAN AND THE CLEAN" (10:10) and to teach the people, and here he listed them specifically.

Much debate has been made over why certain animals were clean and unclean, but no clear explanations are given in Scripture. What is clear is that all animals were "very good" at the end of the creation week (Genesis 1:25, 31), that God gave all animals to humans to eat after the Flood (Genesis 9:3), and that God declared all things clean again in the Church Age (Acts 10:9–16; Romans 14:14). Since no reasons are given, and since these restrictions were only for the nation of Israel (as opposed to the other peoples on earth at the time), we must understand these distinctions not only to be temporary but primarily to force a distinction between holy and profane so that the nation would constantly be reminded that God was set apart from people and they were set apart to God.

---

[4] Constable, *Notes on Leviticus, 2016 edition*, 53.

From land animals, they could eat anything with a split hoof that chewed the cud (vs. 1–8). Specifically forbidden were camels, rock badgers, hares, and pigs. From the sea, they could eat anything that had both fins and scales (vs. 9–12). From the air animals, God was predominantly negative (vs. 13–25). Rather than what they could eat, he gave a long list of what they were to avoid. It seems that these were mostly carrion birds, which eat meat while there is still blood, something that God had forbidden multiple times. This prohibition also included most insects, except for "THE LOCUST OF ANY KIND, THE BALD LOCUST OF ANY KIND, THE CRICKET OF ANY KIND, THE GRASSHOPPER OF ANY KIND."

Coming back to land animals, God began to list many that were not acceptable for food (vs. 26–38). These were mainly those with paws, rodents, and lizards. Touching anything unclean would make a person unclean. Touching the carcass of an unclean animal would make a person unclean. Even if an unclean animal died, fell over, and touched something else, whatever it touched would become unclean.

Death was supposed to be handled carefully by the Israelites (vs. 39–47). Even a clean animal that died would cause a person touching the carcass to become unclean "UNTIL THE EVENING" (when the new day began). The only reason given for all these instructions was that "I AM THE LORD YOUR GOD, AND YOU ARE TO SANCTIFY YOURSELVES AND BE HOLY BECAUSE I AM HOLY."

Chapter twelve deals with the ritual uncleanness of a woman in childbirth. It is important to note that "uncleanness" has to do with the ceremony of Israel and the tabernacle, not with sin or even physical uncleanness. The context must determine which type of uncleanness is at issue. When a Jewish woman gave birth to a child, she was automatically considered unclean for a specified time. Physically, she was unclean for seven days with a son (the same as for her menstrual cycle) and fourteen days with a daughter. Ceremonially, she was unclean for an additional thirty-three days for a son and sixty-six for a daughter.

Again, as with the distinctions of animals to be eaten, no clear reasons are given for the differences between birthing sons and daughters, but a few speculations have been offered. The most obvious is that a son was required to be circumcised on the eighth day. Thus, because the woman was unable to participate in anything holy while she was unclean, at least part of that time had to be shortened to only seven days.

Some have used the doubled time to attack the unfair patriarchal system of the Old Testament, proving that God (or at least this society) did not value males and females equally. The fact that Moses wrote both Genesis, where he recorded both male and female as being created in the image of God, and Leviticus seems to make that unlikely. Additionally, God was the one who gave these instructions, meaning that he, too, would be misogynistic (a charge that is too often thrown at many biblical writers). Finally, the sacrifice the new mother was to offer at the end of the unclean period was the same, regardless of the gender of her child, so that seems to negate that suggestion.

It has been noted frequently and is worth mentioning here, that Joseph and Mary brought two turtledoves to offer at Jesus' circumcision (Luke 2:22–24). According to this passage, this means that they were too poor to afford the "ONE-YEAR-OLD LAMB" (vs. 6).

Chapters thirteen and fourteen do not qualify as "fun reading," since they detail the regulations for determining which skin spots and diseases were clean and unclean. A few points are important to consider here. First, this section was not designed to be a medical textbook or treatment manual. The emphasis of the entire section has to do with the priests determining whether a person was "clean" (able to participate in the sanctuary) or "unclean" (disallowed in the sanctuary). Although they looked for signs of contagiousness, treatment was not their primary goal.[5] Second, skin disease may have made a person "unclean," but that should not be confused with sin. These were not necessarily the results or consequences of sin. Third, although many English translations use "leprosy" here, these rarely refer to what is now known as "true" leprosy (Hansen's disease). Instead, the symptoms described could refer to any number of dermatological issues, including, but not limited to: scabs,

---

[5] While treatment was not the primary concern, God's instructions still included some things that are both logically and medically standard today, such as isolating sick people away from healthy people.

boils, psoriasis, cellulitis, eczema, skin cancer, rashes, burns, and other infections. Even balding could be a concern, depending on the location.

Whenever someone noticed an abnormality in their skin, they were to see a priest. Because physical uncleanness contributed to ritual or ceremonial uncleanness, the purpose was to determine if the person was ritually clean (they could participate in normal Israelite life and worship) or unclean (they were quarantined away from others, in designated places outside of the camp, for some time). The priests would use a series of observations to determine if it was serious: the color of the spot; the color of the hair on the spot; the size and location of the spot; and all of these after several examinations on different days.

The fact that verses 47–58 refer to clothing having infectious diseases makes it obvious that this cannot refer strictly to leprosy, as it is often misunderstood. This section could refer to bodily fluids that had seeped from an infected sore or mildew or anything in between. If the priest determined that it was connected to a contagion, the garment or fabric was to be burned. Otherwise, it could be washed thoroughly and used again.

Chapter fourteen contains God's instructions for how the priests were to deal with a "DISEASED PERSON ON THE DAY OF HIS PURIFICATION" (vs. 1–9). After the priest declared the person to be physically clean, there was a sacrificial process by which he was also made ceremonially clean. On that day, the priest was to bring together "TWO LIVE CLEAN BIRDS, A PIECE OF CEDAR WOOD, A SCRAP OF CRIMSON FABRIC, AND SOME TWIGS OF HYSSOP." The first bird was killed in a pot; the remaining items were dipped in that blood, sprinkled over the healed person, and the live bird was set free. He was required to "WASH HIS CLOTHES, SHAVE OFF ALL HIS HAIR, AND BATHE IN WATER" both that day and one week later.

After this was complete, the next day (eight days after being called physically clean) he was to present "TWO FLAWLESS MALE LAMBS, ONE FLAWLESS YEARLING FEMALE LAMB, THREE-TENTHS OF AN EPHAH OF CHOICE WHEAT FLOUR…MIXED WITH OLIVE OIL, AND ONE LOG OF OLIVE OIL" to the priest at the tabernacle (vs. 10–20). One of the lambs and the olive oil constituted a guilt offering; the oil was used to anoint the newly cleaned person. The rest would be used for a sin offering, burnt offering, and grain offering before the person was considered completely clean. If the person were too poor to afford all of that, God allowed them to bring "ONE MALE LAMB...ONE-TENTH OF AN EPHAH OF CHOICE WHEAT FLOUR MIXED WITH OLIVE OIL...A LOG OF OLIVE OIL, AND TWO TURTLEDOVES OR TWO YOUNG PIGEONS" to cover all of the required sacrifices (vs. 21–32).

As with the garments in 13:47–58, it is possible for something (like mold or mildew) to "infect" a house as well (vs. 33–53). It was the responsibility of the priests to examine these and decide. Depending on what the visible infection did, it could be as simple as having the house scraped and re-plastered, or it could require the house to be torn down and rebuilt. In either case, the priest would follow the same steps with the two birds outside the camp as when a person was first pronounced physically clean.

Chapter fifteen deals with laws concerning four types of bodily discharges, two normal and two abnormal. Verses 1–15 refer to an abnormal discharge or secretion from a man. Commentators are generally agreed that this is probably due to venereal disease. Someone with this disease contaminated anything he sat or laid on, as well as anyone who touched anything contaminated by this man. This type of uncleanness required a sacrifice only for the sick man. Anyone contaminated by him had to wash their clothes, take a bath, and remain ceremonially unclean until the evening when the next day began. He had to wait for eight days after he was pronounced clean, then offer "TWO TURTLEDOVES OR TWO YOUNG PIGEONS," one each as a sin offering and burnt offering.

The second situation was a normal seminal discharge (vs. 16–18). Although this made the man ceremonially unclean until evening and he had to clean up anything that got semen on it, no sacrifices were necessary. This indicates that God did not consider sex itself bad, only that the emission caused ceremonial uncleanness for the rest of the day. This may have been God's way of keeping Israel from falling into the pagan practices of involving sex in worship. Sex is a gift from God to humanity, but it is not an act of worship, so God codified the separation between them.

The third and fourth situations mirror the first two, except they refer to women. When a woman had her regular menstrual cycle, she was considered unclean for seven days (vs. 19–24). This uncleanness would affect anything she sat on and any man she slept with during that time. Because this was normal, her only obligation was to clean herself and anything she contaminated. Constable makes an interesting observation on this seemingly harsh law:

> This law appears very harsh to the modern reader. It appears to consign virtually every woman in Israel to a state of being "untouchable" (unclean) for one week every month. Some authorities, however, believe that women in ancient Israel had menstrual periods far less frequently than modern women. They believe that the youthful, early marriages of Jewish women, delayed weaning (up to the age of two or three) of their babies, and the prevalence of large families made these unclean periods far more infrequent. Those most affected by this law were probably unmarried teenage girls. The result would have been that God-fearing young men would have been wary of making physical contact with them. This law, therefore, would have had the effect of curbing the passions of the young.[6]

The final situation described referred to a woman whose **"DISCHARGE OF BLOOD FLOWS MANY DAYS NOT AT THE TIME OF HER MENSTRUATION"** or longer than her normal period (vs. 25–30). This is similar to the first scenario, when a man had an abnormal discharge, and the solution was the same. A week after her bleeding ended and she was pronounced clean, she was to offer two turtledoves or pigeons as a sin and burnt offering.

Thus, the sick (and potentially contagious) were not allowed to participate in worship ceremonies, and those who had recently had sex could not, which was an obvious distinction from the pagan nations who practiced sex as part of their worship rituals.

---

[6] Constable, *Notes on Leviticus, 2016 edition*, 80.

Chapter sixteen details the requirements for the annual Day of Atonement, *Yom Kippur*. God gave Moses these instructions on the day that Nadab and Abihu died, adding the speculation that they may have tried to enter the Most Holy Place when offering incense in front of it (10:1–2). Here God outlined the only day each year that the Most Holy Place was accessible, only by the high priest, and only as a part of a specific set of sacrifices. Violation of this specific day and method would result in death (vs. 1–2).

After washing himself and putting on clean garments, Aaron (the high priest) was to bring a young bull, two rams, and two goats. One of the goats would be set aside for Yehovah and the other for Azazel.[7] The bull was the sin offering for "HIMSELF AND HIS HOUSEHOLD" (vs. 11). Putting incense on the incense altar to fill the place with smoke, he was unable to see the lid of atonement, "SO THAT HE WILL NOT DIE" (vs. 13); he then sprinkled blood on and in front of the lid.

One of the goats, the one set apart to Yehovah, served as "THE SIN-OFFERING...FOR THE PEOPLE" (vs. 15). Following the same pattern as with the bull, he sacrificed the goat and sprinkled the blood on the atonement lid. No one else was allowed in the Meeting Tent while these sacrifices were taking place (vs. 17). The second live goat was the "scapegoat." Placing his hands on its head, Aaron transferred the sins of the nation to the goat as the substitutionary offering, which was then taken far into the desert by a man designated for this task (vs. 20–22)

As the goat was led away, Aaron washed again and changed his clothes, then sacrificed the two rams as burnt offerings for himself and the people (vs. 23–28). The man who led the scapegoat away was also to wash and change his clothes before returning to camp. The one who finished burning the carcasses of the sin offerings outside the camp was required to do the same.

God commanded that this day be set aside for this purpose annually on the tenth day of the seventh month, almost exactly half a year after the Passover

---

[7] "Azazel" has been translated and interpreted in several ways, most notably as "the scapegoat." It likely refers to the chief goat-demon of the desert (see 17:6), a symbol of Satan's constant battle to accuse and consume God's people for their sins.

(the fourteenth day of the first month). This was a special Sabbath day for everyone in Israel, "BOTH THE NATIVE CITIZEN AND THE RESIDENT FOREIGNER WHO LIVES IN YOUR MIDST" (vs. 29).

Chapter seventeen shifts the emphasis of Leviticus from the nation as a whole to the individual Israelites under the Mosaic Law Code. This is indicated by the repeated phrases "ANY MAN," "THAT MAN," "NO PERSON," "ANY PERSON," and "NO MAN" throughout the rest of the book. The first regulation was that Israelites were not allowed to slaughter certain animals except at the newly-built tabernacle (vs. 1–9). These included oxen, lambs, and goats. Because they were sacrificial animals, this would keep the people from slipping into the pagan practice of demon worship using goats both in sacrifice and bestial practices (as already evidenced by the golden calf incident in Exodus 32).

Eating or drinking blood was also fully prohibited, something that God had banned multiple times before, including (and most importantly) immediately after the Flood (vs. 10–14; see Genesis 9:4). Because God linked blood with the essence of life itself, those who consume blood show disrespect for life.[8] The third command in this chapter had to do with eating meat. If the animal was not slaughtered, but rather died of natural causes (including being killed by another animal), it was legitimate to eat, but the person was unclean until sundown and was required to bathe and wash their clothes (vs. 15–16).

Chapter eighteen continues the commands regarding individual people in Israel. All these commands were tied back to one specific reason: "I AM THE LORD YOUR GOD!" This is repeated six times in this chapter (vs. 2, 4, 5, 6, 21, 30). This, and the reference to Egypt, is reminiscent of the basis of the Ten Commandments (Exodus 20:2). God's people were to be different from the pagans around them and certainly not practice the things from their old way of living in Egypt (vs. 1–5). Because the violation of many of these commands

---

[8] Because this command was given to all humanity long before Israel and the Mosaic Law and is never rescinded in Scripture, we must assume it is still in force for all peoples still today.

resulted in death, God could legitimately say, "ANYONE WHO DOES SO WILL LIVE BY KEEPING THEM."

Sexual practices have always been a part (sometimes an integral part) of pagan religions, and Israel would be surrounded by them, so God laid out clear instructions about sexuality. Adultery was already condemned in the Seventh Commandment, the instruction to respect and protect each other's marriages, but here God broadened it to include other forms of sexual relationships. Addressing specifically the men, God listed fourteen family relations that were too close to him to violate by having sex, plus six other specific situations in which sexual intercourse was prohibited. Verse six seems to be a general reference to any blood relative. The mention of people giving their "CHILDREN AS AN OFFERING TO MOLECH" (vs. 21) does not seem to fit here if it is in reference just to human sacrifice. There must have been a sexual component to Molech worship as well. All these deviant practices were performed routinely by the pagan nations in Canaan, which is the express reason that God wanted Israel to clear them from the land, and he did not want them bringing that filth back into the land once it was purged (vs. 24–30).

Chapter nineteen is an oft-referenced chapter from Leviticus. From a godly standpoint, this is the first time that God specifically laid out his ultimate goal for the Israelites, both as a nation and as individuals: "YOU MUST BE HOLY BECAUSE I, THE LORD YOUR GOD, AM HOLY" (vs. 2). Jesus quoted this when he laid out the requirements for entering his Messianic Kingdom: "SO THEN, BE PERFECT, AS YOUR HEAVENLY FATHER IS PERFECT" (Matthew 5:48), and Peter applied it to the Diaspora Christian Jews who were under increasing persecution for their faith (1 Peter 1:15–16).

The list of commands here is almost proverb-like—quick, one- or two-liners, not necessarily connected with those before or after them. Verses 3–4 quickly review four of the first Five Commandments.

Sacrifices were required to be eaten within a day or two of their offering (vs. 5–8). No single act of worship had a long-term effect. Crops were to be harvested in such a way as to leave some to provide "FOR THE POOR AND THE RESIDENT FOREIGNER" (vs. 9–10). Charity was practiced by the people, when they had the ability, not by the government. Verses 11–14 contain a few more of the Ten Commandments plus several things that seem to be common courtesy toward fellow members of society, including the disabled. Verses 15–18 condemn any kind of judicial system that unfairly treats anyone over another, whether they are poor or rich. The judicial system was based on both the impartiality of the judge and truthful witnesses. People who hate each other are not impartial.

Beginning with verse nineteen, we find another reason that this chapter is quoted frequently, this time by those who interpret the Bible without recognizing proper dispensational distinctions. Many unbelievers love to point out the "hypocrisy" of Christians who do not obey the Bible because they breed different kinds (species) of animals, plant two crops at the same time in their home gardens, and wear clothes made of blended fabrics. Because the entire Mosaic Law ended with Christ (Romans 10:4; Matthew 5:17; Colossians 2:14–15), only those things which are given as commands in the New Testament for churches are binding on us today; these are not.

Although slavery was acceptable under God's law, slaves were still to be treated with respect as human beings. Thus, if a man slept with a female slave who was already engaged to someone else, he had stolen her value from her master and was forced to compensate him (vs. 20–22). (Notice this does not indicate that it was rape, which will be handled later.) Fruit trees were to be allowed to grow for four years before any fruit was taken from them for food (vs. 23–25).

Regular pagan practices were forbidden to the Israelites (vs. 26–31). This included consuming blood, any kind of sorcery, and body-altering.[9] Selling one's daughter to be a temple prostitute was also prohibited, as the last chapter emphasized holiness in sexual practice as well. There was to be no attempt to contact the dead. On the other hand, they were to respect the elderly and

---

[9] Verse 28 is often used by those who are against all kinds of tattoos, but the context makes it apply only for Israelites during the Mosaic Law dispensation and specifically in the context of the pagan practice of contacting the dead.

foreigners who lived among them (vs. 32–34). Honesty in their business dealings was imperative (vs. 35–37).

Chapter twenty addresses sins that carried a heavier penalty, often death at the hands of society. People who disagree with capital punishment often argue that it is not a deterrent for crime. One could respond that God did not necessarily say that it would be, only that it was required to purge wickedness from the community.[10] Any worship of Molech was an abomination to God and required the death of the perpetrator (vs. 1–5). It was so bad that God said that if their society refused to execute the offender, God himself would do it. The same was true with the practice of necromancy (vs. 6, 27). Again, all this came from the command to be holy like God himself (vs. 7–8, 26).

Death was the penalty for cursing one's "FATHER OR MOTHER" (vs. 9). Many of the sexual sins listed in chapter eighteen commanded the death penalty as well (vs. 10–21). Other consequences of these unacceptable unions were shame, excommunication from society, and childlessness. Even the distinction between clean and unclean animals was to help them refrain from slipping into pagan practices and defiling the land God promised to give them.

Chapter twenty-one shifted from commands for the common Israelite to those for the priests. Touching a dead body caused a person to become ceremonially unclean. Because of this, a priest was not allowed to defile himself except in the rare exception of his immediate family (vs. 1–4). Pagan priests would mutilate themselves as part of the mourning ritual, but this was forbidden for Yehovah's priests (vs. 5). The priest's holiness (set-apartness) reflected his position between God and man, so it limited from him some things that other Israelites could do, like take a wife who was previously a prostitute or divorced (vs. 6–9). Additionally, although prostitution was not

---

[10] Because we are not under the Mosaic Law, most of these crimes do not necessarily carry the death penalty today. However, the penalty for murder was given long before the Mosaic Law and should still be in effect today (Genesis 9:5–6).

always punished by death, if the prostitute's father was a priest, then she was to die because she profaned him as well.

Even more stringent than the priests' laws were those for the high priest. He was not permitted to mourn or go near any dead body, even his family, and he was allowed to marry only a virgin from Israel (vs. 10–15).

In the same way that a defective animal was not acceptable to be sacrificed, a priest with a physical defect was not allowed to offer sacrifices (vs. 16–24). Notice that this did not eliminate him from the privileges of being part of the priestly family (e.g., he still ate from the food offered), but he could not fulfill the responsibilities of the priests. Some of the disabilities listed were temporary while others were permanent.

Chapter twenty-two explains that the holy name of Yehovah extended to the priests who served in his name and the offerings made in his name. Because the offerings became holy when they were made, only ceremonially clean priests and their families were allowed to eat the portion dedicated to them (vs. 1–16). This eliminated two other specific groups. First, no unclean priests could eat that food until after sundown and their ritual cleansing (vs. 1–9). God had already given it to them and would withhold it only when they were unclean. Second, no one who was not a priest could eat it, unless he or she was part of the priest's immediate family (vs. 10–13). This restriction extended to slaves purchased by the priest himself and even to a divorced or widowed daughter who had returned to live with her father. If someone did eat the holy food accidentally, he or she was to reimburse the priests for it plus a 20% surcharge (vs. 14–16).

To be acceptable as food for the priests, the offerings had to be flawless when they were offered (vs. 17–25). This was not only true for sin and guilt offerings, because of their role as substitutionary sacrifices, it was also true for "VOTIVE OR FREEWILL OFFERINGS, WHICH THEY PRESENT TO THE LORD AS A BURNT OFFERING." Because the priests lived off the offerings brought by the people, they were not to sacrifice something that they could not keep. The one exception to this rule was that "AN OX OR A SHEEP WITH A LIMB TOO LONG OR STUNTED" was acceptable as a freewill offering but not a votive offering.[11]

God made two interesting stipulations about sacrificing young animals. First, for oxen, sheep, and goats, the animal must be left with its mother for at least one week before it was an acceptable sacrifice. Second, no ox or sheep could be sacrificed on the same day as its offspring (vs. 26–29).

Chapter twenty-three lists seven celebrations[12] God intended for the Israelites to celebrate annually, in addition to the "normal" weekly Sabbath. These were not all to be celebrated the same way, though, as they had different offering, attendance, and work requirements attached to them. Additionally, each annual celebration was assigned to a specific calendar day each year (vs. 4). The weekly Sabbath was observed each Saturday with no required sacrifices. However, the people were not allowed to do any work on the Sabbath because it was God's gift of rest for them (vs. 3).

Passover was held on the fourteenth day of the first month, followed immediately by *Unleavened Bread* for the next seven days (vs. 5–8). During Unleavened Bread, they made sacrifices for seven days and ate bread without yeast. They were prohibited from doing "REGULAR WORK" but not all work. Unleavened Bread was the first of three celebrations that required all Jewish males to attend a gathering (Exodus 23:14–17). *First Fruits* took place the day following Unleavened Bread, representing the early harvest (vs. 9–14). Each family would bring a yearling lamb, unleavened bread, and wine plus a sheaf of grain that the priest would wave in the air before God.

Pentecost (or "the Feast of Weeks") was the second festival the men were required to attend (vs. 15–22). Fifty days after Passover, the spring harvest was in full effect. This grain offering was baked with yeast and was accompanied by "SEVEN FLAWLESS YEARLING LAMBS, ONE YOUNG BULL, AND TWO RAMS" as a burnt

---

[11] A "votive" offering was one that was required for fulfilling a vow. Thus, it was not exactly "freewill" because it was required so the vow was not broken.

[12] These are sometimes called "feasts," because the Hebrew word for "feast" and "festival, celebration" is the same (גח, ḥag). Not all of these were large meals as we might often think of a "feast."

offering, a drink offering, "ONE MALE GOAT FOR A SIN OFFERING AND TWO YEARLING LAMBS FOR A PEACE-OFFERING." No "REGULAR WORK" was allowed on Pentecost, and God re-issued the command that the fields should be harvested in such a way that the poor and foreigners could glean from the corners.

The final three celebrations took place in the seventh month, beginning on the first day. After the exiles returned to Israel (approximately 900 years after Leviticus), a new civil calendar was created, running six months off of the original calendar which became the new "sacred" calendar. The sacred calendar held the feasts outlined in this chapter, whereas the new civil calendar was used for everything else, including government. This is important to understand because Rosh Hashanah, the "civil" new year, occurs six months after the "sacred" new year. Often called *Trumpets*, this first day of the "sacred" seventh month was just a special day of rest for the nation, much like we would celebrate a national holiday (vs. 23–25). It was "announced" by loud trumpet blasts, and the people were not to do their regular work.

Nine days later, the tenth day of the seventh month was Yom Kippur, the *Day of Atonement* (vs. 26–32). The significance and ritual were already explained in detail in chapter sixteen. In short, this was the day that the high priest entered the Most Holy Place to atone for the sins of the nation. It was a solemn day, rather than a celebration, and the people were allowed to do no work at all.

The final annual celebration was called *Booths*, *Tents*, or *Tabernacles* (depending on the English translation). This was a reminder of the Israelite exodus from Egypt (vs. 33–43). Beginning on the fifteenth day of the same month, this lasted seven days, and the people were required to set up and live in temporary shelters or booths. This was the third festival the men were required to attend each year. The first and eighth days of the celebration were "HOLY ASSEMBLY" days, and no regular work was allowed.

Chapter twenty-four contains two parts. The first part describes the lampstand and bread table in the tabernacle. The lampstand was to burn pure olive oil and was not allowed to be extinguished (vs. 1–4). The table contained bread that was made specifically to be eaten by the priests in God's presence and replenished on the weekly Sabbath (vs. 5–9). "The 'lamps' and 'showbread' also represented God to the Israelites as their 'Light' and 'Nourishment.'"[13]

The second part of the chapter records an incident that took place leading to a reminder and enforcement of God's law (vs. 10–23). Two men got into a fight; one was a native Israelite, the other was half-Israelite, half-Egyptian. During the fight, the Egyptian cursed using Yehovah's name—a blatant violation of the Third Commandment. While he was held in custody, God told Moses that the man must be executed for his crime. Lest anyone claim that Moses was being racist against the man, God specifically clarified that anyone, "WHETHER HE IS A RESIDENT FOREIGNER OR A NATIVE CITIZEN," was to be executed for misusing his name. God also used the situation to clarify which acts of violence required death or simple restitution, again noting that the person's ethnicity did not affect the sentence (vs. 17–22). Moses and the people obeyed God and put the man to death.

Chapter twenty-five mentions Mount Sinai for the first time since chapter seven. Each of the final three chapters will underline the fact that all the commandments and regulations laid out in Leviticus were given at Mount Sinai before the nation went up to Canaan. God gave two new regulations to Israel at this time—the Sabbath Year and the Year of Jubilee.

Much like God had commanded the people to rest every seventh day, he now commanded them to let their land rest every seventh year (vs. 1–7). During this Sabbath Year, they were not allowed to sow their fields or prune their vines. They also were not allowed to harvest the way they normally would. Instead, they were to spend the year simply enjoying the produce as God's gift to them, picking what they needed, when they needed it. This is how I imagine Eden was and the New Earth will be. Anything left at the end of the year could be tilled under (or pruned) the following spring to begin a new cycle of growth.

---

[13] Constable, *Notes on Leviticus, 2016 edition*, 125.

In addition to the Sabbath Years, God established a Sabbath Squared Year, "SEVEN TIMES SEVEN YEARS" (vs. 9–12). This was the fiftieth year, the year following the seventh Sabbath Year, beginning with the Day of Atonement that year. Not only were the fields and vines to remain fallow again, but God also gave instructions regarding the people. Business deals for land were calculated based on the depreciation of land between Jubilee years (vs. 13–18) because all land was to be returned to its original owner. This helped safeguard against any Israelite tribe losing their full portion of the land. This was true of rural and village houses as well (vs. 29–34) and those who had to sell part or all their land for financial hardship reasons (vs. 25–28). Essentially, people only leased and rented land and buildings until the next Jubilee year. (Houses within city walls were exempt from this; they were redeemable for only one year.) The reason for this arrangement was that God was truly the owner of the land, and he was simply loaning it to Israel (vs. 23–24).

God anticipated a good question and proved his gracious provision for the people (vs. 19–22). "WHAT WILL WE EAT IN THE SEVENTH YEAR IF WE DO NOT SOW AND GATHER OUR PRODUCE?" God promised that the sixth year (48th in the cycle) would be so plentiful that they would have enough to eat on the Sabbath Year (49th), the Jubilee Year (50th), and the first year of the new cycle, until their harvest came in.

The rest of the chapter deals with how the Israelites were to treat the poor and aliens among them. A fellow Israelite in debt was to be supported by his creditor until the debt could be repaid (vs. 35–38). The creditor could not charge him interest or sell him food for a profit. If a fellow Israelite became so impoverished that he sold himself into indentured slavery, the creditor was limited as to what he could have his countryman do, and the Jubilee Year canceled the debt and freed the man from his slavery (vs. 39–43). God allowed the Israelites to own slaves perpetually, but only if they were from the nations around them or from foreigners who came into their land (vs. 44–46). They were not allowed to enslave fellow Israelites except for the stipulation already given which would release them at the Jubilee. Even if an Israelite indentured himself to a foreigner within Israel, he could be redeemed by a family member, based on the time until the next Jubilee Year (vs. 47–55). At the Jubilee Year, he was released from his slavery. This proves that foreigners in the land of Israel were required to obey the Law, even though they were not Israelites.

Chapter twenty-six contains one of the clearest "if-then" statements God gave to Israel. He began with a summary of nearly the entire book of Leviticus: "YOU MUST NOT MAKE FOR YOURSELVES IDOLS, SO YOU MUST NOT SET UP FOR YOURSELVES A CARVED IMAGE OR A PILLAR, AND YOU MUST NOT PLACE A SCULPTED STONE IN YOUR LAND TO BOW DOWN BEFORE IT, FOR I AM THE LORD YOUR GOD. YOU MUST KEEP MY SABBATHS AND REVERENCE MY SANCTUARY. I AM THE LORD."

In verses 3–13 God gave the good news: "IF YOU WALK IN MY STATUTES AND ARE SURE TO OBEY MY COMMANDMENTS." This was the only condition. They had already exclaimed twice, "All the LORD has said we will do!", and God was ready to put their word to the test. If they perfectly obeyed his Law (including making all the sacrifices when they violated it), then he would protect and provide for them in an unprecedented way. They would have so many crops that they could not harvest them all before it was time to plant again. They would face no harmful animals or enemies. Most of all, God's presence would continually be with them. This was the plan for Eden, and it will finally be realized in Messiah's Kingdom and Eternity.

However, if they did not obey, God promised to discipline them (vs. 14–38). Unlike his blessings and provision, he said that his discipline would graciously come in stages. If they did not respond to one discipline, he would keep adding to it. He would afflict their health, cause drought and famine, and let the land be overrun by wild animals and the surrounding nations. Things would get so bad that the people would even fall back to cannibalism. The amount of death would cause the land to stink as bodies rotted in the streets. Finally, he would exile them to foreign lands so that the land could get the Sabbath rests they did not allow it.

This harsh judgment ends on a positive note, though. God promised that, even when things were at their worst, he would never forget his people (vs. 39–45). Not only would he never allow them to be annihilated, but when the exiles finally turned their hearts back to him, he would return them to their land.

Chapter twenty-seven deals with vows that the people could make to God. These may have been offered freely or made as a result of the discipline outlined in the previous chapter. In any case, once a vow was made, God required that it be fulfilled, and he outlined what vows were legitimate.

> A vow was a promise to give oneself, or another person (as in a dedication of someone), or one's possessions to God, either so He would bestow some blessing, or because He had already bestowed a blessing. People made vows *to do* something or *not to do* something. Vows were normally *temporary*. When a person wanted to get back what he had vowed to God, he had to pay a certain price to the sanctuary to buy back what he had given to God. This constituted "redeeming" what the person *had vowed*. Old Testament examples of people who made vows are Jephthah (Judg. 11:30-31) and Hannah (1 Sam. 1:11). Votive offerings were offerings made in payment of vows.[14]

In verses 1–8 God established the "redemption value" of a person who was vowed or dedicated to God. Many writers (especially modern or postmodern) take great issue with the obvious "discrimination" outlined here. However, the valuation seems to be based on production capability in a primarily agricultural system. Thus, men aged 20–60 had a premium value while women, the elderly, and children decreased in value. It is important to remember that this had to do with production value, not the intrinsic worth of a person. Crimes again people were often sentenced equally—regardless of age, gender, or even ethnicity—because all people are created in God's image.

In addition to people being dedicated to God, other items that could be offered were animals (vs. 9–13), houses (vs. 14–15), and land (vs. 16–25). Land was valued similarly to people, e.g., based on its production capability. Whereas people were evaluated on age and gender, land was evaluated on the amount of time left until the next Jubilee Year (a type of depreciation). Because all firstborn oxen and sheep were automatically dedicated to God, a person could not "double dedicate" one of those animals, using them for an offering

---

[14] Constable, *Notes on Leviticus, 2016 edition*, 140.

(vs. 26–27). Although most vows were temporary, they could be made permanent (vs. 28–29). In this case, no redemption was possible.[15] Even their regular mandatory tithes could be redeemed; however, there was a 20% surcharge that was paid to get the grain or animal back (vs. 30–33).

---

[15] Verse 29 gives the answer to the oft-asked question of whether God really expected Jephthah to kill his own daughter (Judges 11:29–40). If it were a permanent dedication, the answer was yes. If not (which was probably the case due to his rash vow), Jephthah could have redeemed her and not killed her.

Numbers

In Hebrew, the name of this book is בְּמִדְבַּר (*bᵉmidᵉbar*) which means "in the wilderness." This is not only appropriate as it describes where "THE LORD SPOKE TO MOSES" (1:1), it is also the story of the Israelite people for the first forty years after the Exodus. The English title comes from the Septuagint version of the Old Testament. It is Ἀριθμοι (*Arithmoi*) in Greek, referring to the two "numberings" or censuses that bookend the years in the wilderness. Numbers is primarily a historical narrative of the years Israel spent wandering the Arabian wilderness waiting to enter Canaan and contains several favorite or well-known stories about the Jewish people before they entered the land—the spies and the giants, Korah, Balaam, and others. However, it also continues the pattern of Leviticus, outlining God's laws for his chosen nation.

By far, the greatest criticism of Numbers has to do with the two censuses, namely the counts of 603,550 (1:46) and 601,730 (26:51) military-aged men. Many would argue that those numbers are far too large to account for the Israelites who left Egypt and entered Canaan, respectively. Since these are the counts of only the men older than 20 years, when we allow for women and children, there must have been between two and three million people in total. Attempts have been made to reduce these numbers to only a tenth or something else entirely. Surprisingly, Archer (who often sides with more liberal views of the writings) took a hard stance on this issue, spending four pages answering the critics' challenges and defending the literalness of these counts.[1] Most notably, he argues that, without these large numbers, how do we account for Pharaoh's estimation of "THE ISRAELITE PEOPLE, MORE NUMEROUS

---

[1] Gleason L. Archer, *A Survey of Old Testament Introduction, Revised and Expanded* (Moody Press, 1994), 265–269.

AND STRONGER THAN WE ARE" (Exodus 1:9)? Secondly, he calculates that the amount of silver that God required from the Israelites in Exodus 38:25–26 was exactly the amount necessary for 603,550 men. These, plus other arguments, make it impossible to cogently defend a position that does not take these census numbers literally.

The theme of Numbers is the sovereignty and holiness of God. He designed a plan that, had Israel followed, would have assured them success and blessing. However, because of their lack of dependence on him, they lost their blessings and even their lives.

Chapter one records the first census God had Moses take of the newly formed Israelite nation after they had been at Mount Sinai for about eleven months. They were under strict obligation to count "THE NAME OF EVERY INDIVIDUAL MALE" (vs. 2). Literally, this phrase reads "according to the name of every male at their skulls." In other words, despite those who wish to see the final count decreased (sometimes dramatically), God told Moses to take a "headcount" and record their names individually. Thus, whatever number we have is meant to be understood as a literal number.

Moses was not to do this alone. God told him that he and Aaron were to have the help of one chief leader of each of the twelve tribes (vs. 4–16). Verses 20–46 list the twelve tribes numbered (excluding Levi) and conclude a total of 603,500 males. Judah was the largest tribe, by far, and Manasseh the smallest. The Levites were not included in this count because they would not serve in the standing army (vs. 47–54). They were responsible for the assembling, disassembling, and ministry of the tabernacle for the nation. Although not all of the Levites were priests, they all served in the tabernacle and helped the priests. This distinction between the tribes regarding the tabernacle was so strict that "ANY UNAUTHORIZED PERSON WHO APPROACHES IT MUST BE KILLED" (vs. 51).

Chapter two describes the camping and traveling situation for the nation while they were in the wilderness. In addition to having the tribes camp together, God had three tribes join under one larger "tribe," one on each side of the tabernacle which stood in the middle of the camp. On the east side of the tabernacle, under Judah's banner were Issachar and Zebulun. On the south side, under Reuben, were Simeon and Gad. On the west side, under Ephraim, were Manasseh and Benjamin. On the north side, under Dan, were Asher and Naphtali. When the camp moved, the groups would also move in this order. The Levites stayed with the tabernacle in the center of the camp and between the first and last two groups when traveling.

Because no explanation of the camping arrangements is given, commentators have wondered about the reason, looking for certain patterns. For instance, the third group (Ephraim, Manasseh, and Benjamin) were the only tribes from Jacob's wife, Rachel. The fourth group (Dan, Asher, and Naphtali) came through Leah's and Rachel's maids. Whether this contributed to God's design is purely speculative.

Chapter three is the Levite version of chapter two, explaining how the Levites camped and moved. Levi himself had three sons—Gershon, Kohath, and Merari. These became the three sub-tribes of Levi. The Gershonites were responsible for the curtains of the tabernacle and camped on the west side of the tabernacle, between the tabernacle itself and Ephraim's group. The Merarites were responsible for the tabernacle frame, boards, and structure. They camped on the north side near Dan's group. The Kohathites were the tribe Moses and Aaron came from. They were responsible for the tabernacle furniture, including the ark of the covenant. They camped on the south side near Reuben. Moses and his family and Aaron and his family (the actual priests) camped between the tabernacle and Judah on the east side.

Two smaller censuses were taken at this time. The first was from the Levites. Rather than counting army-capable males, they counted all males at least one month old, with a result of 22,000. The second counted all other males in Israel, older than one month but younger than 20 years. This number was 22,273, slightly larger than the Levites. During the Passover in Egypt, God declared that he dedicated to himself all of the Israelite firstborn (Exodus 13:1). At this point, he substituted the tribe of Levi for the rest of the nation. Although all firstborns were still dedicated to him, the Levites would stand in their place in the tabernacle ministry. The difference in the numbers caused a collection to be taken from the people to redeem the lives of the firstborns not covered by male Levites.

Chapter four explains how the Levites were to do their job (outlined in chapter three) of transporting, assembling, and disassembling the tabernacle. First, God had Moses and Aaron do another round of counting. This time only those Levites between the ages of 30 and 50 were included. Only they would serve in the tabernacle ministry. Second, although God had already said which parts of the tabernacle each clan was to carry, the order was particularly important.

No one was allowed in the tabernacle until Aaron and his sons (the priests) had gone in and covered the furniture. If the others went in and tried to carry them uncovered, they would die. Once the pieces were covered, then the Kohathites could remove them. After the furniture had been removed, then the Gershonites could remove the curtains from the inside and outside of the structure. Finally, the Merarites could disassemble the frame walls. It was up to Aaron and his sons to determine the actual work carried out by the clans within God's broad direction.

Chapter five begins a series of laws that God had not yet outlined for the people. Most of these were specific situations, rather than general regulations. This chapter contains three parts. The first, much smaller, was God's command that certain people were required to live outside of the camp, to not defile the others around them (vs. 1–4). These were "EVERY LEPER, EVERYONE WHO HAS A DISCHARGE, AND WHOEVER BECOMES DEFILED BY A CORPSE" (vs. 2). Each of these was a temporary expulsion until they were physically and ceremonially clean again, as outlined in Leviticus.

The second part dealt with a situation in which a person broke God's law toward his fellow man (vs. 5–10). In addition to the sin offering he made at the tabernacle, the offender was required to make restitution for the violation, plus 20% extra to the person he had wronged. If no one in the person's family was left to receive the payment, then it was to go to the priests.

The third part dealt with a marital situation (vs. 11–31). Should a man suspect his wife was having an affair, he could have her faithfulness tested.[2] God designed a physical test that he would use to reveal the truth in which the priest would administer a bitter drink. If she were guilty, God would cause the drink to poison her reproductive system.[3] If she were not guilty, God would protect her from all harm, bringing public embarrassment on her accusing husband instead.

Chapter six outlines the procedures for a special type of vow, the Nazirite vow. *Nazirite* means "consecrated one," and most who took this vow did so temporarily. Only two men were clearly said to have been lifelong Nazirites—Samuel (1 Samuel 1:27–28) and Samson (Judges 13:4–5, 14)—although some teachers believe that John the Baptizer may have been as well. This vow was available for both men and women.

The requirements of the Nazirite vow consisted of three parts (vs. 1–8): 1) do not consume anything from a grapevine, either fruit or drink; 2) do not cut one's hair; and 3) do not come in contact with a dead body, even a close relative. Since the third part was not completely in their control, God made allowance in case a person died right next to him and he touched the body (vs. 9–12). He was required to go through seven days of purification, then shave his head, offer sacrifices, and start the length of his vow over again. The time from before his defilement had been voided. At the end of the vow period, he would bring sacrifices to the tabernacle to offer to Yehovah and shave his head again (vs. 13–21). After this, he was free to eat and drink as before his vow.

The chapter concludes with what has become a well-known blessing (vs. 22–27). God gave the priests a blessing which they could say over the Israelites,

---

[2] Of course, if the affair was known, God had already commanded that both the woman and her lover were to be executed (Leviticus 20:10).

[3] Various translations indicate that the affect could be infertility (NLT) or a miscarriage (CEB, NIV). The NRSV states "when the LORD makes your uterus drop, your womb discharge." This idea comes from the results promised to the woman who was not guilty: "SHE WILL BE FREE OF ILL EFFECTS AND WILL BE ABLE TO BEAR CHILDREN" (vs. 28).

tying the people to the very name of Yehovah. While it is common to hear this offered as a blessing or benediction in churches today, we must do so only with the understanding that the promised blessings are directly connected to the nation's obedience to the Mosaic Law, something that the Body of Christ has nothing to do with. God's peace and protection are offered to the church through our relationship with Christ, not the Mosaic Law or any law code.

Chapter seven is the longest chapter in Numbers by far. It goes back in time to when Moses first assembled the tabernacle and the priests dedicated it (Exodus 40). Verses 1–9 add a piece of information about the transportation of the tabernacle not previously mentioned. Although the furniture pieces were carried with poles, the frame structure, curtains, ropes, etc. were all pulled in ox-drawn carts, which had been contributed by the other tribes. Along with these carts, each tribe gave a significant contribution to the Levites, one each day for twelve days:

> HIS OFFERING WAS ONE SILVER PLATTER WEIGHING 130 SHEKELS, AND ONE SILVER SPRINKLING BOWL WEIGHING 70 SHEKELS, BOTH ACCORDING TO THE SANCTUARY SHEKEL, EACH OF THEM FULL OF FINE FLOUR MIXED WITH OLIVE OIL AS A GRAIN OFFERING; ONE GOLD PAN WEIGHING 10 SHEKELS, FULL OF INCENSE; ONE YOUNG BULL, ONE RAM, AND ONE MALE LAMB IN ITS FIRST YEAR, FOR A BURNT OFFERING; ONE MALE GOAT FOR A PURIFICATION OFFERING; AND FOR THE SACRIFICE OF PEACE OFFERINGS: TWO BULLS, FIVE RAMS, FIVE MALE GOATS, AND FIVE MALE LAMBS IN THEIR FIRST YEAR. (vs. 13–17)

For the next week and a half, the other tribes contributed exactly the same gifts. Together, these made the dedication of the tabernacle a magnificent celebration. Once this procession was completed and Moses had officially accepted the gifts, he entered the tabernacle, and God spoke to him (vs. 89).

Chapter eight records what God spoke to Moses at the end of chapter seven. God's first instruction was that the lampstand was to be focused in such a way that it did not simply light a general area but rather the space directly in front of the lampstand (vs. 1–4).

God's second command, and the majority of the chapter, dealt with the ordination of the Levites to service (vs. 5–22). This goes into greater detail than chapters three and four. A key difference between the ordination of the priests and the Levites is that the leaders of the people were involved with the Levites. Because they were the substitutes for the firstborns of the nation, to be separated to God for ministry, the people participated in their dedication ceremony.

There seems to be a discrepancy between verses 23–26 and 4:47, where God had Moses count the Levites between the ages of 30 and 50 as those who could carry the tabernacle pieces. Here God determined that those "THE AGE OF TWENTY-FIVE YEARS AND UPWARD ONE MAY BEGIN TO JOIN THE COMPANY IN THE WORK OF THE TENT OF MEETING," but they had to retire at the age of fifty. The probable solution is that the first five years were a type of apprenticeship, during which they could "JOIN...IN THE WORK OF" the tabernacle, but they could not yet participate in carrying it.

Chapter nine goes back in time just a little before chapters seven and eight. Moses had not yet assembled the tabernacle for the first time, so God spoke to him in the wilderness rather than from the tent. This chapter contains two sections.

The first section seems to be just another reminder by way of command, but it reveals a supreme act of grace. God told Moses to remind the people that they were to celebrate Passover on the fourteenth day of the first month (vs. 1–5). This was the first Passover since leaving Egypt. It happened that some men were unable to participate in the celebration because they were ceremonially unclean, so they asked Moses why they should be left out (vs. 6–8). He said that he would bring their case to God, which he did. In a most gracious act, God declared that only two reasons could allow someone to celebrate Passover a month later, on the fourteenth day of the second month: ceremonial uncleanness or being away on a journey (vs. 9–14). The extra month would be enough time to become ritually clean again or return from the trip. This gracious allowance made it possible for everyone to participate. However, if someone neglected to participate properly at the proper time, he was found guilty and executed. This applied equally to natural-born citizens and foreigners.

The second section describes the movement of the nation in the wilderness (vs. 15–23). The nation's travel was dependent solely on the *shekinah* glory cloud and fire. Whenever it moved, they moved; whenever it stopped, they stopped. Sometimes the cloud would stop for "MANY DAYS" and rest over the tabernacle. However, no matter whether "IT WAS FOR TWO DAYS, OR A MONTH, OR A YEAR" that it rested, the people assembled the tabernacle and stayed there. "AT THE COMMANDMENT OF THE LORD THEY CAMPED, AND AT THE COMMANDMENT OF THE LORD THEY TRAVELED ON."

Chapter ten records God's final instruction to Moses before Israel moved from Sinai. While they were still camped at God's mountain, there was no reason to signal the people. However, as they began their trek, Moses would need a way to communicate with the nation, so God instructed him to have two long trumpets made (vs. 1–10). These were to be used only by the priests and for five purposes: to assemble the whole community, to assemble just the leaders of the people, to announce when they were to move, to lead the army into battle, and to announce times of national celebration.

Fifty days after Moses began to assemble the tabernacle for the first time, God had the people get up and move from Sinai (vs. 11–28; see Exodus 40:1).[4] It happened just as God had instructed—the cloud moved, the trumpets sounded, and the people moved. The order of the line began with the three tribes associated with Judah, then the Levites carrying the tabernacle frames and curtains. The second set of three tribes, led by Reuben, were followed by the Levites who carried the tabernacle furniture. The final six tribes came up in the back. The exception to this pattern was that the ark of the covenant led the entire process, and the cloud hovered over the ark (vs. 33).

---

[4] This indicates that the entire book of Leviticus and the book of Numbers to this point occurred during this time.

In Exodus 18, Moses' father-in-law gave him some wise counsel about leading the nation, which Moses followed. Exodus 18:27 says that Jethro then returned to his home. Although there is some confusion over exactly who Hobab is here in Numbers 10:29–32, because of the timing, the translations that use "BROTHER-IN-LAW" seem to make more sense. After Jethro (called Reuel here) returned home, Hobab must have stayed with Israel until they prepared to go to Canaan. Moses tried to get him to go with them, and although this text does not say, Judges 1:16 indicates that he did.

The final two verses record a prayer that Moses offered when the cloud moved and when it stopped (vs. 35–36). At the beginning of each leg of the journey, he prayed for God's protection for the people from their enemies. When they stopped, he prayed for God's presence to remain with them. There is an obvious thought of God going before them to fight, then returning to them and dwelling with them. It is a wonderful concept, and certainly necessary for them, but believers have the Holy Spirit indwelling us and the promise that he does not leave and has no need to return.

Chapters eleven and twelve record three specific events during which a complaint arose in Israel. While they were at Sinai, things were good, but as soon as they began to move, discontentment set in, and the grumbling began. The first complaint was general. Although the first leg was only three days (10:33), it wore on them quickly (vs. 1–3). God gave a warning in the form of supernatural fire outside of the camp that burnt up something. They repented, Moses interceded, and they were spared.

When Israel left Egypt, many non-Israelites came with them, which Exodus 12:38 calls "A MIXED MULTITUDE." Although this term is used here in English in verse four, the Hebrew term is used only here in the entire Old Testament and probably refers to a subset of them. Many translations describe them as "rabble" (NASB, NLT, NIV, ESV).[5] It was this group, not the entire nation, that began to long for home and the finer foods they missed (vs. 4–9).

---

[5] The Hebrew word is *saphsuph*, which has a rhythmic quality that may fit the English term "riffraff." (See the NET Bible study note on this verse.)

God had provided them with manna, which was versatile and tasty, yet it was not enough for them. They whipped the people into such an emotional frenzy that Moses could hear entire families crying in their tents about it (vs. 10–15). He was both grieved and infuriated, asking God why he had given him such a great responsibility when he had been reluctant at the beginning. Much like Jonah centuries later, Moses thought it was better to die than to suffer through this role.

God had two parts to his solution for this problem. First, he had Moses gather the seventy elders that Moses had appointed in Exodus 18 at the recommendation of his father-in-law (vs. 16–17, 24–30). Although Moses had selected them to help him, it seems that God had not officially commissioned them yet. So they gathered with Moses at the tabernacle to meet with God. When the Holy Spirit came upon them, they began to prophesy (a singular event, not repeated), displaying God's approval of them. In an interesting story, even two of the men who had not gathered with the rest received the Spirit and began prophesying in the camp, much to Joshua's dismay. When he told Moses about it, he was graciously rebuked for his misplaced loyalty to Moses instead of to God.[6]

God's second solution was to give them more meat than they knew what to do with (vs. 18–23, 31–34). A year earlier, in Exodus 16, God provided quail for them to eat one evening. Manna was their typical provision, but God had already proven that he could provide quail, and he did so again at this point. However, as soon as the rebels bit into the meat, "BEFORE THEY CHEWED IT," God killed them with a plague, displaying both supernatural (and unprecedented) provision and judgment at the same time.

Chapter twelve records the third of three specific complaints, this time against Moses personally. Not only was Moses a leader in Israel, but so were his siblings, Aaron and Miriam. As is often the case, jealousy arose between

---

[6] This theme reoccurs both in Jesus' ministry (Luke 9:49–50) and in Paul's (Philippians 1:15–18).

them against Moses, and they grumbled against him, which displeased God greatly.

Like children before a school principal, God called the three of them to the tabernacle and scolded Aaron and Miriam for their attitudes. Moses, God said, was beyond special to him. Even a prophet would receive only a vision or a dream, but God spoke to Moses face-to-face. It seems that Miriam was the instigator and Aaron the follower (a trait already implied in Exodus 32) because she was immediately inflicted with a severe skin disease. Realizing the severity of the situation, Aaron begged Moses to stop it, and Moses prayed for her healing. In an interesting exchange, God chose to follow his own Law, setting a pattern for the men. Still, in his grace, he gave her the minimum sentence the Law required: seven days' exclusion outside of the camp. After that time, she would have to be inspected by a priest and offer the required sacrifices, just like anyone else. The entire nation was tangibly affected by her sin because they did not travel closer to Canaan while she was sick.

Chapters thirteen and fourteen contain one of the most famous stories in Numbers: the spies enter Canaan. Unfortunately, it is also the most disastrous, the event that caused the second half of Numbers and all of Deuteronomy to even take place. Had the spies and the nation handled this one event differently, they could have entered the land as explained in the book of Joshua, without the long and fatal detour.

As the nation finally approached the southern border of Canaan, God had Moses choose a reconnaissance unit comprised of twelve leaders, one from each tribe (vs. 1–20). Their job was to explore the entire land of Canaan, from south to north, and bring back a report "WHETHER THE PEOPLE WHO LIVE IN IT ARE STRONG OR WEAK, FEW OR MANY, AND WHETHER THE LAND THEY LIVE IN IS GOOD OR BAD, AND WHETHER THE CITIES THEY INHABIT ARE LIKE CAMPS OR FORTIFIED CITIES, AND WHETHER THE LAND IS RICH OR POOR, AND WHETHER OR NOT THERE ARE FORESTS IN IT." They were also supposed to bring back samples of the produce they found.

When the spies went into Canaan, they did exactly as they were told. After thoroughly exploring the land for forty days, they brought back a meticulous report (vs. 21–33). The land was lush, overflowing with fruit and water, fauna and flora. One cluster of grapes they brought with them required two men to carry it. There were also walled cities, strongholds for the existing nations, and that was the problem. The men of one tribe, specifically, were much taller than the others. The family of Anak was tall and strong enough that the only way the spies could describe them was as the Nephilim from Genesis 6:1–4.[7] They concluded that it would be impossible for Israel to take the land. In modern terminology, they said, "Those people would chew us up and spit us out!"

Chapter fourteen shows Israel's response to the spies' report. Shocked and scared, the people began to wail for their lives, wondering again why God had brought them to this place, only to die (vs. 1–4). They feared for their wives and children and even considered replacing Moses as their leader and returning to Egypt. Seeing what had happened, four men fell on their faces before God—Moses, Aaron, and two of the spies, Caleb and Joshua (vs. 5–10). Caleb tried to persuade the people that God would lead them, but they would not listen. They prepared to kill all four of them right there. Then God appeared.

As the *Shekinah* glory filled the area, God threatened to kill them all, offering to start over with Moses' family (vs. 11–19). Moses, again, pleaded on their behalf, noting that God's name and reputation among the nations were at stake. It is noteworthy that Moses did not disagree with God; the rebels needed to die. Their continued disobedience was not good for God's glory either. However, if God killed "THIS ENTIRE PEOPLE AT ONCE," fulfilling his promise to bring them into the land would be impossible right away, also defaming him. Of course, God already knew this, but the people needed to see Moses praying on their behalf.

God agreed and forgave the people, yet he did not withhold the consequences (vs. 20–39). These consequences came in three parts. First, because of Caleb's faithfulness, God rewarded him with his life and with a special inheritance in the land. Second, the people who accepted the bad report

---

[7] There are some scholars who believe that these truly were Nephilim, just like before the Flood, but it is more likely that this was just the spies' description of them.

and turned against God and Moses would die, but not right away. In response to Moses' request, God promised that the people would die over forty years—one year for each day of the spies' mission—never entering the land they longed for; instead, their children would receive it. Third, the ten faithless spies died immediately at the hand of God for leading the people astray.

As humans so often do when faced with consequences, the people tried to change their minds (vs. 40–45). Now they were ready to enter the land, even against Moses' advice. Upon their attempt without God, "THE AMALEKITES AND THE CANAANITES WHO LIVED IN THAT HILL COUNTRY" attacked them, resulting in even more immediate casualties due to their disbelief.

Chapter fifteen is a chapter of grace. During the years of wandering, God continued to give his laws to the nation. The fact that the first of these begins with "WHEN YOU ENTER THE LAND WHERE YOU ARE TO LIVE, WHICH I AM GIVING YOU" (vs. 2) shows that God had not and would not desert his people, and they would eventually take over the land as he had promised.

In verses 1–16, God reiterated his requirement for making an offering. Regardless of who made the offering (citizen or resident foreigner), the reason for the offering (sin, guilt, burnt, freewill, or votive), or the animal being offered (ox, ram, male lamb, or goat), the people were also to bring both bread and wine with them, representing the richness of the land. Additionally, at each new harvest, the people were to make an offering of thanks to God for his provision (vs. 17–21).

Unintentional sins were also handled graciously by God (vs. 22–29). They still required sacrificial payment when discovered, but God was not overly harsh when people sinned without knowing it. Deliberate, willful sin was different (vs. 30–36). When a person knowingly and willfully violated God's law, there was no appeal; the law was firm. By way of example, Moses remembered a time that a man willfully broke the law of Sabbath rest. Even though "picking up firewood" was not specifically codified, it was a blatant violation of the clear "no work" regulation, and God sentenced the man to death.

Knowing that we are a forgetful species, God again graciously built into his law methods to help his people remember to keep their focus on him. Simple things like tassels and strings on their clothing—visible to themselves and those around them—would keep God's law constantly on their minds (vs. 37–41).

Chapters sixteen through eighteen record a series of events that God used to confirm his selection of the Levites to minister in the tabernacle and the family of Aaron, specifically, to serve as his priests. In the Hebrew text, chapter sixteen ends with verse thirty-five, adding the final fifteen verses to the beginning of the English chapter seventeen. Since they are all part of the same events, the chapter division does not make that much of a difference.

Just as Miriam and Aaron had stood against Moses, questioning God's choice as the leader of Israel, Korah (a Levite) and three Reubenites, along with 250 other men, stood up against Aaron as the high priest (vs. 1–3).[8] Once again, Moses quickly interceded for them before God. He gave them a challenge that would prove once-and-for-all whom God had chosen. Rebuking them for being greedy in their desire for authority among the people and personal access to God, Moses told Korah and the 250 Levites he had brought with him to take censers and fill them with incense (vs. 4–11, 16–19). This was the most significant act a priest could perform. In the morning, God would choose between their censers or Aaron's. When Moses summoned Dathan and Abiram, they ignored him, sending the message that he was no one special and that he set himself up as ruler (vs. 12–15). Additionally, they accused him of taking them away from Canaan and driving them into the wilderness.

God had Moses and Aaron warn the people to get away from the tents of Korah, Dathan, and Abiram, so they would not get caught up in their punishment (vs. 20–35). In a similar fashion to Elijah's dual on Mount Carmel (1 Kings 18), Moses declared that his commission from God would be proven by God's response. If his accusers continued to live, Moses was a fraud.

---

[8] Although they accused both Moses and Aaron, it was finally revealed that Aaron and the limited priesthood was Korah's primary target.

However, if something unprecedented took place— "THE EARTH OPENS ITS MOUTH AND SWALLOWS THEM UP ALONG WITH ALL THAT THEY HAVE, AND THEY GO DOWN ALIVE TO THE GRAVE" —then Moses was God's man. Their judgment was immediate. As the onlookers hid in fear, God's fire killed the 250 unsatisfied Levites the same way it had Nadab and Abihu in Leviticus 10.

The last section of chapter sixteen (the beginning of chapter seventeen in Hebrew) concludes the story of the 250 Levites (vs. 36–40). God had Aaron's son, Eleazar, turn the 250 censers into plates that were affixed to the altar. Everyone who saw them, as they brought their sacrifices, would be reminded of God's holiness and the judgment that came on those who violated it. Incredibly, the very next day, the people complained against Moses and Aaron again, charging them with getting rid of Korah and his followers for their own purposes (vs. 41–50). As God began to judge them immediately, sending a plague throughout the people, Moses quickly moved Aaron into position to offer incense, atoning for the rebels. Remarkably, they acted while they were still being accused, and their intercession saved all but 14,700 men.

Chapter seventeen provides one more example of God's obvious choice of Aaron over the others as the high priest. After watching 15,000 of their fellow Israelites die in two days because of their rebellion, twelve leaders of Israel each presented a staff to Moses at God's command. Each tribe was represented, with Aaron standing for Levi. God had Moses bring the staffs into the Most Holy Place overnight, and he would cause one of them to blossom, indicating his choice. The men each had his name carved into his own staff so that the result was obvious. In the morning, not only had Aaron's staff blossomed, it had grown fully mature almonds! God had Aaron's staff remain in the Most Holy Place at the ark as a constant reminder to the people of whom God had chosen.

Chapter eighteen concludes this section regarding the priests. After proving his selection repeatedly, God turned to the priests and Levites to remind them of the great responsibility that was on them. The selection he had just reaffirmed (at the cost of many lives) was a solemn one. First, the

Levites were the designated assistants to the priests (vs. 2–7). They were to minister to the priests, "AS A GIFT FROM THE LORD, TO PERFORM THE DUTIES OF THE TENT OF MEETING." However, they were not allowed to touch the special furniture; only the priests could do that. Anyone else, including Levites, would die.

Along with the responsibility of administrating the sacrifices came the privilege of eating them (vs. 8–19). Because they would have no land of their own in Canaan to grow crops (vs. 20–24), God set aside most of the sacrificial animals and grains to feed the priests, Levites, and their families. Additionally, whenever a firstborn son (human or unclean animal) was born, he was redeemed by paying a fee to the Levites. This provided them with funds to purchase items that were not offered in sacrifice. Firstborn clean animals were sacrificed as God had directed in Exodus and Leviticus. The only stipulation was that even the Levites were not exempt from offering back to God the first tenth of what they received, which was probably given to the priests themselves (vs. 25–32).

Chapter nineteen contains two new laws that work together with each other. The first law concerned the red heifer, a cow that had never been worked with a yoke (vs. 1–10). This heifer was to be slaughtered outside the camp in a specific ritual in front of the priest so that its ashes could be gathered and kept. When necessary, the ashes could be mixed with water to perform purification ceremonies for people and things that had become ceremonially unclean.[9]

As a timely example, since there were about 15,000 newly dead bodies in the camp and many hundreds of thousands were going to die in the wilderness, God directed how the people were to deal with death (vs. 11–22). In short, death made the people and things surrounding it unclean. Whether a person died from natural causes or by violence, touching the dead body or even being

---

[9] At the time of this writing, the lack of a perfect red heifer is one of the only things preventing a new temple from being furnished in Jerusalem because the furniture and utensils cannot yet be purified for use.

in the same tent with it was defiling. It took seven days and two applications of the red heifer ash-water to restore someone so they could approach God again. Even the person who applied the ash-water was unclean until that evening, because of their proximity to an unclean person.

Chapter twenty seems to skip most of Israel's wandering years. Although some commentators believe that Israel came to Kadesh only once and stayed near there (based on Deuteronomy 1:46), it seems clear that this "FIRST MONTH" is a return to Kadesh in "THE FORTIETH YEAR AFTER THE ISRAELITES HAD COME OUT OF THE LAND OF EGYPT" (compare vs. 1, 22–29 with 33:36–38). Essentially, nearly thirty-eight years of Israel's history is ignored as they simply lived and died in the wilderness, waiting for the entire first generation to pass away before they could enter the land.[10]

One wonders how much grumbling and complaining took place during those nearly four decades of nomadic life since the second generation parroted the first generation's mantra— "WHY HAVE YOU BROUGHT US UP FROM EGYPT ONLY TO BRING US TO THIS DREADFUL PLACE? IT IS NO PLACE FOR GRAIN, OR FIGS, OR VINES, OR POMEGRANATES; NOR IS THERE ANY WATER TO DRINK!" (vs. 1–5) After God's continued provision all that time, they still did not trust him. Once again, Moses and Aaron approached God for help in dealing with the people, and once again God chose to provide miraculously (vs. 6–11). He told Moses to speak to a rock, and enough water would come out to supply everyone. However, Moses, in his anger, struck the rock with his staff twice (similar to Exodus 17:1–7) and the water flowed. Because of his attitude and disobedience to God's command, God promised that Moses would not enter Canaan (vs. 12–13).

Unable to enter from Kadesh because of the enemy tribes there, Israel walked around the south side of the Dead Sea toward the eastern side of the Jordan River. Certainly, Moses thought, their relatives from Esau's side of the family (the Edomites) would allow them safe passage (vs. 14–21).

---

[10] It seems that God considered the first year or so out of Egypt, including the time at Mount Sinai, as "time served" toward the full forty years.

Unfortunately, he was wrong. Edom threatened war against Israel if they even crossed their borders, so they continued on a different route.

Making this time even more difficult, just about four months after Miriam's death, Moses lost his brother, Aaron, as well (vs. 22–29). God had him appoint Aaron's son, Eleazar, in his place, then Aaron died and Israel mourned him for a month.

Chapter twenty-one opens with a sad account revealing that the Canaanites were not interested in helping Israel any more than Edom was. As Israel tried another route into the land, they were attacked and some of them were taken prisoner (vs. 1–3). Crying out to God, they asked for complete revenge, which God allowed. Choosing yet another route, they attempted to go around Edom, but it was much longer than they anticipated, and they began complaining again (vs. 4–9). This time, God sent "VENOMOUS SNAKES" to attack them. When the people cried out to God, he had Moses fashion a replica of one of those serpents out of bronze and hang it in the middle of the camp. Anyone who looked to the serpent in faith was healed. Almost 1,500 years later Jesus used this as an example of the requirement to look at him in faith for eternal life because he hung on a cross as well (John 3:14–15).

Verses 10–20 list some of the places they stopped along the way to the east side of the Jordan, where they would eventually enter the land. Once again, when they tried to be good neighbors, asking permission to travel through the Amorites' land, they were refused (vs. 21–35). Like the other Canaanites, King Sihon attacked Israel and lost. Israel took over the entire Amorite land and stayed there for a while. When it was time to move again, King Og of Bashan attacked them and was annihilated.[11]

---

[11] Sihon and Og are mentioned together a few times later in the Old Testament as examples of God's deliverance of Israel during this time (Joshua 2:10; 9:10; 1 Kings 4:19; Nehemiah 9:22; Psalm 135:11).

Chapters twenty-two through twenty-four contain another well-known story from Numbers: the account of Balak and Balaam.[12] In 21:26 we read that Sihon had defeated Moab. Now that Israel had defeated Sihon, the Moabites were naturally afraid that they could be next, so when Israel journeyed up the eastern border of Moab, Balak, their king, had to do something (vs. 1–14).[13] Allying himself with the Midianites, Balak summoned Balaam, a well-known conjuror from near the Euphrates River in Mesopotamia (Abraham's homeland). Balak had only one request: curse Israel so Moab could defeat them. Given God's promise to Abraham (Genesis 12:3), Balak's wording of Balaam's reputation is ironic: "I KNOW THAT WHOEVER YOU BLESS IS BLESSED, AND WHOEVER YOU CURSE IS CURSED" (vs. 6). Balaam was tempted, but he wisely sought divine counsel. Somehow Yehovah spoke to him and informed him that attempting to curse Israel would be a waste, so he refused and sent the messengers of Balak away empty-handed.

Not one to give up, Balak tried again, promising anything Balaam could wish for (vs. 15–21). This piqued Balaam's greed, so he asked Yehovah again what he should do. God permitted him to go, although it was still against his counsel. Additionally, Balaam would be required to say only what God allowed him. In an attempt to teach Balaam the difference between God's permission and God's plan, the messenger of Yehovah (the preincarnate Christ) stood in the path with a sword. Although Balaam's route was blocked, only his donkey could see him; Balaam could not. This caused the donkey to veer off course a couple of times, injuring Balaam, who beat the donkey. Finally, God gave the donkey a voice to speak to Balaam, which finally opened his eyes to the danger he was in.[14] This time Yehovah gave clear permission

---

[12] Outside of the Pentateuch, Balaam appears in these passages: Joshua 13:22; 24:9–10; Nehemiah 13:2; Micah 6:5; 2 Peter 2:15; Jude 11; Revelation 2:14.

[13] Interestingly, the Moabites and Ammonites were relatives to Israel just like the Edomites were. Moab and Ammon (Genesis 19:36–38) were the grandsons of Lot, Abraham's nephew. This made them third cousins to Jacob's sons, the patriarchs of Israel.

[14] Constable cites Wiersbe as wondering if spirits had used animals to speak with Balaam before as the reason this did not seem to affect him (Constable, *Notes on Numbers, 2016 edition*, 88).

for Balaam to continue, noting again that he would say nothing that did not come from God. Upon Balaam's arrival, Balak welcomed him, making sacrifices in Balaam's honor, probably hoping to appease their gods before the dirty work began.

Chapter twenty-three contains the first two of seven "oracles" that Balaam spoke about Israel and her enemies. Balaam thought that following his pagan rituals may help him connect with Yehovah, who would respond favorably to Balaam's desire to curse Israel (vs. 1–13). After Balaam offered seven sacrifices on seven different altars and went up to the highest point available, "GOD MET BALAAM... [AND] PUT A MESSAGE IN BALAAM'S MOUTH." Balaam returned to Balak and relayed God's message of numerical blessing for Israel. Naturally, Balak was furious; he had paid Balaam to curse Israel, but he had blessed them instead. Balaam reminded Balak that he could speak only what God gave him.

Thinking that Balaam may have been overwhelmed by the number of people he saw, Balak took him to a place where he could see only part of the nation (vs. 14–30). Again, Balaam had him build seven altars and offer sacrifices. Again, God met Balaam and gave him a message. Again, Balaam returned and pronounced God's blessing over Israel. This time, rather than speaking of their size, he said that there could be no magic or divination or curse against them, and, rather than being attacked and defeated, Israel would be the attacker and victor over her enemies. All this was based on God's character: "HAS HE SAID, AND WILL HE NOT DO IT? OR HAS HE SPOKEN, AND WILL HE NOT MAKE IT HAPPEN?" Balak was upset again and took Balaam to yet another place to try a third time, building more altars and offering more sacrifices.

Chapter twenty-four continues Balak's attacks on Israel through Balaam. This time Balaam did not follow his previous pattern, going apart to seek answers via secret omens, because God had "hijacked" them (vs. 1–14). Instead, he simply faced the wilderness and waited. Opening his eyes he saw Israel in camp, unaware of their danger, and the Holy Spirit filled Balaam, giving him a third blessing to pronounce. Again, he spoke of Israel's growing strength and power over her enemies and Yehovah's immense blessing on them. Balak had had enough and was ready to fire Balaam. Balaam said again that he was unable to say anything that God did not give to him. This time, however, Balaam was not done. He had four more prophecies to give, starting with Balak and Moab.

Not only would Israel defeat her enemies like a lion, but a particular ruler was going to come—a "STAR" and a "SCEPTER." This one will eventually "CRUSH THE SKULLS OF MOAB" and even overthrow Edom (vs. 15–19). Against the Amalekites, Balaam promised that, even though they were an ancient people, they would be destroyed (vs. 20). Against the Kenites, Balaam said that, although they seemed secure, they would be overtaken by "ASSHUR" or Assyria (vs. 21–22). Finally, against Assyria itself and the other powerful nations, Balaam prophesied that they would not stand before Israel's coming ruler (vs. 23–24). Finished conveying God's oracles, Balaam returned home.

Chapter twenty-five records the final great sin of the first generation of Israelites out of Egypt. This chapter does not include a particular detail that is poignant to the story. According to 24:25, Balaam left Moab, presumably to his own home. However, according to 31:16, it appears that he first went to Midian to continue counseling against Israel. Since he could not curse them, he told the Midianites how to infiltrate them and get Yehovah off of their side.

He planned to have the priestesses and female shrine prostitutes of Midian seduce the Israelite men into the pagan sexual worship of Baal (vs. 1–3), violating at least three of the Ten Commandments—no other gods, no carved religious images, no adultery. When they began to do this, God sent a plague into the camp against the perpetrators and commanded Moses to publicly execute and hang the leaders (vs. 4–5). To this point, it seems that they had kept their sin in Midian itself. However, finally, one man brought a Midianite woman into the Israelite camp, right past the tabernacle where Moses and the priests were praying, and into his tent (vs. 6–9)! Furious, Aaron's grandson, Phinehas, followed them into the tent and ran them through together with a javelin while they were in the act. The high priest's son, thus, began making atonement for the nation. This, along with the execution of the rebel leaders, stopped God's plague, but not before 24,000 men had died.

Because of the passion that Phinehas showed for Yehovah and his holiness, God promised him and his family a special role in ministry and a special relationship with God (vs. 10–14). According to 1 Chronicles 6:4, 8, one of Phinehas' descendants was Zadok, another righteous priest who gained God's favor through an act of faithfulness. God's covenant with Phinehas will be fulfilled in the Millennium through the Zadokite priesthood (Ezekiel 44:15–16).

What made this sin most egregious was that it was done between leaders of both Israel and Midian (through his daughter). Because of this, not only were the Israelite leaders executed, God told Moses to make sure he destroyed Midian as well (vs. 14–18).

Chapter twenty-six is almost a duplicate of chapter one, except that it took place about thirty-eight years later. As he did the first time that Israel was to move into Canaan, God had Moses take a census before the second generation prepared to enter. Comparing the two censuses reveals a few interesting notes. Reuben's tribe recorded a slight decrease in number, along with the reminder that Dathan and Abiram were Reubenites who attempted a mutiny against Moses (vs. 5–11). The Simeonites were cut by almost two-thirds (vs. 12–14; 1:22–23). Some tribes increased (Judah, Zebulun, Dan) or decreased (Gad) by just a little bit. However, Issachar, Manasseh, Benjamin, and Asher increased by a large number, while Ephraim and Naphtali decreased quite a bit. Overall, the military-aged men of Israel decreased from 603,550 to 601,730 in the nearly forty years of wandering, only three-tenths of a percent loss.

Although Judah had five sons, only three of them bore him children (vs. 19–22; see Genesis 38). One of the men from Manasseh "HAD NO SONS, BUT ONLY DAUGHTERS," which would become an issue in the next chapter (vs. 33). The reason for the second census was not only to provide a list of men for the standing army but also to calculate the amount of land each tribe would receive as an inheritance in Canaan (vs. 52–56). Although the Levites increased by 1,000 males during this time, they were not to receive a region for themselves (vs. 57–62). Altogether, every man who was alive at the time of the spies' report in chapter fourteen died in the wilderness except for three: Moses, Caleb, and Joshua, just as God had determined (vs. 63–65).

Chapter twenty-seven contains two parts: a new regulation and a new leader. As noted in the previous chapter, one of the men of Manasseh had five daughters but no sons. As the instructions for the parceling of the land were conveyed, they became concerned and approached Moses about it (vs. 1–11). They feared that, because their father had no sons and daughters did not normally receive an inheritance, their family parcel would be lost. They petitioned Moses to be able to receive the land themselves with a special injunction. When Moses conferred with God, God said that the daughters were correct and that they should receive the land. Additionally, God laid out the "chain of inheritance" in the cases when a man had no sons, daughters, brothers, or uncles to claim his family parcel.

In the second part of the chapter, God had Moses climb up a mountain to see into Canaan, reminding him that he would never enter it because of his sin in taking God's glory by striking the rock instead of speaking to it in chapter twenty (vs. 12–23). While he was on the mountain, Moses prayed that God would not leave Israel without a godly leader, so God told him to stand Joshua before the high priest to be commissioned as God's handpicked leader of Israel, the one to lead them into Canaan. This was to be a public ceremony so that the nation would begin to accept his command immediately. Moses obeyed everything God said.

Chapters twenty-eight and twenty-nine served as a reminder for the Israelites regarding the holy days and special feasts that God had commanded the first generation while they were at Sinai. Even though that generation had died, God did not change his mind about what he expected from the nation, so he had Moses give the details again for the days and exact sacrifices necessary. These celebrations were the following:
- Morning and evening offerings each day (28:1–8)
- Sabbath day offering (28:9–10)
- 1st day of each month (28:11–15)

- Passover; 14th day of the first month (28:16)
- Feast of Unleavened Bread; one week following Passover (28:17–25)
- First Fruits (Feast of Weeks; Pentecost); fifty days following Passover (28:26–31)
- Trumpets; 1st day of the seventh month (29:1–6)
- Yom Kippur (Day of Atonement); 10th day of the seventh month (29:7–11)
- Rosh Hashanah; 15th–22nd day of the seventh month (29:12–38)

According to several commentators, the animals that God commanded to be sacrificed at these special times totaled 1,086 lambs, 113 bulls, 32 rams, and 30 goats annually, plus thousands of pounds of grain and hundreds of gallons of wine and oil. All this was in addition to the burnt, sin, guilt, freewill, and votive offerings made throughout the year (29:39–40). God's law was a bloody system because "ALMOST EVERYTHING WAS PURIFIED WITH BLOOD, AND WITHOUT THE SHEDDING OF BLOOD THERE IS NO FORGIVENESS" (Hebrews 9:22).

Chapter thirty laid out God's regulations on the vows that people could make to him, specifically "RELATING TO A MAN AND HIS WIFE, AND A FATHER AND HIS YOUNG DAUGHTER WHO IS STILL LIVING IN HER FATHER'S HOUSE" (vs. 16). God gave four scenarios in which a person could make a vow or dedication to God.

"IF A MAN MAKES A VOW," then he was obligated to fulfill it (vs. 1–2).

"IF A YOUNG WOMAN WHO IS STILL LIVING IN HER FATHER'S HOUSE MAKES A VOW," there were two options (vs. 3–5). Because she was still under her father's authority, he had the option to void her vow; in this case, she was not obligated to fulfill it. However, if her father knew about it and said nothing, she was under the same obligation as anyone else.

"IF SHE MARRIES A HUSBAND WHILE UNDER A VOW" or if she made a vow as a married woman, the options were the same for her husband as for her father (vs. 6–8). Her husband could void the vow or let it stand.

"EVERY VOW OF A WIDOW OR OF A DIVORCED WOMAN WHICH SHE HAS PLEDGED FOR HERSELF WILL REMAIN INTACT" (vs. 9–15). This held true because her husband had the opportunity to void it before his death or divorce but did not. Therefore, just like a man's vow, the woman's vow stayed in effect before God.

Chapter thirty-one is a follow-up to the events of chapter twenty-five, and it reveals that the killing of another individual, even in a just war directed by God himself, still defiled the killer and required atonement. The Midianites had seduced the Israelites into worshiping their gods, particularly by using the sexual ritual of shrine prostitutes. Even though that had already been taken care of in Israel (25:4–9), God demanded that the Midianites be punished for their part in Israel's sin. To do this, Moses sent an army of 12,000 soldiers (one thousand from each tribe) to attack Midian.[15]

In the ensuing battle, Israel killed five of the Midianite kings and took over their cities (vs. 6–13). They also killed Balaam, who had gone to Midian to help them defeat Israel. After killing all the males in those cities, Israel took captive all the women and children, along with all the animals, bringing them all to Moses and Eleazar to find out what to do with them. However, "MOSES WAS FURIOUS" that they allowed the women to live because many of them were the very ones who had led the Israelite men to the worship of Baal through their sexual rituals (vs. 14–18). So, Moses had all the non-virgins killed, but the virgins he allowed to remain alive and join Israel because they had not been a part of that sin.

Even though God had told them to do this, touching a dead body still made an Israelite ceremonially unclean, so the soldiers had to purify themselves before they could come back to the camp and worship again (vs. 19–24). They also had to purify any weapons and utensils used in the battle by either fire (if it could withstand it) or water. The loot they had taken was to be split between those who physically fought the battle and the rest of the nation (vs. 25–54). There were "**675,000** SHEEP, **72,000** CATTLE, **61,000** DONKEYS, AND **32,000** YOUNG WOMEN WHO HAD NOT EXPERIENCED A MAN'S BED" along with hundreds of pounds

---

[15] Those who attempt to minimize the census numbering have difficulty with this chapter. If they read the census as only a tenth of what Moses wrote (for instance), then it should be read as a tenth here as well, meaning that Moses sent only 1,200 soldiers instead of 12,000.

of gold jewelry and trinkets. Out of this windfall, the gold was given to God at the tabernacle, the Levites received "ONE OF EVERY 50 PEOPLE AND ANIMALS," and the priests were given one of every five hundred. Thus, everyone received a benefit, but the warriors took home a little more because of their involvement. However, not even one Israelite soldier was killed; God gave them a complete victory in what he had commanded them to do.

Chapter thirty-two adds an interesting bit of detail to the story of Israel's preparing to enter Canaan. God had already promised to give the land over to Israel, by helping them defeat the pagan nations that lived there. Additionally, he had said that they were to parcel the land according to the size of each tribe. As the nation was camped on the east side of the Jordan River, the tribes of Reuben and Gad noticed that it was a rich land that could easily support their many herds, so they asked Moses if they could stay there instead of entering the land (vs. 1–5). Moses' pushback against that idea was that they would be getting an inheritance without having to help fight the Canaanites with their brothers (vs. 6–15). He believed that they were just trying to get out of the war, and he compared them to the previous generation who had refused to enter and take Canaan in chapter fourteen.

They responded that this was not their intent at all (vs. 16–19). Rather, if Moses permitted, they promised to establish their families and flocks in the cities they took from the Midianites, from Sihon, and from Og, then send their warriors into Canaan to fight alongside their brothers. Moses was satisfied with this plan and made them swear to not stop fighting and return home until the entire conquest was complete, which they agreed to do (vs. 20–32). If they followed through, they could keep the eastern border of the river; if they did not, they would be required to enter the land and take their inheritance from there.

Chapter thirty-three is Moses' travel journal from Egypt to Canaan. As is recorded in Exodus 12, the Israelites left Egypt "ON THE FIFTEENTH DAY OF THE FIRST MONTH" of the new calendar God created for them (vs. 1–4). While the Egyptians were mourning over and burying their firstborn sons killed in the plague, Israel was leaving Ramses. Verse four also includes the note that the plagues were specially designed to attack Egypt's gods. From there they traveled and camped in many places, three before the Red Sea and eight places afterward, finally coming to rest at Sinai (vs. 5–15). Some of these are recorded in more detail in Exodus 15–19 because of specific events that happened there.

After about a year at Sinai, when they received God's law and built the tabernacle, they moved again, heading north toward Kadesh-Barnea at the southern border of Canaan (vs. 16–36). Moses mentioned twenty campsites before they finally reached Kadesh.

Beginning with verse thirty-seven, Moses skipped journaling the same thirty-eight years of wilderness wandering that he skipped earlier in this book. In every sense, those years were a complete waste for Israel. Not only did an entire generation of people die, but there is no biblical record of anything that they did during that time. From their second approach to Kadesh to the east side of the Jordan River, Israel stopped nine times, including at Mount Hor where Aaron died (vs. 37–49). While in Moab by the Jordan, God told Israel again that their responsibility when entering Canaan was five-fold: "DRIVE OUT ALL THE INHABITANTS OF THE LAND... DESTROY ALL THEIR CARVED IMAGES...DEMOLISH THEIR HIGH PLACES. ...DISPOSSESS THE INHABITANTS OF THE LAND AND...DIVIDE THE LAND BY LOT FOR AN INHERITANCE AMONG YOUR FAMILIES" (vs. 50–56). If they obeyed, God would thoroughly bless them; if not, he promised to do to Israel what he intended to do to the Canaanites.

Chapter thirty-four is primarily a description of the geographical boundaries that God gave to the nine-and-a-half tribes,[16] once they entered Canaan (vs. 1–15). The western and eastern borders were obvious—the Mediterranean Sea and Jordan River, respectively. The southern border ran southwest from the southern-most tip of the Dead Sea to Kadesh, then to the "STREAM OF EGYPT" that serves as an eastern border for Egypt (not the Nile

---

[16] In addition to Reuben and Gad, half of the tribe of Manasseh stayed on the east side of the Jordan River.

River). The northern border ran further north than the Sea of Galilee/Jordan River and over to the Mediterranean Sea.

Although much larger than the area considered the land of Israel today, Constable notes, "This was not the same territory promised to Abraham, but was what God gave the Israelites at their entrance into the land. If they had been obedient to Him, He would have eventually enlarged their borders to include the whole area promised to Abraham."[17] During Solomon's reign, Israel enjoyed the closest fulfillment of God's land promise, but will never experience it fully until the Messianic Kingdom (1 Kings 4).

So that there would be no disputes about the land apportionment (since it was to be kept by the tribes in perpetuity), God chose by name one leader from each tribe (including both Ephraim and Manasseh) to assist Eleazar and Joshua in dividing the land between the tribes (vs. 16–29).

Chapter thirty-five addresses the Levites, who did not receive any of the land of Canaan as an inheritance for their tribe. Instead, God allotted the Levites forty-eight towns spread throughout the other tribes that they could live in (vs. 1–8). The tribes with more land could afford to give more cities than those with less land, and the Levites were to have exclusive grazing rights around their cities for their herds (they did not own enough land for farming). This allowed all the citizens of Israel to have Levites near them to help arbitrate the Law when they could not get to the tabernacle and the priests.

Six of the forty-eight towns were designated as "TOWNS OF REFUGE." The purpose of these towns was to provide a haven for someone who killed someone else unintentionally. In these cases, the killer could take refuge in one of these towns "UNTIL HE HAS STOOD TRIAL BEFORE THE COMMUNITY" so that he could not be killed in revenge. Three of them had to be on each side of the Jordan River to cover the entire nation. If the killer was found to have committed murder, he would be executed under God's Law, as stipulated in the detailed examples that follow (vs. 16–21). Personal vengeance against a murderer was both allowed and encouraged, to quickly purge the sin from the

---

[17] Constable, *Notes on Numbers*, 2016 edition, 120.

land and nation. However, it was to be done quickly and openly, not in secret or by ambush, because this was no better than the original murder.

In case of accidental or even negligent manslaughter, the killer could go to a town of refuge to escape the avenger (vs. 22–29). However, because a life was taken—even unintentionally—the killer (not "murderer") had to remain in the town of refuge until the death of the current high priest. This was the consequence of taking someone's life without malice as a reminder that all people are created in God's image (Genesis 9:5–6). If he left the jurisdiction of that town, the avenger could kill him without consequence. There were no other available options; a murderer must be executed and an innocent killer must stay in the town of refuge (vs. 30–34).

Chapter thirty-six closes the book of Numbers by tackling one more issue related to the daughters of Zelophehad. In chapter twenty-seven, these women approached Moses requesting to receive their father's inheritance because they had no brothers. At God's direction, Moses granted their request.

Now a new question arose. If they were to marry someone from another tribe, the land that was apportioned to them (and their tribe of Manasseh) would be transferred to their husbands and new tribes (vs. 1–4). During the Year of Jubilee, when land would normally have been returned to the previous owner, it would be confirmed under the ownership of the husband's tribe. This was unacceptable because this could drastically diminish the overall land that Manasseh received in the initial allotment.

Once again Moses conferred with God, who explained what he wanted them to do (vs. 5–13). Acknowledging that the Manassehites were correct,[18] God said that in cases such as this (when a man had no sons and passed his inheritance to his daughters), the daughters were free to marry whomever they chose, as long as the men were from their tribe. In this way, they would perpetuate their tribe and keep the tribal lands that God gave them. Very

---

[18] It seems that it must have pleased God to see the Israelites wrestling with the Law, trying to obey it, and coming back to him when they had questions about how to live it out in difficult situations.

clearly God declared, "NO INHERITANCE MAY PASS FROM TRIBE TO TRIBE. BUT EVERY ONE OF THE TRIBES OF THE ISRAELITES MUST RETAIN ITS INHERITANCE." Thus, Numbers ends with a gracious act of God on behalf of his people, helping them understand his Law and his mind while protecting them from losing what he gave them.

Deuteronomy

Deuteronomy is the last of the five books of Moses, comprising the *Torah* (Hebrew, "law") or *Pentateuch* (Greek, "five scrolls"). As with the others, the English name comes from the Greek version. *Deuteronomy* (Δευτερονόμιον, *deuteronomion*) means "second law" and refers to the fact that this book contains the giving of God's law to the second generation of Israelites—the second giving of the law. The Hebrew name is אֵלֶּה הַדְּבָרִים (*'elleh haddebarim*, "these are the words"), the first two words of the Hebrew text.

The authorship of Deuteronomy has come under attack over the past century due to some words and phrases that critics believe would not have been used if Israel were not already established in the land of Canaan, like "beyond the Jordan" to refer to the east side, where Israel was located at the time Moses spoke these words. However, Archer has painstakingly detailed the reasons why Deuteronomy fits squarely where conservative scholars think it should be—approximately 1400 BC.[1] More importantly, Jesus considered Deuteronomy as one of the books of Moses when he referenced the well-known three-part division of the Hebrew text—"THE LAW OF MOSES AND THE PROPHETS AND THE PSALMS" (Luke 24:44).

Deuteronomy plays a significant role in the biblical text. At least three points are worth noting in this introduction. First, it is in Deuteronomy that we find Israel's famous *Shema*: "HEAR, O ISRAEL! THE LORD IS OUR GOD, THE LORD IS ONE!" (6:4) Second, when Jesus was tempted by Satan in the wilderness, all three of his responses began with "It is written" and contained a quote from

---

[1] Gleason L. Archer, *A Survey of Old Testament Introduction, Revised and Expanded* (Moody Press, 1994), 99–112 and 274–283.

Deuteronomy (8:3; 6:16; 6:13; Matthew 4:1–11). Third, although Genesis 15 contains God's covenant promise to Abraham about the land his descendants would inherit, it is not until Deuteronomy 30 that God promised the nation that, after they sinned, he would bring them back to their land from captivity, and they would never be thrown out again. This "Land Covenant" sets up the forever aspect of God's promise to give Israel the land.[2]

The purpose of Deuteronomy was for Moses to reaffirm God's covenant law with the second generation of Israelites after their parents had died in the wilderness. He also encouraged them to obey the law and receive everything God had promised them when they entered the land. This was especially important because Moses knew that he would not personally be leading them into the land, so this was his last opportunity to exert his influence.

Chapters one through three are essentially a brief recap of the entire book of Numbers (and some of Exodus). Some of Moses' listeners were not even born when these events took place, yet throughout his history lesson, Moses referred to the culprits as "you." It was national sin that kept them out of Canaan initially, and this generation had suffered the consequences of wandering, even though they would finally realize their hopes.

With a bit of sarcasm, Moses noted that the journey from Sinai (called Horeb here) should have taken only eleven days but instead, it took more than thirty-eight years ("THE ELEVENTH MONTH OF THE FORTIETH YEAR") after leaving Egypt (vs. 1–5). After having stayed at Sinai for several months, getting the Law and tabernacle instructions from God, and finally building the tabernacle, God told them it was time to move to their new homeland. Moses also reminded them that it was about that time that he had put into place the

---

[2] In older commentaries and study notes, the "Land Covenant" is often erroneously called the "Palestine Covenant" because the land of Israel has been called "Palestine" for centuries. Due to the geopolitical issues concerning Israel and the "Palestinians" and the fact that this covenant deals with the geographical land given to the nation of Israel, we should use the correct title, "Land Covenant."

judicial structure that worked beneath him (vs 6–17; Exodus 18).³ He reminded them that God's law was not just for the citizens of Israel but was to be applied equally and equitably to foreigners who chose to join the nation as well.

Upon reaching Kadesh, God had told Moses to send spies into Canaan and look it over completely (Numbers 13). It seems that the people may have asked for this, which God allowed (vs. 18–25). They discovered that it was everything that God had said. However, the people became afraid of the warrior nations that were already in the land and did not trust God to conquer them like he had promised (vs. 26–33). Because of this, God swore that the military-aged men would die in the wilderness and that the children they were afraid would die in the invasion would be the ones to receive the land (vs. 34–40). Only Caleb and Joshua, the two who encouraged them to take the land, would be allowed to enter it. Even Moses was not allowed to go in. Although he seems to blame the Israelites instead of his own disobedience (vs. 37), it was legitimately their faithlessness that he was reacting to (Numbers 20:1–12). Upon hearing God's sentence against them, the first generation attempted to enter the land after rebelling the first time and lost badly, because God did not go in before them (vs. 41–46).

Chapter two continues Israel's history as told by Moses, picking up when the nation left Kadesh after their defeat and headed back into the wilderness (vs. 1–7). Moses said that they wandered that area "FOR A LONG TIME." At the end of those thirty-eight years, God told them it was time to try again. This time they were to go through the land of Edom, offering to pay for anything they consumed along the way. God reminded them that he had taken care of their every need over the past forty years. After Edom, Israel approached Moab (vs. 8–15). Again, they were to not harass the Moabites, because God had given that land to Lot's descendants (Genesis 19:36–37). God gave them the

---

³ For those who might take issue with the amount of detail that Moses left out here, it should be noted that he had already written Genesis through Numbers, so the detail was preserved. This was meant only to recount specific highlights of those accounts.

same instructions and reason for not acting hostile toward the Ammonites (vs 16–25; Genesis 19:38). However, in the same way that God had cleared the land for Moab and Ammon, he promised to clear out the Amorites before Israel.

Attempting to be conciliatory, Moses used the same tactic with Sihon of the Amorites that he had with Edom, requesting safe passage through their land and offering to pay for anything the people consumed (vs. 26–37). Sihon, however, refused and attacked Israel, but God defeated him with the Israelite army. According to verse thirty-four, Israel's destruction of the Amorites was complete, leaving no survivors, because Sihon was under God's divine judgment.

Chapter three concludes Moses' quick historical tour of the Israelites previous forty years. After defeating Sihon and the Amorites, they faced Og of Bashan north of Canaan in Syria (vs. 1–11; Numbers 21:33–35). Like Sihon, Og was under God's divine judgment, and the Israelites destroyed sixty cities like those the spies said they could never take (Numbers 13:28–29, 32–33). Moses never disputed the enormous size of the warriors that the spies saw; instead, here, he even used that to prove God's faithfulness toward Israel. Og was the last of these Rephaim warriors, and his sarcophagus (often translated as "bed") was "13½ FEET LONG AND 6 FEET WIDE."

During their time of war, God gave Israel much of the land of modern-day Jordan, before they even crossed the Jordan River into Canaan (vs. 12–17). This territory ("Transjordan") was granted to the tribes of Reuben and Gad and half of Manasseh under the condition that their military men entered the land and fought alongside the rest of the nation, while their wives and children remained safe in the cities they had already conquered (vs. 18–22). Once again Moses blamed Israel for God not allowing him to go into the land, but God did allow him to see it from the top of Mount Pisgah, and he commissioned Joshua to be the new leader of the nation (vs. 23–29).

Chapter four is essentially Moses' conclusion to his history lesson of the first three chapters. Because of God's faithfulness to Israel, they needed to pay close attention to his commands, as Moses was about to lay them out formally again (vs. 1–2). Many of them did not see the miracles in Egypt or the Red Sea because they had not been born yet, but they did see what God did for and against them in the wilderness and at Baal Peor, so there were no excuses to not obey God (vs. 3–4). Pointing to the pagan nations around them, Moses noted that they all had gods and laws (this is never disputed), but Yehovah's actions and laws were superior (vs. 7–8).

Some of this generation was younger than twenty years old at Sinai, so they did not die in the wilderness (vs. 9–14). But they were old enough to know what was happening, so Moses reminded them of what they saw and heard there, that their parents had rejected. Especially important was the fact that God never showed himself in any form to the Israelites (vs. 15–20). Had he done so, they would have been tempted to fashion idols in that image. Instead, images were expressly forbidden to them, including things in the creation and the gods of the other nations.[4] Even Moses would not enter the land because of his sin, showing God's lack of favoritism (vs. 21–24).

Moses was careful to point out that entrance did not mean permanence (vs. 25–31). Just because God was leading them into the land, it did not follow that they would be allowed to remain there indefinitely. That was conditioned upon their obedience to God's law. Disobedience would certainly result in expulsion and being scattered among the surrounding pagan nations. However, even there, they would be able to return to Yehovah, and he would restore them. His jealously for Israel cuts both ways: if they abused it, he would punish, but he would always be ready to forgive and restore.

Lest they become prideful for their special position as God's only chosen people since creation, Israel needed to know that the reason for their selection was God's relationship with Abraham, not themselves (vs. 32–40). Had it not been for their connection to Abraham, they would be no different than anyone

---

[4] There is an interesting point here that, by setting Israel apart to himself, Yehovah left the other nations open to demons as their gods. Some scholars believe that he actually assigned supernatural rulers over these nations, at least some of whom are fallen angels (see Deuteronomy 32:8; Psalm 82).

else in the world.⁵ This is what they had been taught, and this is what they needed to never forget.

The chapter concludes with Moses' appointment of the three cities of refuge "IN THE TRANSJORDAN" and a summary of when and where the events of Deuteronomy took place (vs. 41–49).

Chapter five contains a formal repeat of the Ten Commandments that God had given nearly forty years earlier. Although not all of the people were alive at that time, the covenant was with the entire nation that came out of Egypt (Exodus 20:1), not the patriarchs, so it included this generation, and they were bound to it (vs. 1–5).

Although the Ten Commandments in this chapter are not a word-for-word repetition of Exodus 20, they contain the same commands and explanations, when explanations are given (vs. 6–20). The first four have to do with the people's relationship with Yehovah. He was to be their only God. They were to worship him without seeing him and without creating anything that tried to represent him because it could only downsize him in their eyes. They were not to misuse the authority of his name for their own purposes, things he would never authorize (essentially identity theft). Instead, they were to observe the weekly rest he graciously gave them to focus on their relationship with him instead of their own personal, economic, and national pursuits.

The other six commands spoke to their relationships with each other. In the only command with a promise attached, he said that they were to respect their parents because when each succeeding generation did this they would stay true to their foundation. They were to respect each other's lives, marriages, possessions, and reputations. Finally, they were also to control their

---

⁵ This is a significant point regarding Christians as well. Although we are not part of Abraham's physical family, we join his spiritual family through faith in Jesus alone. We, then, are chosen and special as a group because of our individual connection to the chosen men, Abraham and Jesus (see Galatians 3–4).

thoughts about each other, not allowing their attitudes to affect their relationships.[6]

Although God added many other specific laws later, every law came out of this foundational set somehow (vs. 22). When God gave them initially from the mountain, the people were terrified of what they saw and begged Moses to be their mediator with God, which he was until his death, constantly interceding for them and encouraging them to obey (vs. 23–33).

Chapter six is the first of several chapters (through twelve) during which Moses encouraged the people to obey. He used a combination of historical events and laws as reminders for them to hold onto. Much of this is repeated from earlier books (especially Leviticus and Numbers) because Moses knew that they could not hear them too many times. Again, permanence, material provision, and blessings in the land were conditioned solely upon their obedience to God (vs. 1–3). He was able and willing to bless them but would not spoil them if they chose to become ungrateful and rebellious children.

Verse four contains the great *Shema*, the mantra of the orthodox Jew—"HEAR, O ISRAEL! THE LORD IS OUR GOD, THE LORD IS ONE!" (NASB)—and verse five was what Jesus considered the greatest commandment of the entire Law: "YOU MUST LOVE THE LORD YOUR GOD WITH YOUR WHOLE MIND, YOUR WHOLE BEING, AND ALL YOUR STRENGTH."

Because of the importance of the people's obedience and because the covenant was with succeeding generations, it was their responsibility (just as Adam with Eve) to pass these truths and laws on to their children, grandchildren, etc. (vs. 6–9) This way they would not become spoiled children either because they were constantly reminded that everything they were to take possession of was a gift of grace (vs. 10–15). It was not earned, and they needed to remember and remind others that it was God who gave it to them. Their obedience would not only result in material provision; it would also

---

[6] The tenth command is especially noteworthy because it was the only one that could not be prosecuted by anyone except God. Violation of the other commands could result in evidence against the perpetrator in court, but God was concerned about their thoughts as well as their actions.

ensure that God would clear the land before them as well (vs. 16–19). In succeeding generations, they were not only to tell of "THE STIPULATIONS, STATUTES, AND ORDINANCES" that God gave; they were to tie them back to the rescue from Egypt and the great miracles (vs. 20–25). Just as God had been faithful to them, he demanded their faithfulness to him as well.

Chapter seven deals specifically with the land of Canaan that the Israelites were ready to enter and conquer. First, Moses told them that there were seven strong nations already there, but that God promised to conquer them for Israel (vs. 1–6).[7] The spies' report in Numbers 13 was true: these peoples were "MORE NUMEROUS AND POWERFUL THAN" Israel, but that was for God to be concerned with, not them. The total annihilation of these was required because of their extreme wickedness and the temptation that would be for Israel. (They had already fallen into idol worship at least twice since their departure from Egypt.) God wanted them to remain separated to him, so the pagan influences had to be removed.

Second, Moses reminded the people a second time that it was nothing special in them that caused God to choose them (vs. 7–11). Rather, it was because of the promises that he had made to Abraham, Isaac, and Jacob; they were simply the beneficiaries if they would remain loyal to Yehovah. The NET Bible study note on verse fourteen points out the irony between the promise that their obedience would ensure plenty of children and no barrenness, when that was the exact malady that the patriarchs' wives suffered (e.g., Sarah, Rebekah, Rachel). As he told the first generation in Exodus 15:26, Moses promised that God would keep the obedient Israelites from the diseases that they and the Egyptians suffered and, instead, would plague their enemies with them.

---

[7] Sometimes "Canaanites" refers to a specific group, as here, whereas other times it refers to all of the people groups in Canaan, including those listed here. This list points out those who were to be annihilated because of their extreme wickedness. Only these were under divine judgment and were to be destroyed. That was not required of all the people in the land, who could have submitted to Yehovah, fully joining Israel, or could have evacuated before them.

Finally, the people were to utterly destroy everything that had to do with pagan worship in Canaan (vs. 16–26). This included not only the idols themselves, but the altars, the shrines, the poles and banners, and the utensils and vessels used in these wicked practices. Even the clothing, the silver, and the gold were not to be kept, because they had become contaminated by demon worship. When they remembered that Yehovah was the only true God and superior to those they would face, they would not be troubled or scared and would be able to accomplish everything God commanded them.

Digging Deeper: Is God a Genocidal Murderer?

One of the common accusations made against God and the Bible goes something like this:

> *"God in the Old Testament and Jesus in the New Testament are completely different. The Old Testament God is full of anger and murder, while Jesus is full of love and grace. I could never believe in a God that would kill so many innocent people as he did in the Old Testament."*

Let's admit it: God killed or had Israel kill a lot of people during the story of the Old Testament. How does that line up with his command to Israel: "You shall not murder" (Exodus 20:13).

However, two very important points are seldom considered during this debate. First, God authorized Israel to eradicate only certain nations, in a certain place, for a certain reason. Unlike some try to characterize it, Israel did not have a blank check to do whatever they wanted to whomever they did not like.

God was very clear about his reason for destroying certain nations: "YOU MUST UTTERLY ANNIHILATE THEM. MAKE NO TREATY WITH THEM AND SHOW THEM NO MERCY...FOR THEY WILL TURN YOUR SONS AWAY FROM ME TO WORSHIP OTHER GODS." (Deuteronomy 7:2–4)

> To make sure that his people would not turn away from him, God told them to cleanse the pagan nations and their pagan religion from the land. (Of course, Israel did not obey, and they did indeed turn away from God, just as he had warned.)
>
> Second, death was not their only option. The land of Canaan is only about 60 miles (96 km) at its widest point, yet Joshua and the Israelites took more than five years to work their way through the land. Everyone knew they were coming, yet most chose to stay and fight a losing battle instead of either evacuating the land or turning from their wicked paganism to the true God (see Joshua chapter 2).
>
> **Is God a genocidal murderer?** No, he is a God of holy justice who will not allow his people to be led away from himself. And he always offers a chance for people to repent rather than face judgment.

Chapter eight went in the opposite direction of chapter seven. Instead of looking only forward into Canaan, Moses asked the people to remember what God had already done for them during their time in the wilderness. Specifically, he named five miraculous blessings from God:

- Their "CLOTHING DID NOT WEAR OUT" due to the exposure to sun and sand (vs. 4)
- Their feet did not swell from the walking (vs. 4)
- He protected them from "VENOMOUS SERPENTS AND SCORPIONS" (vs. 15)
- He provided water "FROM A FLINT ROCK" (vs. 15)
- He kept them fed "WITH MANNA" (vs. 16)

God also knew the temptation people have to forget the source of blessing, so Moses pointedly reminded them that God "IS THE ONE WHO GIVES ABILITY TO GET WEALTH" (vs. 18).[8] Not only did he promise them the ability to get or create

---

[8] This is a poignant reminder for us today as well.

wealth, but he also promised them a land that was already well-stocked, awaiting their arrival:

> ...A LAND OF BROOKS, SPRINGS, AND FOUNTAINS FLOWING FORTH IN VALLEYS AND HILLS, A LAND OF WHEAT, BARLEY, VINES, FIG TREES, AND POMEGRANATES, OF OLIVE TREES AND HONEY, A LAND WHERE YOU MAY EAT FOOD IN PLENTY AND FIND NO LACK OF ANYTHING, A LAND WHOSE STONES ARE IRON AND FROM WHOSE HILLS YOU CAN MINE COPPER. (vs. 7–9)

For all this, Israel had only two responsibilities—"EAT YOUR FILL AND THEN PRAISE THE LORD YOUR GOD BECAUSE OF THE GOOD LAND HE HAS GIVEN YOU" (vs. 10) and "DO NOT FORGET THE LORD YOUR GOD BY NOT KEEPING HIS COMMANDMENTS, ORDINANCES, AND STATUTES" (vs. 11). Their obedience would bring life, their disobedience death.

It is worth making a special note about verse three. God intentionally used their hunger to instill and grow their humility, and manna was an important part of that. When Jesus quoted this verse during his own wilderness experience (Matthew 4:4), he remembered that "EVERYTHING THAT COMES FROM THE LORD'S MOUTH" includes God's commands as well as his blessings.

Chapter nine shifts Moses' focus again. Instead of emphasizing what Israel had received or was looking to obtain, Moses reminded them of their inherent sinfulness and repeated rebellion. When they entered the land and God destroyed even the giants from before them, they would be tempted to think that it was because of their righteousness that he did that (vs. 1–6). First, he reminded them for a third time that they were chosen because of God's promises "TO YOUR ANCESTORS, TO ABRAHAM, ISAAC, AND JACOB." Second, not only were they just not righteous, they were "A STUBBORN PEOPLE...CONSTANTLY REBELLING AGAINST HIM."

In case they had forgotten just how stubborn they were, Moses pointed out several times they had stood in opposition to God, most notably the episode of the golden calf at Sinai (Exodus 32). He reminded them that God had threatened to pour out all his wrath at that point, utterly destroying them, but Moses interceded on their behalf, exactly as God wanted him to do (vs. 7–21).

They had already tested God at the waters of Marah before that and afterward at "TABERAH, MASSAH, AND KIBROTH HATTAAVAH" and finally at Kadesh-Barnea, when they should have entered Canaan (vs. 22–24). Put frankly, Moses said, "YOU HAVE BEEN REBELLING AGAINST HIM FROM THE VERY FIRST DAY I KNEW YOU!" Even so, Moses continued to pray for them, and God continued to give grace (vs. 25–29).

Chapter ten continues Moses' trip down Israel's memory lane. After Moses shattered the stone tablets with the Ten Commandments on them at the golden calf incident, God wrote out two more (vs. 1–5). These were placed into the ark of the covenant for safe keeping throughout Israel's journeys. During that time God set apart the Levites to carry the ark and minister on behalf of the people. For this reason, they received no inheritance in the land (vs. 6–11). God intended for the nation to enter Canaan and receive the promises he had made to them.

The question, "WHAT DOES THE LORD YOUR GOD REQUIRE OF YOU?" is reminiscent of Micah 6:8. There the prophet appears to have shortened Moses' statement into a summary: "TO DO JUSTICE, TO LOVE KINDNESS, AND TO WALK HUMBLY WITH YOUR GOD." (NASB) Moses' actual command was much more detailed: "TO REVERE HIM, TO OBEY ALL HIS COMMANDMENTS, TO LOVE HIM, TO SERVE HIM WITH ALL YOUR MIND AND BEING, AND TO KEEP THE LORD'S COMMANDMENTS AND STATUTES" (vs. 12–13). The reason for this is because Yehovah is the only God worth worshiping and serving (vs. 14–22). He had chosen Israel, again, because of their ancestors, and he demanded that the people acknowledge and worship him for his perfect character and holiness. He wanted them to treat others the way he treated them—with grace. One small example was the growth he allowed them to have while in Egypt, from only seventy people to as innumerable as the stars.

Chapter eleven concludes Moses' history lesson for the second generation of Israelites with an encouragement to obey God's commands so they could receive his blessings. Moses specifically said that many of those present were old enough to remember the plagues on Egypt, the Red Sea, and the judgments in the wilderness (vs. 1–7). Their children would only hear of such events as reasons to obey Yehovah, but many of these people had seen them, even though they were only children at the time. However, that should have been enough to emblazon God's righteousness on their minds and cause them to want to obey him.

The blessing and material wealth the people would experience in Canaan would be a direct result of their obedience to God (vs. 8–15). Moses said that God would personally tend the land for them, making sure there was plenty of rain at just the right times for the maximum crop harvest and the perfect pasture land. Had they obeyed, they would only have had to reap the benefits of God's work, not toil for themselves. On the other hand, if they disobeyed God, he would withhold rain, crops, and pasture land (vs. 16–17). These were the specific curses for Israel in Canaan, which they experienced almost immediately in Judges. Because their children had not seen God's hand at work, the parents needed to instill these truths into their minds (vs. 18–21). This was the purpose of the instructions in Deuteronomy 6:6–9:

> **THESE WORDS I AM COMMANDING YOU TODAY MUST BE KEPT IN MIND, AND YOU MUST TEACH THEM TO YOUR CHILDREN AND SPEAK OF THEM AS YOU SIT IN YOUR HOUSE, AS YOU WALK ALONG THE ROAD, AS YOU LIE DOWN, AND AS YOU GET UP. YOU SHOULD TIE THEM AS A REMINDER ON YOUR FOREARM AND FASTEN THEM AS SYMBOLS ON YOUR FOREHEAD. INSCRIBE THEM ON THE DOORFRAMES OF YOUR HOUSES AND GATES.**

God also promised that he would drive out their enemies if Israel obeyed him (vs. 22–25). This was not true only in Canaan. God had already promised certain geographical boundaries to Abraham (Genesis 15:18–20) which extended to the Euphrates River. He confirmed that with the nation here as well.

Once they entered the land, they were to stand on two of the mountains—Ebal and Gerizim—and recount all of these blessings and curses publicly to reinforce them amongst themselves (vs. 26–32).

Chapters twelve through twenty-six contain the majority of the actual *deuteronomion*, the second giving of the Mosaic Law. It is not an exact reproduction of the words of Exodus and Leviticus, and it may not even mention every single law previously given; in fact, it often adds detail and explanation in some cases while summarizing in others. Indeed, since the original law was written onto a scroll, Moses could have read it had he wanted to do so. Instead, he intended to remind the people that the law they had been living under for the past thirty-eight years was not changing just because they were about to enter Canaan.

Moses began his review and instruction with a focus on Yehovah's demand for exclusivity in Israel. It was not enough that the Canaanites were to be either slaughtered or evacuated; all their places of pagan worship were to be destroyed as well (vs. 1–4). Not only could the Israelites not worship Yehovah at the existing places, but they were not allowed to be left standing at all. Additionally, God would choose the one place in the entire land that he would allow for his worship, and that would be the only acceptable place (vs. 5–14). All gatherings would be done there, and all sacrifices must be made there. The Levites would minister at the tabernacle there.

That was not to say that all animals could be killed only at that place (vs. 15–19). Although the Israelite diet was highly vegetarian, God allowed them to eat meat whenever they wanted, and it was not necessary to slaughter those at the tabernacle, only the animals used for sacrifice. This would continue to be true as God extended their borders (vs. 20–28). The only stipulation was that they had to drain the blood onto the ground properly before preparing and eating the meat. They were never allowed to eat the blood with the meat.

It was important that the nation worshiped God alone and only in the way that he instructed them (vs. 29–32). He was so strict on this point that he did not even allow them to investigate or study how the pagans practiced their worship. Knowing their methods and rituals would only tempt, entice, and confuse the Israelites from the one proper way that God had already defined and they were being reminded.

Chapter thirteen contains instructions and example situations of what to do when someone tried to institute any kind of pagan worship into Israel. If the instigator was a prophet or seer, and his prophecies did indeed take place, then the people would know that this was a test from God himself (vs. 1–5). A test of a true prophet was that his prophecy would come true (18:21–22). However, that was not the only test. His message had to match God's already-revealed word as well. In this case, if he was telling the people to worship another god, it did not matter if his prophecy came true because his message was not. He was to be executed for inciting rebellion against Yehovah.

A second scenario was if a person's "FULL BROTHER, YOUR SON, YOUR DAUGHTER, YOUR BELOVED WIFE, OR YOUR CLOSEST FRIEND" tried to lead them to worship a false god (vs. 6–11). In this case, it was the person's responsibility to execute the rebel immediately by stoning in the sight of the whole community.

The third scenario was based on a rumor of rebellion (vs. 12–18). In this case, it was important that the people "INVESTIGATE THOROUGHLY AND INQUIRE CAREFULLY" to find out if the rumor was true. God was not interested in lynchings and mob mentality; he is a God of justice. However, if the rumors were confirmed to be true, the execution was to be quick and complete, even to the point of destroying the entire city if necessary.

Chapter fourteen details some of the laws regarding the people's separation to Yehovah and the ceremonial cleanliness that status required. Pagan practices regarding death and dead bodies often included cutting oneself, marking oneself, and shaving specific parts of the head (vs. 1–2). The Israelites were not to participate in any of those rituals.

The dietary laws also had to do with their separation from the pagan society to God (vs. 3–21). Most four-footed cattle and venison was allowed to be eaten at any time. Hooves that were divided into two parts and chewing the cud were the signs that an animal was acceptable. If an animal had only one or the other, it was unclean (such as the camel, hare, rock badger, and pig). Any water animal with both fins and scales was acceptable. A long list of birds was not acceptable, primarily because they were carrion hunters or scavengers. A "corpse" or animal killed but not slaughtered was not clean, although they could sell it to a non-Israelite.⁹ Boiling a young goat in its mother's milk also seems to have had pagan connotations to it, so it was unacceptable as well.¹⁰

They were not to forget to bring their tithes of both crops and herds at the appointed times (vs. 22–29). The primary reasons were that this was a sign of gratitude for God's blessings and that the Levites lived off of these offerings. In some cases it was too far to bring the animals to the place of worship, so God graciously allowed them to convert the tithe into money at home, then purchase the necessary items for their feast at the tabernacle.¹¹ The annual tithe was to be celebrated with the Levites at the tabernacle. The three-year tithe helped provide for the local Levites along with the local poor.

Chapter fifteen opens with the sabbatical year regulations. Every seventh year, all debts were to be canceled and slaves were to be released with a full pardon (vs. 1–6). Moses noted that this applied to Israelite citizens only, not to resident foreigners in the land. However, he also said that there should not have ever been any poor people because God promised to bless them if they obeyed.¹² However, in the case that an Israelite did become poor (which Moses said would happen), it was the responsibility of his fellow Israelites to help him

---

[9] This is an interesting detail because it shows that there was nothing inherently wrong with the animal or meat itself; the restriction was simply God's way of keeping Israel distinct from the surrounding nations. Thus, when the dietary laws went away with the beginning of the church, it was not a change in God's standards or attitude toward the food, only a change in rules—new rules because the old ones were no longer needed. (See Matthew 15:10–20; Acts 10:9–16.)

[10] This is vastly different than the Jewish position held now that dairy and meat cannot even be on the same plate or served during the same course. That is a far extreme position not found in the Mosaic Law.

[11] When Jesus threw the money-changers and animals out of the temple, it was not because their actions were wrong. This was allowed under the Law. It was because they had turned it into a money-making scheme, defrauding their fellow citizens, rather than assisting in their worship.

[12] What a contrast to Jesus' statement that they would always have the poor with them (Matthew 26:11; see Deuteronomy 15:11). Poverty in Israel was a result of disobedience, and Jesus made that statement after he had been rejected, as he prepared the apostles for their new role as founders and leaders of the church.

(vs. 7–11). They were supposed to "GENEROUSLY LEND HIM WHATEVER HE NEEDS" without charging interest. Knowing the selfish temptation to look for loopholes in the law, Moses said that they were not to use the upcoming sabbatical year as an excuse to not help, even knowing that they may never be repaid.

When slaves were released during the sabbatical year, they were not to leave empty-handed (vs. 12–18). Presumably, they became slaves because of poverty, so God required that they not be put back into that state. The master was to send them away with their hands full. There were cases, however, in which the slaves may not have wanted to leave. If they took this option, they would be voluntarily choosing slavery for the rest of their lives. The sabbatical year would no longer have any authority in that situation.[13]

The law of the firstborn remained in effect in Canaan as well (vs. 19–23). The firstborn animals were to be sacrificed and eaten by the family at the place of worship as a celebration of God's blessing. If they were blemished, then they could be eaten at home, like any other animal, as long as they did not eat the blood with it.

Chapters sixteen and seventeen describe the specific practices Yehovah demanded for his worship. The Israelites were to always observe the annual Passover as a reminder of when God rescued them from Egyptian slavery (vs. 1–8). The meal would be eaten at the place of worship, not at home, and all leaven was to be purged from the land first. Additionally, they were to observe the following week of unleavened bread, but that could be done in their homes. Only the Passover itself required the journey to the tabernacle (and later the temple).

The second of three required celebrations was the Festival of Weeks or Pentecost (vs. 9–12). This was a "VOLUNTARY OFFERING THAT" they brought "IN PROPORTION TO HOW HE HAS BLESSED YOU." This celebration was also at the place

---

[13] While it is not a popular opinion today, this regulation shows that slavery in itself is not inherently evil but rather how slaves were treated by their masters can be good or evil. Slavery/servitude in Israel was strictly regulated by God to preserve the human rights of the slaves while allowing the economic benefit for both the master and slave.

of worship. The third festival was *Temporary Shelters* or *Booths* or *Tabernacles* (depending on the translation). This was in the fall to celebrate the later harvest and remind them that they used to live in tents before God brought them into Canaan (vs. 13–17). These three times annually every adult male had to appear at the place of worship with an offering based on God's provision that year.

Part of the proper worship of God was having godly leaders who could interpret God's law and rule justly and fairly (vs. 18–20). The method of worship was also particular (vs. 21–22). They were not allowed to use the shrines or locations that the pagans had already set up, and they were not allowed to construct anything like the pagans had used.

Chapter seventeen continues immediately from chapter sixteen. In addition to not using pagan methods of worshiping God, the people were to offer only animals without any blemish (vs. 1). If anyone practiced the worship of a false god, they were to be executed by the community (vs. 2–7). God was clear that this could not be done without a thorough investigation and at least two confirmed witnesses. He would not allow this to become a "witch hunt" abused by the leaders or fueled by rumors and gossip. Interestingly, this is one of only a few times that the punishment was specifically mentioned to curtail future rebellion. Most punishments were for the crime itself, regardless of whether they might deter future crime.

Verse eight picks up from 16:21–22 on the proper hierarchy of judges throughout Israel (vs. 8–13). There would be times that the local judges would be unable to make decisions for various reasons. In those cases, they were to go to the place of worship and the priest on duty would inquire of God. Whatever he said would be the final law with no chance of appeal. If the people did not obey it, they were to be executed.

Finally, Moses prophesied that the people may one day want to have a human king like the nations around them (vs. 14–20). Although that was not God's plan or desire for them, he would concede to them and give them a king. However, he had four rules for the kings—three negative and one positive. The king was not to amass for himself horses (dependence on his military), wives (dependence on foreign alliances), or silver and gold (dependence on economic wealth). Positively, he was to hand-write a copy of God's law and keep it with him at all times so he could refer to it and make his decisions based upon it. If he did this, God would bless them.

Chapter eighteen has three parts to it: the Levites, more forbidden pagan practices, and the coming Prophet. Of Israel's twelve tribes, Levi would receive no inheritance in the land (vs. 1–8).[14] Although they were granted some grazing rights, for the most part, they lived off of the sacrifices, tithes, and offerings of the people, both what they brought to the place of worship and in the local cities where they ministered. This was not optional or just goodwill by the people; it was commanded by God because of the ministry the Levites performed on behalf of the people.

In addition to not learning the pagan methods or using the pagan places of worship prevalent throughout the land, the Israelites were also not to participate in any of the rituals associated with pagan worship (vs. 9–14). These included but were not limited to child sacrifices or witchcraft and sorcery of any kind. All these required participation with or seeking information from demons, which was (and is still) abhorrent to God.

In place of these practices, God gave the people his prophets to speak for him and to do signs for the people (vs. 15–22). Specifically, he promised to one day send a special Prophet like Moses. The Jewish people continue to look for this Prophet, like they do the Messiah, although Jesus was the fulfillment of this prophecy. Even though Jesus was "like Moses" he was also superior to him (Hebrews 3:1–6). Because the prophet spoke from God, he held the people accountable for what they did with the prophets and their message (see Matthew 23:34–36).

---

[14] Joseph's tribe was split between his two sons, Ephraim and Manasseh, in order to keep twelve tribes. Interestingly, in Revelation 7 a third list of twelve tribes is given. There, Levi stands in place of Dan while Ephraim is called Joseph (as often occurs in the Old Testament as well).

Chapter nineteen begins a series of specific situations that God wanted the people to know. They often begin with "when" or "if" something occurs or should occur. The first had to do with the cities of refuge he would provide for accidental killers (vs. 1–13). The land was to be divided into three equal sections, each having one of these cities. If one person accidentally killed another person, he was to take refuge in one of these cities until it could be confirmed whether it was truly an accident because outside of the city blood revenge was legitimate. This was important because executing an innocent person was as bad as murder, so an investigation was necessary. If the person was found to be a murderer, he was to be executed.

Even in matters not related to murder, a criminal investigation was essential to discover the truth (vs. 14–21). No sentence could be passed legally without at least two credible witnesses. If it was discovered that a person perjured himself to use the law to harm the defendant (a violation of the ninth commandment), the judges were to execute on him whatever he was attempting to do to the defendant. It is in this situation of legal fraud that we find the principle: "YOU MUST NOT SHOW PITY; THE PRINCIPLE WILL BE A LIFE FOR A LIFE, AN EYE FOR AN EYE, A TOOTH FOR A TOOTH, A HAND FOR A HAND, AND A FOOT FOR A FOOT." This is another instance in which God said that the punishment would deter others from doing the same thing.

Chapter twenty reminded the people that they would have to go to war and fight battles as a part of taking the land (vs. 1–9). God would certainly fight for them, but they could not sit back and do nothing. Their responsibility was to be courageous and march forward. However, not everyone was required to go into battle. For those men who had just built a new home or just planted a new vineyard or were just married, God exempted them from military service. He was not taking them into a land of plenty for them to not be able to enjoy it. Additionally, God did not require men who were afraid to go into battle, because they would cause a loss of morale among the other troops.[15] Once

---

[15] God had Gideon follow a similar pattern when he was building his army against the Midianites (Judges 7:1–8).

they knew how many troops they had for each battle, then they could assign the proper number of leaders.[16]

Additionally, with only a few specific exceptions, God did not intend for the Israelites to slaughter every person in Canaan (vs. 10–15). In most cases, they were to offer peace first, at which point the people would become subject to Israel. Only if their offer was declined were they to attack. Even then, they were to let the women and children live, not kill them all. Certain cities, though, were infinitely corrupt, and God demanded that every person in them be killed and all the spoil be destroyed (vs. 16–20).

God gave a curious, yet logical, command regarding when the Israelites were besieging a city. While there, they were not to cut down the fruit trees around the city, because they could eat the fruit both during and after taking the city. "A TREE IN THE FIELD IS NOT HUMAN THAT YOU SHOULD BESIEGE IT!" (vs. 19) Non-fruit-bearing trees, however, could be cut down and used in the battle.

Chapter twenty-one gives a series of hypothetical situations so the people would know how to act properly throughout their daily lives. In the case of a murder, the criminal was to be executed for his crime. But what if no one knows who did it? In this situation, God created a system by which the city elders, judges, and priests ceremonially cleansed and sacrificed a young heifer to make atonement for the heinous crime (vs. 1–9).

In the case of a warrior who was part of an attack on a village or city and who saw a woman he wanted to marry, God allowed him to do that (vs. 10–14). The stipulations required that the woman be allowed to mourn her family and not become a slave. She would have full rights as a wife, including the right to a proper divorce if the man found something about her that he did not like.[17] He was not allowed to enslave her, sell her, or take advantage of her in any way. Contrary to many who criticize God's treatment of Canaanites, this proves that he is and has always been gracious.

---

[16] This is an important general principle about not having "too many chiefs."

[17] Deuteronomy 24:1–4 gives additional information about proper divorces under the Mosaic Law.

In addition to divorce, God also permitted and regulated polygamy in Israel (much to the dismay of many Christians today). Continuing the section on not humiliating wives, if a man had two wives, he might love one more than the other (i.e., Jacob). In this case, he would be tempted to give the firstborn rights to the son of his favorite wife. However, if she did not bear the actual firstborn son, God required that the man not show favoritism in that way (vs. 15–17).

Parents were allowed to have their rebellious sons executed, but only after "THEY DISCIPLINE HIM TO NO AVAIL" and have him stand before the city elders, implying investigation into the accusation (vs. 18–21). The fact that the son is called "STUBBORN AND REBELLIOUS...A GLUTTON AND DRUNKARD" shows that this was not just normal childhood discipline or because the parents were tired of being parents. Corpses were not allowed to be left hanging on a tree overnight (vs. 22–23). Instead, they were to be buried and not be left under God's curse.

Chapter twenty-two continues the application of the law in hypothetical scenarios. Neighbors were to watch out for each other and their possessions, instead of just watching them wander away (vs. 1–4). Dressing in clothes of the opposite gender was forbidden, and this probably speaks to transgender issues rather than just clothing (vs. 5). Verses six through eight show the attitude that the people were to have toward each other and God's creation. They were not to kill both a mother bird and her chicks. Flat roofs were to have a guardrail so that someone did not accidentally fall off.

Because God was giving them the land and produce, he insisted that everything was kept separate: no mixed seeds in the same field, no mixed animals plowing together, and no mixed fabrics in their clothes (vs. 9–12). Although none of these is sinful in itself, it was a reminder of the life of separation that God called Israel to live.

The rest of the chapter has to do with sexual relations (vs. 13–30). Sex is a gift from God, so it should not surprise us that he gave conditions on who could participate and how. Because virginity was valued, a man had the right to expect to marry a virgin. If he discovered that she was not, he had the right to accuse and divorce her. However, this required investigation.[18] If she was proven to be a virgin, the husband owed her father a large sum of money for slandering the man's name, and he was never allowed to divorce her. If it was proven that she was indeed not a virgin, then she was executed for sexual sin as the law prescribed elsewhere.

In the case of adultery, both the man and the woman were to be executed. This was true whether the woman was already married (consummated) or still just engaged (promised in marriage). The spoken clue was that she was complicit because she did not cry for help as if he had raped her. In the case of rape, where the woman was completely innocent and violated, only the man was to be executed. In the case of sex with an unengaged woman, they were to be married and were not allowed to divorce.[19] All forms of incest were forbidden in the law, but Moses here specified marriage and sex with one's stepmother after his father's death or divorce.

Chapter twenty-three continues Moses' instruction in the Law code that Israel was to obey when they entered the land. Ceremonial purity seems to be the theme of these regulations. Certain people were never allowed to participate in public worship because of defective bodies or heritage (vs. 1–8). This emphasized the holiness (transcendent separation) of God. The people included any "MAN WITH CRUSHED OR SEVERED GENITALS" or a "PERSON OF ILLEGITIMATE BIRTH." Ammonites and Moabites and their descendants were excluded,[20] as were Egyptians and Edomites, but only to the third generation.

---

[18] Based on verse seventeen, it seems that her bloody bedsheet from the wedding night was proof of her virginity.

[19] Many people today take issue with this because it could include rape. While this is true, the language does not demand it and the punishment for rape has already been stated. It could mean violation of her family and virginity. To grab ahold of her for the purpose of sex does not necessarily mean rape or non-consensual sex. The phrase "AND THEY ARE DISCOVERED" without her crying out for help is significant.

[20] This must have included only males and any females who did not marry an Israelite man. Ruth was from Moab, and her descendants certainly participated in the public worship of Yehovah (David, Jesus, etc.).

Emissions of bodily fluids, though not sinful, did cause ceremonial uncleanness, so they required ritual purification, even before going to war under God's banner (vs. 9–11). Even though they lived in primitive times compared to modern standards, hygiene was still important, and God required that they bury their excrement outside the camp (vs. 12–14). This contributed to both physical and ceremonial purity.

Concerning specific people, under God's law, runaway slaves were not to be returned to their masters (vs. 15–16). If the master was that bad, God would not force a person to live and work under those conditions. Cultic prostitution was an abomination to God and was never to be part of his worship (vs. 17–18). Interest was not to be charged on a loan to a fellow Israelite, only to non-Israelites (vs. 19–20). Vows to God were to be kept immediately and fully because they were always freely made (vs. 21–23). People were allowed to glean from each other's fields as they walked through because they were from God, but they could not harvest someone else's crops for themselves (vs. 24–25).[21]

Chapter twenty-four opens with God's laws on divorce (vs. 1–4). John Stott described divorce as "a divine concession to human weakness."[22] Although it was never God's design for marriage or mandated, it was allowed under the Mosaic Law (reaffirmed by Jesus in Matthew 19:3–9) and in the New Testament (1 Corinthians 7), always with strict guidelines.[23] Specifically, a man could divorce his wife if something came to his attention about her that she had not disclosed beforehand, and it turned him against her.[24] The divorce would have to be done legally and in writing, releasing her from the marriage.

---

[21] The New Testament gospels records several times that Jesus and his disciples ate as they were walking through a field.

[22] Quoted in Charles Swindoll, *Divorce: When it All Comes Tumbling Down* (Portland: Multnomah, 1981), 20.

[23] I have dealt with this topic in detail in my book, *Marriage, Divorce, and Remarriage: Fresh Help and Hope from the Bible*.

[24] If this were sexual immorality, then she would have been executed, not divorced (22:13–19).

Both were allowed to remarry someone else. However, if the woman's second husband also divorced her, she could never go back to her former husband.

New couples in the first year of marriage were not required to be separated by the husband going into battle (vs. 5). Collateral for loans was legitimate, but not something that would cause the borrower to be unable to provide for his family (vs. 6). Kidnapping, especially with the intent to sell the victim, was a heinous crime worthy of death (vs. 7).

Skin diseases were to be treated carefully, in line with the detailed instructions that God had laid out for the priests (vs. 8–9; see Leviticus 13–14). In the case of a personal loan, the loaner had to accept whatever security the borrower could give (vs. 10–13). If it were his coat or blanket, the loaner had to return it before nightfall. Wages were to be paid at the end of the workday so that the poor did not go hungry (vs. 14–15). Crimes were paid for by the people who committed them (vs. 16). Making sure that the poor in their cities had food and shelter was a priority under God's law (vs. 17–22). This included the widows, orphans, and the "RESIDENT FOREIGNER" who had come to live and work in Israel.

Chapter twenty-five continues the regulations on interpersonal relationships among the Israelites. God had Moses establish both regional and local judges for the people to help them decide cases with God's law (vs. 1–3). Whatever the judge ruled was final, and the people were expected to obey it. Punishments were to be performed by either the judge himself or in his presence. (He could not sentence someone and look the other way, washing his hands of the situation as Pilate attempted to do.) Next to death, the most severe physical punishment was limited to forty lashes.[25]

Work animals were to be treated with care as well (vs. 4). It was unfair for an ox to be kept from eating the grain that it worked to grind. Paul applied this principle to the payment local church elders are to be given for their hard work for their congregation (1 Timothy 5:17–18).

---

[25] Over time they began to give "FORTY LASHES LESS ONE" (2 Corinthians 11:24), so that in case they miscounted, they would not have unintentionally broken the law.

The concept of levirate marriage was important in Israel because of the generational inheritance of the land within the tribes (vs. 5–10). If a man died without bearing children, someone else within the family was required to father a child with his widow in the man's name, to keep his name going. Although this was originally meant to be the man's brother, it could extend further than that (see Ruth 4). If a man was unwilling, it could be considered scandalous because he was rejecting the widow's right to a family inheritance.[26]

Constable notes that the only time in the Pentateuch that punishment by physical mutilation was required was in the case of a woman who intentionally grabbed another man's genitals if he was fighting her husband (vs. 11–12).[27] Not only was this an unfair advantage for her husband, but it was also both indecent and potentially damaging to a fellow Israelite's family line. This type of unfair advantage or dishonesty applied to weights and measures as well (vs. 13–16). God demanded that the people treat each other fairly and justly.

The chapter ends with a reminder that the Amalekites were not just another nation in the land (vs. 17–19). They were especially wicked, and God required that they were utterly destroyed.

Chapter twenty-six concludes Moses' rehearsal of God's Law code for the Israelite nation. When they entered the land, the first harvest of produce was to be given completely over to God at the place of worship (vs. 1–11). It was a special celebration of First Fruits focused on celebrating God's goodness to them in bringing them into the land and the provision that he would grant them there. They were to remember that they came from a family of wanderers (Jacob) and slaves, but God miraculously brought them to this place with far more abundance than they could imagine.

---

[26] This is a strange concept in modern thought, but it was essential for the nation at that time. While it may generate many questions, little detail is given about how it worked in practice. It seems this is another place where polygamy was permitted and the laws about incest (a brother with his sister-in-law) were proven to be situational and practical rather than always a matter of sin.

[27] Constable, *Notes on Deuteronomy, 2021 Edition*, 148.

Every third and sixth year they were to bring a special tithe that was kept in their cities and villages for the local Levites, widows, orphans, and foreign residents there (vs. 12–15). In caring for the poor in this way, not only did they obey God's command, but they were encouraged to ask for even greater blessing in their harvests.

Moses finished his review of these laws with the encouragement to obey them all (vs. 16–19). If the nation would do so, he promised that God would "ELEVATE YOU ABOVE ALL THE NATIONS HE HAS MADE AND YOU WILL RECEIVE PRAISE, FAME, AND HONOR," just as he had promised Abraham (Genesis 12:1–3).

Chapter twenty-seven opens the final section of Deuteronomy, extending through the end of the book. In this section, Moses gave a few final commands and encouragements to the nation, handed over the leadership of the nation to Joshua, and died. Even so, there is a great deal of prophecy and valuable theology in these last several chapters.

The first order of business upon entering Canaan was to go to the most central location (Shechem) where Mt. Ebal and Mt. Gerizim stood (vs. 1–13). There the people were to erect a pillar engraved or painted with God's Law (probably the Ten Commandments). They were also to construct an altar on which they would make burnt sacrifices to God. Then the twelve tribes were to split into two groups—one on each of the two mountains—where they would represent the blessings and curses on the nation based on the laws Moses had given them.

The Levites would call across the valley a series of twelve commands from out of the law, one for each tribe, representing the entire law and the entire nation (vs. 14–26). As they called out each law, and the curse on anyone who broke it, the people were to respond with a loud "Amen," the Hebrew (and Greek) word signifying agreement and assent. In this way, the second generation of Israelites renewed the covenant with God that the first generation had made at Mount Sinai.

Chapter twenty-eight contains a series of both blessings and curses God promised to bring based on the people's obedience or disobedience, respectively, to his law. Although the blessings are given in some detail (vs. 1–14), the curses are much more extensive (vs. 15–68), containing almost four times as many verses. The reason for this is two-fold. First, God wanted the people to know that he would not take their disobedience lightly. Second, he wanted them to know that he was quick to bless and slow to punish. The punishments listed are drawn out, executed little by little if the people continued to rebel. In other words, whereas God promised to give extensive blessings immediately for obedience, his punishment would start small and increase only as their rebellion increased. As horrible as the punishments in this chapter are, we should consider this a wonderful reminder of God's patience and grace toward his people, even under the Mosaic Law.

Both the blessings and the curses would affect their land (abundance or famine), the weather (rain or drought), their families (children or none), animals (offspring or none), enemies (divine protection or utter defeat), physical bodies (healthy or diseased), and their national economy and politics (superpower or "third-world" nation). The major requirement was to not turn away from Yehovah to worship other gods (the first two commandments). The second requirement was to obey the rest of the law. If they failed to do these things, God would not only take away everything that he promised to give them, but he would pour out on them everything that he promised to do to their enemies, including kicking them out of Canaan and scattering them throughout the whole world.[28]

Chapter twenty-nine begins Moses' final plea to the people. To this point he had reviewed God's law, warning them of the dire consequences for disobeying it and the great rewards for obeying it. As he prepared to walk away, he had a few personal things to share with them.

Beginning with Egypt, he quickly reviewed their story of God's deliverance from slavery, natural disaster, and their enemies for forty years (vs. 1–8).

---

[28] Ultimately, his full wrath will be poured out during the 70th week of Daniel's prophecy (Daniel 9:27, often called the "Tribulation"), as he works to turn Israel's national heart back to himself (see Matthew 23:37–39).

However, Moses was concerned for them because, even after all that time, he knew that they still did not understand God or his ways. Moses begged them to obey God, to fulfill the covenant they would renew with him as they began to enjoy his blessings (vs. 9–15). He reminded them that the decisions and actions they made carried long-term consequences, not just in their generation, but even to the many who were not yet born.

Even more than their actions, Moses warned them about their attitudes toward God and his Law (vs. 16–29). He knew that people would be tempted to ignore God's law, thinking that God's patience, grace, and love would not allow him to punish the people. This willful attitude—"I WILL HAVE PEACE THOUGH I CONTINUE TO WALK WITH A STUBBORN SPIRIT"—could not be forgiven, and it would bring consequences to the entire nation if it was allowed to take root and spread.[29] Remarkably, Moses reminded them that they were responsible only for what God had revealed to them to that point, not for things God never told them, a good reminder for all people of every age (vs. 29).

Chapter thirty finally presents Moses' call to action for the nation. To this point, he had spent his time reviewing God's law and the consequences of obeying or disobeying it. He had commanded, taught, and pled with them over it. At long last, it was time for them to make their decision. Moses could do nothing else for them.

"LOOK! I HAVE SET BEFORE YOU TODAY LIFE AND PROSPERITY ON THE ONE HAND, AND DEATH AND DISASTER ON THE OTHER" (vs. 15). Moses knew that this was literally a matter of life and death for the nation. He knew that they were eager to commit to obedience now as they looked into the land and longed for its abundance. He also knew that they would get lazy and take them for granted.

In one of the greatest prophecies of Deuteronomy, Moses declared that they would disobey so long and hard that God would finally banish them from the land, causing them to be exiles in foreign countries (vs. 1–10). However, he also promised that they would not stay there forever. In what is essentially the second half of the great Land Covenant God made with Abraham (see

---

[29] The same thing can happen in a church as well (Hebrews 12:15).

Genesis 15:17–21), God promised that, no matter how far they were scattered, he would eventually bring them back to their land, never to be scattered again. Once returned, they would finally be forever faithful to Yehovah and would experience the full blessings God had always desired and designed to give them. This has never yet happened, and those who interpret the Scriptures literally look forward to the fulfillment of this passage during the Messianic Kingdom (Millennium) and into the Eternal State.

There is an amazing phrase in verse four worth special consideration The NET Bible translates it weakly as "EVEN IF YOUR EXILES ARE IN THE MOST DISTANT LAND." The Hebrew phrase states, "at the extremity of the heavens." Even though Moses could have known nothing about space travel at his point in history, the Spirit-inspired phrasing of this promise includes even those Jews who may be in space or on another planet when God finally brings them back to their land. What an amazing way to see God's hand in the inspiration of Scripture—not revealing more than Moses should have known while not allowing him to write something that would be proven wrong centuries later!

Possibly with a bit of aged frustration, Moses said that it was indeed possible for them to obey God (vs. 11–14). They no longer needed someone to go up to heaven to get God's law or bring it down to them; Moses had done that on Mount Sinai.[30] It was right in front of them, summarized by both Moses and Jesus as the great commandment of love: "LOVE THE **LORD** YOUR **GOD**, TO WALK IN HIS WAYS, AND TO OBEY HIS COMMANDMENTS, HIS STATUTES, AND HIS ORDINANCES." With life and death at stake, Moses begged them, "CHOOSE LIFE SO THAT YOU AND YOUR DESCENDANTS MAY LIVE!"

Chapter thirty-one recounts Moses' final commissioning of Joshua as the new leader of Israel. At 120 years old Moses had spent two-thirds of his life in that Arabian wilderness—forty years shepherding his father-in-law's sheep and forty years shepherding the infant nation. Because of his great failure in Numbers 20:1–13, Moses knew that God would not allow him to take Israel

---

[30] Paul quoted this passage in Romans 10, applying it to Jesus and the gospel of salvation.

into Canaan (vs. 1–8). As he prepared to place the nation in Joshua's hands, he reminded them that although Joshua would stand in front, God was their true fighter. Just as he had destroyed their previous enemies, he would do the same to their future enemies. This should cause Joshua and the nation to have great courage and walk in obedience.

After writing down the entire law (and probably the covenant blessings and curses) onto a scroll, Moses handed it over to the Levites and priests (vs. 9–13). He ordered that it be read to the entire nation during the Festival of Temporary Shelters, when they remembered their time in the wilderness, seven years later in the first sabbatical year. This way, not only would the people standing there be reminded of these things, but children who were born during that time or too young to remember would hear of them, and a third generation would grow up with the foundation they needed to continue following Yehovah.

After Moses' words to the people, God had Moses and Joshua come to the Tent of Meeting so that he could finalize Joshua's commission as well (vs. 14–22). What he told the men, though, was not what they expected to hear: "I KNOW THE INTENTIONS THEY HAVE IN MIND TODAY, EVEN BEFORE I BRING THEM TO THE LAND I HAVE PROMISED." God said that after Moses died and they entered the land, they would immediately begin selling themselves out to other gods. As a result, God would have to fulfill his promises to punish them severely. What heartbreaking news for the men! Even so, God encouraged Joshua that he would be with the young leader, and he gave Moses a song to teach the people so that when they were in exile, they would remember God.

Moses carried the message back to the people, instructing the elders to keep the law scroll by the ark of the covenant and preparing to teach them God's song.

Chapter thirty-two, like Exodus 15, is a song taught by Moses to the nation of Israel. In Exodus 15 it was Moses' song, praising God for his defeat of the Egyptian army at the Red Sea. In this chapter, it was God's song given to Moses so that the people would always know that God had prophesied their rebellion and repentance and his restoration, God's prescient witness that he would use both to testify against them and bring them back.

The song has seven sections, opening with a statement of praise exalting God for his faithfulness (vs. 1–4), followed by the initial declaration of Israel's unfaithfulness to him (vs. 5–6). The third section takes Israel back in time to Genesis 11, when the nations were divided, and Yehovah chose Israel from among the nations for himself (vs. 7–14).[31] Regardless of one's interpretation of the debate in the footnote, no one can deny that Israel is God's "SPECIAL POSSESSION" and "THE PUPIL OF HIS EYE."[32] He plucked them out of obscurity and gave them prominence in both the natural and supernatural worlds.

In response to God's special favor on them, Israel "DESERTED THE GOD WHO MADE HIM" (vs. 15–18). The name *Jeshurun* is a play on the Hebrew verb יָשַׁר (*yashar*), which means "to be upright." Rather than being upright with God as they should have been, Israel breached their covenant and turned to worship the demon gods of the other nations around them. Because of their rebellion, God took steps to punish them (vs. 19–25). As Moses promised in chapter twenty-eight, these punishments began with physical afflictions in the land.

Eventually, as their rebellion increased, God had to fulfill his promise to take them out of the land (vs. 26–38). To do this, he used the very nations that

---

[31] There is a debate in verse eight over how God divided the nations. The Masoretic Hebrew Text reads "according to the number of the sons of Israel," while the Dead Sea Scrolls read "the sons of God," which the LXX translated into "the angels of God." This is the understanding reflected in NET translation *"according to the number of the heavenly assembly."* The difference in understanding is that God either set up the nations of the world in relation to where he would place Israel ("sons of Israel") or that he chose Israel for himself and left the nations to be led/ruled by other divine beings/angels/demons ("sons of God" and "angels of God"). Based on many other passages in both the Old and New Testaments which reveal that the human rulers of this world are under the direction and influence of demons, and based on the immediate following context of vs. 15–18, I prefer the second view and the NET translation.

[32] This is traditionally translated "the apple of his eye," but there is no basis in the Hebrew text. The Hebrew phrase is "the little man," which refers to the reflection a person sees when looking into another person's eye. In this case, it indicates that Israel should see herself when looking at God because he is constantly looking at her.

he had given over to demonic authorities (namely, Assyria and Babylon). This was risky (from a human perspective) because they believed that they had done this in their own power instead of recognizing this as God's judgment. Thus, God promised that he would punish them for their rebellion as well.[33]

The song closes with God's declaration of his superiority over all those other gods (vs. 39–43). He alone holds the power of life and death. He transcends everything to such an extent that he can swear only by himself (see Hebrews 6:13). Even though his people failed him, he made "ATONEMENT FOR HIS LAND AND PEOPLE."

Moses faithfully recorded the song and taught it to the nation (vs. 44–47). God then told him to walk up the mountain where he would look across the Jordan into Canaan but die without stepping foot into it (vs. 48–52).

Chapter thirty-three records Moses' blessing on the nation before his death. Like Jacob before him (Genesis 49), Moses announced God's revelation of his love and law to Israel, then mentioned the tribes by name. A few of his comments are worth noting.

Although he was the firstborn son, Reuben received only an honorable mention, still a result of his sin (Genesis 35:22; 49:3–4). Because of Simeon's and Levi's sin against the men of Shechem (Genesis 34; 49:5–7), Judah became the leader (vs. 7). Moses never mentioned Simeon in this list because his tribe effectively became a subset of Judah (Joshua 19:1–9). However, Levi redeemed themselves by siding with Moses at the golden calf incident (Exodus 32:25–29). Thus, the defenders of the law became the teachers of the law (vs. 8–11).

Joseph, the fourth major patriarch of Genesis, received Moses' longest blessing (vs. 13–17). Not only was he blessed with a double portion of the nation through his two sons, Ephraim and Manasseh, but he also received some of the best portions of the land, including some on the east side of the Jordan River. For the remaining six tribes, Moses gave brief statements of blessing (vs. 18–25). He saved his final comments for the nation as a whole, referring to

---

[33] This is exactly the issue that Habakkuk took up with God when God told him that Babylon was going to be God's tool for punishing Israel.

Israel again as *Jeshurun*, "the upright one," and exalting God as their protector (vs. 26–29).

Chapter thirty-four is possibly the only chapter of 187 in the Pentateuch not originally written by Moses. From the mountain, God allowed Moses to supernaturally see the entire land that Israel would obtain, far beyond what he could see with his naked eye, even though he still had perfect vision (vs. 1–4, 7).

Although it is certainly possible that God had him write the account of his own death, the final comments in this short closing chapter sound much more like a eulogy written by someone who highly respected the greatest leader Israel ever had. He was so close to God that no one else in Israel (except Jesus himself) would ever have the relationship with God that Moses had (vs. 10). His closeness with God is represented in both the fact that God himself buried him (vs. 6) and his final epitaph is that he accomplished everything that "THE LORD HAD SENT HIM TO DO" (vs. 11–12). This, too, is similar to Jesus who, just before his death, declared, "I GLORIFIED YOU ON EARTH BY COMPLETING THE WORK YOU GAVE ME TO DO" (John 17:4). May every man and woman of God step into the Savior's presence with the same confidence.

Joshua

Joshua is the first book in the second section of the Hebrew text, the Prophets (Hebrew, *nevi'im*). It is named after the primary person of the story, Joshua, Moses' faithful right-hand man and God's appointed leader of Israel. Joshua was a man of action, and his book recounts many of those stories in the first half as the nation marched into Canaan and conquered the major strongholds who occupied it. The second half is primarily dedicated to the division of the land of Canaan between the tribes of Israel and Joshua's final words to the nation.

Although it is impossible to date this book exactly, and the writer is never named, it is likely that Joshua himself wrote it. Archer notes several keys pointing to Joshua as the writer: intimate details requiring an eyewitness; cities called by their ancient names instead of newer names; Sidon was still the leading city of Phoenicia rather than Tyre; several "we" passages rather than "they" as if a third person were writing; and more.[1] If Joshua was indeed the writer, then the book dates to the 14th century BC. This, however, does not deny that some things were certainly added later, including the account of Joshua's death and the comment that "ISRAEL WORSHIPED THE LORD THROUGHOUT JOSHUA'S LIFETIME AND AS LONG AS THE ELDERLY MEN WHO OUTLIVED HIM REMAINED ALIVE" (24:31).

Chapter one is nearly an uninterrupted continuation from the end of Deuteronomy. Verse one picks up immediately from Moses' death and Joshua's transition as the new leader of Israel, handpicked by God himself.

---

[1] Gleason L. Archer, *A Survey of Old Testament Introduction, Revised and Expanded* (Moody Press, 1994), 286.

Moses, Aaron, and the generation who had come out of Egypt had lost their privilege to enter the land because of their sin and disobedience. The first generation sinned at Kadesh-Barnea when they refused to enter the land the first time (Numbers 13–14). Moses and Aaron lost their entrance to the land when they hit the rock to bring out water rather than simply speaking to it and placed themselves alongside God as Israel's provider (Numbers 20).

In commissioning Joshua, God made several promises (vs. 3–9). First, everywhere Joshua went he would conquer. Second, the territory would extend to the borders God had promised Abraham in Genesis 15:18–21. Third, no one would be able to resist him. Fourth, God would never leave him. The condition was that Joshua was to faithfully follow God's law, memorize it, obey it, and lead Israel in obeying it.

One specific act of preparation for going into Canaan had to do with the tribes of Reuben, Gad, and half of Manasseh (vs. 10–18). In Numbers 32 these tribes asked Moses if they could stay on the east side of the Jordan River, rather than moving into the land of Canaan with the rest of the nation. Moses finally permitted this provided that their warriors accompanied the rest of the tribes into Canaan and fought alongside their brothers. When called to report for this duty, they told Joshua they intended to fulfill their promise and would follow him wherever he led.

Chapter two continues the account of Joshua's preparation to conquer the land of Canaan and sets the scene for one of the most famous stories of the Old Testament. Jericho was the first major city in the path of Israel's entrance to the land, so they had to conquer it. Joshua sent two spies to find out everything they could about Jericho's defenses (vs. 1–7). Arriving in the city, they spent the night at the home of a prostitute named Rahab. In his *Notes* on Joshua, Constable quotes at least three other sources who note that "a prostitute's or innkeeper's house was the accustomed place for meeting with spies, conspirators, and the like" and "strange men at a harlot's place of business would hardly raise suspicion." Further, he points out that the Jewish historian,

Josephus, called Rahab an innkeeper.[2] Somehow the king of Jericho heard that Israelite spies were at her home, and he commanded her to turn them over to the police, but she refused, saying that they had already left. Because she had hidden them on her rooftop, this was a lie. (See the footnote on Exodus 1 concerning the biblical use of lying in spiritual warfare.)

Unbelievers and skeptics often use the conquest of Canaan as proof of God's malevolence and bloodthirstiness in the Old Testament. *How could God command all these people to be killed, even the women and children? That doesn't sound like a God of love!* However, it is important to notice something Rahab said. In verses 8–14, Rahab told the spies that everyone in the region was "ABSOLUTELY TERRIFIED OF YOU, AND ALL WHO LIVE IN THE LAND ARE CRINGING BEFORE YOU." One might assume that was because Israel's 600,000+ member army was standing at their doors, but that was not so. The reason for their terror was that they "HEARD HOW THE LORD DRIED UP THE WATER OF THE RED SEA AND HOW YOU ANNIHILATED THE TWO AMORITE KINGS, SIHON AND OG, ON THE OTHER SIDE OF THE JORDAN." This is significant because the Red Sea had happened 40 years earlier and the Amorite kings about a year earlier! The Canaanites had been quaking in their boots for four decades knowing that the Israelites were coming for them, and they chose to remain and fight instead of evacuating. They died because they chose to, not because they had to. Later, we discover that Joshua and Israel took approximately seven years to clear Canaan (it had been 45 years since they began their 38-year desert wandering; cf. Deuteronomy 2:14; Joshua 14:7–10), which means that the other cities had time to save themselves as well. (See the article "Digging Deeper: Is God a Genocidal Murderer?" after Deuteronomy 7 for further insight on this.)

Because of her devotion to the true God, Rahab asked that she and her family would be spared in Jericho's certain downfall, but the spies required three proofs of loyalty (vs. 15–24). First, she must hang a scarlet cord from her window, so that the Israelites would know to avoid that home when they attacked. Second, her family must be inside her home during the invasion. Only those inside would be saved. Third, she must not reveal anything about

---

[2] Constable, *Notes on Joshua*, 2015 edition, 15–16.

the spies or let anyone know their plans. When she agreed to all of these conditions, they swore an oath confirming her safety then returned to Joshua, praising God that victory was sure.

Chapters three and four recount the Israelites crossing west over the Jordan River to finally enter Canaan and begin their conquest. After receiving the report from the spies about Jericho, Joshua immediately prepared the nation to enter the land (vs. 1–4). They camped on the banks of the river for three days, during which time Joshua received his orders from God. One of the important things to note throughout this book is the constant communication between Joshua and Yehovah. These were not just dreams and visions, but regular conversations in which Joshua heard God's voice, and sometimes saw the preincarnate Son and responded appropriately.

On the morning they crossed the Jordan the people were to go through a ceremonial cleansing ritual to be prepared to receive what God was going to give them (vs. 5–13). God's plan was simple. The priests would carry the Ark of the Covenant about a half-mile (900m) in front of the people. When they stepped into the river, it would stop flowing and back up, so the people would cross on dry ground. This is significant because most of the people were not yet born when their parents' generation crossed the Red Sea on dry ground (Exodus 14). If the Canaanites were still afraid of that event 40 years earlier (2:10), this similar repeat would solidify Israel's God as the most powerful in their minds.

When the people obeyed, it happened just as God said (vs. 14–17). The priests and ark made their way to the center of the river bed and stood there while the water stopped and the people walked by. A fun detail in verse 15 is that the river was at flood stage. This may be God's inspired advance response to anyone who might claim that the people stepped through during the low, dry season. Without the miracle, anyone trying to cross the river near Jericho would have been washed away and drowned.

Chapter four continues the account from chapter three. God had told Joshua that there needed to be a visible reminder of this event for the succeeding generations to look at and remember what God had done for them that day (vs. 1–7). To accomplish this, God had each of the twelve tribes select one of their men to retrieve a stone from the middle of the river bed, where the priests were standing with the ark. These twelve stones would be placed together into a pile on the west side of the Jordan, where the people entered the land, as a memorial. Whenever their descendants asked about it, the story could be handed down from one generation to the next of "how the water of the Jordan stopped flowing before the ark of the covenant of the LORD." Again, the people obeyed, and at the time of Joshua's writing, probably near the end of his life, the memorial was still standing.

The rest of the chapter finishes with a couple of details introduced in earlier chapters. First, the tribes of Reuben, Gad, and Manasseh, who were staying on the east side of the river, followed through with their promise to send troops into Canaan, adding about 40,000 to the rest of the army that would be staying in the land (vs. 10–14). Second, as soon as the priests stepped up onto dry land the river started to flow again, signifying God's control over creation (vs. 15–18). Third, the memorial was built as God had instructed (vs. 19–24). God orchestrated these things exactly "SO ALL THE NATIONS OF THE EARTH MIGHT RECOGNIZE THE LORD'S POWER AND SO [ISRAEL] MIGHT ALWAYS OBEY THE LORD YOUR GOD."

Chapter four best ends with 5:1, which is a note confirming that what God intended had indeed happened. When the kings in Canaan heard about the Jordan River crossing, it did remind them of the Red Sea crossing, and "THEY LOST THEIR COURAGE AND COULD NOT EVEN BREATHE FOR FEAR OF THE ISRAELITES." As noted before, it makes one wonder why they did not flee and evacuate rather than stand and be destroyed by Yehovah.

Chapter five concludes the preparations necessary before the Israelites could begin their conquest of Canaan. In verses 2–9, a bit of history was necessary. The physical sign of God's covenant that set Abraham apart from the nations around him was the circumcision of his sons (Genesis 17:9–14). The Israelites had done this for 600 years, until the Exodus, when God codified it into his Law. However, they did not continue to circumcise the sons born during the desert wandering, so when the second generation was ready to take the land, God told Joshua that they all needed to be circumcised first (approximately 602,000 men; Numbers 26:51).

In Genesis 34:25, when an entire village was circumcised, the men (understandably) were still in pain after three days. The nation had entered the land "ON THE TENTH DAY OF THE FIRST MONTH" (Joshua 4:19) and celebrated their first Passover in the new land four days later, while they were still healing. Joshua recalled that they ate from the spring produce the next day, at which point the miraculous manna stopped appearing, and they never saw it again (vs. 10–12; see Exodus 16:35).

God knew that Joshua needed one more assurance before beginning his conquest, so he gave him a special message. As Joshua (who had already been circumcised as a baby) stood surveying Jericho, he saw a man standing near him, holding a sword (vs. 13–15). With his army still recuperating, he certainly had cause to be concerned of a possible sneak attack, so he challenged the man as to whose side he was on. His answer was both humbling and thrilling: "I AM THE COMMANDER OF THE LORD'S ARMY. NOW I HAVE ARRIVED!" Joshua must have recognized him and his voice at this point; he had stood by Moses countless times as Moses talked with Yehovah over the previous decades. This was not just a voice from heaven or a dream; the preincarnate Son was standing there, ready to lead all of Heaven's army ahead of Joshua. Joshua asked what God wanted. The reply was simple: submission to Yehovah and worship. "THE PLACE WHERE YOU STAND IS HOLY."

Chapter six records the famous defeat of Jericho, the Israelites' first victory in Canaan. At the end of chapter five, God appeared to Joshua to tell him that the army of Heaven was there. In verses 1–5, God informed Joshua how God would defeat Jericho. The instructions for the Israelite army to walk around the city wall for seven days, carry the ark, and blow the trumpets were meant for them to exhibit their faith in God, not to knock down the walls.

In verses 6–14 Joshua conveyed God's instructions and the army carried them out exactly. The priests carried the Ark of the Covenant ahead of the army, who walked around the city once each day for six days. On the seventh day, they followed the same pattern, except they went around the city seven times. On the final time around, they all gave a loud battle cry and the walls collapsed.

With the walls down, they were instructed to do three things (vs. 17–25). First, all the people and animals were to be killed, and the city was to be burned to the ground. Second, Rahab and everyone in her house were to be spared. Third, all the items of value (gold, silver, bronze, and iron) were to be taken into God's treasury. They were not to be taken by individuals.

Joshua included three final notes (vs. 25–27). First, Rahab continued to live with the Israelites. Later we find out that she became the mother of Boaz, who married Ruth (Matthew 1:5). Second, Joshua put a curse on anyone who tried to rebuild Jericho. Third, as if the Canaanites were not afraid enough because of the Red Sea, the utter defeat of Jericho made Joshua "FAMOUS THROUGHOUT THE LAND." However, most of the inhabitants still chose to stay and fight.

Chapter seven contains the sad story of Israel's first defeat in Canaan. God had specifically commanded that all of the treasure taken from Jericho would be put into God's treasury, not kept by individuals. However, Achan did steal some, which brought God's judgment on the entire nation (vs. 1).

Not knowing about this, Joshua was making plans for the next battle, the city of Ai (vs. 2–5). What they thought was going to be an easy victory became the loss of 36 Israelite men. Joshua went to God to discover the reason for this defeat (vs. 6–9). Like Moses, he was concerned about God's reputation being tarnished in Canaan because of this. It was obvious that something was wrong.

God told Joshua that the people had sinned by taking some of the spoils of Jericho (vs. 10–15). Significantly, God did not automatically point out who the culprit was. Instead, he gave Joshua instructions to narrow down by tribe, then clan, then family. As the men of the nation came before God, he would point out to Joshua when it was time to go to the next level. With more than 600,000 men, this would naturally take a great deal of time, possibly to make the nation keenly aware of the seriousness of the situation and so the offender could confess on his own. Joshua followed God's instructions perfectly (vs. 16–18).

When Achan was finally singled out, Joshua demanded to know what happened (vs. 19–26). Achan said that when he saw the gold, silver, and robe, he took them and hid them in the ground under his tent. He knew it was sin, but he did it anyway. God's penalty for this sin was the death of Achan and his entire family and possessions. They were stoned to death then completely burned, then Joshua put a memorial of stones over that spot as a reminder of God's judgment.

Chapter eight shows the result of Achan's sin being discovered and punished. Rather than sending only 3,000 warriors (7:4) to attack head-on, Joshua sent 30,000 warriors to set an ambush for Ai (vs. 1–9). Joshua would personally lead a contingent against Ai, then pretend to retreat, like the previous time. Again the warriors of Ai would chase them down, celebrating their second victory over Yehovah (something that Jericho could not accomplish), but the ambush troops would capture their city behind them. The plan worked exactly as intended because God was with them this time (vs. 10–23). All the people of Ai were killed, and the city was burnt to the ground.

There were a few instances during Moses' time when God had Moses stand in a particular spot or do something during an event to prove that God was the one fighting for the Israelites. One situation was in Exodus 17:8–16 when Joshua and the Israelites fought the Amalekites. During the battle, Moses was to keep his hands lifted high in the air. While they were lifted, Israel won; when they fell, Israel lost. Aaron and Hur ended up holding Moses' arms for him, and the battle was finally won. In a similar case at Ai, God told Joshua to hold out his "CURVED SWORD" (vs. 18), which he did "UNTIL ISRAEL HAD ANNIHILATED ALL WHO LIVED IN AI" (vs. 26), just as God had promised. The king of Ai was captured alive, and Joshua had him publicly hanged (vs. 29).

The remainder of the chapter describes the fulfillment of Moses' command to the people in Deuteronomy 11:26–32. When the people entered the land, they were to read the book of the Law, setting out both the blessings for obedience and the curses for disobedience on Mounts Gerizim and Ebal. After the victory at Ai, Joshua did what Moses had said (vs. 30–35). They built the altar, offered the sacrifices, and read the whole law in the presence of all of the people. No one in the entire nation was ignorant of what God had said.

Chapter nine records what was probably Joshua's weakest moment as Israel's leader. Through Moses, God had made a distinction between cities that would be far away from Israel's new land and those located within the land (Deuteronomy 20:10–18). If the city was far away, Israel was allowed to make a peace treaty with them, making them Israel's servants. However, for cities within the land, they were to be utterly destroyed so that Israel would not be led astray from the worship of Yehovah.

It seems that this information had been leaked in Canaan, and though most of the cities chose to fight Israel, Gibeon (a Hivite city) did not. Instead, they sent a convoy of ambassadors dressed in worn-out clothing, carrying dry bread and empty, cracked canteens, to "prove" that they had come from a long distance (vs. 1–13). Coming into Israel's camp, they acted weary from their long trip, asking for a peace treaty and recounting all of the wonderful things they had heard that God had done for Israel, all the way back to the Red Sea, just as Rahab had done.

Verses 14–15 are the climax (or trough) of the story. "THE [ISRAELITE] MEN EXAMINED SOME OF THEIR PROVISIONS, BUT THEY FAILED TO ASK THE LORD'S ADVICE." Relying on their own wisdom, Joshua and the elders of Israel "MADE A PEACE TREATY WITH THEM," sealed with an oath to Yehovah.

When Israel approached the Hivite cities only three days later, they discovered the deception (vs. 16–21). Naturally, they were furious, and many in Israel demanded that Joshua break the peace treaty and destroy all of the Hivites. However, because of the oath the leaders took, they refused to break it and call down judgment upon themselves. Instead, they decided to treat the Hivites as long-distance foreigners and made them their servants. Specifically, the Hivites would spend their days chopping wood and carrying water for Israel and God's altar.

Of course, Joshua wanted to know why they had acted out this deception (vs. 22–27). The answer was simply the truth of their previous claim. They knew of God's works on behalf of Israel, and they did not want to die with the others. Yet they knew they were at his mercy, so they humbly said, "SO NOW WE ARE IN YOUR POWER. DO TO US WHAT YOU THINK IS GOOD AND APPROPRIATE." Even with his flaws, Joshua was a godly man, and he kept his promise to them. They remained alive as servants of Israel. What a powerful reminder to seek the Lord for wisdom rather than relying on our own understanding (Proverbs 3:5–6; James 1:5).

Chapter ten explains the ramifications of the peace treaty Joshua made with Gibeon in chapter nine. After hearing of the overwhelming victories at Jericho and Ai and learning that Gibeon, a huge city with many warriors, had joined Israel, the king of Jerusalem created a coalition with four other regional Amorite kings to stop Israel once and for all (vs. 1–5). They decided that their best attack would be against Gibeon because Israel would be forced to fight the whole coalition, rather than one king at a time. Under attack, Gibeon called on Israel for their promised support, which Joshua provided (vs. 6–11). He must have been naturally worried about the enormous battle he was about to enter, but God told him that he would fight for Israel and that Israel would indeed win. Joshua noted that more Amorite warriors were killed by God's large hailstones than by Israelite warriors.

That was not the best part, though. At one point, Joshua prayed for the day to physically be extended, so night did not overtake them before the battle was over (vs. 12–14). In a very specific prayer, he commanded both the sun and the moon to stop at their locations, probably because dusk was quickly approaching. In an unprecedented act of gracious provision, "THE LORD LISTENED TO THE VOICE OF A MAN" (NASB). We should note that many believers and unbelievers alike do not accept this to have taken place literally. They give all kinds of reasons as to why it is not physically and scientifically possible for the earth to stop rotating around the sun. Others use this as proof that the Bible cannot be accepted in matters of science because the sun cannot "stop" since it does not move around the earth. No matter the arguments, they all come back to one premise: the Bible, as written, is not completely trustworthy. Once a person takes this stance, their interpretation will necessarily be flawed. However, the God who created the sun, moon, and earth and put the laws of nature into motion can certainly suspend them when he deems necessary, including stopping the earth's rotation while showering a valley with large hailstones. "IS ANYTHING IMPOSSIBLE FOR THE LORD?" (Genesis 18:14)[3]

When Joshua heard that the five kings were all hiding together in a cave, he ordered them to be locked in until the battle was over (vs. 16–27). Once everyone but a few stragglers was defeated, Joshua brought out the five kings and had them hanged. Their bodies were thrown back into the cave, and it was closed up. "THAT DAY" Joshua began a campaign against all of the cities of those kings and those around them (vs. 28–39). Over the next week, Joshua moved from one fortified city to the next, destroying them as they stood against Yehovah. The refrain is repeated that each one fell like the one before it. Thus, "JOSHUA DEFEATED THE WHOLE [SOUTHERN PART OF THE] LAND…IN ONE CAMPAIGN," then they went back home to rest (vs. 40–43).

Chapter eleven is essentially a replay of chapter ten but in the north. Not learning from the utter destruction of the coalition of the southern kings, King Jabin of Hazor formed a coalition of kings from northern Canaan intent on defeating Israel (vs. 1–5). No matter how many warriors Israel had, facing an army "AS NUMEROUS AS THE SAND ON THE SEASHORE AND…A LARGE NUMBER OF HORSES AND CHARIOTS" must have struck fear into them.

God promised Joshua that Israel would win this battle in a single day and commanded them to hamstring all of the enemy's horses once it was over (vs. 6–15). For some people, this seems cruel, especially since no specific reason is given in this chapter. Why did the horses need to suffer this fate? It likely has to do with God's instructions in Deuteronomy 17:16. Prophesying that the people would one day ask for a king, God instructed that their king "NOT ACCUMULATE HORSES FOR HIMSELF." Doing so would reveal a heart that trusted in military strength rather than on God. Thus, instead of letting Israel keep the war horses, they were to disable them, demonstrating their trust in God. In

---

[3] Again, this seems to be a simplistic, even naïve, response to what is a serious scientific charge. However, the very nature of a miracle is that it temporarily defies natural laws, There is not meant to be a scientific explanation. Rather than suspending belief, the suspense of natural law should bolster faith in God.

one of the best epitaphs of Scripture we read, "JOSHUA DID AS HE WAS TOLD. HE DID NOT IGNORE ANY OF THE COMMANDS THE LORD HAD GIVEN MOSES" (vs. 15).

The rest of the chapter (vs. 16–23) is a summary of the land that Israel conquered from the Negev (far south) to the Lebanon Valley (far north). Verse 18 notes that this took "QUITE SOME TIME." Specifically, it took about seven years to conquer all of Canaan (subtract the 38 years of wandering in the desert in Deuteronomy 2:14 from Caleb's 45 years in Joshua 14:7–10). Only the Gibeonites made peace with Israel; the rest fought and were destroyed. Even the Anakites, whom the spies were deathly afraid of (Numbers 13:28), were no match against Yehovah going before the Israelites.

Chapter twelve brings us to the halfway point of the book and summarizes the end of the desert wandering (Numbers 21) and the first half of Joshua. In verses 1–6 Joshua recounted the defeat of "THE KINGS OF THE LAND...ON THE EAST SIDE OF THE JORDAN." These were taken care of while Moses still led the nation before they crossed into Canaan. These included primarily the Amorites and Rephaites. This land was given to the tribes of Reuben and Gad and half of the tribe of Manasseh.

Verses 7–24 list "A TOTAL OF THIRTY-ONE KINGS" whom Joshua led the people to defeat "ON THE WEST SIDE OF THE JORDAN." These nations included "THE HITTITES, AMORITES, CANAANITES, PERIZZITES, HIVITES, AND JEBUSITES." It is important to note that they conquered only the main fortified strongholds in these regions, not individual villages or even entire nations. It was left to the tribes to clear their lands completely.

Chapter thirteen begins the second half of the book, which details the parceling out and settling of the land of Canaan by the remaining "NINE TRIBES AND THE HALF-TRIBE OF MANASSEH" (vs. 7). Verse one notes that Joshua was very old, but we do not know exactly what that means. According to 24:29, he was 110 years old when he died, when "A LONG TIME PASSED AFTER THE LORD MADE ISRAEL SECURE FROM ALL THEIR ENEMIES" (23:1), and Joshua acknowledged that he was very old. How many years are between chapters 13 and 23 is unknown.

As mentioned in the chapter twelve notes, God said that "A GREAT DEAL OF LAND REMAIN[ED] TO BE CONQUERED." Joshua's job was to lead the nation to break the strongholds of the nations over the land of Canaan. Once the land was parceled out to the tribes, they would be responsible for clearing the remainder of the peoples from their land. The next several chapters (13–19) lay out the borders of the various tribes. The key is to notice that the borders were assigned to the tribes. There was going to be no fighting for land. God had given them the land as a nation, and God divided it out to them through Moses (east of Jordan) and Joshua (west of Jordan).

Sadly, Israel's downfall that would plague them for centuries was already evident here. Speaking of the two-and-a-half eastern tribes, "BUT THE ISRAELITES DID NOT CONQUER THE GESHURITES AND MAACATHITES; GESHUR AND MAACAH LIVE AMONG ISRAEL TO THIS VERY DAY" (when this was written; vs. 13). The book of Judges will show the devastation that occurred because of the peoples that Israel allowed to remain in the land.

Another point of interest is that the tribe of Levi would not receive any land. Chapter 20 will deal with the Levitical cities, but, because they were the priests of God among the people, "THEIR INHERITANCE [WAS] THE SACRIFICIAL OFFERINGS" (vs. 14). In other words, the Levites lived off of the sacrifices and offerings given by the other tribes. More specifically, "THEIR INHERITANCE [WAS] THE LORD GOD OF ISRAEL" himself, as they served him (vs. 33).

Chapter fourteen begins the record of how Canaan was divided among the western tribes. Although verse one says that the territories were assigned by Eleazar, Joshua, and the tribal leaders, verse two clarifies that they determined the boundaries "BY DRAWING LOTS," which was a way to hear from God. It is also clarified that Joseph did not receive an allotment, but his two sons did, Manasseh and Ephraim. Since Levi did not receive an allotment, that balanced the twelve tribal sections.

Verses 6–15 record a special conversation between Caleb and Joshua. These were the only two men who survived the desert-wandering judgment because they faithfully stood against the other ten spies and said that God could be trusted to conquer Canaan for Israel. Because of their faithfulness, even when the entire nation rebelled, they were allowed to enter the land and watch God fulfill exactly what they knew he would.

Caleb reminded Joshua that he was 40 years old when they spied out the land. Forty-five years later he was "STILL AS STRONG AS WHEN MOSES SENT [HIM] OUT" to spy. He had the same energy and was finally ready to conquer the hill country that God promised he could have (Deuteronomy 1:36). Interestingly, the hill country was the home of the Anakites, whom the spies were afraid of when they gave their report (Numbers 13:28). After asking "GOD TO EMPOWER CALEB," Joshua released him to take his land. "THEN THE LAND WAS FREE OF WAR" (vs. 15). What a perfect reward for a faithful man.

Chapters fifteen through nineteen detail the lots apportioned to each of the tribes, including the specific borders and cities included within those borders. Joshua began with Judah, the largest tribe and the most prominent, probably due to Jacob's blessing in Genesis 49:8–12. Judah's land was the southernmost part of Israel, extending east-west between the Dead Sea and the Mediterranean Sea and north-south from the wilderness to Jerusalem (vs. 1–12).

Although he was a Simeonite, Caleb's land fell within Judah's borders (vs. 13). Eventually, all of Simeon would be enveloped by Judah. Caleb had enough land that he was able to bequeath a large portion to his daughter and her husband (vs. 18–19). According to verses 20–62, Judah received more than 100 cities plus their surrounding towns, and the land had areas of desert, hills, and lowlands. However, Judah was "UNABLE TO CONQUER THE JEBUSITES LIVING IN JERUSALEM," and they were still there at the time of the writing of the book (vs. 63).[4]

Chapters sixteen and seventeen address the tribes of Jacob's favorite son, Joseph (Ephraim and Manasseh), and the other prominent family of Israel. Moses had already granted half of Manasseh some land on the eastern side of

---

[4] This argues for an early date for the book's writing. This note had to be added to the text before David's day, when he ran the Jebusites out of Jerusalem.

the Jordan River. The western portion began north of Judah's northern border and extended further north "INTO THE HILL COUNTRY OF BETHEL," between the Jordan and the Mediterranean Sea (16:1–3). Ephraim received the larger, southern portion of this allotment (16:4–9). However, like Judah, they "DID NOT CONQUER THE CANAANITES LIVING IN GEZER," placing them into servitude instead (16:10).

In addition to the two sections east of the Jordan, Manasseh received lots on the west side as well (17:1–6). About seven years earlier, five daughters of Zelophehad, a descendant of Manasseh, had requested that Moses grant them their father's inheritance because he had no sons (Numbers 26:33; 27:1–7; 36:1–6, 10–12). When they brought this request to Eleazar, Joshua, and the elders, they received what Moses had promised to them at God's instruction. Manasseh also did not defeat the Canaanites living in their section of the land (17:7–13).

The two brother-tribes were not happy that they received only "one" share of the land, even though they were considered two tribes (17:14–18). They asked Joshua for more land, but he refused, saying that they had plenty of land, not "JUST ONE TRIBAL ALLOTMENT," but they would have to work for it—clearing out both trees and Canaanites—which they seemed unwilling to do. It is possible they thought, because Joshua was an Ephraimite, that he would be willing to grant them more land as a "favor." Like Caleb, Joshua received a special portion within the borders of his tribe, Ephraim (19:49–51).

Chapters eighteen and nineteen explain how the rest of the land was divided between the seven remaining tribes. Although Eleazar and Joshua were responsible for casting lots to determine which tribe received which piece of land, it seems that it was up to the tribes to come to the leaders to receive it, which the last seven had not done. After the tabernacle had been established at Shiloh for some time, Joshua scolded them for procrastinating in taking their inheritance (18:1–10). His solution was for twenty-one men (three from each of the seven tribes) to explore and map out the remaining land and divide it into seven portions. Then he would draw lots to see which tribe would receive each portion.

Benjamin was drawn first (18:11–28). They received the portion between Judah and Ephraim, with the Jordan River on the east but not quite to the Mediterranean Sea. Their portion included well-known cities such as Jericho, Bethel, and Jerusalem.

Simeon was drawn second (19:1–9). Because Judah's portion ended up being too much for them, Simeon received some of the southernmost parts of Judah's territory on the southwest corner of the land. Zebulun received the third section in the northern part of the country, due west of the Sea of Galilee (19:10–16). They were bordered by the Mediterranean Sea on the west (Genesis 49:13), Asher on the north, Naphtali on the east, and Issachar on the south.

The fourth portion went to Issachar (19:17–23). It was a central strip of land, with the Jordan on the east, Manasseh to the south, and Zebulun and Naphtali to the north. The fifth portion went to Asher, the northernmost allotment (19:24–31). Asher spanned the Mediterranean coastline from Zebulun north to Sidon in Lebanon, with Naphtali on its eastern side. Naphtali was the sixth lot drawn, and they received the remaining land by the Sea of Galilee, north of Issachar and east of Asher (19:32–39). This included the region later known as *Galilee*, which housed Jesus' hometown of Nazareth, Cana, Capernaum, and many other well-known places.

The final lot went to Dan (19:40–48). They were given the lush section between Judah and Ephraim and west of Benjamin, right on the Mediterranean coast. This was the land of the Philistines, including the city of Joppa. Like many of the other tribes, Dan did not conquer the Canaanites in their area. Unlike the others, however, Dan eventually ran away from their allotted portion, finally settling in the far north (even beyond Asher and Naphtali), and their original land was assimilated into Judah (see Judges 18).

Chapter twenty resolves the issue of the cities of refuge. Now that the land had been properly divided among the tribes, the cities of refuge could be assigned. According to this chapter and Numbers 35:9–29, God had told Moses that the Israelites were to choose six cities that would serve as safe havens for people who accidentally killed someone else. Each side of the Jordan

River was to have three cities, and they were to be spaced out throughout the land so that an accidental killer could find sanctuary, safe from the victim's blood avenger, while the case was determined to be either accidental or premeditated. According to the law, if it was premeditated the killer was to be executed for murder. If they determined that it was indeed accidental, the killer was required to remain in the city of refuge until the high priest died. At that time, the killer was free to return to his home, knowing that the blood avenger could not take out his revenge against him (without himself being executed for murder).

On the west side of the Jordan, the cities they chose were Kedesh (Galilee region of Naphtali; north), Shechem (Ephraim; central), and Kiriath Arba (also called Hebron; Judah; south). East of the Jordan, each of the three tribes had one city: Bezer (Reuben), Ramoth-Gilead (Gad), and Golan (Manasseh).

Chapter twenty-one addresses the other special cities that Israel needed—the Levitical cities. Because the Levites did not receive a land inheritance like the other tribes, God told Moses that the nation would set aside certain cities amongst all the tribes. These cities would be where the Levites and their families would live, and they would retain grazing rights immediately surrounding their cities. According to Numbers 35:1–8, they were to receive six cities on the east side of the Jordan River and forty-two on the west side, for a total of forty-eight.

This chapter lists which cities were given to the Levites after the division of the land between the other tribes. Of special note is the fact that all six of the cities of refuge listed in the previous chapter were also Levitical cities. There were three clans within the tribe of Levi—Kohath, Gershon, and Merari—and Kohath was subdivided into the priests (Aaron's family) and non-priests.

The priestly clan of Kohath received "13 CITIES FROM THE TRIBES OF JUDAH, SIMEON, AND BENJAMIN" in the south (vs. 4). The rest of the Kohathites lived in "TEN CITIES FROM THE CLANS OF THE TRIBE OF EPHRAIM, AND FROM THE TRIBE OF DAN AND THE HALF-TRIBE OF MANASSEH" in central Israel (vs. 5, 9–26). This covered about half of the land, including two cities of refuge. The Gershonites received thirteen cities within Issachar, Asher, Naphtali, and the half-tribe of Manasseh in Transjordan, including two cities of refuge (vs. 6, 27–33). The Merari clan received "12 CITIES FROM THE TRIBES OF REUBEN, GAD, AND ZEBULUN," spanning the Jordan and the remaining two cities of refuge (vs. 7, 34–40).

There is some debate over the final three verses of this chapter. Joshua wrote that God faithfully did everything that he had promised, not leaving out one thing, and the people conquered the land and lived in it (vs. 43–45). Since Joshua had already noted repeatedly that the people did not fully conquer the peoples in their respective territories, some charge the Scriptures with being untrue. As is often the case, context clears up the confusion. There was no expectation that the Israelite tribes were to conquer the Canaanites in one fell swoop; this would certainly take time (Exodus 23:27–31). The strongholds had been broken during their previous multi-year campaign, but smaller tribes were scattered throughout the land. God had certainly promised to drive the Canaanites out, but he said that required obedience on the part of the Israelites (Deuteronomy 28:1–14). If they did not obey, one of their punishments would be that the Canaanites would constantly be a trouble for them (Numbers 33:55). The book of Judges records that the nation quickly turned to idolatry after Joshua died and did not drive out the Canaanites, incurring God's promised judgment (Judges 2:6–23). Thus, when Joshua wrote that God had fulfilled everything he promised to the nation, that was true. He brought them into the land, conquering the major strong cities before them, and portioned out the land to them. What they did with it next also received his promise, albeit for judgment instead of blessing.

Chapter twenty-two records what could have turned into the first civil war of the newly planted nation of Israel. After helping their national brothers conquer the Canaanite strongholds, the three Transjordan tribes (Reuben, Gad, and half-Manasseh) were released by Joshua to return home to their families (vs. 1–9). They had fulfilled the promise they made to Moses about not quitting early when he granted them the land on the eastern side of the Jordan River (Numbers 32). Joshua thanked them for their faithfulness and rewarded them with plenty of the spoil taken during the battles. On their way home, just before they crossed out of Canaan/Israel over the Jordan to their land, the men built an altar to God (vs. 10–12). However, when the rest of Israel heard about this, they were furious and made plans to attack the two-and-a-half tribes, eliminating them.

They sent a party consisting of Phineas, the priest, and one leader from each of the ten western tribes to demand repentance for this act of apparent sacrilege (vs. 13–20). They charged them with building an altar distinct from the one at the tabernacle, which would certainly bring God's wrath. Furthermore, this altar stood on the west side of the Jordan, among the ten tribes, rather than on the east side among the "rebel" tribes. How could they do this to their brothers?

Fortunately, it was a simple case of misunderstanding (vs. 21–29). The eastern tribes swore that they had no such thing in mind, to make sacrifices on an altar that God had not commissioned. Instead, they were afraid that, over time, those tribes in Israel would bar the Transjordan tribes from worshiping with them at the tabernacle. This altar was to serve as a memorial for future generations that they, too, were Israelites who worshiped Yehovah properly. Hearing the explanation, the representatives of Israel were satisfied, and they rejoiced together that they had not witnessed the first falling away from the proper worship of God (vs. 30–34).

Chapter twenty-three contains the first half of the farewell address that Joshua made to "ALL ISRAEL, INCLUDING THE ELDERS, RULERS, JUDGES, AND LEADERS" (vs. 2). In this speech, Joshua made three assertions. First, he reminded them of everything God had done for them and said that, if they continued to be loyal to God and obey his law, he would finish driving the Canaanites out of the land (vs. 3–8).

Second, he warned that, if they did not remain loyal to God and instead made "ALLIANCES WITH THESE NATIONS THAT REMAIN NEAR YOU, AND INTERMARRY WITH THEM AND ESTABLISH FRIENDLY RELATIONS WITH THEM," God would not drive out those nations and would instead let Israel disappear from the land (vs. 9–13). Moses had already told this generation that expulsion from the land would be God's punishment if they refused to stay loyal to him (Deuteronomy 29:28), although he promised to bring them back when they finally turned back to him, an event which is still future (Deuteronomy 30:1–10).

Third, because of God's unwavering faithfulness, in the same way that he had fulfilled all his promises to Israel to that point, he would also fulfill all of his curses upon them if they disobeyed him (vs. 14–16). For those who believe that the "God of love" could never punish or curse anyone, they forget that both blessings and curses are bound up in God's faithfulness, and he can never be unfaithful.

Chapter twenty-four concludes the book with the second half of Joshua's farewell speech to Israel. In the first half (chapter 23), Joshua reminded Israel of God's promises and warned them to remain loyal to him. In this chapter, he took it one step further. Rather than simply allowing them to say, "We are willing to do all the words that the LORD has said," which the previous generation said after coming out of Egypt and then failed (Exodus 24:4), Joshua led them in a sort of vow renewal ceremony. He did this in four steps.

First, he reminded them of their history, not just in Egypt but back to Abraham (vs. 1–13). This was important because Moses had already told them that they were not special for their own sake but because of God's promises to Abraham, Isaac, and Jacob (Deuteronomy 7:7–11). So Joshua reminded them of the promises to the patriarchs, then showed how those promises began to be fulfilled. The people of this generation were either children or not yet born when they left Egypt, but many of them still remembered the miracles, and all of them experienced the recent conquest of the land. This section is essentially a summary of the books of Exodus through Joshua, up to their present time.

Second, Joshua gave them a short exhortation to remain loyal to Yehovah (vs. 14–15). His command to "PUT ASIDE THE GODS YOUR ANCESTORS WORSHIPED BEYOND THE EUPHRATES AND IN EGYPT" refers back to Abraham and the generations in Egypt. In verse 15 he challenged them to make their decision. It was similar to Moses' challenge before they entered the land, seven years earlier: "LOOK! I HAVE SET BEFORE YOU TODAY LIFE AND PROSPERITY ON THE ONE HAND, AND DEATH AND DISASTER ON THE OTHER. ... THEREFORE CHOOSE LIFE SO THAT YOU AND YOUR DESCENDANTS MAY LIVE!" (Deuteronomy 30:15, 19)

Third, following their promise to remain faithful to Yehovah (vs. 16–18), Joshua warned them that they would not remain faithful. In fact, Israel's greatest downfall, which led to their captivities, was the worship of false gods.

Fourth, after the people insisted that they really would remain loyal to Yehovah, Joshua drew up a covenant that the people unanimously agreed to (vs. 21–28). This did not supersede the covenant God made through Moses; it was that generation's promise to follow through with that covenant that the previous generation made.

Joshua died at the age of 110, closing what was probably the most faithful time in Israel's history (vs. 29–33). Verse 31 notes that the nation was faithful until that generation died. A final closing note is that Joseph's bones were finally buried in the new land, just as he had requested when he died nearly 500 years earlier (Genesis 50:24–26).

Judges

The book of Judges records one of the worst periods of history for the Israelite nation. God's intention in bringing the nation out of Egyptian captivity into Canaan was to rule as their sole king under a theocracy. The people were to worship and serve him faithfully by living out the Covenant Law they had agreed to, both in Exodus (first generation out of Egypt) and in Deuteronomy and Joshua (second generation). Instead, Judges tells the story of a people who repeatedly refused to live up to their end of the covenant.

In reality, this book should never have been written because the story it contains should never have occurred. During the approximately three hundred years of the judges, the nation went through a "spin cycle" where Israel sinned (failure), God judged them using a foreign nation (punishment), Israel repented (repentance), and God delivered them with one or more judges (deliverance), who then ruled in peace for a period. This repetition of grace in the face of rebellion is the glimmer of light in a dark theme. Sadly, the two verses that best sum up this book are 2:19 and 21:25.

"WHEN A LEADER DIED, THE NEXT GENERATION WOULD AGAIN ACT MORE WICKEDLY THAN THE PREVIOUS ONE." (2:19)

"IN THOSE DAYS ISRAEL HAD NO KING. EACH MAN DID WHAT HE CONSIDERED TO BE RIGHT." (21:25)

We cannot be sure who wrote the book of Judges because no name is attached to it. However, due to verses like 21:25, which seem to indicate that the times of "no king" were in the past, many scholars believe that Samuel compiled Judges later.

Chapter one records the continuation of Israel's conquest of Canaan. "AFTER JOSHUA DIED" was a key turning point in the life of the nation (vs. 1). God had hand-selected Joshua as Israel's leader following Moses' death (Deuteronomy 31:14–22), but no leader was set to replace Joshua, so the nation asked for God's direction. He responded that Judah should be the first to instigate the attack in Canaan, so they requested the help of Simeon and found success in both tribal territories (vs. 2–8). This success included the overthrow of Adoni-Bezek, who claimed to have conquered more than 70 other kings himself. Caleb recruited help to conquer Hebron by offering one of his daughters in marriage to a successful warrior (vs. 9–13). Caleb's daughter and son-in-law also gained more land due to Caleb's later generosity toward them (vs. 14–15). The writer noted that Moses' in-laws also moved into Canaan with the Israelites and lived among the descendants of Judah, in the south (vs. 16–20).

Issachar is the only western tribe not mentioned in the remainder of the chapter. Judah and Simeon defeated their enemies (except those on the coast, because they had iron chariots), but the other tribes did not. The sad refrain throughout vs. 21–33 repeats, "THE MEN OF [THE TRIBE] DID NOT CONQUER THE PEOPLE LIVING IN" their tribal areas. Dan's story was even worse. Rather than simply living among the Canaanites in their area, Dan was rebuffed by the Amorites, who did not allow the Danites to take their allotted land (vs. 34–36).

Chapter two contains a rare public appearance of the "ANGEL OF THE LORD" (a Christophany[1]) to a large group of people at once. This seems to be a flashback to before Joshua's death (vs. 1–5). The writer said that God moved from Gilgal to Bokim, accusing the people of not tearing down the pagan altars as he had commanded them to do (evidence that this was God himself, not just a messenger). They wept for their sin and repented, promising to worship and serve only Yehovah, which they did during Joshua's life. However, when

---

[1] "Christophany" refers to the visible appearance of the Son of God, the second member of the Trinity, before he was incarnated as Jesus.

Joshua and the leaders of his generation died, the people turned away from God (vs. 6–10). This was now the fourth generation out of Egypt. Not only had they not seen the miracles of Egypt, but they also did not have the experiences of the second generation. This generation had only their stories without any real personal experience with God.

Verses 11–19 summarize the rest of the book. For approximately 300 years, the Israelites turned away from God to worship the pagan Baals, so God punished them by sending the nations to plunder and defeat the Israelites. Upon their repentance, God raised men who delivered and then ruled them as judges. This restored peace and prosperity until the judge and that generation died. Sadly, each successive **"GENERATION WOULD AGAIN ACT MORE WICKEDLY THAN THE PREVIOUS ONE."**

The chapter ends with a difficult passage regarding the continued existence of the nations in Canaan (vs. 20–23). The question regards whether God or Joshua left the nations to test the faithfulness of the people. The best interpretation is that God would test Israel with the nations that Joshua left unconquered. The first verses of the next chapter clarify that God did not give them over to Joshua's campaign for two reasons.

Chapter three continues the account from the previous chapter. God did not allow Joshua to conquer all the Canaanite nations for two reasons (vs. 1–4). First, God left them to test Israel's faithfulness. How they responded to the pagan nations around them would reveal whether they would remain faithful to Yehovah. The second reason is a practical result of the first. This generation had not had to fight the Canaanites yet, and their willingness (or lack thereof) to do so would come out of their faithfulness or unfaithfulness. Essentially, God left them some enemies so they had the opportunity to live out their faithfulness to him. Unfortunately, they did the opposite, falling in line with the pagan nations and their worship practices (vs. 5–7).

Verses 8–11 reveal why Othniel received special mention as Caleb's son-in-law in chapter one. After the first punishment by a pagan king, God raised Othniel as Israel's first deliverer and judge. After eight years of subjection,

Othniel delivered Israel and ruled her for forty years. Thus began the pattern for the remainder of the book.

The second judge was Ehud (vs. 12–30). When the Israelites turned from God, he gave them over to King Eglon of Moab for eighteen years. When they finally repented, God used Ehud to deliver them. A favorite Sunday School story recounts that Ehud was a left-handed man. In what sounds like a bad comedy, Eglon's guards allowed Ehud to see Eglon, patting down only his left side but missing the dagger strapped to his right leg. Ehud gained a private audience with Eglon and stabbed him to death, losing his dagger in the king's enormous belly. That day Ehud led the Israelites to a victory over the Moabites, with the resulting peace lasting eighty years. He was followed by Shamgar, who fought the Philistines.

Chapter four tells the story of Deborah and Barak and their defeat of Sisera and the Canaanites. There is nothing in the text that tells when Deborah became a judge or why she was chosen instead of a man, like the other judges. Given her rebuke of Barak's apparent unwillingness to lead, it is possible that no men were willing and able at that time.[2]

For twenty years, the Canaanites, under the direction of General Sisera, had persecuted the Israelites (vs. 1–5). At some point, God directed Barak to go against them with an army of 10,000 men, but he had not done so (vs. 6–11). When Deborah called him out on it, he agreed to lead the charge, but only if she went with him. She agreed, noting that his lack of leadership would be punished by the victory going to a woman rather than to him.

When Sisera saw the army coming out against him, he gathered his troops and chariots and rode out to rout them (vs. 12–16). However, Yehovah fought for Israel, and Sisera's army was destroyed. Sisera got away on foot, looking for refuge with friends. Coming to his friend's tent, Sisera saw the wife, Jael,

---

[2] This should not be taken, as some have done, to prove that women can lead a church today if there are no qualified men. Paul is clear on the qualifications of elders and deacons, that they are to be men. See the notes in *New Testament Chapter by Chapter* for further discussion on Paul's instructions in 1 Timothy 2:8–3:13 and Titus 1:5–9.

and asked for shelter (vs. 17–24). She hid him in her tent, gave him warm milk, and lulled him to sleep. When he was fast asleep, she drove a tent peg through his temples, killing him immediately. When Barak arrived, she showed him Sisera's body. That was the beginning of the end of the Canaanite power over Israel.

Chapter five records the anthem that Deborah and Barak composed after their victory over the Canaanites in chapter four. Verse two is a summary verse of the song, repeated at the end of the first stanza: "WHEN THE PEOPLE ANSWERED THE CALL TO WAR— PRAISE THE LORD!" The first stanza is a generic praise of God for his past actions (vs. 3–9). They sang of God's presence at Sinai, his defeat of Edom, and one of the previous judges, Shamgar. Then they turned to Jael, who would be the heroine of the second stanza.

The rest of the song/chapter recounts the story that just occurred in the previous chapter (vs. 10–31). The first half tells of the army that stood with Barak. Five tribes are named as having stood against the Canaanites—Ephraim, Benjamin, Zebulun, Issachar, and Naphtali—though Barak did not necessarily recruit from all of them (4:6, 10). Reuben, Dan, and Asher were called out as not joining the battle, although it seems Reuben strongly considered it, along with those who lived in Gilead (Transjordan)—Gad and half of Manasseh. Thus, only Judah and Simeon (Levi was not allowed to join battles) are not listed at all. The second half celebrates Jael's courage and strength to kill Sisera when he was vulnerable. In poetic form, Deborah and Barak envisioned Sisera's mother thinking about her son's great victories, while he lay dead in Jael's tent. The chapter closes with a note that Israel had peace for forty years after this.

Chapters six through eight tell the stories surrounding Gideon's rule. After Deborah's forty years of peace, Israel turned away from God again. This time he used the Midianites to punish them. Verses 1–10 describe a situation of nearly complete famine in Israel. Not only did the Midianites and Amalekites take the Israelites' crops, but they also took their animals as well, leaving them nothing. The writer compared them to locusts swarming over the land. When

Israel finally turned back to God after seven years of this, he sent an unnamed prophet to remind them of their wickedness, the reason for their plight. However, because they had turned to him, God would not let the punishment continue.

The angel of the Lord visited Gideon, who was hiding from the Midianites in a winepress while threshing wheat (vs. 11–18). When he addressed Gideon as courageous and said that God would help Gideon defeat Midian, Gideon responded with incredulity. Wasn't this situation God's doing? Would he really help them get out of it? Gideon and his family were small and weak; what could he accomplish? When promised God's presence, he asked for the first of several signs God would grant him. After receiving the supporting sign, he recognized this was truly God and was reassured by God that he would not die (vs. 19–24).

God's first objective was for Gideon to tear down the local Baal statue, set up by his own family (vs. 25–32). Gideon was too afraid to do it until the middle of the night, but he did take servants to help him and followed God's orders exactly. He pulled over the statue, built an altar to Yehovah, cut down the Asherah pole, and used the wood to make a sacrifice to God. The next morning, the damage was discovered and traced back to Gideon. However, his father (maybe beginning to understand the situation) stood up for him, nicknaming him Jerub-Baal, "Let Baal fight" his own battles.

With Gideon's obedience started, God moved him onto the next objective: doing battle with the enemy (vs. 33–40). The nations had come together against Israel and were camped, ready to attack. God had Gideon gather an army to fight them. After summoning men from several tribes, Gideon wanted another sign, his second. He asked God to work two miracles on successive nights with a piece of wool and the dew. God did exactly as Gideon asked, to encourage him in this mission.

Chapter seven records Gideon's battle against the Midianites. Once he had been reassured that God was with him, Gideon was ready to take his 32,000 men to fight. However, God turned the tables on him. God told him his army was too big (vs. 1–8). Gideon was sure that with a big army and God's help, he could win. But God wanted Gideon to rely totally on him, so he had Gideon send home everyone who was scared, reducing the army by two-thirds. However, even 10,000 was too many, so God had Gideon reduce it again. Watching how they drank water from a stream, God showed that only 300 men trusted him implicitly, and they would be Gideon's full army.

Naturally, Gideon's assurance was depleted again, so God offered him another sign (vs. 9–23). Sneaking down into the Midianite camp, Gideon heard one enemy soldier admit to another that he dreamt that Gideon would defeat them. With this confirmation, Gideon surrounded the enemy camp with his 300 men and the element of surprise. The combination of loud noise and unexpected light put the enemy into a panic. Thinking they had been invaded, they began to kill each other. The Israelites (including those originally sent home from the army) chased them down and killed them all.

Chapter eight best begins with 7:24. After the Midianites had been nearly defeated and were on the run, Gideon enlisted the Ephraimites to head off the two generals, Oreb and Zeeb, and kill them, which they did (7:24–25). However, the Ephraimites were upset that they were not included in the battle itself, but Gideon assuaged their insult by praising them for finishing the job (8:1–3).

The battle was not quite finished. Although the immediate Midianite army and generals had been killed, the kings and the rest of their armies were still on the run (vs. 4–12). Chasing them down, Gideon and his men asked for rest and supplies from the residents of Succoth, but they refused, so Gideon promised his revenge on them. When he finally caught the kings and killed the rest of the army, he returned to Succoth, beat the men of the city, then killed them (vs. 13–17). Finally, he killed the Midianite kings, as well, after they admitted to slaughtering Gideon's family (vs. 18–21).

Gideon never saw himself as a judge or king, so when the people offered to subject themselves to a Gideonic dynasty, he refused (vs. 22–27). However, he did take some of the battle spoil for himself and crafted an ephod, which became an idol of worship with Gideon as its "priest." Although "THE LAND HAD REST FOR 40 YEARS," the people were not faithful to God. Gideon married multiple wives and fathered a clan of 70 sons, much like a king would do (vs. 28–32). After his death, the nation returned fully to its idolatry and wickedness (vs. 33–35).

Chapter nine follows Gideon's story with the story of one of his sons, Abimelech, who was born to Gideon's concubine.[3] In 8:35 we read that Israel did not *"TREAT THE FAMILY OF JERUB BAAL FAIRLY,"* and this chapter explains that. When he was grown, Abimelech returned to Shechem, the home of his mother, and proposed that they install him as their ruler, rather than following Gideon's other seventy sons (vs. 1–6). They agreed, and he hired assassins to kill his seventy half-brothers, but the youngest one, Jotham, escaped. When Jotham heard that the people had indeed made Abimelech their ruler, he told a parable to the people, with a thorn bush representing Abimelech as their worst choice and their eventual destroyer (vs. 7–21). However, Jotham told them, God would judge whether they made the correct decision in killing his family and subjecting themselves to Abimelech.

Verse twenty-two says that *"ABIMELECH COMMANDED ISRAEL FOR THREE YEARS."* This is different from the other judges who "ruled" Israel. The word translated "commanded" occurs only here in Judges and only five other times in the Old Testament. It may indicate a type of authoritarian rule. This could be the method God used to create strife between the people and Abimelech (vs. 22–25). The writer clearly states that God was about to bring Jotham's prediction to fulfillment. The Shechemites gave their loyalty to a man named Gaal, who loudly proclaimed his disdain for Abimelech and challenged his rule (vs. 26–41). One of Abimelech's loyal followers informed him of the uprising and suggested that Abimelech ambush the traitors, which he did successfully. The next day he attacked Shechem and killed its citizens and leveled the city (vs. 42–45). The leaders of the city had fled, and Abimelech found them locked in a tower, which he burnt to the ground (vs. 46–49). Finally, he moved to another city and attempted to do the same thing when they took shelter in

---

[3] Although Gideon refused to be Israel's king, he named his son Abimelech, which means "my father is king."

their tower, but a woman dropped a millstone on his head, and he died at his assistant's hand (vs. 50–55). Thus, Jotham's prophecy came true; the people had chosen poorly and suffered the consequences for it (vs. 56–57).

Chapter ten contains two short stories showing the duplicity of the Israelites at this time. In verses 1–5 we find two more judges, Tola and Jair, who ruled Israel for a total of 45 years. Nothing is mentioned about idolatry or wickedness, just the judges. On the other hand, after those two, Israel again turned from Yehovah, choosing to worship gods from a variety of nations, so God handed them over to the Philistines and Ammonites (vs. 6–9). After eighteen years of oppression, it seems that it became especially bad "THAT EIGHTEENTH YEAR," specifically toward those Israelites on the east side of the Jordan in Gilead. When the people cried to God for help, he pushed back. "DID I NOT DELIVER YOU FROM EGYPT, THE AMORITES, THE AMMONITES, THE PHILISTINES, THE SIDONIANS, AMALEK, AND MIDIAN WHEN THEY OPPRESSED YOU?" (vs. 11–12) Since they had continued to turn away from him, what obligation did he have to deliver them again? However, rather than just asking for help or even saying that they had sinned, this time "THEY THREW AWAY THE FOREIGN GODS THEY OWNED AND WORSHIPED THE LORD," so he did deliver them again (vs. 15–16).

Chapter eleven tells the story of Jephthah and his battle against the Ammonites (beginning in 10:17). Like Abimelech, Jephthah's mother was a prostitute, so he did not have a good relationship with his brothers from his father's wife (vs. 1–3). They kicked him out of the house, and he formed a gang of "LAWLESS MEN."

"SOME TIME AFTER THIS," the Ammonites and Israel were at war, and the leaders of Gilead (Jephthah's clan) requested his help (vs. 4–11). When he refused, citing their past disdain for him, they begged him, promising to make him their leader if God granted them success in battle; he agreed to those terms. His first act as commander was to engage the Ammonites diplomatically (vs. 12–28). Asking why they were attacking Israel, he received the response that Ammon believed Israel had taken their land, and they wanted it back. Jephthah returned a message, detailing the true historical record—how Israel had defeated the Amorite king, Sihon, but they never attacked Moab or Ammon. This was true even though these nations tried to use Balaam to curse Israel (Numbers 22–24). If God had protected Israel so far, how did Ammon think they could defeat Israel now?[4] However, "THE AMMONITE KING DISREGARDED THE MESSAGE SENT BY JEPHTHAH."

With Ammon's response, God led Jephthah to take action against them (vs. 29–33). However, before going into battle, Jephthah vowed to God that, if God granted them success, whoever was the first to greet him at home would become a burnt offering to God. God did grant them success, but Jephthah was crushed when, returning home, his only child—a daughter—ran out to greet him first (vs. 34–40).

Much has been written about whether Jephthah fulfilled his vow or if his daughter simply remained a virgin in God's service for the rest of her life (and even why he made that vow at all!). Those who reject that he followed through with his vow literally insist 1) that human sacrifice was always an abomination to God; 2) that the girl's friends (and future generations) bemoaned her virginity, not her death; and 3) that God had established in the law a way to redeem a person who had been dedicated to him (Leviticus 27).

On the other hand, the natural reading of the passage seems to indicate that he did follow through with the sacrifice: 1) He said that he could not break his oath to God; 2) the special time to mourn her virginity with her friends was meaningless if they could mourn it the rest of her life; 3) the annual memorial feast is more appropriate for her death. Most importantly, the text states that, when she returned, "HE DID TO HER AS HE HAD VOWED." Because God had made provision for the redemption of a firstborn, this proves just how little Jephthah (and the entire nation, presumably) knew the Law at this time.

Chapter twelve records another sad turn of events in the wake of Israel's victory over the Ammonites. As they had done with Gideon (chapter eight),

---

[4] Verse 26 contains a rare time reference in Judges. According to Jephthah, Israel had been living in those areas for 300 years. If this refers to when they entered that area before the conquest of Canaan, approximately 1405 BC, Jephthah lived around 1100 BC.

the Ephraimites picked a fight with Jephthah because he had not invited them to join the battle (vs. 1–7). He responded that he had requested their help, but they did not come, so he attacked Ammon without them. (Whether this is true is unknown because the passage did not record it.) So Jephthah attacked Ephraim for their insolence and defeated them. Stationing a blockade at the Jordan River pass, Jephthah's men used the Ephraimites' inability to pronounce the "sh" sound to kill any who tried to escape. Jephthah died after leading Israel for six years.

The rest of this short chapter lists three more judges from various places in Israel but with little detail. "IBZAN OF BETHLEHEM" had at least sixty children and led Israel for seven years (vs. 8–10). "ELON THE ZEBULUNITE" ruled for ten years. Finally, Abdon from Pirathon led for eight years and had a total of seventy sons and grandsons who assisted him.

Chapter thirteen begins the famous story of Samson, who served for twenty years. Samson is the only judge whose story is recorded from birth to death. After forty years of Philistine oppression, God visited an infertile woman from the tribe of Dan and promised her a son to deliver Israel (vs. 1–7). The boy was to be a Nazirite, dedicated to God from his conception, meaning that even his mother had to remain ceremonially clean during her pregnancy (Numbers 6:1–8). When the woman told her husband, Manoah, about the news, he prayed that he would be able to hear it as well and get further information (vs. 8–14). God allowed the messenger to return, but no new information was necessary. They were to follow what he had told the woman originally.

Not knowing he was the angel of the Lord, Manoah asked if the man would stay for a meal (vs. 15–23). The messenger refused but encouraged the couple to present an offering to God. Wishing to honor this "prophet" when the baby was born, Manoah asked him his name. However, the name of God is incomprehensible, so he declined to give it.[5] As the offering burned, the

---

[5] This story offers several reasons to understand the angel of the LORD in the Old Testament to be the preincarnate Son of God.

messenger ascended to heaven in the flame. Realizing who they had been talking with, Manoah became afraid for his life, until his wife encouraged him, noting that they could easily have been killed and that the baby was promised to be born, which he was.

Chapter fourteen reveals that Samson had at least three great weaknesses: women/sex, instant gratification, and anger. The chapter opens with Samson seeing a beautiful woman and demanding that his father arrange a marriage, even though she was a Philistine (vs. 1–4). Although his father resisted, Samson insisted that he should be allowed to marry her. Possibly he argued that, since it was not against his Nazirite vow and not against the Mosaic Law, he would not be in violation of anything. The writer notes that God allowed this and would use it to begin Samson's war with Philistia.

When Manoah finally relented, Samson went to Timnah to meet with his wife-to-be (vs. 5–6). On the way, he was attacked by a young lion, but he easily overpowered it—our first indication of how God intended to use him. Later, passing that way again, he noticed bees making honey in the carcass and took some (vs. 7–9). This is the first record of his breaking the Nazirite vow—touching a dead animal. Additionally, he gave some to his parents to eat, causing them to be defiled as well, but he did not tell them where he got it.

The writer's description of Samson intentionally shows him to be no better than anyone else in Israel at this time— "SHE WAS RIGHT IN SAMSON'S EYES" (ESV) (see 17:6; 21:25). During the wedding feast (which most certainly involved beer and wine, against his Nazirite vow), Samson showed his penchant for showing off. In this case, he offered a riddle to the thirty men in his wedding party (vs. 10–20). If they could answer, he would give them thirty sets of clothes; if not, they would pay him the same.[6] Threatening to burn her and her family, the men persuaded Samson's wife to get the answer for them, so she nagged him until he finally told her. Receiving the answer, they went back to Samson and demanded their reward. Naturally, he knew what had

---

[6] Constable notes that this may indicate that Samson was not only lustful for woman but for clothing and wealth as well.

happened, so he went to Ashkelon (a Philistine city) and killed thirty men to fulfill his bargain. In a moment of self-discipline, he then returned to his father's home to cool down before seeing his wife again. Unbeknownst to him, she had been married off to his best man.

Chapter fifteen takes place "SOMETIME LATER," but it does not state how long. It must have been long enough that the woman's father thought Samson was not coming back, which is why he married her to another man. When Samson did return and discovered that his marriage had ended, he was furious (vs. 1–8). It seems that Samson may have had some remorse or second thoughts about killing those first men, but that was gone this time. Whatever he planned to do, he felt completely justified in doing it. The entire region would suffer his revenge. Catching 150 pairs of jackals, he tied torches to their tails and set them loose in the Philistine wheat harvest, destroying that year's crop. He also burned their "VINEYARDS AND OLIVE GROVES." He intended to starve them. When the Philistines discovered who had done this, they followed through with their initial threat to kill his wife and her family, meaning that nothing she had done to protect herself accomplished anything. Acting in revenge again, Samson killed the men who had killed his wife, then he lived in a cave. He honestly thought that he was done fighting.

When the men of Judah discovered that Samson was living in their territory, they voluntarily acted to turn him over to the Philistines to save themselves from harm (vs. 9–13). There is a sad irony in the fact that the Israelites would rather have gotten rid of God's deliverer than face further potential backlash from their enemies. Approaching Samson they told him their plan. Surprisingly, Samson agreed to be handed over as long as the Jews did not kill him themselves; they promised they would not. When the Philistines saw him, they shouted and rushed to seize him, but God's Spirit empowered him again (vs. 14–17). He snapped the ropes binding him, grabbed a fresh jawbone of a dead donkey (violating his vow again), and killed 1,000 of them, throwing them into a pile. Proving himself a wordsmith again, he taunted their death by naming the place "Jawbone Hill."[7]

Finally, we see the first instance of Samson's recognition of God (vs. 18–20). The battle had left him parched, and he begged God for water, which he provided miraculously. An important note is that Samson had come to recognize that God was empowering him for these battles, and he openly acknowledged that here.

Chapter sixteen concludes Samson's story. Although he led Israel for twenty years, we know almost nothing of his story, save the few situations recorded in these past three chapters. It seems that the Philistines were probably so afraid of him that they left Israel alone for the twenty years that Samson was a threat to them. It was such an odd "relationship" that Samson felt at ease walking into Gaza, a major Philistine port city, and hiring a Philistine prostitute with no repercussions from his enemies (vs. 1–3). Whether or not he knew that they had laid an ambush for him, when he left in the middle of the night, he tore the city gates off their hinges and planted them on a hill opposite the city, maybe just to prove he could.

Once again his sexual desire drove him toward another Philistine woman, Delilah (vs. 4–20). Discovering that he had fallen for her, "THE RULERS OF THE PHILISTINES" offered her "1,100 SILVER PIECES" each. Constable notes that this offer "was a fortune since a person could live comfortably on '10 [pieces] . . . of silver' a year (17:10)."[8] It seems that Samson thought that Delilah was simply playing a game with him. Each time she asked for the source of his strength, he gave her a wrong answer. When she tried it, he jumped up, showed his strength, and laughed. It seems unlikely that he would have ever told her the truth if he believed that his enemies were involved.

However, he finally did reveal his secret; his hair was the last part of his vow that he had never violated. His honesty was evident, and she demanded payment from the Philistines while she watched his hair fall to the floor. When

---

[7] Constable, *Notes on Judges, 2016 Edition*, 112.

[8] Constable, *Notes on Judges, 2016 Edition*, 114.

she called again, as she had before, that the Philistines were upon him, he thought the game was still in play, not realizing that God had left him, although he had left God so long before. The Philistines had finally captured their prize, and they led him away in chains, gouging out his eyes in triumph (vs. 21–22). Locked in prison, performing the most menial task possible, Samson finally repented and turned to Yehovah. As his hair grew, his attitude softened, and God turned toward him again.

One day, when the Philistine crowds wanted to laugh at him in sport, he asked God for the opportunity to die as a martyr in his holy war (vs. 23–31). Resting against the pillars which held up the roof porch where so many had gathered to laugh at him, Samson prayed for strength—the only time he is recorded to have done so—and pulled the pillars down, collapsing the roof on himself and others. There were three thousand on the roof alone, in addition to the others in the stadium. Sadly, the number killed that day accounted for more Philistines than in Samson's twenty years of leading Israel. He wasted so many years enjoying his status as a threat that he never actually delivered his nation from enemy control as the other judges had done.

Chapter seventeen begins the first of the last two stories in Judges. No date is given for this narrative, only that "ISRAEL HAD NO KING" yet (vs. 6). However, while the abject moral depravity displayed may indicate that this was later in the historical timeline, the lack of a Danite homeland may imply earlier (18:1). A man named Micah had stolen "1,100 PIECES OF SILVER" from his mother (vs. 1–6). When she pronounced a curse on the thief, he confessed and returned the money. Because of his honesty, she dedicated the money to God but promptly used it to purchase or make idols, which Micah put into a shrine in his house.

At an unknown point, Micah met a young Levite from Bethlehem (vs. 7–13). He was traveling to find another place to live and minister when Micah hired him to serve in his house at his shrine. They agreed to an annual wage, and the Levite moved in with Micah, becoming "LIKE A SON TO" him. In addition to Micah being wrong to create and worship idols and this Levite being wrong to agree to serve Micah and his idols as a priest in the name of

Yehovah, Micah was also wrong to think that having a Levite on his payroll would bring God's blessings.

Chapter eighteen continues the story of Micah and his hired Levite. At this point in Israel's history, the tribe of Dan had been run out of their allotted territory by the Amorites, but they had not yet settled elsewhere (1:34; Joshua 19:40–48). Verse one contains the second reference in this story to the fact that Israel did not yet have a king (17:6; 18:1). This supports the idea that the book of Judges was compiled later, possibly by Samuel, after the monarchy had begun. To find a homeland, the Danites sent five men to spy out the land of Canaan to see what might be suitable for them (vs. 1–6). Leaving the hill country in their originally allotted land, they entered the Ephraimite hill country and came to the home of Micah and his hired Levite. After hearing the Levite's story, the men asked him to gain an oracle from God, indicating if their search for land would be successful. The Levite (with or without God's approval) said that it would be.

When they reached the far northern part of the land, they found a peaceful area that was remote enough that the inhabitants did not have military allies (vs. 7–10). This encouraged them, so they returned home and confidently told their brothers to attack that peaceful area and claim it. Six hundred Danite soldiers began the march north (vs. 11–20). Coming again through Ephraim, they passed the house of the Levite, which the original spies told them contained a great deal of silver in idols. While the six hundred soldiers kept the Levite occupied at the gate, the spies broke in and stole the idols. When he protested, they argued that it would be better for him to serve a whole tribe rather than just one family, so he agreed to go with them.

When Micah discovered what had taken place, he and his neighbors hurried after them (vs. 21–26). Catching up with them, he accused them of stealing his idols and his priest. However, the Danites threatened to kill him if he crossed them, so they went their separate ways. When the Danites arrived at Laish in the north, they attacked and killed its inhabitants and took over the land, renaming it Dan (vs. 27–31). They established a place of worship there, and, sadly, it was Moses' descendants who **"SERVED AS PRIESTS FOR THE TRIBE OF**

DAN UNTIL THE TIME OF THE EXILE." Which "exile" is referred to is unknown. Constable notes that, if the Assyrian captivity is meant (722 BC, nearly 400 years after this event), this note must have been added to the book much later.[9] This blatant unfaithfulness to God and his established structure of worship is sometimes credited for the fact that Dan is missing from the list of tribes in Revelation 7, where he is replaced by Levi.

Chapter nineteen begins with the statement, "IN THOSE DAYS ISRAEL HAD NO KING" (vs. 1), the third time in as many chapters. This transitional sentence separates the story of the next three chapters from the past two, although some of the details are similar. So, the "LEVITE LIVING TEMPORARILY IN THE REMOTE REGION OF THE EPHRAIMITE HILL COUNTRY" was probably not Jonathan from the previous story (although he possibly could have been).[10] This Levite had a concubine from Bethlehem who had left him for some reason, returning to her father's home. The NASB says that she "PLAYED THE HARLOT AGAINST HIM" (vs. 2). The NET says "SHE GOT ANGRY AT HIM," with the study note that the verb could mean "to be a prostitute" or "to be angry; to hate." No matter the reason, he wanted her back, but he waited four months before going to get her, "HOPING HE COULD CONVINCE HER TO RETURN" (vs. 3).

For nearly a week, his father-in-law convinced him to stay, but they finally started their return trip home (vs. 4–9). Leaving in the evening, they approached Jerusalem (still under pagan control), but he wanted to keep going, thinking they would be safer in an Israelite town (vs. 10–15). They arrived at Gibeah and settled in the town square, but no one offered them hospitality, except for an old man who was coming home from the field (vs. 16–21). In an account that is strikingly similar to Sodom and Gomorrah in Genesis 19, the men of the city surrounded the house, demanding that the old man send the Levite out so they could sexually abuse him (vs. 22–26). They offered the man's daughter and the Levite's concubine, but the citizens refused,

---

[9] Constable, *Notes on Judges, 2016 Edition*, 134.

[10] Judges 20:28 notes that Aaron's grandson, Phineas, was still alive and serving as priest at this time, making it early in the judges' period.

threatening to break down the door. Rashly, the Levite grabbed his concubine and tossed her out to the mob, who raped her all night long, throughout the city. At dawn, when they finally released her, she collapsed at the door of the old man's house. When the Levite prepared to leave in the morning and told her to get up, she was unresponsive, so he put her on his donkey and finished the journey (vs. 27–30). Upon returning to his home, he dismembered her, cutting her into twelve pieces, and sent one piece to each of the twelve tribes of Israel. (Whether she was dead that morning, died along the way home, or died at his hands is not stated.) Upon receiving the body part, and presumably an explanatory note, the Israelites were incensed and gathered to decide what should be done.

Chapter twenty opens with the Israelite assembly called to determine how to respond to the Levite's story of what happened in Gibeah (vs. 1–7). Verse one notes that nearly everyone was represented from within the land of Israel and across the Jordan (Reuben, Gad, and half of Manasseh), totaling 400,000 soldiers. At their assembly, they had the Levite recount what had happened. (Naturally, he left out the part that he had thrown the woman to the mob.)

The Israelites swore that the offenders would die, so they sent ten percent of their army to get supplies and meet the rest at Gibeah, where they would attack (vs. 8–11). Hoping to minimize the disaster, they sent word to the leaders of Benjamin to hand over the criminals, but they refused, mobilizing their own army instead—26,700 against 400,000 (vs. 12–17). The Israelites did not expect this response and asked God who should lead an attack against the entire tribe of Benjamin; Judah was his response (vs 18). The next morning, when they met in battle, the Benjaminites killed 22,000 Israelites (vs. 19–23). Confused, they approached God again, asking if they should continue their campaign. He said yes, so they attacked again the next morning, losing another 18,000 men (vs. 24–28). This time, when they approached God, they did so with great humility and sorrow. Offering sacrifices, they finally asked if they should even be waging this war against a fellow tribe. This time God responded that he would "HAND THEM OVER" to them. It seems as if God allowed the Benjaminites to kill so many others as punishment for the Israelites' sin in not seeking his wisdom at the beginning. Now they had finally sought him, rather than simply seeking his help for their revenge.

With God's blessing and promised help, the Israelites set up an "AMBUSH OUTSIDE GIBEAH" and "ATTACKED ...THE NEXT DAY" (vs. 29–35). Although they lost thirty men this time, the Israelites killed 25,100 men of Benjamin (out of the original 26,700) in the first wave. The rest of the day was filled with battles in every town and city, nearly annihilating Benjamin (vs. 36–48). Only 600 Benjaminite men survived.

Chapter twenty-one concludes both the story of Benjamin's near demise and the book of Judges. The writer included a new detail about the meeting at Mizpah a few days earlier. In addition to swearing that they would kill the perpetrators of the crime against the Levite's concubine, they had also sworn to not allow their daughters to marry any man of Benjamin (vs. 1–7). When the battle was finally over, the people realized what had happened: they had nearly killed off an entire tribe and had left them without means to marry anyone except pagans, something God had forbidden. They assembled again to determine how to correct it. Discovering that no one from Jabesh Gilead had joined the assembly when the oath was made, they sent soldiers against them, killing everyone except four hundred virgins, whom they brought back for the Benjaminites (vs. 8–12).

Still needing to provide two hundred more wives, the Israelites instructed the Benjaminites to ambush and kidnap that many virgins from Shiloh when they passed by (vs. 13–22). Since they were kidnapped, their family was not in danger of breaking their oath to not give their daughters away in marriage (vs. 23–25). Thus, the book ends with every person doing "WHAT HE CONSIDERED TO BE RIGHT," rather than trusting and obeying God. Not only was there no king, but there was also little-to-no respect for Yehovah and his law.

Ruth

The book of Ruth is a short, but important, story about the history of Israel and, more specifically, the family line of David. The date of the story and the date of its writing may have been separated by up to a few hundred years. The story itself took place "DURING THE TIME OF THE JUDGES" (1:1; c. 1374–1054 BC), but the family tree could not have been linked to David (one of the major themes of the story) until during or after his reign in 1010–971 BC.

Ruth's story illustrates the great truth of the Kinsman-Redeemer. In a similar way that Boaz claimed Ruth for himself when she had nowhere else to go, Jesus has claimed believers for himself because we have nowhere else to turn to receive forgiveness for sin and eternal life. In the same way that Boaz was required to be a relative to redeem Ruth, Jesus had to become human to redeem humankind. Additionally, since Jesus is the long-anticipated "son of David" (the Messiah), it is significant that Ruth appears as one of only four women (not including Mary) recorded in his genealogy (Matthew 1:5).

Although the book is one continuous story, the chapter divisions serve as acts or scenes in a play, each one revealing or hinting at the next part of the story's progression.

Chapter one sets the stage for the story. At some point during one of the famines "DURING THE TIME OF THE JUDGES," a family left Bethlehem to find food in Moab (vs. 1–6). Elimelech and Naomi had two sons, each of whom married a Moabite—Orpah and Ruth.[1] Over time, all three of the men died in Moab,

---

[1] The Moabites were descendants of the incestuous relationship between Lot and his oldest daughter (Genesis 19:36–37). Since Lot was the nephew of Abraham, the

leaving behind the women as widows. When Israel finally returned to God in one of their cycles (see the introduction to Judges for more information), he allowed the harvest to return, ending the famine. Noami, the mother-in-law of the other two, decided that she would return to her family home in Bethlehem.

There is no mention of children from either of the Moabite wives, even though they had been married for approximately ten years. Naomi, however, was old, so Orpah and Ruth offered to return with her (vs. 7–13). Naomi insisted that they return to their own homes. She had nothing left to give to them, including more sons to marry. They would be better off under their fathers' care until they could marry again. No matter how much they pled with her, she insisted that they stay with their families in Moab.

Finally, Orpah did return home, but Ruth refused (vs. 14–17). In what has become the most famous statement of the book, Ruth declared her loyalty: "WHEREVER YOU GO, I WILL GO. WHEREVER YOU LIVE, I WILL LIVE. YOUR PEOPLE WILL BECOME MY PEOPLE, AND YOUR GOD WILL BECOME MY GOD." Naomi finally conceded, and the two of them journeyed to Bethlehem together. Upon their return, Naomi responded to the village women's welcome by asking them to call her "Mara," which means "bitter," because the tragedy she had suffered, apparently at the hand of God, was bitter to her (vs. 19–22). Setting the scene for act two, the writer noted that the summer barley harvest had just begun.

Chapter two opens with the introduction of a new character, Boaz. He was a relative of Elimelech's and a *"WEALTHY, PROMINENT MAN"* (vs. 1). Verse two continues the narrative left off from chapter one. The women needed food, and Naomi was presumably too old to do manual labor, so she sent Ruth to glean barley in the fields (vs. 2–3). According to the Mosaic Law, Jewish field owners were required to leave some of their harvest in the fields and on

---

grandfather of Jacob (Israel), the Israelites and Moabites were distant relatives. According to the book of Numbers, the Moabites showed hostility toward Israel as Moses led them on the east side of the Jordan River to enter Canaan.

the vines for the poor to glean (Leviticus 19:9–10; 23:22).² Ruth obeyed Naomi and went to work in a nearby field. According to the narrator, "SHE JUST HAPPENED TO END UP IN THE PORTION OF THE FIELD BELONGING TO BOAZ."

In addition to being wealthy and prominent, Boaz was also a considerate and detailed man. Although Bethlehem was never a big city, it seems Boaz knew every poor person because he immediately noticed a new young woman gleaning with the other poor people, someone he did not recognize (vs. 4–7). Discovering Ruth's identity as Naomi's daughter and Mahlon's widow, Boaz knew that he was responsible to take care of them as Elimelech's extended family. Calling her aside, Boaz told Ruth that she must never leave his field to glean elsewhere and that she was to gather alongside his workers rather than getting only the leftovers with the other poor people (vs. 8–13). This would assure that she would never find too little. As if that were not enough, he invited her to eat lunch with him and his workers, and he commissioned his chief harvesters to intentionally drop ears of grain in front of her so that she could gather more for the time she worked (vs. 14–17). Altogether, in a single day, Ruth gathered "ABOUT THIRTY POUNDS OF BARLEY," after cleaning and processing!

Upon returning home to Naomi, Ruth told her everything that had happened and her encounters with Boaz (vs. 18–23). Naomi immediately recognized his name and told Ruth to do everything that he told her. Not only would this keep Ruth physically safe, but it would ensure their survival.

Chapter three seems to continue the narrative, but the context changes, indicating a later time.³ Naomi was still concerned about Ruth's long-term care, so she developed a plan that would hopefully lead Boaz to marry Ruth

---

² This was one of the ways God provided for all the Jewish people, no matter their economic status. It is worth noting that this is not the same as the civil government taking from some people to give to others. These poor people received nothing if they did not go out to work for it.

³ Even though the Hebrew text does not specifically show it, a few English Bibles indicate this with an opening phrase: "At that time" (NET), "One day" (NLT, NIV). Others simply include "then" (NASB, ESV, KJV).

(vs. 1–5). One night while Boaz was "WINNOWING BARLEY" by himself, Noami told Ruth to clean herself, put on perfume, and get dressed up, then go to Boaz's threshing floor after he had fallen asleep. Once there, she was to "UNCOVER HIS LEGS AND LIE DOWN BESIDE HIM." He would know what this meant and would give her further instructions.[4]

As had become typical, Ruth obeyed Naomi "AND DID EVERYTHING HER MOTHER-IN-LAW INSTRUCTED HER TO DO" (vs. 6–10). Boaz was asleep when Ruth approached him, and her actions startled him awake. Realizing a woman was with him and what she was doing, he demanded to know who she was. Discovering that it was Ruth, he knew her intentions and what Naomi wanted from him. However, there was a problem (vs. 11–16). Another relative was closer than Boaz, and he had the first right of refusal by law. Nevertheless, Boaz promised to take care of it and to take care of Ruth and Naomi. Before dawn, Boaz sent Ruth back home with sixty more pounds of processed barley. This was certainly meant to protect both of their reputations from any small-town rumor of sexual scandal. When Ruth reported everything to Naomi, she was satisfied that Boaz would do exactly as he promised (vs. 17–18).

Chapter four concludes the book and Ruth's story. Outside of this book, her name appears again only in Matthew 1:5. Boaz fulfilled his promise to find out whether the closer relative would claim his right to marry Ruth (vs. 1–12). Following both God's law and the customs of his day, Boaz gathered some of the village leaders to witness the transaction and waited for his relative to enter the village.[5]

---

[4] Many scholars admit that "uncover his legs" is probably a euphemism for his genitals here. Exactly what Ruth was to do is unclear, but there is no direct mention of sexual activity, which would have violated Mosaic Law until they were married. It is more likely that we should see this as only a symbolic expression of submission and request for marriage rather than improper sexual contact.

[5] Constable points out the significance that the relative is never named. By refusing to exercise his right and responsibility as the closest relative, he forfeited having his name recorded, not only in Scripture, but as the ancestor of David (vs. 22) and, ultimately, the Messiah (Matthew 1:5).

There is some debate over Boaz's discussion with the other man. In 3:13 Boaz seemed to indicate that it would be the man's choice to marry Ruth. In 4:4–5, however, Boaz seemed to make the marriage to her as a condition for redeeming Elimelech's family property from Naomi (see Deuteronomy 25:5–10). The man may not have known that Mahlon had a widow, and Boaz used that to his advantage, knowing that the relative would want the land but not Mahlon's widow. When that important detail came to light, the relative refused all of it, allowing Boaz to legally and freely claim both the land and Ruth, which he did in front of the village leaders (vs. 6–10). They witnessed the transaction and invoked the names of Yehovah, Jacob (Israel), and Judah, asking God to bless Boaz and Ruth forever (vs. 11–12).

God honored this request by giving the couple a son (vs. 13–17). Not only did this promote the family line, but it also comforted Naomi in her old age. This son became the grandfather of none other than King David.[6] The final verses indicate that the book of Ruth was written either during or after David's reign or that someone appended them to the book at that time. Thus, the story ends with Boaz fulfilling his role as the Kinsman-Redeemer of his family, foreshadowing the one who would come from heaven to be born in the same village and take on human nature so he could become the Kinsman-Redeemer of the entire world—Jesus the Messiah, son of David, and descendant of Boaz and Ruth.

---

[6] Assuming the line of Boaz–Obed–Jesse–David had no unmentioned gaps, then this story took place near the end of the judges' period, possibly around the same time as the beginning of 1 Samuel.

1 Samuel

The four books of Samuel and Kings were originally only two books about Israel's kings and kingdoms. Although many would declare David to be the most important figure in both of the books named after Samuel, it was Samuel with whom God spoke regularly once again—the first one since Moses and Joshua (the judges seemed to be much less frequent), and it was Samuel who anointed both Saul and David as Israel's kings. This puts Samuel as a superior character in the narrative, even though his personal story is found in less than one-quarter of the overall content.

When the Hebrew Bible was translated into Greek (the Septuagint), the translators divided Samuel and Kings into two books each, calling them *1–4 Kingdoms*. About 600 years later, Jerome placed Samuel's name back on the first two books in his *Vulgate* translation (the Jews had retained Samuel's name), and 1–2 Samuel and 1–2 Kings have remained the same since.

First Samuel contains the story of Samuel's life and the establishment of the monarchy in Israel. There is a special emphasis on how this monarchy went against God's design and plan for Israel, yet he allowed it to take place, even with the establishment of Saul, who never followed Yehovah from the beginning. We are also reminded of the sad truths that a godly man (like Samuel) is not necessarily a godly father and that a godly father (Eli, David) does not necessarily produce godly sons.

Although Samuel probably wrote much of 1–2 Samuel himself, a great deal took place after his death and has been attributed to Nathan and Gad. This first book spans about 95 years, from Samuel's birth (c. 1105 BC)[1] until Saul's death and the beginning of David's reign (c. 1010 BC).

Chapter one introduces the backstory of Samuel's life. His father was an Ephraimite and had two wives (vs. 1–2). For some reason, Hannah (Samuel's mother), was unable to have children without God's intervention. This is possibly the reason Elkanah married a second time. A Jew reading or hearing this story would likely think of the other great women in Israel's history who were barren until blessed by God with special children, e.g., Sarah and Isaac, Rebekah and Jacob, Rachael and Joseph. This did not assuage Hannah's grief, though, and she repeatedly prayed to God, asking for children, much to her husband's dismay (vs. 3–8).

During one particular visit to the tabernacle, Hannah went alone to the house of God to pray again (vs. 9–14). She was praying so intensely that her mouth was moving without sound. (Prayer is often much more audible in Jewish contexts.) This led the old priest, Eli, to think that she was drunk, and he scolded her for it. She responded that she was not drunk but that she was praying for a son, whom she would dedicate to God's service if her request was granted (vs. 15–20). With this new understanding, Eli blessed her and her plea. After she returned home, God did grant her request, and she became pregnant with a son.

After Samuel's birth, Hannah stayed at home during her husband's visits to the tabernacle until Samuel was weaned (vs. 21–28). At that time she took him to Eli and reminded him of the prayer and promise she had made a few years earlier.

Chapter two divides naturally into three sections. In the first section, Hannah prayed to God, thanking him for her son and dedicating Samuel back to God's service (vs. 1–11). Long before David wrote his songs of lament and

---

[1] Some scholars put Samuel's birth as much as 20 years earlier, lengthening the time frame of 1 Samuel.

imprecatory psalms,[2] Hannah asked for God to protect her and judge those who stood against her and her son. In poetic form, she praised God, exalting him above the wicked. The writer notes that from that time, Samuel lived and grew up in the tabernacle, under the care and training of Israel's high priest, Eli.

The second section shifts from Samuel to Eli and his sons (vs. 12–26). Eli was the high priest of the tabernacle, and his sons, Hophni and Phineas, served as priests also. They are described as "WICKED MEN" who "DID NOT ACKNOWLEDGE THE LORD'S AUTHORITY." They took more than their assigned portion of the sacrifices, sometimes even before the offerings were burned. They demanded sex with female worshippers, much like the pagan worship practices around them. To make it worse, Eli knew about these things but did nothing to stop them. In contrast, Samuel served faithfully, growing in "FAVOR BOTH WITH THE LORD AND WITH PEOPLE" (see Luke 2:52). His parents would visit regularly, and he eventually had three brothers and two sisters.

In the third section, an unnamed "MAN OF GOD" visited Eli to bring news that God had taken away the priestly service from Eli's family because of the disgrace his sons had brought on it (vs. 27–36). Additionally, he would not have any descendants who would live to old age, and they would have to rely on a new priestly line to even survive. As a confirming sign that this prophecy was from God, Eli's two wicked sons would die in a single day.

Chapter three's opening statement is more than a passing comment; it is an indictment on the chapter of the judges that was coming to a close: "RECEIVING A MESSAGE FROM THE LORD WAS RARE IN THOSE DAYS; REVELATORY VISIONS WERE INFREQUENT" (vs. 1). God, who had spoken so closely with Moses and Joshua, had been relatively silent for nearly three hundred years as Israel spiraled downward spiritually and morally. The few good judges that they had were no comparison to the relationship Samuel would have with God.

---

[2] An "imprecatory" psalm or song is one written against someone else, usually the writer's enemies. It often includes a curse or a call for the destruction of the song's subject. Some of the major imprecatory psalms include Psalms 5, 10, 17, 35, 58, 59, 69, 70, 79, 83, 109, 129, 137, and 140.

One evening, when Samuel was just a boy, he heard a voice calling to him (vs. 2–14). Mistakenly thinking it was Eli calling for help, he ran to Eli to discover it was not him. After doing this a second time, Eli finally realized that it was God calling Samuel, so he instructed the boy on how to answer Yehovah appropriately. The third time, Samuel answered, and God told him that he was going to take away the priesthood from Eli in judgment. In the morning, Eli insisted that Samuel tell him what God had said, which he did, reluctantly (vs. 15–18). Eli did not hold this against Samuel but rather accepted God's punishment for his and his sons' sins.

The chapter ends with a series of statements describing Samuel and his ministry. First, he "CONTINUED TO GROW, AND THE LORD WAS WITH HIM" (vs. 19). This is similar to Luke's description of how Jesus grew and matured (Luke 2:52). Second, "NONE OF HIS PROPHECIES FELL TO THE GROUND UNFULFILLED." Although "prophecies" here could refer to any of Samuel's words or teachings, the next sentence clarifies that it referred to his primary role as God's spokesman to Israel: "ALL ISRAEL...REALIZED THAT SAMUEL WAS CONFIRMED AS A PROPHET OF THE LORD" (vs. 20). This opened regular communication between Yehovah and Israel again. The chapter best ends with the first half of 4:1, summarizing Samuel's role: "SAMUEL REVEALED THE WORD OF THE LORD TO ALL ISRAEL."

Chapter four records the first of several downward steps in this new period in Israel's history. This chapter completes the record of God's prophecy against Eli and does not mention Samuel at all. The Philistines were still Israel's primary enemies during this time (Samuel was born during Samson's time), and they came against Israel to attack again, this time defeating them (vs. 1–2). The Israelites determined that they lost because God was not helping them, so they decided to carry the ark of the covenant to their next battle (vs. 3–4). Contributing to this superstitious action were Eli's sons, who accompanied the ark into battle. The Israelite army gave a great shout when they saw the ark, thinking it would solve all of their problems (vs. 5–9). However, it tipped off their actions to the Philistines, who lamented that they could not withstand Israel's God. More than 350 years later, they were still talking about the miracles of the Exodus, but instead of giving up, they fought even harder, and God gave them victory over Israel. Not only were 30,000 Israelite soldiers killed, but Eli's sons also died and the ark was captured and taken to Philistia (vs. 10–11).

Whether Eli approved of the ark's journey into battle is unknown, but he was concerned about its safe return (vs. 12–13). When a survivor ran back from the battlefield, and Eli asked how it went, the man gave Eli four pieces of bad news: "ISRAEL HAS FLED FROM THE PHILISTINES! THE ARMY HAS SUFFERED A GREAT DEFEAT! YOUR TWO SONS, HOPHNI AND PHINEAS, ARE DEAD! THE ARK OF GOD HAS BEEN CAPTURED!" (vs. 14–17). Upon hearing about the ark, Eli fell over in his chair—possibly due to a stroke or heart attack—"BROKE HIS NECK AND DIED" (vs. 18). When Phineas' wife heard the news, she went into stressed labor and died shortly after giving birth (vs. 19–22). Before she died, she named her son Ichabod, which means "Where is the glory?", referring to the glory of God leaving Israel.

Chapter five contains the funny story of what happened after the Philistines had captured the ark of the covenant in chapter four. Conquering another tribe or nation was viewed to be the conquest of that people's gods as well. So, as was their custom, the Philistines took the ark and placed it in the temple of Dagon, their god, to show his superiority over Yehovah (vs. 1–2). However, the next morning, they found Dagon face down in his own temple before Yehovah's ark (vs. 3). Undeterred, they repositioned the idol. The next morning, not only had Dagon fallen again, but this time his head and "TWO HANDS WERE SHEARED OFF AND WERE LYING AT THE THRESHOLD" (vs. 4). This started a superstition among the priests of Dagon (vs. 5). Additionally, God struck the residents of Ashdod with painful sores (vs. 6).

Naturally, the Philistines were afraid and no longer wanted the ark in their midst, but not so much that they wanted to send it back to Israel yet, so they moved it to another Philistine city, Gath (vs. 7–8). However, God attacked the citizens of Gath as well, "SO THEY SENT THE ARK OF GOD TO EKRON" (vs. 9–10). The people in Ekron, though, would not take it in fear for their own lives, so they arranged to send the ark back to Israel (vs. 11–12). Many Philistines died or were struck with painful sores during the seven months that the ark was in their land (6:1).

Chapter six records the result of God's attack on the Philistines for capturing the ark of the covenant. After the ark "HAD BEEN IN THE LAND OF THE PHILISTINES FOR SEVEN MONTHS," they finally attempted to decide how and where to return it to Israel (vs. 1–4). All agreed that it needed to go, but they thought they needed to send it back with a kind of guilt offering. They decided to fashion five mice and five copies of their sores out of gold and send them with the ark, one for each city affected (vs. 5–6, 17–18). This seems funny to us, but they seriously thought this could rid them of God's punishment.

> The Hebrew word translated "broke out" occurs only here [5:9] in the Old Testament (v. 9). The Septuagint translators interpreted it accurately as "groin." These tumors were apparently most prominent in the groin area, hence the English translation "hemorrhoids." Tumors in the groin are a symptom of bubonic plague. Since the Philistines associated mice with this plague (6:4-5), and mice carry bubonic plague, it seems clear that the hand of Yahweh sent this particular affliction on them. Josephus wrote that vomiting and dysentery plagued the people, which may have been accompanying symptoms.[3]
>
> Probably the Philistines intended that the models would trigger sympathetic magic, that is, that they would accomplish what they wanted when they did a similar thing. By sending the models out of their country they hoped the tumors and mice would depart too.[4]

Out of respect, they placed the ark on a cart, which was hauled by two cows that had "NEVER HAD A YOKE PLACED ON THEM" (vs. 7–12). They also had to have borne calves, which were taken away from them. This was a final test, similar to Gideon's fleece (Judges 6:36–40). If the cows kept moving to Israel

---

[3] Constable, *Notes on 1 Samuel*, 2016 edition, 36.
[4] Constable, 37–38.

with the ark, the Philistines would know the attacks were from Yehovah. However, if the cows returned to their stalls and calves, they would know that it was a coincidence, and they intended to keep the ark. "THE COWS WENT DIRECTLY ON THE ROAD TO BETH SHEMESH. THEY...TURNED NEITHER TO THE RIGHT NOR TO THE LEFT."

Under the watchful eye of five Philistine leaders, the people of Beth Shemesh welcomed the ark, using the cart as firewood and the cows as their sacrifice on an altar to God in front of the ark (vs. 13–16). However, because many of the people opened and looked into the ark, God killed 50,070[5] Israelites that day as well (6:19–7:1). In fear, they asked that the ark be moved to Kiriath Jearim, where it was placed under the care of Eleazar.

Chapter seven brings attention back to Samuel for the first time since chapter three. It seems best to read verse one along with chapter six and to begin the new narrative with verse two.[6] There is a twenty-year gap between verses one and two during which the ark stayed in Kiriath Jearim. After this time, the people began to long for Yehovah again, so Samuel led them in national repentance (vs. 3–6). This included removing all of their idols and gathering for public confession.

When the Philistines heard that the Israelites had gathered at Mizpah, they attacked them there, probably hoping that they would finish destroying them (vs. 7–11). The Israelites thought the same thing and cried to Samuel to pray on their behalf. He did, offering a lamb as a whole burnt offering. Because of their repentance, "THE LORD THUNDERED LOUDLY AGAINST THE PHILISTINES," and they were thoroughly routed. Samuel placed a memorial stone there and called it *Ebenezer*, which is Hebrew for "rock of help" (vs. 12–14). Not only were the Philistines defeated at that battle, but they never attacked Israel again during Samuel's life, and the Israelite cities they had captured were returned to Israel's

---

[5] Some modern translations read only "70" here, instead of 50,070. Constable and the NET Study Bible note that a few more recent Hebrew manuscripts have only 70, and Josephus records the same number.

[6] The paragraph markings in the Hebrew Masoretic text agree with this more logical division.

control. "THERE WAS ALSO PEACE BETWEEN ISRAEL AND THE AMORITES." Samuel lived and judged Israel in Ramah for the rest of his life (vs. 15–17).

Chapter eight is another turning point in Israelite history. Much like Eli's sons, Samuel's sons were not righteous when he appointed them as judges in Israel (vs. 1–3). The solution of Israel's elders was that Samuel should establish a king. The final phrase in their request is key: "JUST LIKE ALL THE OTHER NATIONS HAVE" (vs. 4–5). Samuel was, naturally, disappointed; he saw this as a rejection of his authority and leadership, but God told him that was not the case: "IT IS NOT YOU THAT THEY HAVE REJECTED, BUT IT IS ME THAT THEY HAVE REJECTED AS THEIR KING" (vs 6–9). God authorized Samuel to appoint a king for them while warning them of the ramifications of their decision.

Samuel did try to warn them of the harsh realities of a monarchy—taxes, authoritarianism, wars, servitude—but they refused to listen (vs. 10–20). He wanted them to understand that, if they went through with this, God would let it take its natural course. When they begged him to deliver them, he would not listen. None of this changed their minds; they wanted to "BE LIKE ALL THE OTHER NATIONS." This was the real issue; they had rejected Yehovah's rule. When Samuel returned to the Lord for direction, the response was simple: "DO AS THEY SAY AND INSTALL A KING OVER THEM" (vs. 21–22).

Chapter nine is the introduction to the man who would become the first king of Israel. Saul was young, tall, dark, and handsome, and he came from a prominent family from Benjamin (vs. 1–2). One day some of the family donkeys wandered off, and Saul's father sent him and a servant to find them (vs. 3–4). They crisscrossed the region for so long that Saul was afraid his father would stop worrying about the donkeys and send a search party for the men, so he decided to return home (vs. 5–10). However, the servant noted that a well-known prophet lived nearby. Perhaps he could help them find the donkeys. Saul had in his pocket "A QUARTER SHEKEL OF SILVER." The *Baker Encyclopedia of the Bible* lists a shekel as 12 grams, so he had about three grams.[7] He thought that would be enough to pay for the prophet's services. (This says something about how the people viewed God's prophets.) Verse nine gives an interesting perspective on the time of 1 Samuel's writing. This account was written long enough after the event that some common verbiage had changed; prophets were no longer called "seers" by the time 1 Samuel was written.

It seems that Saul did not know Samuel yet. On their way into town, the men asked where they could find the prophet, and some girls told them to look at the high place, where the sacrifice was about to be offered (vs. 11–18). Little did Saul know that God had already told Samuel that Saul was coming and that Samuel was to anoint him as the king. When Samuel saw Saul, God confirmed he was the man and that he would deliver Israel from the Philistines. Making himself known to Saul, Samuel told him to not worry about the donkeys and invited the men to eat with him (vs. 19–24). As Saul and his servant prepared to leave, Samuel told the servant to go ahead so he could talk with Saul and deliver God's message to him (vs. 25–27).

Chapter ten continues the conversation between Samuel and Saul from the last chapter. Pouring oil on Saul's head, Samuel told him that God had chosen him to be the new king over Israel (vs. 1–8). This was a shock to Saul, so Samuel sent him home but gave him three obvious signs that would confirm that this message was from God. First, Saul would meet two men near Rachel's tomb who would tell him that the donkeys had been found and that his father was worried about him. Second, he would meet three men at the tree of Tabor. They would have with them three goats, three loaves of bread, and some wine. They would give Saul two of the loaves. Third, Saul was to go from there to Gibeah. There he would see a procession of prophets prophesying. God's Spirit would come on Saul, and he would prophesy with them. Note that the fulfillment of these signs was dependent on Saul's

---

[7] Walter A. Elwell and Barry J. Beitzel, *Baker Encyclopedia of the Bible* (Grand Rapids, MI: Baker Book House, 1988), 2:2136.

obedience to go in a certain direction. Had he not gone past Rachel's tomb, Tabor, or Gibeah, he would not have received the confirming signs.

However, he did go in that direction, and immediately "GOD CHANGED HIS INMOST PERSON" (vs. 9–16).[8] Each of the signs was fulfilled as prophesied. When he returned home, he told his uncle only about the donkeys but nothing about being king or the signs. Although he and Saul already knew the outcome, when Samuel gathered the people together to appoint a king for them (vs. 17–22), he cast lots to publicly show that God was making the decision. When the lot fell to Saul, he could not be found because he was hiding. Placing Saul in front of the people, Samuel reminded the people what God had previously said about having a king(vs. 23–27; Deuteronomy 17:14–20). He even wrote it down for them, but they were too excited about having such a good-looking king that they did not listen. However, not everyone was happy about the selection.

Chapter eleven contains a strange story, but it seems to catapult Saul into his position as the leader in Israel. (Notice that Saul was plowing a field, not reigning as king, when this event occurred.) The Ammonites, under a man named Nahash[9], "MARCHED AGAINST JABESH GILEAD" (vs. 1–3). Afraid for their lives, the residents of Jabesh Gilead asked to make a treaty with Nahash, who agreed under one condition: he wanted to gouge the right eye out of every man for the explicit purpose of humiliating Israel. The weird part is that the men agreed, as long as they could not find someone within Israel to protect them within seven days.

---

[8] Salvation has always and only been by grace through faith, and this simple act of Saul's faith, resulting in a changed heart, may be compared to Genesis 15:6, where "Abram believed the LORD, and the Lord credited it as righteousness to him." While Saul's later life does not look like someone who trusted God, this passage clearly indicates that God changed Saul's heart, at least in this moment. The Hebrew text reads, "and God turned/changed for him another heart." Saul was not the same man after this experience as before it.

[9] Interestingly, the Hebrew word *nahash* means "serpent" and is the same word used in Genesis 3. This may indicate something about this man's character.

When this news reached Saul's city, the others wept in fear, but Saul became furious (vs. 4–8). In an episode reminiscent of the Levite and concubine in Judges 19, Saul cut up two oxen and sent their pieces throughout the land with this message: "Anyone who does not follow Samuel and me into battle will suffer the loss of their oxen in the same way." This mobilized an army of 300,000 Israelites. He sent the messengers back to Jabesh Gilead with the promise that they would be rescued the following day (vs. 9–15). The next day Saul led the army against the Ammonites and defeated them so badly that no survivor had even one other person to flee with. Some of Saul's men wanted to kill those who were against his kingship, but Saul let them be. They offered sacrifices to God and officially crowned Saul as their king.

Chapter twelve is essentially Samuel's farewell speech to the nation. In verses 1–5 he challenged the people to offer even one example of how he had harmed them or what he had taken from them unjustly, but they could point to nothing. There was nothing in his entire ministry that gave them just cause to demand a king. He then proceeded to give a history lesson, pointing out many of the ways that God had acted on behalf of his people (vs. 6–11). Time and time again for nearly four hundred years God had delivered them from their oppressors using men like Moses, Aaron, Gideon, Barak, Jephthah, and even himself. Yet when they faced another enemy in Nahash, they rejected God and demanded a human ruler, and God allowed it, but not indiscriminately (vs. 12–15). If they would obey his law, God would bless them and their king, but if not, he would personally stand against them, from whom no one could deliver them.

As a sign that he was indeed speaking for God—that their demand for a king was a rejection of Yehovah—Samuel asked God to make it thunder and rain (vs. 16–19). Because it was harvest time, the rain could have been disastrous rather than a blessing, possibly a symbol of judgment that would come if they did not repent. Faced with their sin and imminent loss of their crops, the people cried out to God, acknowledging their sin. Samuel encouraged them that God had not turned against them (vs. 20–25). Even though his perfect design did not include a human king, he would still bless them if they obeyed, but if they disobeyed, they would be destroyed.

Chapter thirteen opens with a textual issue. "Verse one contains a textual corruption in the Hebrew text. There the verse reads, 'Saul was . . . years old when he began to reign, and he reigned . . . two years over Israel.'"[10] The ellipses here show where two numbers are missing in the Hebrew text, which has led to a great debate that is reflected in the major English translations.[11] Acts 13:21 says that Saul ruled for forty years, so if the second missing number refers to his total reign, then it is easy to fill in that blank. However, some scholars believe that it may refer to just his reign up to the story in this chapter, in which case we are still left with a problem. Because Saul's son, Jonathan, was old enough to lead a military unit (vs. 2), it seems likely that Saul must have been at least forty years old at this point.[12]

Jonathan had attacked a Philistine military outpost, which then mobilized the Philistine army against Israel (vs. 1–8). Saul called for the Israelites to band together against the Philistines at Gilgal, but they were afraid, so many of them hid. In 10:8, Samuel had told Saul that when he went to Gilgal, he should wait for Samuel for seven days.[13] After seven days, Samuel had not yet come, so Saul became impatient, because "THE ARMY BEGAN TO ABANDON SAUL."

Knowing that it was important to have God with him in battle, Saul took it upon himself to offer a burnt sacrifice to God without Samuel (vs. 9–14).

---

[10] Contsable, *Notes in 1 Samuel, 2016 Edition*, 61.

[11] The KJV and ESV do not fill in the ellipses counting "one" year of his reign (not his age), then "two" years until this campaign. The NASB, NIV, HCSB, and NLT have "thirty" and "forty-two" years, respectively. The NET offers "thirty" and "forty" years. The NET Study Bible notes at https://netbible.org provide a great explanation of the different translation options.

[12] This interpretation conservatively assumes that Saul was twenty years old when Jonathan was born and that Jonathan was twenty years old during this campaign.

[13] This may indicate that the time between chapters 10 and 13 was not that far apart, meaning that this incident took place early in Saul's reign. Alternatively, it could simply have been a prophecy that when Saul did go down to Gilgal (something he did not know he was going to do), he should wait for Samuel before doing anything.

When Samuel arrived, he rebuked Saul for overstepping his authority. The penalty, Samuel said, was that Saul would not have a royal dynasty. God took the kingdom away from Saul's family and would give it to someone who would obey him. Samuel turned and left Saul with his army, so Saul gathered everyone and everything he had, which totaled only 600 men (vs. 15–22). The writer notes the historical fact that the Philistines had a monopoly on ironsmithing in that region, so the Israelites were reliant on them for any of their iron goods (like "PLOWSHARES, CUTTING INSTRUMENTS, AXES, AND SICKLES"), even to sharpen them. However, that meant that no one in Israel's army had a sword or spear, except for Saul and Jonathan.

Chapter fourteen tells of the great victory in Saul's battle against the Philistines. According to 13:23, the Philistines had set up a garrison at a pass, so Jonathan took it upon himself and his armor-bearer to attack them (vs. 1–15). Although he did not let anyone know what they were about to do, Jonathan did want to make sure that God would bless this move, so he devised a test. If the enemies challenged them when they saw Jonathan, he knew that God would grant a victory. Otherwise, he would not follow through. As he expected, the Philistines began to mock them when they appeared. "LOOK! THE HEBREWS ARE COMING OUT OF THE HOLES IN WHICH THEY HID THEMSELVES. COME ON UP TO US SO WE CAN TEACH YOU A THING OR TWO!" This was Jonathan's cue, so he attacked and defeated the twenty soldiers stationed there. God used this to strike fear within the entire Philistine army.

When Saul saw the Philistines beginning to run away, he took roll call to discover who was no longer with them, discovering only Jonathan and his armor-bearer missing (vs. 16–23). As more Philistines fled, Saul called for the priest to determine if they should chase them down, which they did. Even the Israelites who had hidden from Saul joined in the pursuit.

The rest of the chapter reveals a bit of Saul's personality and attitude (vs. 24–45). He had made his men take an oath to not eat anything until that evening. Of course, this meant that they were not nourished for the battle, so they expended themselves chasing the Philistines. When they saw honey in the forest, everyone faithfully kept their oath and did not eat it. However,

Jonathan was not there to hear or agree to the oath, so he ate some. When he was told about the oath, Jonathan derided it, saying that Saul was only hurting the army. When the army did attack the Philistine camp, they were famished and began to eat everything in sight, including raw meat with its blood, which was against God's Law. In an effort to save his men, Saul built a makeshift altar to slaughter the animals before God so the men could eat them. When he sought God's instructions on whether to continue their pursuit, God did not respond, which Saul took as a sign that someone had sinned. Ultimately, the lot fell on Jonathan, who confessed that he had eaten honey in the forest. When Saul commanded Jonathan to be executed, the army defended him, saying that it was because of Jonathan that the battle had been won, so Saul relented.

Verses 46–52 serve as a summary of Saul's reign and family. He had three sons and two daughters. Once his reign was established (another indication that this event was still early in his rule), he was at war with various nations, especially the Philistines, throughout his entire reign. Because of this, he instituted a perpetual draft, conscripting into the army "ANYONE WHO WAS A WARRIOR OR A BRAVE INDIVIDUAL."

Chapter fifteen records the second instance when Saul went directly against God's law or command. God had Samuel tell Saul to attack the Amalekites and destroy everything—"MAN, WOMAN, CHILD, INFANT, OX, SHEEP, CAMEL, AND DONKEY ALIKE." Nothing was to be saved. This was God's promised judgment for their rejection of Israel approximately 400 years earlier during the Exodus (vs. 1–9).[14] During his attack on the Amalekites, Saul graciously allowed the Kenites to escape because they were not under God's judgment. When Saul attacked, they did defeat the Amalekites. "HOWEVER, SAUL AND THE ARMY SPARED AGAG, ALONG WITH THE BEST OF THE FLOCK, THE CATTLE, THE FATLINGS, AND THE LAMBS, AS WELL AS EVERYTHING ELSE THAT WAS OF VALUE. THEY WERE NOT

---

[14] Because Israel was to be a "come and see" nation, Yehovah's representative to the Gentile nations around them, these 400 years was an act of grace on the Amalekites, not judging them until this point.

WILLING TO SLAUGHTER THEM. BUT THEY DID SLAUGHTER EVERYTHING THAT WAS DESPISED AND WORTHLESS."

This brought God's immediate response and judgment (vs. 10–23). He sent Samuel to confront Saul for his sin, but Saul insisted that he had followed God's instructions. Twice he blamed the army for keeping some of the animals, but he said they were going to be sacrificed to God. In a statement that is repeated in one form or another throughout the prophets, Samuel told Saul, "OBEDIENCE IS BETTER THAN SACRIFICE." Doing anything else is essentially idolatry because it places one's allegiance to someone other than Yehovah. Because God had already taken a dynasty away from Saul, his punishment this time was that God rejected him as king of Israel. Though Saul would certainly rule for many more years, God would anoint another king now and be with him, rather than with Saul.

This scared Saul, and he began to confess his sin, but it was too late (vs. 24–31). As Samuel turned away, Saul grabbed his robe and tore it. Samuel said that this symbolized God tearing the kingdom from Saul. However, upon Saul's pleading, Samuel reluctantly agreed to return with Saul to help him save face in Israel. However, there was one thing left to do. Agag, the Amalekite king, thought that he had been spared, but Samuel personally killed him with all the brutality the Amalekites usually used (vs. 32–35). For the rest of his life, Samuel never saw Saul again.

Chapter sixteen records the fulfillment of God's rejection of Saul. Samuel must have continued to mourn for Saul because God told him to stop so that he could anoint another man to be king (vs. 1–3). Samuel was concerned because God told him to go to Bethlehem, which required him to travel directly through Saul's hometown. If Saul heard of it, he would certainly try to stop Samuel. God told Samuel to take a heifer with him for a sacrifice. If Saul asked, Samuel could legitimately say that he was going there to offer a sacrifice.[15]

---

[15] This is such an interesting conversation because some people might think God told Samuel to be deceitful or unethical. In reality, this situation is similar to Rahab

God sent him to the home of Jesse, who had seven sons (vs. 4–11). On a humorous note, the elders of Bethlehem were afraid to meet with Samuel for some reason. It may have been because "Samuel had gained a reputation as an executioner since he had killed Agag."[16] Samuel had Jesse call his sons to stand before him so that God could point out his selection for the new king. In a moment of humanity, Samuel almost made the same mistake that the people had made with Saul. He saw that Eliab, Jesse's oldest son, was tall and handsome and assumed that he was God's choice. Samuel had to learn, even in his old age, that God is far more concerned with a person's heart than his outward appearance. However, after observing seven sons, God had not chosen any of them. When Samuel asked if Jesse had any others, he commented that there was indeed one more, but he was just a shepherd. Surprisingly, he was God's choice, and Samuel anointed him that day (vs. 12–13). Thus, the first mention of David records his selection and God's Spirit coming on him.[17]

The rest of the chapter sets up the juxtaposition between Saul and David. God's Spirit had come on David and left Saul (vs. 14–23). In his place, Saul became tormented by a different kind of spirit. Whether this was a demon or another type of mental-emotional-spiritual affliction is unclear. Judging from his later actions, it may have been a kind of recurring paranoia that was eased by David's music. If this was the case, then Saul may serve as a concrete example of God's giving people over to their depraved minds (Romans 1:18–32). David became important to Saul for this type of mental relief, though it seems that Saul did not know him well outside of this capacity yet (see 17:55–58).

---

and the Israelite spies (Joshua 2:1–7) and the Egyptian midwives (Exodus 1:15–21). Saul was God's enemy at this point, and if it required Samuel to trick him by not telling him the entire plan, that was justifiable so that God's plan was carried out. Let us not forget that this is spiritual warfare, and enemies at war do not share their battle plans with each other.

[16] Constable, *Notes on 1 Samuel, 2016 Edition*, 80.

[17] The two instances of his name in Ruth 4:17, 22 were written much later, after David was king and his name and story became significant.

Chapter seventeen contains one of the most famous stories of the Bible. The phrase "David and Goliath" is used throughout the secular culture to describe the ultimate struggle between great and small, strong and weak, champion and underdog. Although they had retreated from the previous battle in chapter fourteen, the Philistines were far from defeated. Once again they came against Israel, and the two sides stood across the valley of Elah opposite each other (vs. 1–3). Rather than simply attacking Israel, the Philistines sent out their champion, Goliath, to taunt and challenge the Israelite soldiers (vs. 4–11). Saul was "HEAD AND SHOULDERS" taller than the other Israelites (9:2), yet Goliath seemed to dwarf even him, standing almost ten feet tall.[18] The battle would be one-on-one, winner-take-all between the sole champion warrior of each side. Goliath's height, coupled with his enormous weapons, struck fear throughout the entire Israelite army.

In what would be pure coincidence without God's sovereignty, Jesse sent David to the battlefront to check on his older brothers, take them supplies, and bring back a report to Jesse (vs. 12–19). Although he was still playing music for Saul whenever necessary, David's job was primarily with the sheep (vs. 20–25). By the time David found his brothers, Goliath had been issuing his challenge for forty days, but David finally heard it for the first time.[19] Asking about the challenge, he discovered that no one was willing to fight Goliath, even though Saul had offered a great reward to anyone who could beat him (vs. 26–37). Although his brothers accused him of being prideful, David honestly wondered why no one had stood up to the giant, especially since he was mocking Yehovah. Determined to do something about it, he approached Saul and offered to fight. Naturally, Saul refused, but David insisted, citing his experiences fighting lions and bears in the pastures. More than that, he knew that God would fight for his own name.

---

[18] The Hebrew text reads "six cubits and a span," which would be more than 9 1/2 feet, but some scholars believe this to be either a copying error or exaggeration and that he was closer to seven feet tall.

[19] This indicates that Saul's need for David's music was not that regular, if David had not been there for more than one month.

Saul finally began to outfit David with his royal armor, but it did not fit (vs. 38–49). Gathering the tools he was familiar with—his sling and a few stones—David ran to meet Goliath. Invoking Yehovah's name in the face of Goliath's stream of insults, David threw one stone that embedded itself in the giant's forehead. "DAVID PREVAILED OVER THE PHILISTINE WITH JUST THE SLING AND THE STONE" (vs. 50–54). He cut off Goliath's head with the giant's own sword and brought it back to the Israelite camp. Seeing their champion dead, the Philistines ran, chased by the Israelite soldiers, who slaughtered them along the way. Saul, still in the camp, began to investigate who David was.[20]

Chapter eighteen describes the fallout from David's victory over Goliath. Immediately after the battle, Saul no longer allowed David to return home, and David became close friends—essentially brothers—with Saul's son, Jonathan (vs. 1–4). Something in David caused Jonathan to create a deep bond with him to the point that he gave David his royal clothing, a sign of submission to the young man. With his new experience in battle, David became a sensation throughout Israel, finding success in every mission Saul sent him on. Eventually, Saul promoted him to captain over all the soldiers (vs. 5–9). However, as David's fame grew, it took away from Saul's reputation, and Saul began to resent David for it.

One day Saul attempted to silence the voices by killing David with a spear while he played the music that Saul's tormented mind needed (see the notes on chapter sixteen regarding the "EVIL SPIRIT"); this happened "ON TWO DIFFERENT OCCASIONS" (vs. 10–16). Saul knew that God was with David now, giving him these victories. The more success David had, the more the people loved him, and the more Saul hated him.

Unable to kill David himself, Saul tried something else (vs. 17–30). He offered to let David marry his oldest daughter, as long as he continued to fight the Philistines, knowing that they would eventually kill David for him, but

---

[20] Although he knew David from his music, Saul likely did not take much personal interest in David or his family until this event, at which point he became very interested.

David refused. However, Saul's other daughter, Michal, actually loved David. When Saul found out, he was sure she would turn David over to him, so he started a whisper campaign so David would hear that Saul genuinely wanted him to marry Michal and become his son-in-law. The only condition was that David was to kill 100 Philistines and bring their foreskins to Saul as "payment." David agreed and, instead, killed 200 Philistine soldiers. This convinced Saul that David was a threat and needed to be eliminated.

Chapter nineteen records Saul's first all-out attempt to have David assassinated (vs. 1). Since he was unable to do it himself, he "TOLD HIS SON JONATHAN AND ALL HIS SERVANTS TO KILL DAVID." Naturally, Jonathan was unwilling to do this, and he warned David to hide until he could discover from Saul exactly why he wanted David dead (vs. 2–5). Jonathan calmly and logically explained to Saul that David had not injured him in any way; in fact, he had fought the battles that Saul would not fight, which only helped him. Saul was convinced and promised that David would be safe again (vs. 6–10). However, the next time David defeated more Philistines, Saul became afraid of him and tried to kill him again with his spear. (This may have been the second time mentioned in 18:11.)

This time there was no talking Saul out of his plan (vs. 11–17). He sent men to kill David at home, but Michal helped him escape through a window. She told the men that David was sick in bed, and let them peek in the doorway to see the man-sized lump under the blanket.[21] When they reported this to Saul, he demanded that they bring David, bed and all. At that point, they discovered that he was not there. Saul was furious with his daughter, who lied by saying David forced her to help him escape.

From this time on, David was on the run for his life until Saul's death (vs. 18–24). He first went to Ramah to take refuge with Samuel. When this news was reported to Saul, he sent his men to get David, but they were filled with

---

[21] The fact that David and Michal had a man-sized *teraphim*, "A HOUSEHOLD IDOL," in their home is never explained.

the Holy Spirit and began to prophesy. Finally, Saul himself went to Ramah, and the same thing happened to him.

Chapter twenty records the event that finalized in David's mind the truth that Saul would never let him live. While Saul and his men were under the influence of the Holy Spirit (19:20–24), David ran again and met with Jonathan (vs. 1–4). David honestly wanted to know what he had done to cause Saul to want to kill him. Jonathan thought he was exaggerating, but Saul had hidden this from Jonathan.

Together they developed a plan to determine whether David would ever be safe there (vs. 5–23). Jonathan would cover for him when David did not attend a banquet with Saul. If Saul simply accepted Jonathan's story, they knew David was safe, but if he did not, David was never to return. Jonathan would report the outcome through code language that only David would know. When the time came, Saul asked about David's lack of attendance and became infuriated with Jonathan's story, calling him a traitor for letting David leave (vs. 24–31). When Jonathan attempted to stick up for David, Saul tried to kill him as well (vs. 32–33). So, Jonathan went into the field where David was hiding and shot three arrows far into the distance, telling his servant that they were further away (vs. 34–42). This was code that David needed to escape. Jonathan sent the servant back home, then embraced David, sending him away in friendship.

Chapter twenty-one begins with the last half of 20:42 in the Hebrew text. When David left Jonathan, he traveled a few miles to Nob to see Ahimelech the local priest (vs. 1–3). Positively, David's first stop was with the priest of God; negatively, he had not yet learned to trust God to protect him, so he fabricated a lie about being on a short-notice mission from the king so he could explain 1) the lack of soldiers with him, 2) his lack of provisions, and 3) his lack of weapons. Ahimelech did not have much, but David asked if he could have any leftover "HOLY BREAD," the bread made daily for the priests (vs. 4–6; Exodus 25:23–30). After verifying that David's "men" were ceremonially clean, Ahimelech gave that to him. He also gave him Goliath's sword, since that was the only weapon he had available (vs. 8–9). The writer noted that one of Saul's servants, Doeg, happened to be in Nob and saw David talking with Ahimelech.

With the few provisions and the sword, David left Nob and went into the Philistine city of Gath, Goliath's hometown (vs. 10–15). When he realized that they recognized him as one who had killed thousands of Philistines, he was afraid and forgot to trust God again. He pretended to have gone insane and was so convincing that the Philistine king did not even want him in his city.

Chapter twenty-two concludes the part of the story that began in chapter twenty-one. Leaving Gath, David continued going south and hid in a cave in Adullam (vs. 1–5). There he was joined by his family and 400 men who were not happy with the political or economic situation in Israel. In some ways, David was beginning to be the real-life version of Robin Hood. He was afraid that Saul might harm his family to get to him, so he took his parents further south into Moab (Jesse's grandmother was Ruth from Moab, Ruth 4:13–17) and asked the king to provide refuge for them there. Although he planned to stay in a fortress nearby, God sent the prophet, Gad, to tell him to return to Judah.

Meanwhile, Saul was becoming increasingly paranoid (possibly the mental/emotional/spiritual condition that David's music had previously soothed) to the point that he accused his guards of being on David's payroll and not telling him that Jonathan had helped David set an ambush for Saul, of which there is no record (vs. 6–8). At this point, Doeg stood up and informed Saul that he had seen David with Ahimelech the priest, who had given him bread and Goliath's sword (vs. 9–15). Saul immediately called a meeting with Ahimelech and the other priests of his family, accusing them of aiding the fugitive. Ahimelech tried to stick up for David (as Jonathan had done multiple times). This was not the first time he had helped David, and it always helped Saul's cause as well. His explanation did not satisfy Saul, who ordered his men to slaughter all of the priests (vs. 16–23). Wisely, they refused, but Doeg was happy to ingratiate the king. That day he killed "**85** MEN WHO WORE THE LINEN EPHOD" (priests) along with all the "MEN AND WOMEN, CHILDREN AND INFANTS,

OXEN, DONKEYS, AND SHEEP" in Nob. One of Ahimelech's sons escaped and ran to report the slaughter to David, who felt guilty for those deaths because he saw Doeg there and knew that he would cause trouble. This was the event that led to him writing Psalm 52.

Chapter twenty-three records the first major pursuit that Saul took to hunt down and kill David. David learned that the Philistines had attacked the Israelite village of Keilah, so he asked God if he could go fight them and deliver his countrymen (vs. 1–6). God allowed this and gave David a complete victory. This was also where Abiathar caught up with him.

While they were there, someone reported their location to Saul, who came after David (vs. 7–12). Because of their poor strategic position, David asked God two questions: Would Saul come to get him there, and would the Keilahites turn him over to Saul? God's answers reveal one amazing aspect of his omniscience—that God knows both potential and actual events. God responded that, yes, Saul would come there and, yes, they would hand him over to Saul. With this information, David left Keilah, so Saul did not complete his journey. This means that the new answers to the questions were no—Saul did not go there and David was not handed over. This does not mean that God was wrong. Had David stayed there, that is exactly what would have happened. Because David left, the potential event did not become actual.[22]

From there, David went into the desert of Ziph, where Saul pursued him again but could not find him (vs. 13–15). Jonathan did find him, though, and they renewed their covenant together (vs. 16–20). Even Jonathan knew that David would be the next king, though he thought he would be David's second-in-command. The Ziphites also knew where David was and reported his location to Saul. (This was the occasion of Psalm 54.) Saul asked them to find his precise location and track his movements so that he could finally catch

---

[22] This is a great example that disproves determinism, the concept that God's sovereignty and omniscience necessarily means causation. Had God's original answers been decrees, David would certainly have been turned over to Saul. Instead, God gave him insight into what could happen and left David the option to change the course of events.

him, which they agreed to do (vs. 21–29). As Saul hunted, David and his growing army moved from one place to another. It looked like Saul had finally cornered David, but the Philistines had attacked Israel, and Saul had to return to fight them, allowing David to take refuge at En-Gedi.

Chapter twenty-four records David's first opportunity to take the throne from Saul. After fighting with the Philistines, Saul heard that David was at En-Gedi, so he pursued him there (vs. 1–7). En-Gedi is a large region with many large caves, so searching them all would take time. One day during the search, Saul went into a random cave to relieve himself, the very cave where David was hiding. Encouraged by his men to kill Saul right there, David quietly cut off a piece from the hem of Saul's robe. Even this caused him to feel guilty for touching the king at all; after all, God had still anointed Saul as Israel's king.

To assuage his guilt, David followed Saul out of the cave (vs. 8–15). When Saul was a safe distance away, David called out to him, using the terms "LORD...KING...FATHER." He asked why Saul hated him and wanted to kill him when he had always served him faithfully. He pointed to Saul's robe as evidence that he did not intend to kill Saul, even though he could have. Finally, he asked Saul to let God be the arbiter and judge if he had harmed Saul.

Saul's response seems like genuine repentance (vs. 16–22). Calling him "MY SON," He acknowledged that David would be the heir to the throne and that he had been wrong to hunt him. He only asked that David would not eradicate his family or his name when David became the king. David swore an oath that he would not, so Saul returned home. David, though, stayed at the fortress in En-Gedi.

Chapter twenty-five opens with a passing comment about Samuel's death, then turns attention back to David (vs. 1). If it were not for Saul's attempt to communicate with his spirit later, this would be the last mention of Samuel in the book. Unlike many other previous chapters, which contain a series of events, this chapter records one complete story of David's interaction with Nabal, whose name means "fool" or "foolish." Nabal was a wealthy, but harsh, man with a "WISE AND BEAUTIFUL" wife named Abigail (vs. 2–8). David's men had been kind to Nabal's shepherds before this time, so David sent a message to Nabal carrying a blessing on him and asking if he could spare anything for David's cause. Nabal's response was nothing like David expected (vs. 9–13). He denied even knowing David's name, which was unlikely given his prominence as Israel's chief warrior, and then accused the messengers of running away from their masters to seek their own profit. When David heard this report, he was infuriated and prepared to attack Nabal with about four hundred men.

The report of Nabal's message found its way to Abigail, who heard about David's response as well (vs. 14–19). Knowing her husband, she quickly moved into action to appease David without her husband's knowledge.[23] She gathered a banquet's-worth of food and sent it ahead with some servants to David, then she followed behind. When she finally met up with him, she fell down and begged for the lives of her husband and his entire organization (vs. 20–31). She even accepted full responsibility for the situation, stating that she would have acted immediately had she known about David's request. She asked for forgiveness for her family and for God's curse on David's enemies. Finally, acknowledging his coming reign, she simply asked for mercy when he did begin to rule.

David's response was humble and gracious (vs. 32–35). He admitted that she was right and he would have been wrong to carry out his plans. He promised to grant her the peace she desired. When Abigail returned home, Nabal was drunk at a party, so she left him alone. The next morning, she told Nabal everything that had happened, and he had a stroke or heart attack that God used to kill him ten days later (vs. 36–38). When David heard this, he praised God for his actions and asked Abigail to be his wife (vs. 39–44). She agreed and joined him at his fortress. The chapter ends with a note that Abigail

---

[23] Abigail is a great example of a wife's role in marriage. She was there to help him, and, in this case, he did not even know that he needed help, but she stepped in anyway.

was David's third wife, although Saul had taken Michal from David and had given her to another man instead.[24]

Chapter twenty-six gives the account of David's second opportunity to kill Saul. Based on the information from the scouts of Ziph (see 23:19–23), Saul came against David again, this time with 3,000 soldiers (vs. 1–4). One evening, while Saul was asleep, David and Abishai sneaked into his camp to gain reconnaissance information (vs. 5–8). What they found shocked them: Saul was asleep with a spear near his head, completely vulnerable to any attack! Abishai urged David to let him kill Saul with one jab, but David refused. As in the earlier situation (24:1–7), David could not bring himself to assassinate God's anointed king, but he did take Saul's spear and water jug (vs. 9–12).

As before, once he was a safe distance away, he called to them, this time to Saul's general, Abner (vs. 13–16). Accusing him of not protecting Saul, David proved how easily he could have killed him. Once again, hearing David's voice and plea for justice, Saul felt remorse for his actions but did not fully repent (vs. 17–25). He promised that he would not kill David and invited him to come back home. However, when Saul and his army left, David stayed where he was, unconvinced.

Chapter twenty-seven opens with David's mindset after his encounter with Saul. He knew that Saul was unchanged and would eventually kill him when he had the chance, so he continued to strategize for his safety (vs. 1). The only solution he could imagine was to hide among the Philistines, so he returned to King Achish in Gath. The last time he was here, he had pretended to be insane so that the Philistines would not kill him (21:10–15). This time he had a different plan.

Rather than hiding from the Philistines, David boldly approached Achish with an offer of partnership (vs. 2–8). He promised that he would not be in

---

[24] Interestingly, there is nothing in verse 43 indicating whether David's choice to have multiple wives was a positive or negative thing. God neither condones nor condemns David's marriages here, only records them as a statement of fact.

the way and asked the king for a place where he and his army could live in peace. For the next "YEAR AND FOUR MONTHS," they lived in Ziklag, attacking the surrounding villages and tribes. When Achish asked about his activities, David lied, saying that they were attacking some of the outlying villages of Judah (vs. 9–12). This caused Achish to begin to trust David, believing that he had finally turned against Israel. In reality, David was slowly and methodically wiping out Philistine villages, leaving no witnesses to report what was really happening.

Chapter twenty-eight begins the final story of the book and the end of Saul's reign. Whereas the last chapter covered more than one year, the next four chapters together span only a few days. While David lived in Ziklag, the Philistines once again "GATHERED THEIR TROOPS FOR WAR IN ORDER TO FIGHT ISRAEL" (vs. 1–2). Based on the false information that David had been attacking Israelite villages (27:10–12), King Achish assumed that David would certainly fight alongside him. When David did not outright reject that option, Achish made him his bodyguard.

The rest of the chapter focuses attention back on Saul, who was at a complete loss without the Holy Spirit, Samuel, or David. Though God had forbidden under the Law any communication with the dead (Leviticus 20:6; Deuteronomy 18:9–14) and Saul had all those who practiced such things removed from Israel, he was desperate. He had tried to get a response from God from both priests and prophets, but God had remained silent (vs. 3–7). His only option, he believed, was to contact Samuel's spirit, so he searched for someone in Israel who still did that. When his servants directed him to a woman in Endor, he disguised himself and paid her a visit at night, asking her to call up someone from the dead (vs. 8–11). When she hesitated, he used Yehovah's name in an oath to guarantee her innocence.[25] As soon as he said Samuel's name, she immediately became aware of several things (vs. 12–14). First, she recognized that it was Saul who stood before her. Second, she

---

[25] This is a clear violation of the third commandment. Saul misused God's name to accomplish something that went against God's law and character.

realized that this would be no ordinary conjuring; she played no role in it. Third, rather than a demon or hoax, she saw Samuel himself.

In an amazing act of both grace and judgment, God allowed Saul to speak with Samuel's spirit, the only occurrence of this happening anywhere in Scripture (vs. 15–19).[26] After scolding Saul for this act of disobedience against both God and Samuel, Samuel proceeded to remind Saul that God had torn the kingdom away from him, and he prophesied that Saul and his sons would die the next day. In a twist of irony, Saul had desperately wanted to see Samuel, and Samuel said that they would be reunited within 24 hours. This message sent Saul into a panic-induced depression (vs. 20–25). Lying flat on the ground, he refused to move or eat until his servants and the woman begged him to do so. He finally ate and returned to camp.

Chapter twenty-nine turns the story back to the Philistine camp, before the events of the previous chapter. As they lined up in their standard battle formation for inspection, the commanders noticed David and his men in the rear, alongside King Achish (vs. 1–5). When they complained to Achish, he defended David. "I HAVE FOUND NO FAULT WITH HIM FROM THE DAY OF HIS DEFECTION UNTIL THE PRESENT TIME!" The commanders responded with the well-known song of David's past victories over them, indicating that he would kill them from behind, accusing him of espionage.

Although he was sad to do it, Achish told David that he would not allow him to fight with the Philistines in this battle (vs. 6–11). The text does not say this explicitly, but it was most certainly an act of God, who kept David from having to fight his countrymen. Feigning frustration at the situation, David asked if he had ever done anything to garner the king's distrust. He had not, but the other commanders insisted that David not come along, so the king sent him and his men back.

---

[26] This also provides the biblical teaching against annihilationism, the belief that people cease to exist after death. Samuel's spirit recognized Saul, retained his memory of his earthly life, and communicated in Saul's language a new prophecy from God.

Chapter thirty is David's story that was occurring at the same time as Saul's visit to Endor in chapter twenty-eight. After three days, David and his men returned from where the Philistines were gathering, back to their home in Ziklag, to find it vacant and burned (vs. 1–8). The Amalekites had responded to David's attacks on them (27:8) by raiding the outlying Philistine and Israelite villages while those men were preparing for battle. After a time of weeping for their families, the men wanted to kill David, but he called for the priest and asked God what they should do.

God promised that David would completely rescue his people if he pursued the Amalekites, so he and his men took off after them (vs. 9–15). Along the way, they came across a slave who had been left behind by the Amalekites. David gave him food and water and asked if he could lead them to the Amalekite camp. He promised he would, as long as they did not hand him back over to them. When they found the enemies, they were spread out over the plain gorging themselves on the loot they had stolen (vs. 16–20). For the next 24 hours, David and 400 of his men slaughtered them; only about 400 soldiers escaped. David rescue all of the people and everything that was not eaten. When they returned to the 200 men who did not accompany them on the raid, David's men refused to share the spoils with them (vs. 21–25). David immediately corrected them, saying that they all should receive a portion since it was God who won the battle for them. Additionally, when they returned home, David sent some of the plunder to his friends across Judah (vs. 26–30). This began to ingratiate him again as a strong warrior with God on his side.

Chapter thirty-one concludes the first book of Samuel and Saul's story. Though God fought for David and delivered the Amalekites to him, he did not fight with Saul's army. "THE MEN OF ISRAEL FLED FROM THE PHILISTINES AND MANY OF THEM FELL DEAD ON MOUNT GILBOA" (vs. 1–3). Three of the casualties were Saul's sons, including Jonathan, just as Samuel had prophesied (28:19). Saul had also been spotted by the Philistine archers and had been wounded. Not wanting to die at the hands of the Philistine warriors, Saul asked his armor-bearer to kill him, but the man refused (vs. 4–6). Saul saw no other option but to kill himself, which he did, and his armor-bearer did as well. Thus, as Samuel said, Saul and his sons died that day.

If the citizens of Israel had any hope, it was in Saul. When they saw the army scattered and found Saul dead, they all ran, leaving their homes and cities, which the Philistines immediately occupied (vs. 7). As the Philistines began to loot the corpses, they came across Saul and his sons (vs. 8–13). They took the bodies back to the temple of their gods in triumph and hung them on the walls. However, men from Jabesh Gilead, Saul's hometown, stole back the bodies at night, burned them, then buried their bones and fasted in mourning for a week. Thus, Saul's reign and life ended in tragedy and shame.

2 Samuel

Second Samuel, or the Second Book of the Kingdoms, picks up immediately where 1 Samuel stopped, with the story of King Saul's death and burial. Only a couple of days separate the two books and the division is unnecessary, as is revealed in the fact that they were originally one book. (See the introduction to 1 Samuel for more information.) Dating some of the events in this book proves difficult because so many things are summarized or representative of longer periods. Some of these will be mentioned in the notes. The entire book revolves around David's reign as king over Israel—his coronation, victories, and sins—to the point just short of his death. Thus, this book spans about forty years.

Chapter one continues the story from 1 Samuel 31. King Saul and his three sons had all died in battle against the Philistines, while David and his men were defeating the Amalekites and regaining control of Ziklag. They had been in Ziklag for two days before news of the tragedy made it to them. Ironically, it was an Amalekite—the same people David had just defeated—who brought him the news of Saul.

The young man's story, though, did not match the account in 1 Samuel 31. Rather than Saul asking his armor-bearer to kill him and being refused, this man said that Saul asked him, and he did it (vs. 3–10). It seems this was an obvious attempt to ingratiate himself with David, especially since he was an Amalekite, because he said that he brought Saul's crown and royal jewelry for David to wear.

In what had to be a shock for the young man, who expected a reward for his allegiance to David, David tore his clothes in mourning and demanded why this man thought he had any right to touch God's king (vs. 11–16). David himself, who had already been anointed, had refrained from killing Saul twice, but this pagan thought he should do it? David had him executed on his own confession, believing the story, then wept for his loss.

David's song in response to Saul's death is amazing (vs. 17–27). His grief over Jonathan is understandable since they were close friends. Saul wanted him dead, though, and tried many times over several years to do it. The Amalekite had every reason to think that David would be overjoyed to hear that Saul was finally dead, but he was still David's king, ex-father-in-law, and one-time friend. David commanded that this song be recorded in the book of Yasher ("THE UPRIGHT ONE") and that people learn it and not forget Saul.

Chapter two shows the maturity that David had gained in his years running from Saul. The natural thing to do would have been to go to Saul's home and immediately take the throne. Samuel had anointed him, and Saul had repeatedly acknowledged that David would be the next king. What else was necessary? Instead, David asked God if he should even leave Ziklag (in Philistine territory) and move back to Judah (vs. 1–4)![1] God agreed and told him to go to Hebron, which is where he was anointed king over Judah. When he heard that the men of Jabesh Gilead (Saul's home region) were the ones who had taken care of Saul's body, David sent them his blessing, winning their support as well (vs. 5–7).

While David was making those movements, Saul's general, Abner, took things into his own hands, setting up Ish Bosheth (one of Saul's sons) as the king in Saul's place (vs. 8–11).[2] It seems that it took Abner about five years to even get Ish Boseth a following, then he ruled his little region for only two years.[3] The rest of the chapter details the battle between Abner (the real power

---

[1] Even though there was officially only one kingdom at this time, the distinction between Judah (not just the tribe) and Israel is evident already in this chapter.

[2] The fact that Ish Bosheth was 40 years old (2:10), yet was Jonathan's younger brother, and the fact that David was only 30 years old (5:4), reveals the wide age disparity between Jonathan and David, possibly twenty years or more.

[3] According to 2:11 and chapter four, David reigned from Hebron for 7 ½ years, but Ish Bosheth seems to have reigned only the last two of those.

behind Ish Bosheth) and David, and specifically David's general, Joab. At one particular battle, they set up a match between twelve men from each side, who killed each other like gladiators (vs. 12–16). When Abner and his men fled, Joab and his two brothers chased them down with their men. Joab's brother, Asahel personally went after Abner, who warned him to chase someone else or he would die (vs. 17–23). However, Asahel continued his pursuit, so Abner killed him with the blunt end of his spear. This, of course, caused Joab to pursue him (2:24–3:1). Abner had the high ground and asked Joab, "Why are we causing brothers to kill each other?" Joab thought the question sensible, called off his pursuit and went home. The day's casualties were 19 on David's side but 360 on Abner's.

Chapter three concludes the story of chapter two with a statement on the condition of the two sides. Even though that particular battle was over, the war continued, and David kept getting stronger, while Abner grew weaker (vs. 1). Verses 2–5 give a sad and shocking look into David's home life at this time. Readers already know that David had two wives—Ahinoam and Abigail. Now we learn that during the seven years in Hebron he married at least four more, and each of the six gave him a son!

For seven years Abner fought David for control of Israel until one day Ish Bosheth accused Abner of sleeping with one of Saul's concubines (vs. 6–11). This accusation of disloyalty (though he never denied it) infuriated Abner to the point that he was done fighting for and supporting Ish Bosheth. Abner said he would turn everything and everyone in Israel over to David, and it was not an idle threat. He immediately contacted David to talk about how to make it happen (vs. 12–21). Probably as a kind of test to see if this was genuine, David said that he would not even talk to Abner unless he arranged to have David's first wife, Michal, returned to him, which Abner did. This action gained David's trust, and they had a meal together to discuss the transfer of power.

When Joab heard of Abner's meal with David and that David let him leave in peace, he became upset (vs. 22–25). How could David not kill him when he had the chance? He was an archrival and the man who had murdered Joab's brother! Discreetly, Joab sent a message to call Abner back to Hebron, but without David's knowledge or permission (vs. 26–27). When he returned, Joab took him aside and killed him. Even if this was justified as revenge for his brother, Constable notes that this took place in Hebron, one of the Levitical cities of refuge, where God had expressly forbidden revenge to be carried out.[4] This action caused David to mourn again, as it could have sabotaged his work to unite Israel under his rule (vs. 28–39). As his eulogy reveals, David also had great respect for Abner, who was a man of greater character than Joab. By making a public display of mourning, distancing himself from Abner's murder, and pronouncing a curse on Joab's descendants, David gained the respect and support of Israel anyway. "IN FACT, EVERYTHING THE KING DID PLEASED ALL THE PEOPLE."

Chapter four is a short chapter that adds a new twist to the story of Ish Bosheth and introduces a new person who will become important later. When the news of Abner's death reached Ish Bosheth, he became afraid because Abner was the true leader (vs. 1–3, 5–7). One day while Ish Bosheth was resting in his bed, two of Saul's raiding party captains sneaked into his room, stabbed him, then cut off his head. Much like the Amalekite in chapter one, they thought they had done a great deed for David, and they proudly traveled through the night to see him and present Ish Bosheth's head as a trophy.

These were not men of godly character and could not understand David's outrage (vs. 8–12). Several years earlier, during one of Saul's lucid moments when he recognized David as God's next anointed ruler, he had asked David to make sure to preserve his family and his name when David became king, and David gladly agreed (1 Samuel 24:21–22). This act by these two men went against everything that David had sworn to Saul. Invoking the story of the Amalekite, he considered them even less honorable, had them executed, and buried Ish Bosheth's head with Abner.

Verse four makes a passing mention that Jonathan had a five-year-old son when he died named Mephibosheth. At that time, he was dropped by his nurse, which injured him, causing him to become crippled in both legs. Why

---

[4] Constable, *Notes on 2 Samuel, 2016 edition,* 19.

this is important is not fully known until chapter nine, where we find that he was the last surviving member of Saul's family. Thus, no one was left to claim Saul's throne, leaving David's path to complete rule wide open.

Chapter five contains three distinct sections that are not necessarily chronological. The first section records the conclusion of David's battle with Saul's family (vs. 1–5). With Ish Bosheth dead and Mephibosheth presumably dead or in hiding (the text has not yet made clear which), the rest of Israel came to David to submit to his rule. This section ends with a summary statement of David's entire reign, both in Hebron and Jerusalem.

The second section tells how David conquered Jerusalem (vs. 6–16). It was still under Jebusite control at this time (Joshua 15:63), but David wanted it as his capital, so he went up to attack it. The Jebusites were certain he could never win and taunted that even their blind and lame could defend it. After he defeated them, it seems that the Israelites mockingly called all Jebusites "the blind and lame" from that time on, and they were not permitted in David's palace. This section also ends with a summarization of David's reign, this time from the perspective of his family. After moving into Jerusalem, David took more women as both wives and concubines, who gave him even more sons. Although God had expressly forbidden for Israel's kings to multiply wives for themselves (Deuteronomy 17:17), he continued to bless David as his chosen king. However, several parts of this book will show that David and his family did not escape the consequences of this sin.

The third section tells of his encounter with the Philistines (vs. 17–25). Upon hearing that David was the new king over all Israel, the Philistines attempted to defeat him, probably considering him a traitor. (He appeared to be on their side against Saul for more than a year, 1 Samuel 27:7.) God told David that he should attack them because he would win, which he did. In another attempt, God had David circle around behind them and defeat them again. Nothing in the text tells exactly when these two battles took place, only that it was after he had secured the throne. Thus, this section, too, could be a representative summary of David's fight with the Philistines during his reign.

Chapter six records an event that was twenty years in the making. In 1 Samuel 5–7, the Philistines captured the ark of the covenant, and God punished them for doing so, causing them to send it back to Israel, where it stayed in Kiriath Jearim (another name for Baalah, 1 Chronicles 13:6) for twenty years (1 Samuel 7:2). Finally, after all that time, David decided to bring it to Jerusalem, where he was king (vs. 1–5). He led a parade of 30,000 men to retrieve it, following behind it as it rode on a new cart pulled by oxen. At one point, the oxen stumbled, and Uzzah reached out to stabilize the ark. However, when he touched it, God immediately killed him because no one was allowed to touch it. This sent a wave of fear throughout the procession, and they stopped at the house of Obed-Edom for three months until they could decide what to do with it (vs. 6–11).

Hearing that Obed-Edom's family was being blessed because they were housing the ark, David once again intended to bring it to Jerusalem (vs. 12–23). This time, rather than putting it on a cart, he had men carry it, as God intended. Before they left, "DAVID SACRIFICED AN OX AND A FATLING CALF." As they marched, David danced and sang before it, all the way into and through Jerusalem. Arriving at their destination, David offered more sacrifices to welcome the ark, and God's presence, to its new home. He also gave a blessing over all the people and handed out gifts of food. Returning home, David was accosted by his wife, Michal, who called him a fool for dancing that way in public. David responded that how he looked to God mattered more than how he looked to other people, including her. The final verse gives God's impression of her contempt for David: he allowed her to have "NO CHILDREN TO THE DAY OF HER DEATH."

Chapter seven contains one of the key covenant promises of the Old Testament: the Davidic Covenant. Some time had passed, and God had given David and the nation peace, so David's mind considered ways of honoring God (vs. 1–7). Noticing the disparity between his cedar-paneled palace and the tent housing the ark, David planned to build a temple for God and received approval from Nathan, God's prophet. However, Nathan had not received that approval from God. That night God gave him this message for David: "In all the centuries I have been with Israel, I have never asked for a cedar house."

Playing off the key word "house," God said that, instead of David building him a house, God would build David a house—a royal dynasty that would never end (vs. 8–16). He reminded David where he came from—the sheep pasture—and that he had won David's battles for him. Although he did not deserve anything else, God promised him more. God would treat David's heir like his own son, including giving discipline when necessary. However, David's son, Solomon, could not reign forever, so we find the ultimate fulfillment in David's greatest son, Jesus, who will be the eternal king (Luke 1:30–33; Matthew 1:1).

The rest of the chapter contains David's prayer in response to God's promise (vs. 18–29). In this prayer, David addressed God in several different ways:

- Seven times with the extended name אֲדֹנָי יְהוִה (*'adonai yehvih*), translated once in the NET Bible as "**LORD GOD**" (verse 19) and as "**SOVEREIGN LORD**" in verses 18, 19, 20, 22, 28, and 29
- Twice with the title יְהוָה צְבָאוֹת (*yehvah tsaba'oth*) translated "LORD of Heaven's Armies" in verses 26 and 27 (also used by God in verse eight)
- Once each with just God's name יְהוָה (*yehvah*, verse 24) and the more common יְהוָה אֱלֹהִים (*yehvah 'elohim*, "**LORD GOD**," verse 25)

In his prayer, David admitted that he did not deserve this great honor, but he thanked God for his past faithfulness—toward Israel, generally, and David, specifically—and asked him to completely fulfill this covenant, so that his name would never be tarnished throughout the nations.

Chapter eight concludes the first major section of 2 Samuel, which summaries David's military campaigns and the establishment of his kingdom. Verse one begins, "**LATER DAVID DEFEATED THE PHILISTINES AND SUBDUED THEM**" ("now after this," NASB), but 7:1 says that God had already given him relief

"FROM ALL HIS ENEMIES ON ALL SIDES," before stating the Davidic Covenant. Probably, this chapter took place along with chapters five and six, before chapter seven, but it is recorded here as a final summary.

In addition to the Philistines (vs. 1; 5:25), God allowed David to defeat the Moabites, the Arameans (Syrians), the Ammonites, the Amalekites, and the Edomites (vs. 1–2, 12–14). Thus, all the nations surrounding the land of Israel became subject to David. He reduced their armies and plundered their gold, silver, and bronze which he dedicated to God. (These would later be used by Solomon in the Temple.) The reason for this success was because "THE LORD PROTECTED DAVID WHEREVER HE CAMPAIGNED" (vs. 14). He was a great king for Israel and "GUARANTEED JUSTICE FOR ALL HIS PEOPLE" (vs. 15). Unfortunately, as the next many chapters will show, his personal and family life was not as stable. Verses 16–18 give a summary of key people in David's administration.

Chapter nine returns to the story which was briefly mentioned in 4:4. When Jonathan died, he had a five-year-old son named, Mephibosheth, who was injured, leaving him crippled in both feet. This chapter probably took place at least fifteen years later (nearly halfway through David's reign), since Mephibosheth had "A YOUNG SON" by this point (vs. 12). After David had defeated his enemies, moved the ark to Jerusalem, and built himself a palace there, he went in search of anyone left from Saul's family whom he could bless (vs. 1). One of Saul's servants was still around, so David asked him the same thing, and he said that Jonathan did have a son who survived (vs. 2–4). David was thrilled and sent for him at once.

When Mephibosheth appeared before David, he bowed low and called himself a "DEAD DOG" (vs. 5–8). David offered him the greatest honor he could—a spot at David's own table. Additionally, he awarded everything that was owned by Saul's family to Mephibosheth and commanded the servant, Ziba, and his family to serve him by working the family land and providing for his every need (vs. 9–10). David treated Mephibosheth like one of his sons, and he lived the rest of his life under David's care (vs. 11–13).

Chapter ten seems to have taken place earlier in David's reign since 1) he had not yet defeated the Ammonites (see chapter eight) and 2) they did not even seem to fear him yet. The previous king of Ammon was an ally of David's, so when he died, David offered a show of respect to the king's son, by sending a delegation to Ammon (vs. 1–3). However, the new king's advisers (much like Rehoboam's later, 1 Kings 12:6–11) did not trust David and gave him bad counsel. They accused David's messengers of espionage, so the king humiliated them by shaving their beards and cutting off the lower halves of their robes before sending them back to David (vs. 4–5). When they discovered that they had upset David, they sent 34,000 soldiers against him, so he responded by sending his entire army (vs. 6–8).

Immediately, Joab noticed that the Ammonite coalition had separated into two groups and that he would have to fight on two fronts (vs. 9–14). He took an elite unit to face the Arameans and left the rest of the army with his brother to fight the larger Ammonite force. They agreed that they would unite their forces if one side began to be defeated. Instead, the Arameans quickly ran from Joab's men, causing the Ammonites to do the same. The Arameans, though, were not through (vs. 15–19). As they marshaled reinforcements, David took his army to meet them and soundly defeated them, so that "THEY MADE PEACE WITH ISRAEL AND BECAME SUBJECTS OF ISRAEL" and would not help the Ammonites in the future.

Chapter eleven opens the following spring after David had defeated the Arameans, but while the Ammonites were still his enemies. Rather than leading the army himself, as he did against Aram (10:17), David sent Joab out with the army to fight the Ammonites, setting David up for the greatest personal failure he is widely known for.[5] Much has been written about how much Bathsheba was complicit in the affair—whether she was an innocent victim of the king's royal decree or a willing seductress, bathing in the open

---

[5] Unfortunately, David is known in the secular world for his sin with Bathsheba just as much as (and possibly more than) his battle with Goliath.

under his window. The text indicates neither clearly, so we must not take a firm stance.

The fact is that she *was* bathing where David could see her from his window (vs. 1–5). This was her ceremonial cleansing, seven days after her menstrual cycle (Leviticus 15:19–30), which means she was probably at her peak time for pregnancy. Following the well-known pattern from Genesis 3:6, David saw her, desired her, and took her for himself. Within a few weeks to a month, she confirmed that she had become pregnant and sent word to David.[6]

To cover up this sin, David sent for her husband, Uriah, to come home from the battle (vs. 6–13). At first, David simply tried to talk Uriah into going home to his wife, but he would not; instead, he slept with the servants. The second night, David got him drunk, but he still would not go home. Finally, David sent him back to the battle with a private message for Joab: send Uriah to the front line, then pull back, and let him be killed (vs. 14–21). Joab must have thought that would be too obvious, so he sent a small group too close to the city, and they were all killed. When he sent his report of this to David, he made sure the messenger specifically mentioned that Uriah had died with that group (vs. 22–25). David could respond with only a sad cliché: "Well, you never know who will die in battle."

David allowed Bathsheba the full mourning period for her husband, then brought her into his harem as one of his wives (vs. 26–27). "BUT WHAT DAVID HAD DONE UPSET THE LORD."

Chapter twelve records God's response to David's series of sins, which "UPSET THE LORD" (11:27). Many months had passed before God sent the prophet Nathan to announce David's sin and punishment (vs. 1–6). Whether the parable was from God or Nathan is inconsequential because it had the intended effect. The story was of two men—one rich, one poor. The rich man had everything he could want, but the poor man had only one lamb that was like family to him. Rather than eating from his abundance, the rich man stole

---

[6] She could not have been too far along or David's plan to make the baby seem to be Uriah's would not work.

the poor man's lamb and served it to his guest. David was furious and rightly declared that the payment was to be four lambs (Exodus 22:1), even though in David's emotional opinion the man deserved death. David's crimes, however—adultery and murder—actually did carry the death penalty.

Nathan's accusation—"YOU ARE THAT MAN!"—was met with David's immediate and sincere confession and repentance (vs. 7–14). Like the rich man, David had everything he could possibly want, including more wives than necessary; he was wrong to steal his neighbor's wife, too (also a violation of the tenth commandment).[7] However, unlike Saul, who never truly repented for his sins, God forgave David because of his repentance. (Psalm 32:3–4 may refer to the previous year during which he hid these sins, while Psalm 51 contains his confession prayer.) David would not die, but his family would be plagued with the consequences of his sin. Although David's sins were done secretly, his punishments would be in the sight of all Israel and the surrounding nations. Additionally, and most immediately, David and Bathsheba's illegitimate son would die.[8]

For the next seven days, while the baby was ill, David fasted and prayed for God to spare the baby's life (vs. 15–23). To the amazement of his servants, when David heard that the baby did not live, he cleaned up, worshipped God, and ate a meal. Incredulously, they asked why he would fast and pray during the baby's sickness but not after his death. Very simply, David admitted that, although God had not shown pity on the baby by preserving his life and the baby would not come back to life, David would one day die, just like his son, and would rejoin him.

---

[7] Some note that it was God who gave Saul's wives to David and that he could have had more if he would have simply asked instead of taking them forcibly or for political reasons.

[8] This is a troublesome passage because elsewhere God says that he does not punish children for the sins of their fathers (Deuteronomy 24:16; Ezekiel 18:20). It seems that, because royal children were often just a way to extend a king's dynasty, killing the child was both a personal and political loss for David, while the doctrine of the resurrection promises life for the child in eternity. So, while the child was not allowed to grow up, he will live forever.

Those who attempt to make David's statement, "I WILL GO TO HIM, BUT HE CANNOT RETURN TO ME!" mean that he will rejoin his son "in heaven someday" overestimate ancient knowledge of the resurrection and afterlife. While David certainly believed in a future kingdom full of resurrected saints, he was most likely simply referring to the grave here: "My son went to the grave, and one day so will I."

Constable notes that, since the boy's name is never mentioned and the naming took place on the eighth day at the circumcision, it's possible that these were the only seven days of the boy's life, and that he died nameless and uncircumcised.[9] When David consoled Bathsheba, she became pregnant again (vs. 24–25). David named this boy Solomon (built from the Hebrew word, *shalom*, "peace"), but Nathan, at God's command, called him Jedidiah, which means "beloved of Yehovah." A comparison of 3:2–5 and 5:14–16 with 1 Chronicles 3:5 shows that Solomon was probably David's seventh son.[10]

Verses 26–31 pick up and finish the story left off in 11:25, probably during the time between chapters eleven and twelve. Joab did conquer the Ammonite royal city, this time with David in the lead. All the captives were pressed into hard labor under David's rule.

Chapter thirteen begins a new section of 2 Samuel in which God's promise that David's family would fall apart because of his sin takes place. Sadly, as David's sin included covetousness, sexual sin, and murder, this chapter, spanning five years, contains them all as well.

According to 3:2–3, Amnon was David's oldest son and Absalom his second. At some point after chapter twelve, Amnon fell in love with his half-sister, Tamar, Absalom's sister (vs. 1–2).[11] Each night he went to bed thinking of her; each morning he awoke frustrated for not having her, but she was a

---

[9] Constable, *Notes on 2 Samuel, 2016 Edition*, 62.

[10] Although Solomon is listed last in both passages, it seems more likely that he was David and Bathsheba's first living son.

[11] Interestingly, this is not the first Tamar who was sexually violated by a man from David's family (Genesis 38).

virgin. One day his cousin, Jonadab, suggested that Amnon pretend to be sick and ask David to send Tamar to nurse him (vs. 3–6). Then he could seduce her. Amnon agreed and carried out the plan, so David sent Tamar to Amnon's house. Kicking everyone out of his room, Amnon tried to seduce Tamar, but she refused, attempting to talk him out of it (vs. 7–16). She even suggested that he get permission from David first, but instead, he raped her. Faced with what he had done and her resistance, his love turned to hate, and he tried to send her away, but once again, she attempted to talk him out of it. Twice the text states, "HE REFUSED TO LISTEN TO HER." When she would not leave, he finally had her locked out of his room (vs. 17–22). She went home, crying to her brother, Absalom, who told her to not worry about it. David's response was only grief, not correction, but Absalom began to plan his revenge.

"TWO YEARS LATER," Absalom invited the king and his servants to a feast during the sheep-shearing event (vs. 23–27). When David repeatedly refused, Absalom asked that David would at least require Amnon to attend, which he did, sending all his sons along. Absalom saw this as his opportunity to exact the revenge he had been planning, so he told his servants that, when Amnon was drunk, they were to kill him (vs. 28–29). When they did so, the other royal sons must have thought that they were next, because they all ran back to Jerusalem. Somehow word made it to David that Absalom had killed all David's sons, but Jonadab corrected this rumor, stating that it was only Amnon (vs. 30–33). He also made sure that David knew this was purely Absalom's revenge, which he had talked about openly for two years. As his brothers reached Jerusalem, Absalom ran to his grandfather in Geshur, near the Sea of Galilee (vs. 34–38; 3:3). David treated Amnon's death like Bathsheba's infant son; he was consoled and moved on. But for the next three years, David longed to see Absalom again.

Chapter fourteen continues the saga between David and Absalom with more deception pushed onto the king. After three years, Joab knew that David wanted to see Absalom, but he also knew that he would not do it, so he devised a plan (vs. 1–3). He found a wise woman from Tekoa (a town in Judah; Amos' hometown), who would play the role for him, and he gave her the script. As with Nathan's parable in chapter eleven, the story the woman told David evoked an emotional response, but he did not see through it immediately (vs. 4–11). She said that she was a widow with two sons, but one son had killed the other. The community wanted to execute him, but he was in hiding. She asked that the king would allow him to return without revenge being taken on him, going so far as to ask him to swear with God's name. When David agreed, she asked if she could speak on another matter, which he also allowed (vs. 12–20). She used her story to ask why David would save her son but not his own. He immediately knew that it was Joab who had put her up to this, which she confirmed.

David told Joab that he was permitted to bring Absalom back to Jerusalem, but David refused to see him for two more years (vs. 21–24, 28–32). This confused Absalom, who attempted to find out the reason from Joab, but he would not respond to Absalom's messages. Finally, Absalom had Joab's barley field set on fire to get his attention, which it did. Absalom asked why Joab had brought him back to Jerusalem if he would not get to see David. Joab relayed the message to David, who finally relented and saw Absalom.

Verses 25–27 provide an interesting aside about Absalom that will be important over the next few chapters. His description reminds the reader of other well-known men from Israel's history. Like Saul, Absalom was a handsome man. Like Samson, he had a great mane of hair, which he shaved every year. He also had a "VERY ATTRACTIVE" daughter, whom he named Tamar, probably after his sister. He was also the heir-apparent to David's throne.

Chapter fifteen begins the story of Absalom's attempt to overthrow David and take his throne. The two years he spent in Jerusalem without David's forgiveness must have built into him a resentment that he intended to correct, but not by confession or repentance as David had done. For "FOUR YEARS" Absalom began to build a coalition that would follow him against David (vs. 1–9). He "WON THE LOYALTY OF THE CITIZENS OF ISRAEL" by pretending to be their sole representative to the king, painting David as out-of-touch with the common man. Finally, when he thought he had enough support, Absalom approached David with a fake request to go to Hebron and fulfill a vow to God; David let him go.

On his way out of Jerusalem, Absalom took a contingency of 200 men, although they did not know what he had planned (vs. 10–12). He sent word throughout Israel that, when the horn sounded in Hebron, it would mean that he had become king there. "THE CONSPIRACY WAS GAINING MOMENTUM, AND THE PEOPLE WERE STARTING TO SIDE WITH ABSALOM," including one of David's advisors. When the news reached David that Absalom had taken over Hebron (where David had first ruled as well, 5:1–5), he knew that his life was in jeopardy, so he began to evacuate Jerusalem (vs. 13–22). Although he left ten concubines there, about 600 men followed him, along with his servants and family. He tried to get others to stay behind, but some would not.

He met with Zadok the priest and, after offering sacrifices to God, David told him to return to Jerusalem with the Levites (vs. 23–31). No one knew what the future would hold, but David knew that if God would continue to be faithful to him, he would return to Jerusalem. In the interim, Zadok could serve as David's eyes and ears in Jerusalem under Absalom. David convinced one more friend, Hushai, to remain as well (vs. 32–37). Not only would he be able to keep David apprised of what was happening in Jerusalem, but David also hoped that Hushai would become a counselor to Absalom and offset the evil advice he was getting from others.

Chapter sixteen opens with David meeting another friend as he traveled (vs. 1–4). Mephibosheth's servant, Ziba (9:1–13), met David with supplies for him and his people. When David asked him about Mephibosheth, Ziba said that he had stayed in Jerusalem, thinking that Saul's family would reclaim the throne. Knowing that Mephibosheth would die if he opposed Absalom, David thanked Ziba for his friendship by making him Mephibosheth's sole heir.

Arriving at Bahurim, David ran into another one of Saul's extended relatives (vs. 5–14). Seeing David coming and knowing what was happening in Jerusalem, Shimei threw both insults and rocks at David, cursing him for overthrowing Saul's reign. When Abishai wanted to kill him, David held him back. With his own son trying to kill him, this man was unimportant. David thought that perhaps even God had led him to do this.

Back in Jerusalem, David's friend, Hushai, did meet with Absalom and convinced him that he wanted to continue to serve whoever was on the throne, not just David (vs. 15–23). Ahithophel was a valuable counselor to both David and Absalom, almost prophetic, so Absalom asked him what his first action in Jerusalem should be. In fulfillment of God's prophecy in 12:11–12, he told Absalom to have sex with the concubines that David had left behind and to do it on the roof of the palace, so that everyone could see that he was now in charge, and the people would follow him.[12] Absalom followed Ahithophel's counsel.

Chapter seventeen opens with the second piece of counsel from Ahithophel to Absalom (vs. 1–6). He suggested that Absalom give him an army of 12,000 men to pursue David. He promised to kill only David and bring back the deserters. Although Absalom liked the idea, he decided to see what Hushai would say first. Hushai disagreed immediately, saying "AHITHOPHEL'S ADVICE IS NOT SOUND THIS TIME" (vs. 7–14). He warned that Ahithophel had underestimated David's prowess and cunning as a warrior and that he would never find David. In fact, David would probably attack first, and Absalom's men would lose their morale. Instead, Absalom himself should lead the attack—not with just 12,000 but with as many men as he could gather from all Israel. Rather than trying to find and kill only David, they should swarm into his camp and kill everyone; no one should be left alive. Only then could Absalom be certain that his rule was guaranteed. Absalom listened to Hushai over Ahithophel, "SO THAT THE **LORD** COULD BRING DISASTER ON ABSALOM."

As David had instructed, Zadok passed along the news to David through a series of different people and secret meetings (vs. 15–20). Unfortunately, one of Absalom's informants saw one of these meetings and sent word back to Absalom. Much like Joshua's spies in Jericho, David's men had to hide in a

---

[12] "Conquering" the previous king's harem was a common method of exerting a new king's rule in the ancient world.

well while Absalom's men searched for them. When they asked the woman where David's men were, she said they had already left, so Absalom's men returned to Jerusalem. David's men quickly returned to him with news of Absalom's plans, so they all went to the east side of the Jordan River (vs. 21–22). When Ahithophel heard that Absalom had rejected his plan in favor of Hushai's, he realized that he was no longer a valued voice in the palace, so he went home and hanged himself (vs. 23). With Absalom in pursuit, David and his group moved to Mahanaim, where friends met them with fresh supplies (vs. 24–29).

Chapter eighteen records David's attack on Absalom's army and the end of the coup. Although the writer did not record the number of soldiers in David's army, he had enough that he was able to section them into battalions of hundreds and thousands (vs. 1–5). He then divided the entire force into three sections under the leadership of Joab, Abishai, and Ittai. Against his desire, the soldiers insisted that David remain behind instead of leading the troops. "YOU ARE LIKE 10,000 OF US! SO IT IS BETTER IF YOU REMAIN IN THE CITY FOR SUPPORT." However, he commanded his generals that nothing was to be done to harm Absalom.

The battle was gruesome, and 20,000 Israelites died in the civil war (vs. 6–8). The note that "THE FOREST CONSUMED MORE SOLDIERS THAN THE SWORD DEVOURED THAT DAY" is curious. Did God somehow cause even the trees to fight for David? Nothing in the text clarifies this intriguing statement. When Absalom accidentally stumbled across a regiment of David's men, he turned to flee on his mule, but he got caught up in an oak tree (vs. 9). Although it does not explicitly state it, the fact that he was hanging by his head makes it clear that his long hair must have been caught in the branches. When a soldier told Joab about it, he questioned why the soldier did not kill Absalom where he hung (vs. 10–15). The soldier reminded Joab of David's instructions regarding Absalom, but Joab ignored him, rushed to the scene, and ran Absalom through with three spears, leaving him for dead. Joab's armor-bearers killed Absalom there. Joab blew the sound for the army to halt, then threw Absalom's body into a pit and covered him with rocks, calling the place "Absalom's Memorial" (vs. 16–18).

Ahimaaz, one of Zadok's sons, wanted to tell David the good news that the war was over, but Joab refused, knowing that David would not receive Absalom's death as good news (vs. 19–27). Instead, he told a foreigner (a Cushite) to relay the message. Ahimaaz would not be refused, so he asked again. When given permission, he ran to David, passing the Cushite. Seeing only one messenger, rather than a retreating army, David thought the news would be good. He was further convinced when he saw it was Ahimaaz. However, Ahimaaz told him only that David had won (vs. 28–33). When the Cushite came, rejoicing over Absalom's demise, David fell into deep sorrow, weeping over his son and would not be consoled.

Chapter nineteen concludes the story of Absalom's attempted coup. When Joab and the army heard that David was weeping over his son rather than rejoicing in the victory, the soldiers quietly slipped away to their homes (vs. 1–8). This upset Joab, so he approached the king and wisely told David that, by responding in this way, he had unintentionally shown that Absalom was more important to him than the people who had just saved his life. Admitting that Joab was right, David cleaned up and sat again in the city gate to receive his army. But they had all gone home.

Naturally, there was a great deal of confusion and concern throughout Israel (vs. 9–15). Most of the northern tribes (Israel) and part of Judah had supported Absalom; how would David respond to them? David had no intention of alienating or dividing Israel any further. He graciously asked why they had not welcomed him back, rather than accusing them of leaving him in the first place. Coming back across the Jordan River, David was met by Ziba and his men, who welcomed him (vs. 15–23). Shortly afterward, Shimei approached him as well. He was embarrassed and apologetic for his reaction earlier when he called out insults and threw rocks at David. Abishai (again) wanted to kill him right there, but David did not allow it. No one else would die in Israel that day.

Next, Mephibosheth came out to meet David (vs. 24–30). Earlier, Ziba had told David that Mephibosheth was hoping that the civil war would return the crown to Saul's family. However, the writer noted that Mephibosheth had been in mourning during this war, and he rejected the charge against him, saying that the only reason he did not join David's army was that he was lame. David had already given everything belonging to Saul's family to Ziba, but he offered to split it with Mephibosheth as well, but he refused, saying that David's life (and subsequent generosity) was enough for him.

Finally, David met with Barzillai, an old friend, who had helped him in Mahanaim as he ran from Absalom (vs. 31–40). Wishing to extend his gratitude for the help, David invited Barzillai to return to Jerusalem with him as David's guest. Barzillai refused, because of his age, but suggested that another man, Kimham, take his place. Barzillai's speech is worth noting because it reminds us that people have always faced some of the same ailments that come with advanced age: slowed thinking, loss of taste, and loss of hearing (vs. 35).

The final few verses are almost humorous, as the men of Israel and Judah got into an argument about who supported David the most (vs. 41–43). Judah thought they did because he was their blood relative, and they fought with him. Israel thought they did because they had more tribes and welcomed him back right away. Ironically, for all the arguing, it was a unifying situation.

Chapter twenty recounts the sole protest against David's return as king over all Israel. Sheba, a Benjaminite, refused to acknowledge David's rule and was able to get the men from Israel (northern tribes) to follow him and go home, while the men from Judah (southern tribes) stayed with David (vs. 1–2). The note that David confined the ten concubines refers to the ones Absalom had slept with on the roof of the palace (vs. 3–4). Whether David had turned back to God in his sexual life or if he no longer considered them his own is unclear, but they were considered as widows for the rest of their lives; David was dead to them. Absalom had also appointed Amasa over the army when Joab fled with David (17:25). Now that David returned, he kept Amasa on and sent him to gather the men of Judah, but he took too long to return, so David turned to Abishai to take care of Sheba for him (vs. 5–7).

Even though he was no longer in command, Joab went with Abishai and the army (vs. 8–10). When Amasa approached them, Joab pretended to greet him, but instead stabbed him in the stomach and killed him. The comment that Joab's dagger fell out of his waist is confusing. The NET Study note quotes Josephus who "suggested that as Joab approached Amasa he deliberately caused the dagger to fall to the ground at an opportune moment as though by accident. When he bent over and picked it up, he then stabbed Amasa with it."[13] Another option is that Joab had two daggers, which the NET Bible seems to favor in verse 10 by stating that there was a "KNIFE IN JOAB'S OTHER HAND." Whatever happened, Joab used a kiss to betray an ally (cf. Judas Iscariot) and furthered his murderous career. As Joab's men passed Amasa lying on the ground in his own blood, they noticed that he was still struggling to live, so they stopped to look at him (vs. 11–13). Not wanting this to slow them down, one of the men dragged his body into the woods.

Sheba managed to stay in front of Joab and Abishai and finally took refuge in the city of Abel (vs. 14–22). When they besieged the city, a "WISE WOMAN" asked why they meant to destroy such an important city in Israel. Joab convinced her that he was after only Sheba, not the city, and that he would leave if they handed Sheba over to him. The city rulers agreed, chopped off his head, and threw it over the wall to Joab, who took it back to David as a prize. The final few verses list the names of David's council in Jerusalem (vs. 23–26).

Chapter twenty-one through the end of the book contains a handful of events that took place at various times during David's reign. It seems this chapter must have occurred during the first half of David's career for at least three reasons. First, his mercy on Mephibosheth is linked with his actions here (see the notes on chapter nine). Second, it seems unlikely that David would have waited very long to obtain the bones of Saul and Jonathan. Third, it seems unlikely that God would hold off a three-year famine for Saul's sin and place it very far into David's rule.

---

[13] NET Study Bible, note 13; 2 Samuel 20:8

When David finally asked God the reason for the famine, he learned that it was because of Saul's sin against the Gibeonites (vs. 1–3). He quickly called them together to find out how to make restitution to them, but they were not interested in a monetary reward (vs. 4–9). They simply wanted to exact legal revenge on seven of Saul's descendants for the deaths of their family members; David readily agreed, though he spared Jonathan's son, Mephibosheth. Since it was during the barley harvest, they did not expect rain right away. However, the mother of two of those executed kept the corpses out but protected them from carrion birds and wild animals until the rain came again, proving that God's law had been satisfied (vs. 10–14). When David heard of this, he took Saul's and Jonathan's bones, along with those of the seven men killed, and buried them together properly.

Verses 15–22 tell of four other giant Philistines, like Goliath, who fought against David later during his reign. David's men would not allow him to fight, because of his status as king. Instead, these giants were killed by Abishai, Sibbekai, Elhanan, and Jonathan (David's nephew). The giants are called the "DESCENDANTS OF RAPHA" and could be connected to the Rephaim (Rephaites), such as Og (Deuteronomy 3:11).[14]

Chapter twenty-two is a song that David sang "WHEN THE LORD RESCUED HIM FROM THE POWER OF ALL HIS ENEMIES, INCLUDING SAUL" (vs. 1). It is repeated, along with the same title, in Psalm 18. See the notes there for a full treatment of this song.

> This psalm records David's own expression of the theological message the writer of Samuel expounded historically. Yahweh is King, and He blesses those who submit to His authority in many ways. Verse 21 is perhaps the key verse. David learned the truths expressed in this psalm

---

[14] There is quite a bit of debate over exactly who the Rephaim were. Some scholars see them as connected to (either literally or just in the ancients' minds) the Nephilim of Genesis 6:4. See Numbers 13–14 for the Israelite spies' conclusion that the giants in Canaan were Nephilim.

and evidently composed it rather early in his career (vv. 1, 20-24; cf. the superscription of Psalm 18).[15]

Chapter twenty-three contains "THE FINAL WORDS OF DAVID," probably his last official statement or testament (vs. 1). He called this an "ORACLE" and boldly claimed, "THE LORD'S SPIRIT SPOKE THROUGH ME; HIS WORD WAS ON MY TONGUE. THE GOD OF ISRAEL...SPOKE TO ME." (vs. 2–3). Constable notes that this verse holds in the Old Testament the same standing as 2 Timothy 3:16; Hebrews 2:1–2; and 2 Peter 1:19–21 do in the New Testament regarding the inspiration of the text.[16]

What God spoke to David helped him rule God's people fairly, so that he became a light for them (vs. 4; see 21:17; Psalm 119:105). He celebrated the covenant promise that God had made to him, that his royal dynasty would last forever, while still acknowledging that all his deliverance and blessing came from God (vs. 5). In a refrain similar to many of his psalms, he spoke of wicked people as under God's judgment and those who should be avoided by God's people (vs. 6–7).

Verses 8–39 list 37 men who were a part of David's elite fighting group. But more than simply a list of names, God chose to preserve an epitaph for each one—either a character trait or an extraordinary act of bravery or courage. The purpose seems to be two-fold. First, we marvel at what a small band of men can accomplish who are dedicated to God and God's mission. Second, we wonder at what God can do with a few people who are dedicated to him. This section truly demonstrates the supernatural bond between a man who acts and God who empowers him.

Chapter twenty-four concludes this book and David's reign with a bittersweet story. The accounts of this chapter and 1 Chronicles 21 seem to be conflicting.

---

[15] Constable, *Notes on 2 Samuel, 2016 Edition*, 94.
[16] Ibid, 94.

> "THE LORD'S ANGER AGAIN RAGED AGAINST ISRAEL, AND HE INCITED DAVID AGAINST THEM, SAYING, 'GO COUNT ISRAEL AND JUDAH.'" (vs. 1)

> "AN ADVERSARY OPPOSED ISRAEL, INCITING DAVID TO COUNT HOW MANY WARRIORS ISRAEL HAD." (1 Chronicles 21:1)

Whose fault was this? It seems that God was upset with Israel for a reason which is not given, so he allowed "an adversary"[17] to mobilize against David, which led him to count his troops. It seems that he did this without asking God first, showing his reliance on his army instead of God for protection. Interestingly, even Joab recognized that something was wrong and that this could bring God's judgment on them, but David insisted (vs. 3–4). After nearly ten months of counting every eligible male in Israel (plenty of time for David to repent and stop the census), Joab returned with the report that David had 1.3 million warriors available to him—800,000 in Israel and 500,000 in Judah (vs. 5–9).

Again, the account in 1 Chronicles 21:5–6 is slightly different from the numbers given here. That passage records "1,100,000 SWORD-WIELDING SOLDIERS; JUDAH ALONE HAD 470,000." Most commentators attribute this to the fact that David's standing army had about 300,000 soldiers (Israel) and 30,000 (Judah), which 1 Chronicles adds to the 800,000, plus 470,000 others who were available throughout Israel as needed.[18]

David's action did displease God, and David knew it (vs. 10–12). When he asked God for forgiveness, he discovered it was too little, too late. He had nearly ten months to repent, but he had not. Now he had to face the punishment for his sin. Graciously, God allowed David to choose the punishment: seven years of famine, three months of running from his enemies, or three days of nationwide plague (vs. 13–17). David chose the plague,

---

[17] The Hebrew word for adversary is שָׂטָן (satan), which is why some English translations put "Satan" in 1 Chronicles 21:1. However, the word does not always necessarily mean Satan, the fallen angel, and can mean any adversary, including a person or nation. Whether Satan, the angel, was the adversary God used is unknown.

[18] This suggestion is found in Keil & Delitszch, Constable, and the *Bible Knowledge Commentary*, among others.

thinking that he would rather be hurt by God than by man. God's messenger of death spread throughout the land and killed 70,000 men. However, God did not allow the angel to attack Jerusalem, because David (who it seems could see it coming) pled for their lives, even if it required his own.

The book ends with David offering a sacrifice to God at the very place that the angel of death had stopped (vs. 18–25). When the owner of the place saw David coming, he was afraid and asked what David wanted. Hearing that he wanted to offer a sacrifice there to stop the plague, the man was ready to give David both the land and the animals to slaughter, but in a statement of humility and great respect for God, David declared, "I WILL NOT OFFER TO THE LORD MY GOD BURNT SACRIFICES THAT COST ME NOTHING." His sin had cost the lives of 70,000 men, and this affected him greatly. He purchased the land and oxen, offered the sacrifices, and God stopped the plague. This was the last act of David recorded in Scripture, except for officially appointing Solomon as his successor in the next book.

1 Kings

First Kings is the first half of the original Second Book of the Kingdoms (see the introduction to 1 Samuel for more information). It begins with the death of King David and Solomon's installation as the third king over united Israel. Of the twenty-two chapters in the book, half are dedicated to Solomon's reign and half to the first 80 years of the divided kingdom.

The theme of 1 Kings should have been the Golden Age of Israel under Solomon's leadership and royal dynasty. Instead, because he failed to stay faithful to Yehovah, the theme becomes division as the nation was divided into two and many Israelites turned to other gods.

Much of the content of 1–2 Kings was compiled from the official royal records of the kingdoms of Israel and Judah, but we do not know who chose which records to include and did the compilation. Benware gives this concise summary of the evidence:

> It is generally agreed by commentators that the content of 1 and 2 Kings was compiled before the captivity of Judah, with the final editing taking place in the captivity period. Some believe that the author was a Jewish captive living in Babylon, whereas others point to the prophet Jeremiah as the most likely candidate. In either case, the date of writing would be about 600–575 BC.[1]

---

[1] Paul N. Benware, *Survey of the Old Testament, Revised* (Chicago: Moody Press, 1993), 115.

Chapter one finishes David's story and begins Solomon's. Although David was old and possibly bed-ridden, he had not yet officially named his successor to the throne (vs. 1–4). His health was failing to the point that he could no longer stay warm and needed a full-time nurse to take care of him.[2]

Since a successor had not been installed and David's firstborn son, Absalom, had been killed, Adonijah (his second son) assumed the crown for himself (vs. 5–10). He formed a coalition of some of David's key leaders (but not all of them) and his brothers (but not Solomon) and went to En Rogel, where he offered sacrifices and made himself king. Nathan heard about this and informed Bathsheba, prompting her to take the news to David so that he would fulfill his promise to appoint Solomon as the true king (vs. 11–21). Nathan planned that immediately after she gave this news to David, he would arrive and verify her report.

The plan worked exactly as Nathan thought, and they got David's promise that Solomon would be appointed immediately (vs. 22–31). David summoned the men that Adonijah had ignored—Nathan (prophet), Benaiah (military), and Zadok (priest) —and had them take Solomon to Gihon (vs. 32–40). He was to ride on David's mule and be accompanied by David's elite fighting force (also ignored by Adonijah) into Jerusalem, where David put him on the throne. When Adonijah and his guests heard what had happened, they fled for their lives (vs. 41–53). Adonijah sought asylum from Solomon at God's altar, but Solomon promised that he would not kill him for this treachery and sent him home.

Chapter two records what Solomon did about several men who had hurt David, which fully secured the nation under his reign. Just before he died, David pointed out two enemies and some friends to Solomon (vs. 1–11). Before Solomon's famous prayer for wisdom (chapter three), David recognized that this young man was already wise and could take the actions necessary and appropriate. Joab had turned against generals Abner and Amasa, even though

---

[2] Interestingly, his advisors thought that having sex with a young woman, rather than one of his wives, would help, but he did not do that.

David had shown them grace.³ Shimei had threatened David's life, even though he cowered when David had survived Absalom's coup. Both men needed to be handled. "THE SONS OF BARZILLAI" were David's friends and allies, and he wanted Solomon to reward them for their faithfulness to him. After setting Solomon up to rule, David died, having ruled God's people for forty years.

Solomon went to work right away, removing the men who were his greatest threats. Although he had already shown mercy to Adonijah, the request (coming through his own mother) that Solomon would allow his brother to have David's newest concubine, Abishag (1:3), was a subtle form of treason.⁴ Solomon saw through it and had Benaiah execute Adonijah (vs. 13–25).

Next, Solomon dealt with Abiathar, the priest (vs. 26–27). Because of his position and his long friendship with David, even though he supported Adonijah, Solomon dismissed him from his position and allowed him to return home. Abiathar must have still been from the priestly line of Eli because the writer noted that his replacement fulfilled God's prophecy against Eli. Solomon appointed godly Zadok as the new priest of Israel (vs. 35).

When news reached Joab that Solomon was cleaning house, he ran to the altar to find asylum there, like Adonijah did (vs. 28–35). However, Solomon did not intend to grant him mercy. He sent Benaiah to kill Joab, but because he was at the altar, Benaiah hesitated. Joab had declared, "I will die here," so Solomon said, "DO AS HE SAID." Benaiah executed Joab in front of God's altar, and Solomon appointed him to take Joab's place as general of the army.

Finally, Solomon addressed Shimei (vs. 36–46). He offered him his life as long as he remained in Jerusalem for as long as he lived; if he left Jerusalem for any reason he would die. Shimei accepted this proposal and moved to Jerusalem. "THREE YEARS LATER," however, in a routine act of going to Gath to retrieve some runaway slaves, Shimei forgot his promise to Solomon. When

---

³ David does not even mention Joab's murder of Absalom here.

⁴ Sleeping with a king's concubines was like a claim of succession to that king's throne. See Absalom's act in 2 Samuel 16:20–22.

Solomon heard of it, he sent word to Shimei that he had broken his oath and had Benaiah execute him as well. Thus, Solomon's rule was confirmed, and David's internal enemies were all defeated.

Chapter three contains two of the most famous stories of Solomon's reign, both having to do with his extraordinary wisdom. Early in his reign Solomon married the Pharoah's daughter in a political alliance (vs. 1–3).[5] The reason this was mentioned was to point out that the Temple had not yet been built, so Solomon and the Israelites offered sacrifices on high hills throughout Israel, rather than just at the ark of the covenant. This is the background for the first story of Solomon's wisdom.

Solomon had gone to Gibeon to offer sacrifices, apparently one of his favorite places (vs. 4–15). While he was there, he had a dream in which God told him to ask for whatever he wanted. David had already noted Solomon's wisdom, which is on display when he humbly asked for more wisdom from God, especially the ability to make correct judicial decisions for Israel. Because he did not ask for personal wealth or long life, God granted him both the wisdom he sought and the personal wealth he did not request, promising that Solomon would be the wisest and greatest king the world had ever seen. However, God gave one condition: "IF YOU FOLLOW MY INSTRUCTIONS BY OBEYING MY RULES AND REGULATIONS, JUST AS YOUR FATHER DAVID DID, THEN I WILL GRANT YOU LONG LIFE" (vs. 14). When Solomon awoke, he returned to Jerusalem to offer sacrifices before the ark of the covenant.

The second story of this chapter highlights just one example of Solomon's wisdom, a story that people still invoke today (vs. 16–28). Two prostitutes brought one baby to Solomon, each claiming that the baby was hers and that the baby of the other one had died. His proposed solution was to cut the baby in half, so both walked away with something. However, the real mother was willing to give up the baby rather than see him killed. This proved that she was his true mother, and Solomon left the baby with her. "WHEN ALL ISRAEL

---

[5] Many scholars believe that she may be the woman referred to in the Song of Solomon.

HEARD ABOUT THE JUDICIAL DECISION WHICH THE KING HAD RENDERED, THEY RESPECTED THE KING, FOR THEY REALIZED THAT HE POSSESSED DIVINE WISDOM TO MAKE JUDICIAL DECISIONS."

Chapter four gives a summary of Solomon, his ruling council, and his activities that brought the world to his doorstep. That this record spans Solomon's entire rule, not just what he did immediately, is shown by the fact that two of the regional governors named had married Solomon's daughters, and that these governors were tasked with bringing taxes from their region to Solomon's treasury once each year, indicating an ongoing system.

The Hebrew text ends the chapter with verse twenty, putting the next fourteen verses at the beginning of chapter five, summarizing Solomon's reign with a happy and healthy nation, filled with countless people, just as God had promised Abraham (Genesis 15:5; 22:17). Most English Bibles keep chapter four going, with the remaining fourteen verses summarizing Solomon's lifetime activities.

God had promised Abraham a tract of land from the river of Egypt to the Euphrates River (Genesis 15:18). Under Solomon's rule, Israel did subdue, collect tribute, and rule over the nations in that area, but it was never considered part of Israel, as the specific mention of "FROM DAN TO BEER SHEBA" (a common reference to Israel proper) indicates (vs. 21–25). Solomon's royal court was so large that they consumed daily 180 bushels of flour, 360 bushels of grain, 30 calves[6], 100 sheep, "NOT TO MENTION RAMS, GAZELLES, DEER, AND WELL-FED BIRDS." His army size is not given, but the cavalry consisted of 12,000 chariot horses.

Personally, Solomon was a philosopher, scholar, teacher, and writer—the original Renaissance Man. "HE COMPOSED 3,000 PROVERBS AND 1,005 SONGS. HE PRODUCED MANUALS ON BOTANY, DESCRIBING EVERY KIND OF PLANT, FROM THE CEDARS OF LEBANON TO THE HYSSOP THAT GROWS ON WALLS. HE ALSO PRODUCED MANUALS ON BIOLOGY, DESCRIBING ANIMALS, BIRDS, INSECTS, AND FISH." He outdebated the wisest

---

[6] The distinction between farm-raised and free-range calves is fascinating, especially giving the debates about how food is grown in our modern time.

men from around the world, and people visited Jerusalem from far and wide just to hear him lecture.

Chapter five records the beginning of Solomon's Temple project. Shortly after Solomon became king, David's friend, King Hiram of Tyre, sent messengers to Jerusalem to celebrate Solomon's new reign and to continue the treaty that Hiram had with David (vs. 1–6). Solomon was impressed with Hiram's loyalty and sent word that he wanted to hire Hiram to supply the materials for the Temple Solomon was going to build. He told Hiram to name his price.

Equally impressed with Solomon's generosity, Hiram promised to supply everything Solomon needed, including the tradesmen to help with the construction (vs. 7–12). His price was to keep his royal court fed, so Solomon sent him 120,000 bushels of wheat and 120,000 gallons of olive oil annually.[7] Solomon showed his prowess in construction management as well, making sure his workers were well-paid, had benefits, and that there were enough supervisors to keep the project and more than 180,000 workmen on track (vs. 13–18).

Chapter six lists much of the detail work that Solomon built into the Temple. Verse one gives a key date for biblical history. Solomon began to build the Temple "IN THE FOUR HUNDRED AND EIGHTIETH YEAR AFTER THE ISRAELITES LEFT EGYPT, IN THE FOURTH YEAR OF SOLOMON'S REIGN OVER ISRAEL, DURING THE MONTH ZIV (THE SECOND MONTH)" (vs. 1). This is important because we can date the fourth year of Solomon's reign using extrabiblical historical records to about 967 BC. Adding 480 years brings the Exodus to about 1447 BC, much earlier than liberal scholars want to place it.[8]

---

[7] Based on the numbers given in chapter four, this was about two-thirds of the grain that Solomon's court used.

[8] Due to the methods that ancient civilizations used to track the reign of individual kings (some counted the first year as "year zero"; some counted it as "year one"; some did not count a partial first year at all), this has a margin of error of about two years.

Unlike the Second Temple (completed in 515 BC under Zerubbabel's supervision after the exile), which Herod remodeled into a monstrosity during Jesus' time (John 2:20), and unlike the Millennial Temple that Ezekiel saw (Ezekiel 40–48), Solomon's Temple was small, much smaller than most modern church buildings and even some American homes. It was not meant to be a place of corporate gathering or worship, like a church building. It was modeled after the instructions God gave Moses for the Tabernacle / Tent of Meeting, the place where the priests would serve at the altar. The Temple itself measured only "90 FEET LONG, 30 FEET WIDE, AND 45 FEET HIGH" (about 2,700 ft^2 or 250 m^2). Around this Solomon added a porch and walls with side rooms attached.

An interesting note about the work environment was that Solomon did not allow any stone cutting on the Temple grounds; that was all done in the quarries and only finished rock was shipped to the Temple (vs. 7). "THE INSIDE OF THE TEMPLE WAS ALL CEDAR AND WAS ADORNED WITH CARVINGS OF ROUND ORNAMENTS AND OF FLOWERS IN BLOOM" (vs. 18).

Attached to the back of the Temple proper was the Most Holy Place, where the ark of the covenant would be housed. God promised Solomon that if he continued to obey, then God's presence would reside in that Temple on the ark, as he had in the desert with Moses. Everything inside the Temple and Most Holy Place was plated with gold to emphasize the brilliance of God's presence. In addition to the cherubim sculpted into the lid of the ark (Exodus 25:17–22), Solomon commissioned two cherubim to be sculpted to stand at the entrance to the Most Holy Place. They each stood 15 feet high and had a 15-foot wingspan so that their outstretched wings touched the outer walls and touched one another in the middle of the entrance. The high priest had to walk beneath the wings to enter the Most Holy Place. "ON ALL THE WALLS AROUND THE TEMPLE [including the doors and pillars inside], INSIDE AND OUT, HE CARVED CHERUBIM, PALM TREES, AND FLOWERS IN BLOOM." The entire project took seven-and-a-half years to complete, from foundation to grand opening.

The conservative date usually given for the Exodus is 1445 BC, which fits within that margin. Modern liberal scholars prefer to date the Exodus at least 200 years later.

Chapter seven begins as if it were going to describe Solomon's palace, but that is only a minor part of the chapter (vs. 1–12). The writer noted that Solomon took 13 years to build three palaces: one for his throne room and "HALL OF JUDGMENT," one for himself, and one for his Egyptian bride. He used the same type of materials and architecture for these buildings as he had for the Temple. It seems they were all "150 FEET LONG, 75 FEET WIDE, AND 45 FEET HIGH," or more than 11,000 square feet (1,020 m²), about four times the area of the Temple.

The rest of the chapter is dedicated to the furnishings of the Temple, done by the ingenious skill of Hiram himself. In Exodus 25–30 God had directed Moses to equip the Tabernacle with specific pieces of furniture, each with a special purpose. It seems that Solomon took these instructions and "upgraded" them, making them larger than the originals and, in some cases, making more than the original called for.

For instance, God designed a bronze basin in which the priests were to wash before and while on duty. Since no dimensions are given in Exodus 30:17–21, Solomon made his 15 feet in diameter, holding 12,000 gallons of water! It was so big that he named it "The Sea."[9] He also commissioned ten smaller basins that lined the Temple area. Everything was covered with sculptured pomegranates and lilies. He also crafted "LIONS, BULLS, AND CHERUBIM...DECORATIVE WREATHS...AND PALM TREES." It must have been a beautiful sight. There was so much bronze used in these furnishings and sculptures that "THEY DID NOT WEIGH THE BRONZE" to see how much they used. The other tables and lampstands that God ordered were also recreated with extraordinary detail work but in gold.

---

[9] This account reveals the intelligence and accuracy of Solomon and his workers. Although we know that circumference is usually calculated as a circle's diameter times 3.14 (C=πd), the fact that the circumference of "the Sea" was three times the diameter and called a circle is brilliant. Some liberals may try to attack this as a mathematical error in the Bible, but given the fact that they were not working with decimals, it is a great example of accuracy in the ancient biblical record.

Chapter eight records Solomon's dedication of the Temple. The Temple would have been useless without God's presence, so the first order of business was to move the ark of the covenant from where David housed it in Jerusalem into the Temple's Most Holy Place. Solomon led a parade of people to retrieve the ark, and the priests carried it and the other furniture to the Temple (vs. 1–5). Solomon and the people had gone ahead to wait for them and sacrificed countless animals to God.

When they arrived at the Temple, the priests carried the ark into the Most Holy Place and closed the curtain behind them, but the carrying poles stuck out a little bit (vs. 6–11). In addition to the tablets of the Law, Hebrews 9:4 states that the ark also contained Aaron's staff and a jar of manna (Exodus 16:32–34; Numbers 17:10–11) When God's glory filled the area, it was like a cloud of thick smoke, so that the priests could not even see to carry out their duties.

Verses 12–21 contain the blessing that Solomon spoke over the nation before turning to the altar and offering a long prayer to God, which makes up most of the chapter (vs. 22–53). In his prayer, Solomon noted several key principles. First, he gave thanks that God had fulfilled his promise in putting Solomon on David's throne and asked that he would continue to fulfill the eternal covenant that he had made with David (2 Samuel 7:8–16). Second, he recognized that God transcends the whole universe, much more than the little house Solomon had built him. God's choice to be there was an act of grace and faithfulness, not obligation, so Solomon asked for his continued protection of Israel.

Third, in the longest section of the prayer, Solomon admitted that no one is sinless and that Israel would certainly turn away from God in the future. Loosely following the structure of the curses from Deuteronomy 28:15–68, Solomon asked that when God was required to carry out his promised punishments that he would also be quick to forgive when Israel returned to him. The history of Israel, as shown in 1 and 2 Kings and the prophets, proves that God answered Solomon's honest prayer. Fourth, Solomon acknowledged that Israel was special only because God had chosen them, not because there is anything inherently special about them. However, since God had chosen them, they were infinitely special.

Following his prayer, Solomon turned to the people and announced another blessing on them, encouraging them to obey God and his laws, so that the punishments would never have to occur. He then proceeded to officiate a fourteen-day celebration, during which time they made so many voluntary sacrifices that they had to move to the Temple's front lawn because the altar was too small to hold them all.

Verse 65 contains what some literary purists might call a mistake. Writers and narrators usually refrain from putting themselves into whatever story they are writing, opting to use the third person (he/she/it/they/them) as a third-party observer of the events taking place. The writer(s) of 1 Kings usually did this as well, but in verse 65, possibly caught up in the moment, he used the phrase "THE LORD OUR GOD," identifying himself with the Israelites celebrating that day. This phrase is found only in this chapter in 1 Kings. Solomon used it three times in his prayer (vs. 57, 59, 61), which may be why the writer—possibly recording as Solomon prayed—used it just a few verses later himself. Rather than an error, it is an inspired personal touch from someone who stood there, participating, that day.

Chapter nine tells two sad accounts of Solomon about midway through his reign. He had spent twenty years building the Temple and his palace, after which God "APPEARED TO SOLOMON A SECOND TIME" (vs. 1–9). In this meeting, God acknowledged that he had done everything Solomon had asked and God had previously promised; now it was time for Solomon to uphold his end of the deal. God had made a covenant with David that he would always have an heir to the throne of Israel, but he also said that he would punish David's sons who sin (2 Samuel 7:8–16). In this vision, God reminded Solomon of this and promised that he would bless him if he obeyed and punish him if he disobeyed. For those who know the story, this is sad because we can see that God would have to follow through with his punishments.

The second sad account has to do with Solomon's dealings with Hiram (vs. 10–14). It seems that Hiram had fronted much of the cost of Solomon's building projects before Solomon gained his immense wealth. In a kind of repayment, Solomon deeded twenty cities of Israel to Hiram. This was bad for at least two reasons. First, the land of Israel was God's inheritance to the nation of Israel, and it was not to change hands.[10] Even as the king, Solomon had no right to simply give it away to a foreign nation. Second, it appears that it was not even that good of a deal. When Hiram inspected the cities, they were worthless to him, and he felt that Solomon had cheated him. The writer noted that Hiram had given Solomon more than $150,000,000 (current value) in gold.

The rest of the chapter gives details about the work crews that Solomon used for the building projects (vs. 15–28). Solomon built much more than just the Temple and his palace. He fortified Jerusalem, rebuilt cities, and constructed other palaces and buildings. Because there were still Canaanites living in the land, he forced them to be manual laborers and put the Israelites in charge of them. The writer noted that Solomon personally offered sacrifices to God three times a year at the Temple in Jerusalem. He made that his center of worship, though he would build others later. A note about Solomon's navy is also mentioned.[11]

Chapter ten tells of the famous visit of "THE QUEEN OF SHEBA." Sheba seems to have been in the far southern part of the Arabian Peninsula, modern-day Yemen, as much as 1,400 miles away from Jerusalem.[12] She was close enough to have heard of Solomon yet far enough away to not have regular dealings with him, so she traveled to Jerusalem "WITH A GREAT DISPLAY OF POMP" and many gifts (vs. 1–13). She brought with her some of the greatest questions and riddles she had, and he solved them quickly and easily. The combination of his wisdom and wealth both amazed and impressed her, with the exact result that

---

[10] Every 50th year (the year of Jubilee, Leviticus 25:10), everything was return to its original owners, even if it had been sold off in debt.

[11] Modern archaeology is finding evidence that Solomon's navy may have traveled as far as North and South America.

[12] If this is the true location of ancient Sheba, it indicates how far the story of Solomon was known.

it was supposed to have: she praised Yehovah, the God of Israel. She gave Solomon immense wealth, and he gave her many treasures in return.

The rest of the chapter summarizes Solomon's wealth and influence (vs. 14–29). He received nearly a billion dollars' worth of gold every year in taxes, tariffs, and tribute. This contributed to the artwork and detail in his palaces. His throne was decorated with ivory and gold and had statues of lions in front and beside it. He was so wealthy that silver was almost worthless (it was "AS PLENTIFUL IN JERUSALEM AS STONES"), and he used gold even for his cups and flatware. People from all over the world came to Jerusalem to hear him lecture and to bring local items to him. He paid what amounted to pennies for both horses and chariots, the best of Egypt.[13] This is a wonderful preview of what it will be like in the Millennial Kingdom.

Chapter eleven concludes the story of Solomon and tells of his final downfall. In addition to breaking God's law by purchasing horses from Egypt, Solomon also married many women from foreign countries for political alliances (vs. 1–13; Deuteronomy 17:17)[14]. Just as God had warned, "HIS WIVES HAD A POWERFUL INFLUENCE OVER HIM...[AND] SHIFTED HIS ALLEGIANCE TO OTHER GODS." Not only did he allow his wives to worship their tribal gods, but he also encouraged it by building shrines and altars for them, including the "DETESTABLE" Milcom and Chemosh.[15] Ultimately, he turned from Yehovah, recognizing him as only one of many other gods. Because of this, God told Solomon that he would do exactly as he promised for Solomon's disloyalty. For David's sake, God did not take the kingdom from Solomon but promised that he would take it from his son, leaving him only Judah and one other tribe. The other ten would go with another king.

For the rest of Solomon's reign, God brought certain enemies against him (vs. 14–25). "HADAD THE EDOMITE" was the lone Edomite survivor from David's

---

[13] This was contrary to God's instructions on two counts. He was not to amass horses for himself and was not to purchase any horses from Egypt (Deuteronomy 17:16).

[14] Although "700 ROYAL WIVES AND 300 CONCUBINES" seems a little excessive.

[15] Both of these gods required human sacrifices.

campaign against them. He grew up in Egypt and sought revenge against Solomon from the south. **"Rezon son of Eliada"** put together a raiding party against Solomon from Syria in the north. From within his own borders, Solomon's threat was Jeroboam, an Ephraimite. During Solomon's building projects, he had made Jeroboam one of his supervisors. One day a prophet told Jeroboam that God would give him ten tribes of Israel to rule, after taking them from Solomon's son, because of Solomon's sin.[16] Solomon found out about this and tried to have Jeroboam killed, but he escaped to Egypt until Solomon's death.

Thus, Solomon's story began and ended with opposition to his rule. The first was not his fault but the last was due to his sin. After ruling for forty years—some of the best of Israel's national history—he died, and the kingdom went to his son, Rehoboam.

Chapter twelve opens with the crowning of Rehoboam, Solomon's son, as king over Israel, in Shechem, which was in central Israel (vs. 1–5). Jeroboam returned from Egypt for this event and led the nation to plea for leniency from the new king. Solomon's building projects caused the people to work hard for a long time, and they asked if Rehoboam would lighten their load. He told them to return in three days for his answer.

Rather than seeking wisdom from God, Rehoboam sought counsel from two groups—the old men who had served Solomon and the young men he had grown up with. The old men urged him to lighten the people's work, which would guarantee their voluntary allegiance. The young men said he should beat them into submission. Rehoboam took the advice of his friends and told the nation he would be harsher than his father. In a surprising mutiny, the nation turned against him and crowned Jeroboam as their king (vs. 6–20). The writer noted that **"Israel has been in rebellion against the Davidic dynasty to this very day"** (vs. 19). He also declared that this was the method God used

---

[16] Even though God made this promise to Jeroboam, he included the fact that this humiliation of David's family would not last forever because of the eternal Davidic Covenant.

to fulfill his threat against Solomon and promise to Jeroboam. Rehoboam intended to attack the rebellious tribes with men from Judah and Benjamin, but God did not allow it (vs. 21–24).

Jeroboam was convinced that if the people had to continue to go to Jerusalem to worship God in the Temple, they could be persuaded to return to Rehoboam (vs. 25–33). His solution was to create two golden calves and declare that these were the "GODS WHO BROUGHT YOU UP FROM THE LAND OF EGYPT." Word-for-word in Hebrew, this was the identical statement that Aaron made at the foot of Mount Sinai when he made the golden calf in Exodus 32:4. Jeroboam placed one calf in Bethel (central Israel) and one in Dan (northern Israel). Additionally, he built other shrines, installed priests who were not Levites, and added a feast day that God had not commanded.

Chapter thirteen continues Jeroboam's story from chapter twelve. On "THE FIFTEENTH DAY OF THE EIGHTH MONTH" (12:33), Jeroboam created a festival for the golden calves he built. While he was sacrificing to them, an unnamed prophet from Judah stood before Jeroboam in Bethel and announced that one day a king would be born to David's family; his name would be Josiah, and he would undo the idolatry that Jeroboam had caused. Because this prophecy was so far in advance (Josiah would not reign for almost 300 years), the prophet gave a "near" prophecy to authenticate that he was from God.[17] He declared that the altar in front of him would split open and the ashes fall to the ground. Jeroboam furiously pointed at him, demanding his arrest, and his hand shriveled up as he pointed. The altar did split, as the prophet had said, and Jeroboam pled with him to ask God to restore his hand, which he did. When Jeroboam invited the prophet home for a meal, the man said that God had explicitly told him to not eat or drink anything there, and he left.

"NOW THERE WAS AN OLD PROPHET LIVING IN BETHEL" (vs. 11–19). When he heard what had happened at Jeroboam's altar, he went after the younger

---

[17] Prophecies far in the future often came with prophecies much closer. If the close one came true, then the people could be assured that the far one was from God and would come true as well.

prophet and invited him back to his home for a meal. When the man again protested that God had told him to not eat there, the old prophet lied, saying that God's angel had authorized it, so the man returned with the old prophet.[18] In the middle of the meal, God used the old prophet to announce the young man's sin and punishment (vs. 20–22). After the meal, the young prophet went on his way but was attacked and killed by a lion (vs. 23–32). When the old prophet heard it, he rushed to the site to find the lion and donkey standing there together by the corpse. "THE LION HAD NEITHER EATEN THE CORPSE NOR ATTACKED THE DONKEY." The old man gathered the body and buried it in his own tomb, with instructions that he should be buried next to the young man.

None of this changed Jeroboam's ways, and he continued to act wickedly in Israel and even appointed anyone to be a priest who wanted to be. Not only was Jeroboam punished for this, but his entire dynasty was "DESTROYED FROM THE FACE OF THE EARTH."

Chapter fourteen tells the end of both Jeroboam's and Rehoboam's reigns. Jeroboam's son, Abijah, fell ill, so Jeroboam sent his wife (in disguise) to Ahijah the prophet who had told him of God's plan to make him king (vs. 1–18). He had hoped to get a good word from the prophet if he did not know that Jeroboam's wife was the one asking, but God had already told Ahijah that she was coming in disguise. The word God gave him for her was that the boy would die when she returned home. He also condemned Jeroboam for his wickedness and promised that not a single male descendant would live, eventually wiping out his dynasty. Finally, he prophesied that Israel would be scattered as exiles in foreign countries because of their sin, just as God had promised in Deuteronomy 28. When the woman returned home, her son died

---

[18] The NET Study Bible note attempts to explain why the old man lied. "The motives and actions of the old prophet are difficult to understand. The old man's response to the prophet's death (see vv. 26–32) suggests he did not trick him with malicious intent. The old prophet probably wanted the honor of entertaining such a celebrity, or perhaps simply desired some social interaction with a fellow prophet."

immediately, just as the prophet had said. This was the last story of Jeroboam recorded in this book (vs. 19–20).

Returning to Rehoboam's story, all that God recorded was that he ruled for seventeen years, about five fewer than Jeroboam, and that he led Judah in more wicked idolatry and practices than even Solomon had done (vs. 21–31). Only five years into Rehoboam's reign, King Shishak of Egypt invaded Jerusalem and seized all the treasures that Solomon had placed in the Temple and palace. The specific mention of the 500 gold shields in 10:16–17 serves to reveal that Rehoboam was just a cheap imitation of his father. He attempted a show of wealth and power by replacing the gold shields with bronze shields that were paraded around when he was present. He remained at war with Jeroboam for his entire reign and both were succeeded by their sons.

Chapter fifteen begins the succession of kings of Judah (the southern kingdom) and Israel (the northern kingdom), which will last for the remainder of the book. After Rehoboam's death, his son, Abijah, became Judah's next king for three years (vs. 1–8). He ruled the same way as Rehoboam, continuing the wicked practices of idolatry throughout the land. However, the writer noted that God did not punish the entire dynasty, the way he did Jeroboam's, because of his promise to David. In a remarkable epitaph, God recorded that David's incident surrounding Uriah the Hittite was the only time that David had disregarded God's law.

After Abijah's death, his son, Asa, ruled Judah for 41 years (vs. 9–24). He was a godly king, after the pattern of David. Not only did he destroy the idols and get rid of the cultic prostitutes, but he also deposed his own grandmother from being queen because of her involvement in the paganism. He did not tear down every shrine, but he was still faithful to Yehovah. During his reign, he battled with Israel, especially King Baasha. At one point, he even paid Assyria to align with him against Israel, breaking their alliance with Israel. This caused Israel to retreat for a time.

Nadab, Jeroboam's son, was a short-lived ruler of Israel (vs. 25–32). He was wicked like his father and was assassinated by Baasha, who proceeded to kill all of Jeroboam's family, fulfilling God's prophecy against Jeroboam. Baasha also led Israel to sin, but God allowed him to rule for twenty-four years (vs. 33–34).

Chapter sixteen is the darkest spot in 1 Kings to this point. While godly Asa was reigning over Judah for 42 years, six kings ruled over Israel, all wicked. God sent a message to Baasha that was similar to Jeroboam's: you are wicked, so you and your family will die violently (vs. 1–7). Baasha's son, Elah, became king after him, but he ruled for only two years before being assassinated in a drunken stupor by Zimri (vs. 8–14). Zimri killed all of Baasha's family as God had prophesied.

Zimri's reign lasted only seven days before the news broke that he killed Elah (vs. 15–20). A military coup overthrew him, putting Omri as their king, and Zimri killed himself by setting his palace on fire. Omri did have opposition, but his opponent died, and Omri became the outright king of Israel (vs. 21–28). Although he ruled for twelve years, it is at this point that we read the first of two scathing indictments from God: "OMRI DID MORE EVIL IN THE SIGHT OF THE LORD THAN ALL WHO WERE BEFORE HIM." That means he was worse than Jeroboam, Nadab, Baasha, Elah, and Zimri—all of whom were wicked kings, some bad enough to have had God's curse on them. As if that were not enough, upon Omri's death, his son, Ahab, became king over Israel and reigned for twenty-two years (vs. 29–33). "AHAB SON OF OMRI DID MORE EVIL IN THE SIGHT OF THE LORD THAN ALL WHO WERE BEFORE HIM." For 32 years Israel was ruled by two kings—father and son—who were exponentially worse than their predecessors. Ahab went as far as marrying Jezebel, a pagan priestess from Sidon. He built a temple and altar to Baal and worshiped him, completely ignoring Yehovah.

The chapter ends with a note showing how evil things were at this time. A man decided that he wanted to rebuild Jericho, against the explicit instructions of God (vs. 34). When he did, his oldest son died when the foundation was laid and his youngest when the gates were installed. Joshua had cursed Jericho 500 years earlier (Joshua 6:26), and it turned out to be prophetic.

Chapter seventeen continues the story of Israel under King Ahab, adding a new player, the prophet Elijah. There is never any introduction given for Elijah, except that he was "FROM TISHBE IN GILEAD" (vs. 1–6). We know nothing about him until he comes on the scene with a message for Ahab: "THERE WILL BE NO DEW OR RAIN IN THE YEARS AHEAD UNLESS I GIVE THE COMMAND." God told him to hide in a valley near the Jordan River, where God used ravens to bring food for him.

When Elijah's source of water dried up because of the drought, God sent him about 100 miles north, outside of Israel, to Zarephath in Sidon, where God would take care of him through the help of a widow (vs. 7–16). When he arrived, he saw the widow gathering wood for a fire and asked for a drink of water. When she complied, he also asked for a piece of bread. This she refused, saying she had only enough flour and oil to make a small piece for herself and her son before they died. Elijah assured her that, if she would trust him and give him bread first, her flour and oil would never run out throughout the drought/famine. She agreed and God continued to provide for them.

During this time, the widow's son became ill (vs. 17–24). Superstitiously, she blamed Elijah for bringing this pain with him, so he took the boy upstairs and prayed over his body, that God would restore his health, which he did. Presented with her healed son, the widow believed that Elijah was a true prophet of God.

Chapter eighteen records the famous showdown between Elijah and the prophets of Baal, who were supported by Ahab and Jezebel. During "THE THIRD YEAR OF THE FAMINE," God sent Elijah back into Israel to see Ahab so that rain could come again (vs. 1–15). This could only happen if the people returned to Yehovah, so Elijah knew that a confrontation had to take place. On his way, Elijah came across Obadiah[19], a faithful servant of God, who had hidden 100 of God's priests while Jezebel was hunting them down to kill them. He and Ahab were looking for any land that was still good for grazing their animals.

---

[19] It is unlikely that this is the Obadiah who wrote the short book in the Old Testament by that name.

When he saw Elijah, Obadiah was glad to see him, until Elijah told him to announce Elijah's arrival. Obadiah was afraid that God would spirit Elijah away and that Ahab would kill Obadiah, but Elijah swore, "I WILL MAKE AN APPEARANCE BEFORE HIM TODAY."

Elijah told Ahab to gather the 450 prophets of Baal and another 400 prophets of Asherah (Jezebel's private group) and meet him, along with all Israel, at Mount Carmel (vs. 16–24). Once everyone was gathered, he challenged them to a test of deity. The false prophets and Elijah would both build an altar to their gods and sacrifice a bull on it. Whichever deity could send fire down to burn the sacrifice would be known as the true God. The people considered this a fair test.

Elijah let the prophets of Baal go first because they were the majority (vs. 25–29). All day, they danced and yelled and mutilated themselves in the face of Elijah's mockery, but Baal never responded. When evening came, at the time when the evening offering should have been made to Yehovah, Elijah reinforced the altar to Yehovah that was there (vs. 30–40). He used twelve stones, signifying the twelve tribes of Israel. He dug a trench around the altar, killed the bull, and put it on top, then had other men pour so much water all over it that it filled the trench. In a simple prayer, he asked Yehovah to prove himself by sending fire from heaven, which he did. Not only did the fire light the soaked wood and animal, but it also burnt up the bull, the wood, the stones, the dirt, and the water! The people were convinced, and Elijah had them slaughter the false prophets.

It seems that Ahab may have been rationing food because of the drought/famine, so Elijah told him to celebrate by having a feast when they heard the thunder (vs. 41–46). Elijah went higher up the mountain to pray. Seven times he had his servant look for signs of rain until he finally saw a small cloud coming off the Mediterranean Sea. Ahab and Elijah both took off for the palace, but God enabled Elijah to run faster than Ahab's chariot could take him.

Chapter nineteen reveals the weak, human side of Elijah. After the strong victory over Baal and Asherah (and by proxy, Ahab and Jezebel) at Mount

Carmel, Elijah probably felt invincible. When Ahab told Jezebel what had happened, though, she sent a message to Elijah threatening to murder him, so he and his servant ran for their lives (vs. 1–8). Elijah left his servant in Beer Sheba and went another day into the desert, where God met him. An angelic messenger (possibly the pre-incarnate Jesus) gave him food and water twice before sending him further south. It was enough to sustain him **"40 DAYS AND 40 NIGHTS UNTIL HE REACHED HOREB, THE MOUNTAIN OF GOD"** (better known as Mount Sinai).

After staying the night in a cave there, Elijah finally heard from God (vs. 9–18). God asked him, **"WHY ARE YOU HERE, ELIJAH?"** God did not need the information; he needed Elijah to speak for himself. Elijah complained that he had done everything God wanted, but he was alone and on the run for his life. God told him to stand and wait until he passed by. First, there was a violent wind, then an earthquake, then a fire, but God did not show up in any of these. Finally, there was **"A SOFT WHISPER,"** which caused Elijah to go out of the cave. There God asked the same question, and Elijah gave the same answer as before.

This time God gave Elijah three tasks: 1) go to Damascus **"AND ANOINT HAZAEL KING OVER SYRIA"**; 2) **"ANOINT JEHU SON OF NIMSHI KING OVER ISRAEL"**; 3) and anoint **"ELISHA SON OF SHAPHAT FROM ABEL MEHOLAH TO"** succeed Elijah as God's prophet. Together, they would kill God's enemies throughout the region. God also told him that he was not alone; there were still 7,000 people in Israel loyal to Yehovah. Elijah did as God had commanded him, and Elisha joined him as his assistant (vs. 19–21).

Chapter twenty gives a peek into a gracious act from God for the wicked King Ahab of Israel. Even though God had already described him as the most wicked king of Israel to this point (16:30, 33), God still would not let Israel be annihilated. Ben Hadad, king of Syria, put together a coalition with 32 other kings to attack Israel (vs. 1–12). He sent messengers to Ahab stating that he was going to strip all the gold and silver, **"AS WELL AS THE BEST OF YOUR WIVES AND SONS."** Ahab simply agreed, so Ben Hadad became bolder. He said that he would send his men through Ahab's own house to grab anything they wanted.

At this point, Ahab sought advice from the leaders of Israel, who told him to not give in. When he refused Ben Hadad and warned him of becoming overconfident, the Syrian king ordered the attack. However, his men were drunk.

God sent a prophet to Ahab, telling him to attack Ben Hadad's army right away (vs. 13–21). Ahab gathered a little more than 7,000 men and attacked the Syrian coalition, totally defeating them. Once again the prophet went to Ahab, this time to have him build up his defenses because Ben Hadad would return (vs. 22–28). The reason for Ben Hadad's second attempt was bad advice. He was told that Yehovah had power only in the mountains but not on the plains, so the king should attack Israel from the plains.[20] Gathering 127,000 men, Ben Hadad marched out again. However, God took the insult personally and had the prophet tell Ahab that he would defeat Syria again.

In one day the small Israelite army killed 100,000 Syrian soldiers (vs. 29–34). The other 27,000 fled to find refuge in a city, but it collapsed and killed them, too. Ben Hadad sent his messengers to make a peace treaty with Ahab, which he did. In a bizarre drama, the prophet had someone wound him so that he could appear to be a wounded soldier from Ahab's army (vs. 35–43). When the king passed by, the disguised prophet pretended to have lost a prisoner, which should have cost him his life or a fine. When Ahab said that he had stated his own punishment, the prophet declared that Ahab would be the one to pay with his life for not killing the Syrian king, after God had given him over to Ahab.

Chapter twenty-one gives insight into how wicked Jezebel was and how much Ahab and other leaders were under her influence and control. Next to Ahab's palace was a vineyard owned by Naboth (vs. 1–3). Ahab wanted the land for a garden, so he offered Naboth a better piece of land in trade, or he would purchase it outright. There seems to be nothing sinister or evil in the

---

[20] Many false gods of ancient civilizations had power only at certain times or in certain locations, so it would not strike Ben Hadad as odd to hear that Israel's God was a mountain god who was weak in the plains.

transaction Ahab offered. However, according to the Mosaic Law, inherited land was to stay within the family, and Naboth attempted to use God's law to politely decline Ahab's offer. Ahab went home and pouted, refusing to eat, until Jezebel asked him what was wrong (vs. 4–7). When he told her what happened, she could not believe that the king would be refused so easily, so she promised to take care of it.

She wrote instructions for the local leaders to bring two false witnesses against Naboth, accusing him of cursing God and the king (vs. 8–16). Cursing God brought the death sentence, and Naboth was unjustly arrested, tried, and executed. Jezebel returned to Ahab and told him to go take Naboth's land. God sent Elijah to Ahab with the news that, because of his crimes, his dynasty would be eradicated and his blood would be spilled on Naboth's land. Elijah also said that Jezebel would be eaten by wild dogs, knowing that she was the true instigator of the crime. Verse 25 gives one of the worst descriptions of anyone in Scripture: "THERE HAD NEVER BEEN ANYONE LIKE AHAB, WHO WAS FIRMLY COMMITTED TO DOING EVIL IN THE SIGHT OF THE LORD, URGED ON BY HIS WIFE JEZEBEL." Ahab did show humble remorse for what happened, so God graciously lightened his sentence, stating that his judgment on Ahab's dynasty would be carried out on his son rather than on Ahab himself.

Chapter twenty-two concludes this book and the lives of three more kings. Jehoshaphat was introduced briefly in 15:24 as Asa's son who succeeded him as the fourth king of Judah. He became king "IN THE FOURTH YEAR" of Ahab's reign over Israel (vs. 41). After Ahab's defeat of Syria, there was peace between Israel and Judah for three years (vs. 1–9). During the third year, Jehoshaphat visited Ahab, who proposed that they attack Syria together. All of Ahab's prophets said that they would win, but Jehoshaphat wanted to hear from one of Yehovah's prophets. Ahab knew of one, Micaiah, but did not like him, because he always prophesied against him.

Finally, Jehoshaphat convinced Ahab to let Micaiah come (vs. 10–14). The false prophets were still predicting the utter defeat of Syria, and Ahab's messengers suggested to Micaiah that he go along with the rest. He declared, "AS CERTAINLY AS THE LORD LIVES, I WILL SAY WHAT THE LORD TELLS ME TO SAY."

When he arrived and was asked for a message from God, he surprisingly agreed with the other prophets (vs. 15–28). However, when pressed to make sure he was telling the truth, he admitted that God's real message was that Israel would be defeated and scattered. The reason for the deception was that God allowed an angelic messenger to deceive the king and lead him to his defeat. Ahab ordered that Micaiah be put into prison until he returned from battle. Micaiah remarked, "IF YOU REALLY DO SAFELY RETURN, THEN THE LORD HAS NOT SPOKEN THROUGH ME."

Ahab cunningly convinced Jehoshaphat to wear his royal robes into battle while Ahab disguised himself (vs. 29–40). Naturally, he thought that they would kill Jehoshaphat, but Ahab would escape. This almost happened until the Syrians discovered that it was not Ahab dressed in his royal attire. In what can only be attributed to God's direction, an anonymous Syrian archer randomly shot an arrow that pierced Ahab's armor, causing him to bleed out in his chariot. When they took him back home and buried him, they washed out the chariot, and "THE DOGS LICKED HIS BLOOD, WHILE THE PROSTITUTES BATHED, IN KEEPING WITH THE LORD'S MESSAGE THAT HE HAD SPOKEN." Ahab's son, Ahaziah, succeeded him and ruled for two years, but he was just as wicked as his father (vs. 51–53).

Jehoshaphat ruled for twenty-five years (vs. 41–50). Like his father, Asa, he was a godly king, who attempted to continue the religious reforms that Asa had started. When he died, his son, Jehoram (or Joram), became king.

2 Kings

This book concludes the Books of the Kingdoms, the story of the kings and kingdoms of Israel and Judah. (See the introductory notes of 1 Samuel for more detail about the Books of the Kingdoms.) Second Kings spans a little more than 260 years and details the fall of both kingdoms into their respective captivities. This makes captivity the theme of the book. Israel's northern kingdom marched into captivity more quickly than Judah, as one king after another rejected God. Judah had a few godly kings, which put off their fall for about one hundred years more, but eventually, God sent them into exile for their sin as well. Isaiah, Jeremiah, and most of the Minor Prophets fit chronologically into 2 Kings, even if they are not mentioned in the book.

Chapter one continues immediately from the end of 1 Kings (since they were originally combined as one book). King Ahab's son, Amaziah, was injured, so he sent messengers to hear from Baal Zebub (a pagan god) whether he would survive (vs. 1–4). God sent Elijah to intercept the messengers with the message that the king's lack of faith showed in not coming to Yehovah, so he would die. When they returned to Amaziah with the message, he asked for a description of the prophet, whom he correctly identified as Elijah (vs. 5–8).

The king sent a captain with fifty soldiers to bring Elijah to him, but Elijah called fire from heaven to consume them (vs. 9–12). This happened a second time as well. When the third captain arrived, he begged for his life, recognizing that Elijah was a true prophet of God, so God had Elijah go with him (vs. 13–15). When he arrived at the king's palace, Elijah gave Amaziah the same message he had sent earlier, and the king died just as God had said (vs. 16–18).

His brother, Jehoram, became king in his place, during the second year of King Jehoram of Judah's reign.[1]

Chapter two records the transition from Elijah to Elisha (and the source of the phrase "passing of the mantle). It seems that God had revealed to the other prophets that he would take Elijah away on a specific day, so each place Elijah and Elisha went, they asked if he knew that (vs. 1–6). Each time they moved to a new location, Elijah told Elisha to stay there, and each time Elisha refused, invoking God's name, showing his loyalty to Elijah while he lived.

Finally, the two prepared to cross the Jordan River (vs. 7–13). Elijah hit the water with his cloak and parted it so they could walk across. (Fifty other prophets stood and watched.) Elijah asked Elisha if he had any requests before Elijah left. Elisha requested that God give him a double portion of the prophetic power that Elijah had. Of course, Elijah could not guarantee this, but he gave a final prophecy that, if Elisha saw him leave, then God would grant his request. As they talked a fiery chariot with horses went between them and a whirlwind took Elijah away.

Elisha picked up Elijah's cloak from the ground, walked back to the river, and hit it, calling out "WHERE IS THE LORD, THE GOD OF ELIJAH?" (vs. 14–18). The water parted, allowing him to walk across and verifying to him and the other prophets watching his position as God's chief prophet in Elijah's place. For some reason, the prophets thought that the wind may have dropped off Elijah somewhere else, so they insisted on sending a search party for him, against Elisha's instruction.[2] Finally, he let them search, but they found nothing.

The chapter closes with two immediate examples of Elisha's new power (vs. 19–25). In Jericho, the leaders asked him to do something about the water source, which was killing their crops. He put salt into the water and declared

---

[1] Yes, two men named Jehoram reigned at the same time. Sometimes one of them is called "Joram" to eliminate confusion.

[2] There are some scholars today who also think that Elijah was transported to another location and lived there for the remainder of his natural life. Based on Elisha's response to the idea and the precedent of Enoch in Genesis 5, the most common conservative belief is that Elijah was taken from earth.

that God had purified it. The second instance was when a group of forty-two young boys disrespected him, blatantly and repeatedly. He called God's judgment on them, which took the form of two female bears mauling them to death.

> The two brief episodes recorded in vv. 19–25 demonstrate Elisha's authority and prove that he is the legitimate prophetic heir of Elijah. He has the capacity to bring life and blessing to those who recognize his authority, or death and judgment to those who reject him.[3]

Chapter three picks up from the end of chapter one, continuing the story of Israel's new king, Jehoram (vs. 1–3). Although he was still evil like Jeroboam, he was not as bad as Ahab and Jezebel. As mentioned in 1:1, Moab rebelled against Israel after Ahab's death, so Jehoram asked King Jehoshaphat of Judah if he would go to war with him against Moab (vs. 4–12). Jehoshaphat agreed, and they added the king of Edom as well. After seven days they ran out of water, and Jehoram grew anxious. Much like during his coalition with Ahab, Jehoshaphat sought direction from a prophet of God, and he was pointed to Elisha.

When the kings visited him, Elisha said he would have dismissed Jehoram immediately if not for Jehoshaphat's presence (vs. 13–19). He told them to dig cisterns throughout the land and in the morning they would have water. Additionally, God would give the Moabites over to them as well. However, they needed to destroy the land of Moab and tear down every city, stone by stone. Sure enough, in the morning there was plenty of water (vs. 20–27). From the angle that the Moabites saw it, the water looked like blood, and the king assumed the coalition had turned on itself, so he sent his men to plunder. However, the armies of Israel, Judah, and Edom were ready and thoroughly defeated them. They also destroyed the land and cities as God had said. Only one city remained, and the king of Moab sacrificed his son as a burnt offering to his god there on the wall.

Verse 27 is difficult to interpret because it does not state the source of the anger against Israel. The NET Bible interprets it to mean "DIVINE ANGER," but

---

[3] NET Study Bible notes on 2 Kings 2:25

this does not make sense in the context. It is more likely that the king of Moab displayed his anger toward Israel by burning his son. This showed his defeat, so the Israelites and Edomites went home, fully satisfied that they had won.[4]

Chapter four contains four stories with five miracles that God did through Elisha. There is no specific chronological connection with the surrounding events of the kings, so we cannot place it on the timeline precisely.

In the first story, one of the other prophets died, leaving his wife and two sons with so much debt that the creditor was going to take the sons as slaves until the debt could be paid (vs. 1–7). The widow had nothing but "A SMALL JAR OF OLIVE OIL" and asked Elisha for help. He told her to have her sons borrow as many containers as they could from their neighbors. She was then to pour the olive oil into all of the containers, filling them up. She could then sell the oil and pay the debt.

The second story contains two miracles. Elisha traveled through Shumen regularly, where an older couple had a nice space (vs. 8–17). The woman invited Elisha for a meal, and he stopped there whenever he was in town, so they built a room for him to stay as well. Because of their generosity, he asked if he could do something nice to repay them, but they declined. His servant, Gehazi, noted that the husband was old and they had no son, so Elisha told the woman to expect a son that time next year, which did happen.

One day, several years later, the boy ran out to the field to see his father but complained about a headache, so his father sent him back home where he died on his mother's lap. She laid him on the bed in Elisha's room, then sent a message to her husband asking for a servant and donkey so she could go see Elisha, but she would not tell him why. When she finally found the prophet, she also refused to tell Gehazi but fell at Elisha's feet. He was confused because God had not revealed to him what this was about. When she told him the story, Elisha sent Gehazi running ahead, while he traveled with the woman. When they reached the house, Gehazi reported that the boy was indeed dead.

---

[4] This view seems to make the most sense, and it is the common translation of most major English Bibles. Constable takes this view in his commentary as well.

Elisha went up to the room and laid over the boy, and God brought him back to life.

The third story occurred during a famine, one of the promised results of God's judgment for rebellion against him (vs. 38–41). Some prophets had visited Elisha, so he put on a pot of stew. Someone unintentionally put poisonous plants into the stew, threatening the lives of everyone there, but Elisha added flour and declared that God had purified it. In the fourth story, a man brought a gift of food to Elisha, who told him to give it to a hundred people there (vs. 42–44). When the man objected to the small amount feeding so many people, Elisha said that God had promised more than enough, plus leftovers, which is exactly what happened (similar to Jesus' miracles feeding the 5,000+ Jews and 4,000+ Gentiles).

Chapter five records the famous story of Elisha and Naaman, "THE COMMANDER OF THE KING OF SYRIA'S ARMY." He was well-respected because of his military prowess (granted by God), and somehow obtained an Israelite girl as a servant for his wife (vs. 1–3). He also had a skin disease, traditionally translated as "leprosy."[5] One day the girl mentioned to Naaman's wife that if he could see the prophet who lived in Samaria, he could be healed. When Naaman told his king of this news, the king sent a letter and large gift to the king of Israel (vs. 4–7). The letter simply said that this gift was in payment for Naaman's healing. When the king read this, he took it as an act of aggression from Syria. He could not cure this commander, could he? (Which king of Israel this was is never mentioned, so the assumption is the last one named, Jehoram.)

When Elisha heard Jehoram's interpretation of the letter instead of coming to Elisha, he sent a message to the king telling him to have Naaman report to Elisha (vs. 8–14). This would prove to Jehoram that Elisha was a true prophet of God. When Naaman arrived, Elisha sent out a servant with the instructions

---

[5] Today, leprosy is called "Hansen's disease." It is unlikely that every instance of "leprosy" in the Old Testament was Hansen's. It is probably a catch-all term for several types of skin disease.

that Naaman was to wash seven times in the Jordan River to be healed. This infuriated him, probably for several reasons: 1) Elisha did not receive him personally; 2) he did not do an incantation or invoke Yehovah's name on Naaman's behalf; 3) he could have jumped in any water in Syria if that was all it took. As Naaman stormed away, his servant wisely pointed out that he would have done anything Elisha said, so why not try. Humbly, Naaman washed seven times in the Jordan River and came out completely healed!

Rushing back to Elisha's house, Naaman asked what he could pay for his healing, but Elisha repeatedly refused any payment at all because Naaman had come to the faith in Yehovah as the only true God (vs. 15–19).[6] Somewhat superstitiously, Naaman asked for a load of dirt that he could take back to Syria with him, so he could worship Yehovah on Israel's soil, even in his foreign country. He also asked for a permanent pardon for the sin he would commit of standing in Rimmon's temple with his king when his king worshiped there. Elisha granted him both requests.

As Naaman left, Gehazi decided that Elisha was wrong to not accept Naaman's generosity, so he ran after him (vs. 19–27). Naaman saw him coming, so he stopped his chariot and asked if everything was okay. Gehazi lied about unexpected visitors coming to Elisha and asked Naaman for some silver and clothes for them. Naaman gladly gave him twice the silver he asked for and the clothes, and Gehazi took them back to his home. When Elisha asked where he had been, he lied, but Elisha said, *"I WAS THERE IN SPIRIT,"* and it was not appropriate for Gehazi to take from Naaman. Because of that sin, Naaman's skin disease was given to Gehazi and his descendants forever.

Chapters six and seven tell one story in two parts of a time when Syria was attacking Israel. It opens with another seemingly random story about a miracle that Elisha did (6:1–7). The place where the prophets met was getting too small, so they asked Elisha if they could build a bigger building, and he agreed, so they went to the Jordan River to cut down trees. While one man

---

[6] How different from the response of many so-called healers today, who often take everything from those who flock to them.

was chopping, his ax head flew into the river. He called out to Elisha because he had borrowed it from someone else. Elisha threw a branch into the river at the spot where the tool had gone in, and it floated, so they could get it.

The first story of Syria's attack on Israel is funny (6:8–14). Ben Hadad, Syria's king, was planning to ambush Israelite soldiers, but God kept giving Elisha the coordinates, and he passed them on to Israel's king, so they avoided the traps. Naturally, Ben Hadad thought he had a spy, but someone told him that the information was coming from Elisha, so he sent an army to get him.

The next morning Elisha's servant saw the army surrounding them and was afraid, but Elisha asked God to help him see the invisible angelic army surrounding their enemies (6:15–19). He then asked God to blind the Syrians, and he went outside and told them that he would lead them to Elisha. Instead, he led them right into Samaria, surrounded by the Israelite army. Jehoram asked if he should kill them all, but in an act of grace, Elisha said to throw them a banquet and send them home (6:20–23).

Although Ben Hadad stopped sending raiding parties, he eventually attacked Israel again, this time besieging Samaria (6:24–25). With food supplies cut off, people paid exorbitant prices for a donkey's head or a scoop of dove dung for food. It was so bad that one woman stopped the king one day and said that she and a friend had made a deal to eat her son one day and the other woman's the next (6:26–31). She was complaining to the king because the other woman had hidden her son, after eating the first woman's son. The king was furious and swore to kill Elisha.

Elisha was at home with the city elders when the king's assassin came for him (6:32–7:2). He had told them to block the door because a man was coming to kill him. When the man arrived, he blamed God for the disaster that Israel was facing, but Elisha said that by the next morning, there would be so much food in Samaria that it would cost almost nothing to buy. Of course, the man could not believe that God could accomplish such a feat, and Elisha said that he would see it but not partake of it.

That day, four Israelite men were outside of Samaria because they had a kind of skin disease that caused them to live outside the city (7:3–11). They decided to go to the Syrian camp, thinking they would either live or die there, but they would certainly die in Samaria. When they reached the camp, they found it completely deserted by people but full of animals, food, and wealth. The writer noted that God had made noises in the surrounding hills that made the Syrians think they were under attack, so they fled. The sick men ate their fill and took some of the spoils before thinking that they should inform their king, so they did.

The king thought that it might be a trap, so he sent two men to see if they could find the Syrians in the surrounding hills (7:12–16). What they found, instead, was a trail of clothes and equipment that the Syrians dropped on their way back home. When they told the king, all Samaria raided the Syrian camp and plundered it. There was so much food that people had to pay almost nothing, just as Elisha had said. However, the king's messenger, who had said that God could never do it, was trampled to death by the crowd of people at the city gate. Thus, just as God had said, he saw it happen but was not able to partake of it.

Chapter eight records two stories about Elisha and two new kings of Judah. At some point, God told Elisha that there would be a famine in the Shunem region, where he often stayed with the family whose son had died and come back to life (vs. 1–6). As a good friend, Elisha told the woman to move until the famine passed, which she did. When they returned to claim their property, Gehazi was talking to the king at that moment about some of Elisha's greatest acts, and the king pressed her to tell her whole story. Afterward, he willingly gave them back all their property and assigned a servant to take care of anything they needed.

The second story about Elisha also concerned Ben Hadad, king of Syria (vs. 7–15). Ben Hadad sent one of his officials, Hazael, to ask Elisha if he would recover from an illness. Elisha said that Hazael could tell him "yes" but that Ben Hadad would actually die.[7] Elisha began to weep, explaining that he saw

---

[7] This is one of several places throughout Scripture where God condoned or even commanded someone to lie to an enemy. See the notes on Exodus 1 for further discussion and examples.

the terrible things that Hazael would do to Israel because God said he would be the next king of Syria.[8] When he returned to Ben Hadad, Hazael told the king that he would recover, then suffocated him, and Hazael became the new king of Syria.

After godly Jehoshaphat died, the next two kings of Judah were evil (vs. 16–29). The writer noted that Jehoram (also called Joram) had "MARRIED AHAB'S DAUGHTER," who led him astray. Under his reign, Edom broke free from Judah's rule. Jehoram ruled for eight years, then his son, Ahaziah, ruled for one year. Still related to Ahab and his dynasty, he was also wicked. However, God did not wipe out their dynasty as he often did in Israel, because they were still part of David's eternal dynasty under God's covenant promise.

Chapter nine tells of how God finally destroyed Ahab's dynasty and Queen Jezebel. When Joram/Jehoram, the king of Israel, was wounded in battle against the Syrians, he went home to recover and Ahaziah, the king of Judah, visited him. While they were off the front lines, Elisha sent a prophet to anoint Jehu, one of Joram's officers, as the new king of Israel (vs. 1–13). The prophet's message was that God would use Jehu to kill the rest of Ahab's sons, and Jezebel's corpse would be eaten by dogs instead of being buried. After the prophet left and Jehu told his fellow officers what happened, they immediately accepted him, and he began to make plans against Joram.

Jehu took off with some men to go meet Joram and Ahaziah (vs. 14–21). When the sentry saw troops coming back from battle, Joram sent a messenger out to meet them. Because the messenger stayed with the troops instead of returning immediately with a report, Joram sent another who did the same thing. Finally, the sentry figured out it was Jehu (he was a bad chariot driver) and told Joram, who rode out with Ahaziah to meet him. When Joram asked if everything was all right, Jehu responded, "HOW CAN EVERYTHING BE ALL RIGHT AS LONG AS YOUR MOTHER JEZEBEL PROMOTES IDOLATRY AND PAGAN PRACTICES?" (vs. 22–29) Joram knew it was a trap, warned Ahaziah, and turned his chariot

---

[8] Hazael was one of the three men God told Elijah to anoint in 1 Kings 19:15. We have no record when he did that.

around to run away, but Jehu shot him in the back with an arrow, killing him. His body was dumped in the field that once belonged to Naboth (see 1 Kings 21). Ahaziah turned and ran, too, and he was also shot, but Jehu had him buried as a member of David's family.

When Jehu entered the city, Jezebel dressed up and put on makeup for him, apparently to seduce him into keeping her as his queen (vs. 30–37). He did not fall for her trick, though, and asked if anyone in the house was on his side. "TWO OR THREE EUNUCHS" responded, and he told them to push her out of the window, which they did. After Jehu had gone into the city and eaten a meal, he told some men to go outside to bury Jezebel, but they found that dogs had eaten everything but her "SKULL, FEET, AND PALMS OF THE HANDS," just as Elijah had prophesied.

Chapter ten finishes the story of Ahab's family. With Joram and Jezebel both dead, Jehu wrote a letter to the leaders in Samaria, Israel's capital city, and told them to put the best of Ahab's seventy sons on the throne to defend his family's name (vs. 1–5). Having heard the news of what he had done to Joram and Ahaziah, they were afraid and said that they were his subjects. If that was true, he replied, their first task was to kill all of Ahab's sons and send him their heads as proof (vs. 6–11). They did exactly as he said the next day, and he accepted them as his subjects, noting that God had fulfilled his promised judgment against Ahab's family. Jehu proceeded to kill "ALL WHO WERE LEFT OF AHAB'S FAMILY IN JEZREEL, AND ALL HIS NOBLES, CLOSE FRIENDS, AND PRIESTS." On his way from Jezreel to Samaria, Jehu also came across Ahaziah's family and had them executed as well because they were still related to Ahab, then killed all the remaining family in Samaria, finishing off Ahab's entire dynasty (vs. 12–17).

In Samaria, Jehu gathered the people and said that he would worship Baal far more than Ahab did, but he was intentionally deceiving them (vs. 18–28). Promising "A GREAT SACRIFICE TO BAAL," he commanded that all of Baal's priests, prophets, and servants attend, and he led them into Baal's temple, but he did not let any servant of Yehovah inside. Once they were all there and celebrating, Jehu had them killed and the temple destroyed. "SO JEHU

ERADICATED BAAL WORSHIP FROM ISRAEL." Although Israel had no godly kings, Jehu accomplished more for Yehovah than any of the others. He reigned for twenty-eight years, but he did not completely turn Israel back to Yehovah.

Chapter eleven introduces the next king of Judah and explains how he survived. Ahaziah's mother intended to wipe out the rest of the dynasty so that she could rule in his place without fear of any family rivals (vs. 1–3).[9] However, Amaziah had an infant son named Joash (or Jehoash), who was the rightful heir to the throne, so Amaziah's sister took the baby and hid him "IN THE LORD'S TEMPLE" with the priest, Jehoiada.

After about six years, Jehoiada decided it was time to reveal the true king (vs. 4–8). He brought together the commanders of the royal and Temple guards and made them swear an oath of allegiance to God and possibly to the king, which they all did. He then presented young Joash to them. Jehoiada knew that the boy would need constant protection until his enemies were defeated, so he set up a rotation of the guards so that there was always one unit protecting him in the Temple. The commanders did as Jehoiada instructed and continued to report to him (vs. 9–12). How long they did this is not recorded here, until Jehoiada brought the boy out and presented him to the people as their king, but it must not have been very long because "JEHOASH WAS SEVEN YEARS OLD WHEN HE BEGAN TO REIGN" (vs. 21).

When Athaliah heard the noise, she left the palace and joined the crowd to see what was happening (vs. 13–21). She immediately recognized what had taken place and tried to start a riot, calling it a conspiracy and treason by Jehoiada. However, the priest had the guards seize her, take her outside the Temple, and execute her. Anyone who followed them was to be executed as well. He also "DREW UP A COVENANT BETWEEN THE LORD AND THE KING AND PEOPLE" stating that they would once again follow Yehovah. They kept their word immediately by destroying Baal's temple and altar and killing Baal's priest. At seven years old, Jehoash became the youngest king of Judah.

---

[9] From a spiritual standpoint, this was another attempt by Satan to wipe out the Davidic line so that Messiah could not be born.

Chapter twelve tells of Jehoash's (Joash's) reign in Judah. Because he was only seven years old when he took the throne, the godly priest, Jehoiada, became his counselor and teacher (vs. 1–3). However, they still allowed people to offer sacrifices at the shrines dotted throughout Judah, instead of tearing them down. One of the actions Jehoiada immediately authorized was the repairs that the Temple badly needed (vs. 4–5). Jehoash allowed the priests to use the silver from the treasury to make the repairs themselves. However, after twenty-three years, they had kept taking silver, but the repairs were not completed, so he stopped them (vs. 6–8). Instead of taking more of the existing funds and doing the work themselves, Jehoiada put a locked box next to the altar for people to give voluntary offerings toward the Temple repair. When it was full, he hired craftsmen to do the work, and they completed it (vs. 9–16). The writer makes an interesting note that no audits were taken because the people who disbursed the funds were honest.[10]

Sadly, Jehoash did not stand against the Syrian army or ask God for help when Hazael attacked Jerusalem (vs. 17–21). Instead, he gathered together "ALL THE SACRED ITEMS THAT HIS ANCESTORS JEHOSHAPHAT, JEHORAM, AND AHAZIAH, KINGS OF JUDAH, HAD CONSECRATED," along with some gifts of his own, and sent them to Hazael to buy him off. The Syrians stopped their attack, but it was not a victory for Judah. After reigning for forty years, Jehoash was murdered by two of his own men.

Chapter thirteen introduces the next two kings of Israel and has the potential for confusion because some of the men mentioned had the same names as others or had the names of their grandfathers. Jehoash of Judah had reigned for twenty-three years when Jehoahaz became king of Israel (vs. 1–9). Jehoahaz was evil like Jeroboam, so God gave Israel over to Hazael of Syria. However, Jehoahaz turned to God for mercy, and he did deliver them from Syria again, but they still did not turn from their wickedness and idolatry.

---

[10] This is one of those descriptive stories, not necessarily a prescription or a best-practice that we should follow today.

When Jehoahaz died, his son Joash of Israel, not the Joash/Jehoash from the previous chapter) succeeded him as king.

Joash of Israel reigned for the last three years of Joash of Judah's reign (vs. 10–13). He, too, was evil, as the kings of Israel before him, although he unsuccessfully tried to prevent a civil war with Amaziah, the next king of Judah. When Joash of Israel died, his son, Jeroboam[11], succeeded him.

While Joash reigned in Israel, Elisha became sick and was about to die, so Joash visited him and wept for him (vs. 14–21). Elisha's final prophecy was that God would allow Joash to destroy Syria. To show him, Elisha had Joash shoot an arrow out of the east window. The arrow symbolized the victory that God would give. Then he had Joash grab other arrows and strike the ground (or shoot them at the ground), which he did three times. Elisha was upset because he did not use all the arrows (symbolizing total victory) and declared that Joash would defeat Syria only three times instead of total annihilation.

After Elisha's death, God did one more miracle through him. One day, while some men were burying a dead body, a Moabite raiding party came through, so they tossed the body into Elisha's nearby tomb instead of burying it. When the body touched Elisha's bones, the man came back from the dead.

Hazael continued to harass Israel and Judah throughout Jehoahaz's reign, but because of his covenant with David, God never let them defeat Judah (vs. 22–25). When Hazael died, his son Ben Hadad succeeded him, and Joash of Israel defeated him three times, just as Elisha said.

Chapter fourteen tells of the civil war between Israel and Judah. Amaziah of Judah was not an evil king but not one we would call a godly king (vs. 1–6). "HE DID WHAT THE LORD APPROVED, BUT NOT LIKE DAVID HIS ANCESTOR HAD DONE." He did follow the Law and execute only his father's murderers and not their entire families as many rulers would do.

---

[11] For our purposes, we will identify Joash's son as Jeroboam II, to distinguish him from Jeroboam, the first king of Israel after the kingdom divided following Solomon's death.

After a successful war against Edom, Amaziah became overconfident and challenged Jehoash of Israel to battle as well (vs. 7–14). Not wishing a civil war, Jehoash refused, telling the young Amaziah to not become arrogant, because Israel would easily defeat Judah. Amaziah would not listen, so Jehoash attacked and thoroughly defeated Judah, capturing Amaziah and breaking part of Jerusalem's wall. Fifteen years after Jehoash of Israel's death, Amaziah was assassinated, and his son, Azariah, succeeded him (vs. 15–22).

Jehoash's son, Jeroboam II, became king of Israel and reigned for forty-one years (vs. 23–29). Even though he was a wicked king, God allowed him to have a strong military and restore the borders of Israel from previous wars with Syria. It was during his reign that the prophet Jonah ministered (vs. 25). Because Israel was in such a weakened state, God used Jeroboam II to strengthen them again, so that they would not be destroyed. When Jeroboam II died, his son, Zechariah, replaced him.

Chapter fifteen lists a series of kings of Israel that ruled during Azariah (also called Uzziah) of Judah's reign because he was king of Judah for fifty-two years (vs. 1–7). Little detail about him is given in this chapter, except that he was a good king (not extremely godly) like his father, and that he had a skin disease. His son, Jotham, co-ruled with him during at least part of his reign before he became king upon Azariah's death.

Five different kings ruled in Israel during Azariah's reign over Judah. After Jeroboam II's death, Zechariah ruled in Israel for six months before he was assassinated (vs. 8–12). He was the fourth, and last, in Jehu's dynasty, as God had prophesied (10:30). Shallum ruled Israel for only one month before he was killed by Menahem, a wicked, ruthless man (vs. 13–16).

Menahem's reign of twelve years was marred by an Assyrian invasion (vs. 17–22). Menahem paid off the Assyrians with about 75,000 pounds (34,000 kg) of silver that he obtained by taxing the wealthy Israelites. After his death, his son, Pekahiah, ruled Israel for two years (vs. 23–26). He, too, was evil and was assassinated. Pekah took his place as king and ruled for twenty years (vs. 27–31). Pekah began his reign the year before Azariah of Judah died. Israel was invaded again by Assyria during Pekah's reign, and they captured much Israelite land and took many of the people captive.

After Azariah's fifty-two-year reign, his son and co-ruler, Jotham, became the king of Judah (vs. 32–38). Like several kings before him, he followed Yehovah, but he did not eliminate the shrines across Judah where people continued to offer pagan sacrifices.

Chapter sixteen is the story of Jotham's son, Ahaz. He was a wicked king in Judah who broke from the pattern of the previous four kings who at least tried to serve God (vs. 1–4). Ahaz was blatant in his rejection of Yehovah, publicly worshiping pagan gods and even practicing the pagan ritual of sacrificing one of his sons in fire. According to 15:37, God prompted Pekah of Israel and Rezin of Syria to team up against Judah. Rather than turning to Yehovah, Ahaz contacted the Assyrians to help him (vs. 5–9).[12] The Assyrians conquered Damascus, the Syrian capital, and killed King Rezin.

When Ahaz went to Assyria to meet with Tiglath-pileser in Damascus, he was impressed with the altar there and commissioned a duplicate to be built in Jerusalem (vs. 10–20). By the time he returned to Judah, the new altar was complete, and he replaced Solomon's altar with the new one and commanded that all the normal sacrifices to Yehovah be offered on the new altar. He also dismantled several other pieces of furniture that Solomon had in the Temple. After sixteen years, Ahaz died and was succeeded by Hezekiah.

Chapter seventeen is the sad story of the fall of Israel. Hoshea was the last king of Israel, and he reigned for nine years (vs. 1–6). Although he had paid off Shalmaneser of Assyria to leave Israel alone, he planned to team up with the Egyptians to revolt against Assyria, but they found out. Shalmaneser marched through Israel, "CAPTURED SAMARIA AND DEPORTED THE PEOPLE OF ISRAEL

---

[12] It was this event that prompted the famous "Christmas" passage of Isaiah 7, where Isaiah said that Ahaz's sign from God would be a young woman giving birth to a son and calling him Emmanuel. While this would ultimately be fulfilled by Mary and Jesus, something must have happened during Ahaz's day to fulfill the sign for him, too.

TO ASSYRIA," ending the northern kingdom of Israel. This took place in 722 BC.

The rest of the chapter is the official indictment from God against Israel. In verses 7–23, the writer reviewed the previous 200 years of Israel's history, since Jeroboam became king in 931 BC. They lived in open rebellion against Yehovah, worshiping many other gods all over the land, even to the point of making child sacrifices. Additionally, they blasphemed Yehovah by somehow insinuating that he approved of their actions. Even though God had sent several prophets (like Elijah, Elisha, Hosea, Amos, Isaiah), they did not listen to them and continued their rejection of God. "THEY COPIED THE PRACTICES OF THE SURROUNDING NATIONS IN BLATANT DISREGARD OF THE LORD'S COMMAND" (vs. 15). It was for their idolatry and pagan worship that God sent them into captivity. He had already taken Israel away from David's dynasty because of Solomon's pagan worship; now he shut down that part of Israel completely.

After removing the Israelites from their land, the Assyrian king replaced them with people from other nations that he had conquered (vs. 24–33). However, Yehovah sees the land of Israel as sacred, not just the people, so when the foreigners worshiped their gods and not Yehovah at all, he sent lions in to kill them. This prompted Shalmaneser to send one Israelite priest back to the land to teach them the proper ways to worship Yehovah in addition to their other gods. For some reason, God allowed this arrangement to continue, even though it was simply for show.

The chapter concludes with a review of the commands that God had given Israel when he gave them the land of Canaan, that they should worship him alone, but even to the day that the writer was penning the Books of the Kingdoms, the people tried "WORSHIPING THE LORD AND AT THE SAME TIME SERVING THEIR IDOLS" (vs. 34–41).

Chapter eighteen introduces one of the two best kings that Judah ever had. (Josiah in chapters 22–23 was the other.) Hezekiah was a godly man, like David (vs. 1–12). Unlike his predecessors, who allowed pagan worship outside of Jerusalem, Hezekiah tore down every shrine, pillar, and Asherah pole used for idolatry. We find out here that the bronze serpent that Moses had made in the desert 700 years earlier (Numbers 21:9) had survived, and the people were worshiping that, too! God recorded that, in the matter of trusting Yehovah, "THERE WAS NONE LIKE HIM AMONG THE KINGS OF JUDAH EITHER BEFORE OR AFTER." Hezekiah also broke Judah's treaty with Assyria, and it was during his reign that the northern kingdom was taken into captivity.

Beginning with verse thirteen and going through the next chapter, this passage is repeated nearly word-for-word in Isaiah 36–37. "THE FOURTEENTH YEAR OF KING HEZEKIAH'S REIGN" would have been about 702–701 BC.[13] Secular world history records that Sennacherib captured everything that he besieged except Jerusalem; this account explains why. As was common, both kings sent their aids to meet (vs. 17–18). Sennacherib's message was simple: surrender or die. However, he did not stop there. Much like Goliath (1 Samuel 17) and Nebuchadnezzar (Daniel 3), he did not challenge only Hezekiah or Judah, he challenged Yehovah.

After declaring that Egypt would turn on them if Hezekiah asked them for help, Sennacherib's spokesman said that Yehovah was powerless before the Assyrian army (vs. 19–25, 29–35). After all, Hezekiah himself had eliminated all the altars except for the one in the Temple in Jerusalem. That must have weakened Yehovah and made him upset with Hezekiah (a natural misunderstanding from a pagan worshiper). Not only that, but not one of the other tribal gods that Assyria previously faced had been able to protect their nations, including Samaria.[14] As if that were not enough, the official invoked God's name himself, claiming that Yehovah had told Assyria they were to punish Hezekiah, probably for tearing down the other altars!

---

[13] To make sense of these dates, we must understand the ancient practice of co-regency. Kings would often serve for years as subordinate to their fathers (as the "co-king/co-regent") and later with their sons being the co-regents. Hezekiah ruled as co-regent under Ahaz for 14 years (729–715 BC, during which time Israel was captured by Assyria), then as king for 29 years (until 686 BC). During his last eleven years, Hezekiah's son, Manasseh, served as his co-regent before his own reign began.

[14] It is not insignificant that Israel had turned so far away from Yehovah that Sennacherib did not recognize Yehovah as Israel's God. He considered Yehovah to be the God only of Judah (southern kingdom) but not Israel (northern kingdom).

Surely it would be much better if they simply surrendered. He even went so far as to yell in Hebrew to the guards on the wall, trying to convince them that Hezekiah was only deceiving them and that Yehovah could never protect them (vs. 26–28). After the meeting, Hezekiah's advisers accurately reported what Sennacherib's man had said and done (vs. 37).

Chapter nineteen records Hezekiah's response to Sennacherib's threat. He and his officials went into the Temple in sackcloth to inquire from God (vs. 1–4). It is a powerful passage of trust in the true and living God. Hezekiah sent a message to Isaiah asking him for a message from God. Hezekiah was especially grieved over the "INSULTS" that were made against God and his name. He asked Isaiah to pray for God to punish Assyria for that and to rescue his people. God responded that he would personally cause Sennacherib to return home and would kill him there, delivering Jerusalem from both attack and defeat (vs. 5–7).

When Sennacherib's spokesman heard that Sennacherib had left Jerusalem without attacking, he threw a final insult at Hezekiah: "Don't think this is the end. Your God cannot save you! None of them have!" (vs. 8–13) It seems that this message was on official letterhead because Hezekiah once again approached God (vs. 14–20). After a time of worship, exalting Yehovah as the only true God, he asked God to avenge his name that Assyria had attacked with both slander and libel.

God sent his response through Isaiah again (vs. 21–29). He promised that everything that Judah feared and Assyria threatened would not take place. How dare he stand in Yehovah's city and insult him to his face! Sennacherib may have defeated many kingdoms, but it was all within God's allowance and overall plan.[15] God told Sennacherib, "I KNOW WHERE YOU LIVE," and he would certainly step in, contrary to what Sennacherib thought.

Addressing Hezekiah once again, God gave him a sign that what he had just promised would certainly come true. Instead of starving to death due to a

---

[15] This is the same basis as when Jesus told Pilate, "YOU WOULD HAVE NO AUTHORITY OVER ME AT ALL, UNLESS IT WAS GIVEN TO YOU FROM ABOVE" (John 19:11).

long siege or being taken captive, God promised that the people of Judah would eat crops from their fields for the next three years (with an implied indefiniteness), and they would raise their children there. The phrase, "THE ZEAL OF THE LORD OF HEAVEN'S ARMIES WILL ACCOMPLISH THIS," is similar to Isaiah 9:7 (identical in the parallel account in Isaiah 37:32), when God gave the sign of Immanuel to Ahaz about 30 years earlier.

Not only would Sennacherib not capture Jerusalem, but he also would never attack or besiege it. God would take him back to his own land. He did this by sending "THE ANGEL OF THE LORD" to slaughter 185,000 Assyrian soldiers in one night (vs. 35–37). This sent Sennacherib back to Nineveh, where he was eventually assassinated by his own sons (approximately 20 years later).

Chapter twenty is said to have occurred "IN THOSE DAYS," i.e., during Sennacherib's threat of attack. However, this event took place before chapters 18–19, since God's initial promise to protect Judah from Sennacherib must have taken place before Sennacherib returned to Assyria. This is likely the reason Hezekiah was so certain that God would respond to Assyria's threats.

Hezekiah was on his deathbed. Unlike Christians today, he had no guarantee of an immediate afterlife with God. Additionally, with the threat of Assyria on his doorstep, he must have been afraid that he would die and Judah would be lost. He reminded God of how faithful he had been in helping turn Judah back to God and asked if God would grant him more time (vs. 1–3). God's response should not confuse us or be assumed as a contradiction. Yes, he had Isaiah tell Hezekiah that he was going to die. Yet, when Hezekiah asked for more time, God granted it (vs. 4). This speaks to the fact that God does listen to prayer and that every detail of every event is not planned from the beginning as many people believe. Had Hezekiah not prayed and requested more time, he would have died as God had originally said.[16]

---

[16] We see a similar situation with David in 1 Samuel 23:9–13, when God told him that he would be handed over to Saul by the leaders of Keilah. However, taking that as a warning, David did not go to Keilah and thus was not arrested and killed there. See the notes at that passage for a longer discussion about God's omniscience and the flexibility of world events.

Not only did God promise to add 15 years to Hezekiah's life, but he also promised to protect Jerusalem from the Assyrian threat (vs. 4–6). Unlike his father, Ahaz, who refused to ask for a sign (Isaiah 7:11–12), Hezekiah was not shy at all. He wanted to know how he could be sure that this was true. Isaiah said that "THE SHADOW...ON THE STAIRS OF AHAZ" would "GO BACK TEN STEPS," and it did (vs. 7–11).[17]

Somehow the king of Babylon "HEARD THAT HEZEKIAH WAS ILL" so he sent an envoy with gifts and letters of well-wishing (vs. 12–13). Hezekiah was so glad about the gesture that he proceeded to show the Babylonians around his palace and the Temple. The Hebrew text of verse thirteen says, "There was not a thing which Hezekiah did not show in his house and in all his dominion" (my translation).

Second Chronicles 32:24–25 reveals that Hezekiah's heart was not right with God after his recovery. Securing a strong ally against Assyria was his true motive for being so friendly with Babylon (2 Chronicles 32:31). He showed his lack of trust in God's promise that he would protect Judah himself, so God sent Isaiah with a message (vs. 14–18). When asked who the visitors were and what they saw, Hezekiah was happy to tell him the truth. Solemnly, Isaiah announced that Hezekiah had just secured his nation's fate. Everything that he showed off would one day end up in Babylon, including some of his descendants, who would stand as eunuchs in the Babylonian palace. This took place about 100 years later when Nebuchadnezzar invaded Judah three times between 605 and 586 BC (see Daniel 1).

Hezekiah's response is both confusing and discouraging (vs. 19). Rather than deep repentance or prayer and weeping, as with God's previous message concerning his impending death, Hezekiah simply accepted God's decision, commenting that at least it would not take place during his lifetime. He did not weep over God's people or Jerusalem, only his own life. Although he was

---

[17] The fact that it was specifically the "shadow" that would move has been the source of great debate. Did the entire Sun/earth change that much or did God move only the shadow without affecting the planets? There is no way to know. However, Constable notes the irony that God offered Ahaz a sign even from the heavens that he refused.

one of the few godly kings in Judah, Hezekiah died with this as his last story preserved in Scripture (vs. 20–21).

Chapter twenty-one gives a short history of two wicked kings of Judah—Manasseh and Amon. In contrast to good King Azariah (Uzziah) who reigned in Judah for fifty-two years, Manasseh ruled for fifty-five years, but he was evil (vs. 1–9).[18] He undid everything that Hezekiah had done regarding pagan worship—rebuilt the shrines, Asherah poles, and altars. But he went further. He also practiced star worship, child sacrifice, divination, and necromancy. He even put an idol in the Temple! He killed so many innocent people that Jerusalem was stained with their blood (vs. 16). Under Manasseh, Judah "SINNED MORE THAN THE NATIONS WHOM THE LORD HAD DESTROYED FROM BEFORE THE ISRAELITES."

Because of this, God had his prophets announce the fall of Judah, like Israel had fallen (vs. 10–15). Although Babylon is not named here, Manasseh had certainly heard of what Isaiah told Hezekiah about Babylon's coming invasion in 20:16–18. It is interesting to consider that Manasseh's reign may have been part of God's judgment on Judah because of Hezekiah's sin in courting Babylon. Since Manasseh began to rule when he was eleven years old (vs. 1), he was not born until after Hezekiah's sickness and recovery. Had Hezekiah died rather than gaining 15 more years, he would never have turned to Babylon for help, and Manasseh would never have been born.

Unlike other kings, verse 17 notes the rest of Manasseh's actions were recorded upon his death, "AS WELL AS THE SINFUL ACTS HE COMMITTED" (vs. 17–18). Manasseh's son, Amon, ruled next (vs. 19–26). He was wicked as well, continuing the pagan practices that Manasseh had established. Amon reigned only two years before he was assassinated, and his son, Josiah, took the throne.

Chapter twenty-two begins the story of Josiah, the last godly king of Judah. He was only eight years old when he became king, and much like Jehoash of Judah before him, a wise and godly priest counseled him in the

---

[18] Second Chronicles 33 records his repentance that 2 Kings does not.

ways of Yehovah (vs. 1–7). As Jehoash did before, Josiah commissioned the Temple to be rebuilt, using the silver brought by the people to pay for it. Unlike the first time, however, Josiah had the work done by professional tradesmen from the beginning and did not require an audit of the foremen disbursing the funds.

During the renovation, "HILKIAH THE HIGH PRIEST INFORMED SHAPHAN THE SCRIBE" that he had found "THE SCROLL OF THE LAW" in the Temple (vs. 8–13). When Shaphan read it and realized it was the Mosaic Law,[19] he went to Josiah with a progress report on the Temple and read to him from the scroll. Josiah was devastated and insisted that they find a prophet who could give them a message from God. The people had obviously not obeyed Yehovah, and the scroll said that they were to be judged. Josiah's men did find a prophetess who told them that the judgment must take place (vs. 14–20). However, because Josiah had humbled himself immediately when he read the law, God promised that the destruction would take place after his time and that he would die in peace.

Chapter twenty-three is a bittersweet section of the book. On the one hand, followers of Yehovah can celebrate the deep cleaning that Josiah did throughout all Judah and even into Israel. After renewing their covenant with God to follow him only (vs. 1–3), the next twenty-one verses describe, in detail, what Josiah tore down from the wicked kings before him (vs. 4–24). Some of these were already listed as having been installed by Manasseh, but chapter twenty-one did not tell even a short version of the story. Everywhere Josiah turned there was another altar, another shrine, another Asherah pole. The people were participating in the worship of every god from the nations around them, every celestial body in the sky, and every demon they had heard of. Cultic prostitution was rampant. In addition to the things Manasseh had

---

[19] Or at least part of it. Since Deuteronomy lists the blessings and curses of what God would do with the nation of Israel in the land, it is likely at least part of the scroll (if not the entire thing) was Deuteronomy.

done, there were still leftovers from Solomon and Jeroboam, hundreds of years earlier!

More than all of that, Josiah discovered that Israel was supposed to celebrate the Passover annually, something that had not been done "SINCE THE DAYS OF THE JUDGES; IT WAS NEGLECTED FOR THE ENTIRE PERIOD OF THE KINGS OF ISRAEL AND JUDAH" (vs. 21–23). This does not mean that they had completely ignored the Passover all that time, but that it was not performed strictly according to the law as Josiah insisted.[20]

The best epitaph Josiah could have received is found in verse twenty-five: "NO KING BEFORE OR AFTER REPENTED BEFORE THE LORD AS HE DID, WITH HIS WHOLE HEART, SOUL, AND BEING IN ACCORDANCE WITH THE WHOLE LAW OF MOSES." However, even his reforms did not turn God's plan away from Judah's destruction (vs. 26–30). Josiah died in battle attempting to prevent Pharaoh Necho from helping the Assyrians.

Josiah's son, Jehoahaz, took his place as king, but he was wicked and reigned only three months (vs. 31–37). Necho imprisoned Jehoahaz in Egypt, where he died, and made Jehoahaz's son, Eliakim, the king instead. Necho changed Eliakim's name to Jehoiakim. He ruled under Necho over Jerusalem for eleven years and had to tax the people heavily to pay the tribute to Necho.

Chapter twenty-four is the beginning of the end for the kingdom of Judah. It was during Jehoiakim's rule that Nebuchadnezzar invaded Israel for the first time in 605 BC (vs. 1–7). Daniel and his friends were included in this first deportation (Daniel 1:1–7). This was the fulfillment of the promise God made to Hezekiah, that his descendants would stand in the Babylonian court as eunuchs (2 Kings 20:16–18). When Jehoiakim died, his son, Jehoiachin, became king. Pharaoh Necho did not attempt to take over Jehoiachin because Nebuchadnezzar had already defeated Necho and that would have been seen as a revolt against the Babylonian king.

---

[20] Second Chronicles 30 tells that a form of Passover was held under Hezekiah, but it was not done exactly according to the Mosaic Law.

Jehoiachin reigned only three months before Nebuchadnezzar sent his army into Jerusalem a second time in 597 BC (vs. 8–17). It was at this time that he made a second, much larger, deportation. Not only was Jehoiachin taken prisoner, but "ALL THE RESIDENTS OF JERUSALEM, INCLUDING ALL THE OFFICIALS AND ALL THE SOLDIERS (10,000 PEOPLE IN ALL). THIS INCLUDED ALL THE CRAFTSMEN AND THOSE WHO WORKED WITH METAL. NO ONE WAS LEFT EXCEPT FOR THE POOREST AMONG THE PEOPLE OF THE LAND." Nebuchadnezzar also stripped the Temple of everything of value, including the gold items Solomon had put there. Finally, he installed Jehoiachin's uncle as the new king and renamed him, Zedekiah. It was under Zedekiah that Judah finally fell to Babylon (vs. 18–20).

Chapter twenty-five concludes the story, not just of 2 Kings, but also of the kingdom of Judah, which was the last kingdom of Israel to stand under a Jewish king until Messiah reigns in the future Millennial Kingdom. Jeremiah 37–40 and 52 give more detail about the events, leading some scholars to think that Jeremiah or his writings contributed to 2 Kings.[21]

Toward the end of Zedekiah's reign, Nebuchadnezzar came to Jerusalem one more time and besieged it for almost a year and a half (vs. 1–7). When the situation became so grave that there was nothing left in Jerusalem to eat, the people attempted to flee, but they were captured by Nebuchadnezzar's men. Zedekiah was forced to watch the execution of his sons, then his eyes were gouged out, and he was taken as a prisoner to Babylon. During the eleven years of Zedekiah's rule, the population of Jerusalem had grown again, so in this final deportation (586 BC), Nebuchadnezzar wiped out nearly everything. He burned the palace, houses, and the Temple and tore down the city wall. Only the poorest of the poor were left; everyone else either escaped to Egypt (some of whom kidnapped Jeremiah and took him with them) or were carried off to Babylon.

---

[21] If you are reading the Bible as chronological history, the two books that continue and conclude the historical narrative after 2 Kings are Ezra and Nehemiah. See the section entitled "Introduction to the Old Testament" at the beginning of this book for more information about where the chronology of the Old Testament can be found.

Everything that was in the Temple that the Babylonians had either overlooked or simply did not take previously (like the bronze items), they broke down and took this time (vs. 13–17). All of the royal advisers and the priests were hunted down and executed (vs. 18–21). Nebuchadnezzar appointed a governor, Gedaliah, to oversee the people who were left (vs. 22–26). Because he was Jewish, some of the military officers who had gone into hiding came to him, hoping that he would guarantee their safety. He said that he would if they submitted to Babylon. They did not like that response and had him assassinated, then they fled to Egypt.

The book ends on a positive note, however (vs. 27–30). Thirty-seven years later, Jehoiachin was still a prisoner in Babylon. When Evil-Merodach became king in Babylon, he pardoned Jehoiachin, gave him a ruling position over the exiles in Babylon, and provided for him for the rest of his life. Thus ends the story of the kingdoms of Israel.

1 Chronicles

Like the books of Samuel and Kings, the Chronicles were originally one book with the Hebrew name דברי הימים (*debarim hayamim*), "the words of the days." Archer notes that, since the Septuagint (the Greek translation of the Old Testament done in the 2nd and 3rd centuries BC) has them divided into two books, that must have been done in the Hebrew text already.[1] The break between 1 and 2 Chronicles is approximately the same as between 2 Samuel and 1 Kings, which is a natural division between the reigns of David and Solomon.

Many people often assume that Chronicles is simply a slightly-altered repeat of Samuel and Kings. While there is certainly some borrowed or repeated material (from Genesis as well), that is a gross misunderstanding of both the content and purpose of Chronicles. Written much later (possibly by Ezra after Israel's return from captivity), the accounts in Chronicles span the entire history of Israel, beginning with Adam, and place a special focus on the Abrahamic and Davidic Covenants. Thus, for instance, Saul's reign comprises only one short chapter, while David's spans nineteen. Additionally, once Israel was divided into northern and southern kingdoms, 2 Kings tells the history almost equally about both kingdoms, while 2 Chronicles focuses primarily on David's dynasty in the southern kingdom, ignoring much of the northern kingdom.

Another perspective is to see that the books of Samuel and Kings are more political-historical, while Chronicles is emphatically spiritual-historical. In other words, whereas Samuel and Kings have more of a human perspective on

---

[1] Gleason L. Archer, *A Survey of Old Testament Introduction, Revised and Expanded* (Moody Press, 1994), 449.

the events recorded, Chronicles offers God's perspective on many of the same events, helping us understand their bigger picture. This accounts for the infamous nine-chapter genealogy which begins 1 Chronicles. It moves quickly through about 3,000 years from Adam to David, because it connects the nation of Israel and David's dynasty back through Judah to Abraham.

Liberal scholars like to point to the discrepancies between the earlier books and Chronicles, especially when it comes to large numbers. After explaining much of the detail about some of these, Archer succinctly wrote:

> In the light of all this evidence it is impossible to construct an airtight case proving any original discrepancy between the autograph manuscript of Chronicles and the relevant passages in the other canonical books. It is safe to say that all the so-called discrepancies that have been alleged are capable of resolution either by textual criticism or by contextual exegesis.[2]

Chapter one contains a specialized genealogy that was probably compiled from the lists in Genesis chapters five and ten, along with other historical records. The first few verses cover the nearly 1,700 years between Adam and Noah's sons (vs. 1–4). The next section briefly lists the Gentile nations that came from Japheth and Ham (vs. 5–16), before coming to Seth's family line, which was the author's goal.

The writer again passed quickly through Shem's line until he reached his second major personality after Adam: Abraham (vs. 17–27). At this point, the genealogy slows down considerably. Officially, Abraham had only two sons: Ishmael and Isaac (vs. 28). Although Genesis 25:1 does not specifically state it, verse 32 here calls Keturah a concubine of Abraham, not a wife (Genesis 25:6 records that he had multiple concubines), meaning that her sons did not share

---

[2] Gleason L. Archer, *A Survey of Old Testament Introduction, Revised and Expanded* (Moody Press, 1994), 455.

a legal inheritance with Sarah's.[3] After listing Ishmael's and Keturah's descendants (vs. 29–33), the writer came to Isaac.

Isaac had two sons, Esau and Israel (vs. 34). A point of significance was the writer's refusal to use Jacob's name in the genealogy.[4] Esau's genealogy received considerably more space than any of the other non-Jewish families (vs. 35–54). This is probably due to the closeness in both familial and geographical proximity between the brothers' descendants and because Edom (Esau's nation) was a perennial enemy with Israel for centuries.

Chapter two finally comes to the writer's primary focus of his genealogies: "THE SONS OF ISRAEL" (vs. 1–2). The naming of Jacob's twelve sons is odd. The first six named were Leah's, which is to be expected as she was his first wife and Reuben was his first son. His other wife was Rachel (his favorite), who gave birth to Joseph and Benjamin. Rachel's maid, Bilhah, bore Dan and Naphtali; Leah's maid, Zilpah, bore Gad and Asher. Dan's placement before Joseph seems out of place. However, Constable quoted Keil to explain:

> That a different place is assigned to Dan, viz. before the sons of Rachel, from that which he holds in the list in [Genesis 35:23ff.], is perhaps to be accounted for by Rachel's wishing the son of her maid Bilhah to be accounted her own [see Genesis 30:3-6].[5]

In other words, Bilhah's first son was supposed to be credited to Rachel who could not have children. Thus, the three sons named after Leah's were Bilhah's first (Dan) followed by Rachel's biological sons (Joseph and Benjamin). Although he was not the firstborn or the birthright holder, the

---

[3] Although Ishmael was not biologically Sarah's son, the arrangement between Sarah and Hagar was supposed to be that Hagar's son would legally be Sarah's, because she was barren. When Isaac was born, Ishmael lost the position of heir, but Abraham did not relegate him to the status of a concubine's son.

[4] In fact, in the books of Chronicles, the name "Jacob" occurs only twice (16:13, 17), both in reference to Jacob the man, not his nation.

[5] Keil quoted in Constable, *Notes on 1 Chronicles, 2016 Edition*, 11.

writer listed Judah's family first because it was through him that the royal Davidic (and Messianic) line came (vs. 3–55; Genesis 49:10). Although the writer tended to skip some of the negative aspects of Israel's history, he usually did so only when it did not further his purpose of recording God's covenantal promises. Because the Davidic line came through Judah's son, Perez, the writer had to record the sins of Er and Onan and Judah's relationship with Tamar (vs. 3–4).

Some of the more notable descendants of Judah (aside from David) were Achan, who stole items from Jericho and brought judgment on his house (Joshua 7); the Kenites descended from Jericho's Rahab (spelled "Rechab" in vs. 55); and Bezalel, the master craftsman who led the work on the Tabernacle in the wilderness (vs. 20; Exodus 31:1–5).

Chapter three brings the reader to the most famous of Judah's descendants (at the time of writing[6]): David. When David was ruling in Hebron, he had six sons by six different women (vs. 1–9). Once he became king over all Israel and moved to Jerusalem, his wives gave him thirteen more sons; four of these were Bathsheba's (including Solomon and Nathan, from whom Joseph and Mary, respectively, came; see Matthew 1 and Luke 3). David also had other sons and daughters by his concubines but only one daughter, Tamar, from a wife. (According to 2 Samuel 13:1, Tamar was Absalom's full sister.)

Staying true to his purpose of recording the Davidic family line, the writer concludes this chapter by listing the sons of Solomon, the one through whom the Davidic Covenant was fulfilled (vs. 10–24). In addition to the kings of Judah also found in 1 and 2 Kings, the writer included at least five generations from after Israel's return from exile (vs. 19–24), beginning with Shenazzer and Zerubbabel from Ezra 1–2.[7]

---

[6] Further revelation confirms Jesus of Nazareth as the promised Messiah, the son of David.

[7] This proves that the compilation of Chronicles was much later than the books of Samuel and Kings.

The original readers of Chronicles, freshly transplanted into the Promised Land from Babylonian captivity, were having an identity crisis. They needed to remember what they were and what God intended for them to be. They lived in a culture that wanted to use them for its own ends. By piecing together name lists from the previous historical books of the Old Testament, and perhaps other sources, the writer was able to preach the meaning of his people's history. This he continued to do throughout Chronicles.[8]

Chapter four comes back to Judah's family to point out a few more prominent people before moving on to the other descendants of Jacob. Probably two of the most famous verses in 1 Chronicles in recent days are verses 9–10, the prayer of Jabez. Ironically, as he "WAS MORE RESPECTED THAN HIS BROTHERS," this genealogy does not list who his brothers or father were.

The last two notable Judahites were Othniel and Caleb. Joshua 15:17 is unclear whether Othniel was Caleb's brother or nephew, but verses 13–15 here seem to exclude them from being brothers. Caleb was one of the two faithful spies (along with Joshua) who went into Canaan for Moses and believed Israel could take the land (Numbers 13–14). He and Joshua finally did conquer the land after Israel's years wandering the desert (Joshua 15). Othniel was younger than twenty years old (if he was even born) when the spies went into Canaan since he survived the wandering years. He was also part of the army during the conquest of Canaan and the first judge of Israel after Joshua's death (Judges 3:9).

The rest of chapter four gives the descendants of Jacob's second son, Simeon (vs. 24–43). The reason for Simeon's relative weakness among the other tribes of Israel is explained by the fact that most of the sons from the first few generations had few children to perpetuate the family line.

Chapter five contains the family lines of the two-and-a-half tribes that stayed on the east side of the Jordan River, rather than receiving their inheritance within the borders of Canaan (Numbers 32). Verses 1–2 confirm

---

[8] Constable, *Notes on 1 Chronicles, 2016 Edition*, 13.

what the observant reader of Genesis infers. Although Reuben was the firstborn son of Jacob, he gave up his birthright by sleeping with his father's concubine (Rachel's maid; Genesis 35:22; 49:3–4). Joseph was Jacob's favorite son, so he received the birthright, including a double portion of the inheritance, represented by having two tribes—Ephraim and Manasseh. Reuben was the largest of the Transjordan tribes, extending "AS FAR AS THE ENTRANCE TO THE WILDERNESS THAT STRETCHES TO THE EUPHRATES RIVER" (vs. 3–9).

Gad also lived east of the Jordan (vs. 10–22). Little is recorded about them, except for the war they waged with Reuben against the Hagrites and their allies. God helped them defeat this enemy, and they captured many animals and 100,000 people.

"THE HALF-TRIBE OF MANASSEH" is charged with falling away from Yehovah and worshiping the pagan gods around them (vs. 23–26). All these tribes were attacked by the Assyrian king, Tiglath-Pileser III,[9] and finally conquered by his successor, Shalmaneser V, in 722 BC.[10]

Chapter six records the family of Levi.[11] Levi had three sons—Gershom, Kohath, and Merari—each of whom had many descendants (vs. 1–3). Moses, Aaron, and Miriam were from the Kohath clan. The reason these clans were important was because of the various duties assigned to them. In Numbers 3, we see that Moses divided out the responsibilities surrounding the Tabernacle to these clans. The Gershonites were responsible for setting up, tearing down, and carrying the curtains, ropes, etc. The Merarites were responsible for the framework of the Tabernacle. The Kohathites took care of the furniture inside the Tabernacle, including the Ark of the Covenant. Within the Kohathite clan was Aaron's family who served as the priests, including the high priest.

---

[9] Also called Tilgath-Pilneser (Hebrew spelling in verse six) and Pul (vs. 26).

[10] Shalmaneser V died in 722 BC, the year Israel fell, and his successor, Sargon II, claimed the conquest of Israel for himself.

[11] The Hebrew text includes the first fifteen verses along with chapter five, making chapter six begin with the second time the writer said, "THE SONS OF LEVI."

This chapter includes the detail that David selected certain of the Levites to serve as music ministers in the Tabernacle and, later, the Temple (vs. 31–47). These included Heman, Asaph, and Ethan, whose names appear in the Psalms. Because God did not grant the Levites any tribal land of their own, they received cities within each of the other tribes, where they served the spiritual needs of their fellow Israelites on a more local level than just the Temple in Jerusalem (vs. 54–80).

Chapter seven concludes the genealogy of Israel with Issachar, Benjamin, Naphtali, the other half of Manasseh, Ephraim, and Asher. A few points are worth considering here. First, Naphtali was given one line, only four sons, and no further lineage. Second, Dan and Zebulun were not included at all. Constable suggests that this was because of their lack of size and influence after the captivity.[12] Furthermore, since the writer included both sons of Joseph (and both halves of Manasseh separately) and Levi, he needed to remove two tribes to keep the number twelve. Dan was the most idolatrous of the tribes, which may point to his being ignored here.[13]

Chapter eight begins and ends as if it were just an expanded listing of Benjamin's tribe, but, in context, the purpose of this genealogy is discovered in verse thirty-three: "NER WAS THE FATHER OF KISH, AND KISH WAS THE FATHER OF SAUL," the first king of Israel. Moreover, Benjamin sided with Judah to stay true to the Davidic line, so the writer would naturally emphasize this tribe as well, even though the promised king would come from Judah.

Chapter nine ends the major genealogical section with verse one, pointing to the fact that 1) there were other record books with official genealogies and 2) the writer used and referenced them. While this chapter does certainly include more family lines, these are less "ancient history" than the previous chapters were. Instead, these were "recent history" for the Chronicler, because

---

[12] Constable, *Notes on 1 Chronicles, 2016 Edition*, 17.

[13] Dan is also left out of the list in Revelation 7.

they focused on those who resettled the land after the exile. As the book of Ezra also records, some of the first people back in the land were "ISRAELITES, PRIESTS, LEVITES, AND TEMPLE SERVANTS" (vs. 2). He was especially interested in three tribal families—Judah, Benjamin, and Joseph (represented by Ephraim and Manasseh).

Chapter ten begins the narrative for the rest of the book. As noted in the Introduction, the writer did not intend to simply repeat the content of the books of Samuel and Kings. His was a special purpose that required only certain content. The other detail could be read in the other books.

> In all of Chronicles the writer assumed his readers' acquaintance with the other Old Testament historical books. This is especially true regarding what Samuel and Kings contain. These books, or at least the information in them, appears to have been well known by the returning exiles.[14]

As much as the writer wanted to stay with the Davidic dynasty and God's covenantal promises, he could not simply overlook Saul's reign. So, even though he had already given Saul's family line (chapter eight), he still needed to briefly address the king. However, rather than recounting any part of his reign, the writer skipped directly to Saul's death and the subsequent defeat of Israel at the hands of the Philistines (vs. 1–7; 1 Samuel 31). He also included the humiliation of Saul's and his sons' corpses at the hands of the Philistines and their rescue by the men of Jabesh Gilead (vs. 8–14). "HE DID NOT SEEK THE LORD'S GUIDANCE, SO THE LORD KILLED HIM AND TRANSFERRED THE KINGDOM TO DAVID SON OF JESSE."

Chapter eleven gives only a summary of David's reign, first in Hebron, then in Jerusalem (vs. 1–9). True to his purpose, the writer attributed David's

---

[14] Constable, *Notes on 1 Chronicles, 2016 Edition*, 20.

greatness to God. "DAVID'S POWER STEADILY GREW, FOR THE LORD OF HEAVEN'S ARMIES WAS WITH HIM."

Most of the chapter is dedicated to the warriors who served alongside David. First, the writer mentioned the "THREE ELITE WARRIORS" who stood out above the rest (vs. 10–25). Although only one was named, Eleazar, both Abishai and Benaiah gained fame within the three, even though they were not part of the three. Additionally, there were thirty "MIGHTY WARRIORS" (vs. 26–47) plus others who served David well.

As noted in the introduction to 1 Chronicles, there are some places where large numbers differ between the Chronicles and the books of Samuel and Kings. These variants could have occurred for several reasons. The account of Jashobeam killing 300 men (vs. 11) or 800 men (2 Samuel 23:8) is one of these instances. At this point, it is impossible to determine which number is correct. The most logical conclusion is that the number "300" was mistakenly copied in 1 Chronicles 11:11 since that is the same number attributed to Abishai later in verse 20 as well. In this case, the correct number is preserved in 2 Samuel.[15]

Chapter twelve continues the record of David's fighting men, particularly from his time at Ziklag (vs. 1–7). These men joined him early on "WHEN HE WAS BANISHED FROM THE PRESENCE OF SAUL." Two unique features are given about these men. First, they were ambidextrous in their use of both bow and arrow and slings. Second, they were Benjaminites, the same tribe as Saul.

Some Gadites also joined David (vs. 8–22). These are said to have been experts with spears and shields and military leaders over groups of hundreds and thousands. He also had men from Benjamin, Judah, Manasseh, and the other tribes. During his time waiting out Saul, "EACH DAY MEN CAME TO HELP DAVID UNTIL HIS ARMY BECAME VERY LARGE." Eventually, David had more than 337,000 warriors with him, from every tribe of Israel (including Levi), who supported making him king (vs. 23–40).

---

[15] Since Samuel was written much earlier than Chronicles and reads "800," it would be much more likely for the scribe to make the unintentional copy error in Chronicles than for someone to inflate the number in Samuel at a later date.

Chapter thirteen parallels 2 Samuel 5–6 when David called all Israel to support him as king in Hebron. After reigning for seven years there, he moved to Jerusalem and wanted to move the ark of the covenant there as well. He had a new cart prepared to move the ark from Kiriath Jearam, where it stayed under Saul's reign, but along the way, the oxen stumbled, and the ark looked like it was going to fall. A man named Uzzah reached out to protect the ark, but he touched the side of it, something even the priests were not allowed to do. Immediately, God executed him for this breach of God's transcendent holiness. This scared and angered David, so he housed the ark with Obed-Edom for three months, during which time God blessed the man's home.

Chapter fourteen parallels 2 Samuel 5:11–25. Once David was settled in Jerusalem, King Hiram of Tyre sent him messengers and materials to build a palace there (vs. 1–2). As was noted earlier in his genealogy, David married many wives and had thirteen more sons plus daughters born there (vs. 3–7). Twice the Philistines invaded the Valley of Rephaim (vs. 8–17). The first time, God had David attack them directly, and he defeated them. The second time, God told him to ambush them from the back, while God attacked them from the front. This victory secured David's reputation, not only in Israel but throughout all the surrounding nations.

Chapter fifteen tells how the ark finally came to Jerusalem. Although David did not build the Temple, he did build a tent to replace the one that had traveled through the desert some 400 years earlier (vs. 1). Realizing his error in not having the Levites carry the ark the first time, he remedied that, gathering the men from Aaron's family and having them consecrate themselves before God and use the poles as God had instructed Moses (vs. 2–15).

He also assigned other Levites to accompany the ark "AS MUSICIANS" (vs. 16–24). Heman, Asaph, and Ethan, along with many others, sang and played instruments as the parade marched from Obed-Edom's house into Jerusalem. As they marched, David also danced and sang before it. Arriving at their destination, David offered more sacrifices to welcome the ark, and God's presence, to its new home. With less detail than 2 Samuel 6, the writer notes only that David's wife, Michal (noted as "SAUL'S DAUGHTER"), "DESPISED HIM" for his dancing.

Chapter sixteen continues the story of the ark's move to Jerusalem (vs. 1–6). Once the ark was in place, David offered a blessing over all the people and handed out gifts of food. He also appointed a new troupe of musicians to serve before the ark regularly. These included songwriters and singers, stringed instruments, cymbals, and trumpets. Although there was some music involved in the original duties of the Levites, David (a musician himself) expanded this ministry.

The "SONG OF THANKS" in verses 7–36 is a compilation from three psalms (with some variations), none of which are titled in the Psalms, but seem to have been written by David—Psalm 105:1–15 (vs. 7–22); Psalm 96:2–13 (vs. 23–33); Psalm 106:1, 47–48 (vs. 34–36). The chapter concludes with David's instructions to the priests and musicians, who served both in Jerusalem at the ark and in Gibeon, where Moses' Tabernacle still stood (vs. 37–43). "THEN ALL THE PEOPLE RETURNED TO THEIR HOMES, AND DAVID WENT TO PRONOUNCE A BLESSING ON HIS FAMILY."

Chapter seventeen finds its parallel in 2 Samuel 7, the great Davidic Covenant, one of only a few eternal covenants in Scripture. Some time had passed, and God had given David and the nation peace, so David's mind considered ways to honor God (vs. 1–6). Noticing the disparity between his cedar-paneled palace and the tent housing the ark, David planned to build a temple for God and received approval from Nathan, God's prophet. However, Nathan's message had not come from God. That night God gave him this message for David: "In all the centuries I have been with Israel, I have never asked, 'WHY HAVE YOU NOT BUILT ME A HOUSE MADE FROM CEDAR?'"

Playing off the keyword "house," God said that, instead of David building him a house, God would build David a house—a royal dynasty that would never end (vs. 7–15). He reminded David where he came from—the sheep pasture—and that he had won David's battles for him. Although he did not deserve anything else, God promised him more. God would treat David's heir like his own son.[16] However, David's son, Solomon, could not reign forever, so we find the ultimate fulfillment in Jesus as the eternal king (Luke 1:30–33; Matthew 1:1).

The rest of the chapter contains David's prayer in response to God's promise (vs. 16–27). In this prayer, David addressed God in several different ways[17]:

- Six times with God's covenantal name יְהוָה (*yehovah*, verse 19, 20, 22, 23, 26, 27)
- Twice with the combination יְהוָה אֱלֹהִים (*yehovah 'elohim*, "LORD God," verses 16, 17)
- Once with the title יְהוָה צְבָאוֹת (*yehovah tseba'oth*) translated "LORD of Heaven's Armies" (traditionally "LORD of hosts") in verse 24 (also used by God of himself in verse seven)

In this prayer, David admitted that he was not deserving of this great honor, but thanked God for his past faithfulness—toward Israel, generally, and David, specifically—and asked him to completely fulfill this covenant, so that God's name would never be tarnished throughout the nations.

Chapter eighteen gives a summary review of some of David's military campaigns and the establishment of his kingdom. In addition to the Philistines (vs. 1), God allowed David to defeat the Moabites, the Arameans (Syrians), the Ammonites, the Amalekites, and the Edomites, as far as the Euphrates River (vs. 2–3, 11). Thus, all the nations surrounding the land of Israel became subject to David. He reduced their armies and plundered their gold, silver, and bronze which he dedicated to God. (These would later be used by Solomon in the Temple.) The reason for this success was because **"THE LORD PROTECTED**

---

[16] The writer did not include God's statement that he would discipline David's son if necessary, like in 2 Samuel 7:14, because he was focusing on the positive covenantal promises only. Additionally, it may be that the 1 Chronicles version emphasizes the Messiah while the 2 Samuel version emphasizes Solomon.

[17] The use of names and titles is very different from the 2 Samuel passage (see the notes there).

DAVID WHEREVER HE CAMPAIGNED" (vs. 6, 13). He was a great king for Israel and "GUARANTEED JUSTICE FOR ALL HIS PEOPLE" (vs. 14). Verses 14–17 give a summary of key people in David's administration.

Chapter nineteen gives an example of David's military wisdom and generosity. Even though he had defeated the Ammonites (18:11), he kept friendly relationships with them, so when "KING NAHASH OF THE AMMONITES DIED AND HIS SON SUCCEEDED HIM," David sent messengers to show his respect and sympathy (vs. 1–2).

However, the new king's advisers (much like Rehoboam's later in 1 Kings 12:6–11) did not trust David and gave him bad counsel (vs. 3–5). They accused David's messengers of espionage, so the king humiliated them by shaving their beards and cutting off the lower halves of their robes (leaving the men mostly naked) before sending them back to David (vs. 4–5). When they discovered that they had upset David, they hired 32,000 chariots to join their coalition armies against him, so he responded by sending his entire army (vs. 6–8).

Immediately, Joab noticed that the Ammonite coalition had separated into two groups and that he would have to fight on two fronts (vs. 9–15). He took an elite unit to face the Arameans and left the rest of the army with his brother to fight the larger Ammonite force. They agreed that they would unite their forces if one side began to be defeated. Instead, the Arameans quickly ran from Joab's men, causing the Ammonites to do the same. The Arameans, though, were not through (vs. 16–19). As they marshaled reinforcements, David took his army to meet them and soundly defeated them, so that "THEY MADE PEACE WITH DAVID AND BECAME HIS SUBJECTS" and would not help the Ammonites in the future.

Chapter twenty skips the most infamous of David's personal stories, that of his affair with Bathsheba and the murder of her husband, Uriah (2 Samuel 11). Although the writer understandably wanted to focus on the positive aspects of God's covenant with David, the fact that both Solomon and Nathan (Joseph's and Mary's ancestors, respectively) were sons of Bathsheba, seems to make her an important part of the covenantal story.

Instead, the writer focused on David's victories, closing a small section about David's battles in chapters 18–20. After the problem with the Ammonites in the last chapter, David sent Joab to take their capital city (vs. 1–3). As a matter of practice, David did not kill all of the captives but instead "MADE THEM LABOR WITH SAWS, IRON PICKS, AND AXES."

Verses 4–8 tell of a few more battles between David and the Philistines. Goliath was not the only giant (or mutant) from that nation. Not only did he have brothers of enormous size, but there was also another "LARGE MAN WHO HAD SIX FINGERS ON EACH HAND AND SIX TOES ON EACH FOOT."

Chapter twenty-one is the parallel passage of 2 Samuel 24, presenting what appears to be a contradiction in the Scriptures.

> "AN ADVERSARY OPPOSED ISRAEL, INCITING DAVID TO COUNT HOW MANY WARRIORS ISRAEL HAD." (vs. 1)

> "THE LORD'S ANGER AGAIN RAGED AGAINST ISRAEL, AND HE INCITED DAVID AGAINST THEM, SAYING, 'GO COUNT ISRAEL AND JUDAH.'" (2 Samuel 24:1)

Whose fault was this? It seems that God was upset with Israel for a reason which is not given, so he allowed "an adversary"[18] to mobilize against David, which led him to take a census of Israel to count how many troops were available. It appears that he did this without asking God first, showing his reliance on his army instead of God for protection. Interestingly, even Joab recognized that something was wrong and that this could bring God's judgment on them, but David insisted (vs. 3–4). Second Samuel 24:8 says this took nearly ten months to complete. Joab returned with the report that David had 1.3 million warriors available to him—800,000 in Israel and 500,000 in Judah (vs. 5–9). The count here is slightly different from the 2 Samuel

---

[18] The Hebrew word for adversary is שָׂטָן (satan), which is why some English translations put "Satan" in verse one. However, the word does not always necessarily mean Satan, the fallen angel, and can refer to any adversary, including a person or a nation. See the notes on 2 Samuel 24 for a larger discussion.

numbers. This passage records "1,100,000 SWORD-WIELDING SOLDIERS; JUDAH ALONE HAD 470,000." Most commentators attribute the difference to the fact that David's standing army had about 300,000 soldiers (Israel) and 30,000 (Judah) which this writer added to 2 Samuel's count of 800,000 and 470,000 others, respectively, who were available throughout Israel as needed.[19]

David's action did displease God, and David knew it (vs. 7–8). When he asked God for forgiveness, he discovered it was too little, too late. He had nearly ten months to repent, but he had not done so. Now he had to face the punishment for his sin. Graciously, God allowed David to choose the punishment: seven years of famine, three months running from his enemy, or three days of nationwide plague (vs. 9–14). David chose the plague, thinking that he would rather be hurt by God than by man. God's messenger of death spread throughout the land and killed 70,000 men. However, God did not allow the angel to attack Jerusalem, because David (who could apparently see it coming) pled for their lives, even if it required his own in return (vs. 15–17).

The chapter ends with David offering a sacrifice to God at the very place that the angel of death had stopped (vs. 18–27). It seems that the owner of the place saw the messenger of death as well and hid. He reappeared when David came, and hearing that David wanted to offer a sacrifice there to stop the plague, the man was ready to give David both the land and the animals to slaughter. However, in a statement of great humility and respect for God, David declared, "I WILL NOT OFFER TO THE LORD WHAT BELONGS TO YOU OR OFFER A BURNT SACRIFICE THAT COST ME NOTHING." His sin had cost the lives of 70,000 men, and this affected him greatly. He purchased the land and oxen, offered the sacrifices, and God stopped the plague. From that time, David never visited the Tabernacle again, fearing the angel of the Lord (21:28–22:1). Instead, he sacrificed only at the new site, which would become the location of Solomon's Temple.

---

[19] This suggestion is found in Keil & Delitszch, Constable, and the *Bible Knowledge Commentary*, among others.

Chapter twenty-two has no parallel in Samuel or Kings. We know that David wanted to build a temple for God, but God refused and said that David's son would build it instead (17:1–15). However, that did not deter David from helping prepare. He began to gather gold, silver, bronze, and cedar so that Solomon would have enough building material (vs. 1–5). He also took Solomon aside and told him everything that God said, including the news that God had given Solomon his name (vs. 6–10). At a minimum, depending on the modern value of "**100,000 TALENTS OF GOLD [AND] 1,000,000 TALENTS OF SILVER,**"[20] David had set aside more than 33,000 tons of gold and silver "AND SO MUCH BRONZE AND IRON IT CANNOT BE WEIGHED, AS WELL AS WOOD AND STONES," and many skilled workers (vs. 11–16). However, he said that the key was for Solomon to continue to obey God and his law to receive God's continued blessing. David also made sure that his officials agreed to support Solomon (vs. 17–19). He was excited about them being able to move the ark and the Tabernacle furnishings into the new Temple.

Chapters twenty-three through twenty-six contain David's instructions to the Levites for the setup of the coming Temple's new serving teams. Although he primarily retained the structure God gave Moses in the wilderness, since there was no need for groups to carry the tent and furnishings around anymore, David kept them in their assigned family groups but gave them new jobs for the stationary site in Jerusalem (23:25–26). He also counted the Levites from twenty years old instead of thirty years (23:27). They were to start their ministry with the ark and continue when Solomon finally built the Temple. He appointed Temple workers, officials and judges, gatekeepers, and some to play instruments (23:1–6).

Aaron's descendants were the priests, but there were many more Levites than just the priests. Moses had assigned the Gershonites to the interior of the Tabernacle, those who carried the furniture and served the priests (23:7–24). In the new system, the Gershonites were "TO HELP AARON'S DESCENDANTS IN THE

---

[20] A "talent" could refer to a few different weight values, depending on the nation and time frame in which the word was used. The NET Study Bible notes that these talents could have weighed between 67 and 130 pounds (30–60 kg).

SERVICE OF THE LORD'S TEMPLE" (23:28–32). This meant that they kept things clean, made and put out fresh bread, and kept everything in its proper place for the priests to use. Next to the priestly work itself, this was the most important role in the Temple service. "THEY WERE IN CHARGE OF THE MEETING TENT AND THE HOLY PLACE, AND HELPED THEIR RELATIVES, THE DESCENDANTS OF AARON, IN THE SERVICE OF THE LORD'S TEMPLE."

One of the key systems David established was a rotation of twenty-four teams (24:1–19). These teams were based on the family clans within the Levitic tribe, and they drew lots to determine the order of the teams. Each rotation, priests from the assigned clan would serve in the Temple. Based on the number of men in any given clan, it could be several years before the same priest served again.[21] The other non-priest Levites also cast lots to be put into their rotations as well (24:19–31).

David also assigned the Temple musicians in a twenty-four-team rotation, based on the families headed by Heman, Asaph, and Jeduthun (25:1–31). The note that they were "TO PROPHESY AS THEY PLAYED STRING INSTRUMENTS" is interesting (25:1). Referring to both Miriam and Deborah, the two prophetesses of the Old Testament, Constable sees that composing music and leading worship fit the role of prophet at that time. "In any case, the definition of 'prophet' should probably be understood to mean 'worship leader,' not in the restricted sense of a song-leader, but of a person who also passed along messages (songs) that God had inspired."[22] We know that these three men composed and several of the psalms God inspired for Scripture.[23]

There was a need to protect the Temple grounds from those who should not enter it, so David also created a system of guards for the gates and the

---

[21] This is the explanation of why it was so special that Zechariah finally served in the Temple as an old man in Luke 1:8. It was conceivable that there would be so many men from Aaron's line that a man may serve as priest only once in his lifetime or even not at all!

[22] Constable, *Notes on 1 Chronicles, 2016 Edition*, 37.

[23] Asaph wrote Psalms 50 and 73–83, and Heman wrote Psalm 88. If Jeduthun is another name for Ethan, then he wrote Psalm 89. Otherwise, Jeduthun is listed as the music director in Psalms 39, 62, and 77.

storehouses (26:1–22). "Each day there were six Levites posted on the east, four on the north, and four on the south. At the storehouses they were posted in pairs. At the court on the west there were four posted on the road and two at the court." One of Moses' descendants was the supervisor of the storehouses (26:23–28). In the storehouses were items that David had consecrated to God, especially those items taken in battle, as well as things given by Samuel, Saul, Abner, and Joab.

Finally, the rest of the Levites, who were not assigned positions at the Temple site, were spread out throughout the tribes of Israel to serve as officials and judges on spiritual matters (26:29–32). They lived in the cities that Moses had established so the Israelites did not have to travel to Jerusalem for every spiritual matter or to find an arbitrator in matters regarding the Law. David also found some non-Levites whom he tapped to serve in royal and religious matters that were outside the purview of the God-ordained Levitic responsibilities.

Chapter twenty-seven contains "A list of Israelite family leaders and commanders of units of a thousand and a hundred, as well as their officers who served the king in various matters" (vs. 1). Each division had 24,000 men and was assigned to serve one month out of the year. Some of the leaders, like Benaiah, were trusted warriors who had served with David a long time. Others were just commanders over the warriors from each of the twelve tribes. As God had ordered Moses (Numbers 1:1–3; 26:1–4), David counted all the men twenty years and older who could serve in the standing army.[24] If this is the same census as reported in chapter twenty-one, then Joab "started to count the men but did not finish" because he did not count Levi or Benjamin (21:6). This, and the resultant plague, may have been the reason that the number was never recorded in "The Annals of King David," another historical record that the writer of Chronicles used as a source. The rest of the chapter lists the

---

[24] For an unknown reason, the leaders of Levi and both half-tribes of Manasseh were listed, but Gad and Asher were left out.

leaders of the team who guarded and took care of David's personal property and served in other various positions in David's government (vs. 25–34).

Chapters twenty-eight and twenty-nine record David's final charge to the nation of Israel, his commission of Solomon as king, and his death. This is information that is not included in the parallel account in 1 Kings, but it expands the record in 1 Kings 1.

After gathering all the officials of Israel (probably those listed or alluded to in the previous five chapters), David stood and gave his speech. He began by reviewing the circumstances surrounding the Temple, especially the covenant that God had made with him (28:1–8). This is the third time that the writer included the Davidic Covenant (17:1–15; 22:6–10). This is a major purpose of this writing, to remind the post-exilic Jews of the promises that God had made to Israel and David, and to spur them on in their rebuilding project.[25]

Next, David addressed Solomon (28:9–21). He charged him to continue to obey God and not be turned away (something Solomon did not follow). David also handed him the blueprints for everything he had planned for the Temple. This included not only the building itself, but all of the furnishing, utensils, and decorations, along with the system he had prescribed for the Levites. Interestingly, although 1 Kings seems to imply that Solomon designed it and 1 Chronicles that David did, in 28:19, David claimed that God had given him "INSIGHT REGARDING THE DETAILS OF THE BLUEPRINTS." Depending on how much insight this included, it may be comparable to the detailed directions God had originally given to Moses for the Tabernacle (Exodus 25–28, 30, especially 25:40; Hebrews 8:5).

Turning back to "THE ENTIRE ASSEMBLY," David stood Solomon before the people as his successor to the throne and the one who was to build the Temple (29:1–9). Because this Temple was not for a man but for God, David publicly bequeathed his entire fortune to the project, in addition to what he had already set aside for Solomon's use. Then, in a stroke of brilliant leadership, he asked,

---

[25] See Ezra, Haggai, and Zechariah for more detail about the circumstances that were happening and the people for whom the Chronicles were written.

"**WHO ELSE WANTS TO CONTRIBUTE TO THE LORD TODAY?**" The people willingly and gladly donated millions more in gold, silver, bronze, iron, and precious gems. David prayed a prayer of praise and thanksgiving and blessing to God, asking that he would guide Solomon in obedience, and the assembly responded with great praise (29:10–20). The next day they celebrated again, sacrificing thousands of animals to God, which they ate in a great feast (29:21–25). This may be the noise referenced in 1 Kings 1:38–48.

The book ends with a summary of David's reign (29:26–30). He reigned for a total of forty years (and some months), and God blessed him greatly. Most importantly, God fulfilled his promise of putting Solomon on David's throne, the beginning of the eternal dynasty. The writer closed by referencing three more of his sources, the writings of Samuel, Nathan, and Gad.

2 Chronicles

This is the second half of the original Book of Chronicles (see the introduction to 1 Chronicles for more information). Starting with the beginning of Solomon's reign, it parallels but is not an exact repetition of 1 and 2 Kings. Since the purpose of the Chronicles is to emphasize God's faithfulness in keeping his promises to David, many of the events of the northern kingdom (Israel) from the Kings were left out of this account, allowing it to be much shorter. Second Chronicles covers Solomon's reign, the split between the northern and southern kingdoms, and the exiles to Assyria and Babylon. With little exception, each of the kings is given one chapter with a few specific events of their reigns. Chronicles is also the last book in the order of the Hebrew Scriptures, so this closed the Bible of Jesus and the apostles.

Chapter one opens with Solomon's first covenantal act as king. Although the ark of the covenant was in Jerusalem (where David had moved it), the rest of the Tabernacle, including the altar, was in Gibeon, so Solomon went there to worship God and "OFFERED UP 1,000 BURNT SACRIFICES" (vs. 1–6). "THAT NIGHT GOD APPEARED TO" him and made his famous offer: "Ask for anything you wish from me" (vs. 7–13). Solomon's reply was one of wisdom and humility. He acknowledged God's faithfulness and asked for the wisdom to rule well and make the right decisions for God's people. God granted him not only what he asked but also the many things that he did not ask—"RICHES, WEALTH, AND HONOR SURPASSING THAT OF ANY KING BEFORE OR AFTER" him. However, contrary to God's explicit instructions in Deuteronomy 17:16, Solomon "ACCUMULATED CHARIOTS AND HORSES...FROM EGYPT" (vs. 14–17).

Chapter two details the preparations that Solomon made to begin work on the Temple that David had wanted to build. Twice the writer noted that "SOLOMON HAD 70,000 COMMON LABORERS AND 80,000 STONECUTTERS IN THE HILLS, IN ADDITION TO 3,600 SUPERVISORS" (vs. 2, 17–18). These were not Jews but instead "ALL THE MALE RESIDENT FOREIGNERS IN THE LAND OF ISRAEL."

He sent a letter to King Huram (Hiram) of Tyre, asking for both men and supplies, in addition to what David had already set aside for him (vs. 3–10). Specifically, he wanted "A MAN WHO IS SKILLED IN WORKING WITH GOLD, SILVER, BRONZE, AND IRON, AS WELL AS PURPLE-, CRIMSON-, AND BLUE-COLORED FABRICS, AND WHO KNOWS HOW TO ENGRAVE." In response, Huram sent his own son (Huram Abi means "my father is Huram" in Hebrew).

Solomon was both wise and honest enough to know that this Temple would "REALLY BE ONLY A PLACE TO OFFER SACRIFICES" to God, because even "THE SKY AND THE HIGHEST HEAVENS CANNOT CONTAIN HIM." Huram replied that Yehovah was truly great and had blessed Israel by giving them David, and now Solomon, as their kings (vs. 11–16). So, he sent everything that Solomon had requested, and Solomon paid what he promised.

Chapters three and four provide a summary of the detail that Solomon put into the Temple. (See the notes on 1 Kings 6–7 for more detail.) Unique to this writer is the face that Solomon built the Temple on Mount Moriah (3:1). Not only is this the location where David sacrificed to God after the plague of 1 Chronicles 21, but this was also possibly the location where Abraham had offered Isaac as a sacrifice to God (Genesis 22:2). If so, then the writer was making a strong connection between the Davidic Covenant (2 Samuel 7:8–16) and the Abrahamic Covenant (Genesis 12:1–3), which God reinforced to Abraham at that time. This would have been especially helpful to the Jews in post-exilic Jerusalem as they worked to rebuild the city and Temple.

Solomon built the Temple according to the specifications that David had given him and set everything in order (1 Chronicles 28:11–12, 18–19). "WHEN SOLOMON HAD FINISHED CONSTRUCTING THE LORD'S TEMPLE, HE PUT THE HOLY ITEMS THAT BELONGED TO HIS FATHER DAVID (THE SILVER, GOLD, AND ALL THE OTHER ARTICLES) IN THE TREASURIES OF GOD'S TEMPLE" (2 Chronicles 5:1).

Chapters five through seven record Solomon's dedication of the Temple. The Temple would have been useless without God's presence, so the first order of business was to move the ark of the covenant from where David housed it in Jerusalem into the new Temple's Most Holy Place. Gathering together "THE LEADERS OF THE ISRAELITE TRIBES AND FAMILIES," Solomon led a parade of people to retrieve the ark, and the priests carried it and the other furniture to the Temple (5:2–6). Solomon and the people went ahead to wait for them and sacrificed countless animals to God.

When they arrived at the Temple, the priests carried the ark into the Most Holy Place and closed the curtain behind them, but the carrying poles stuck out a little bit (5:7–10). Somewhere along the line, Aaron's rod and the jar of manna had been lost, leaving only the stone tablets of the law inside the ark.[1] When God's glory filled the area, it was like a cloud of thick smoke, so that the priests could not even see to carry out their duties (5:11–14).

Solomon's blessing for the nation begins in chapter six after he publicly announced that this building was God's Temple (6:1–11). For the fourth time since 1 Chronicles 17, the writer reviewed the Davidic Covenant, focusing on the promise that David's son would build the Temple and succeed David to his throne. Solomon then turned and gave a long prayer to God, which spans the rest of the chapter (6:12–42). In his prayer, Solomon noted several key principles. First, he gave thanks that God had fulfilled his promise in putting Solomon on David's throne and asked that he would continue to fulfill the eternal covenant that he had made with David (2 Samuel 7:8–16). This is the fifth time the writer came back to the Davidic Covenant. Second, he recognized that God transcends the whole universe, much more than the little house Solomon had built him. God's choice to be there was an act of grace and faithfulness, not obligation, so Solomon asked for the continued protection of Israel.

Third, in the longest section of the prayer, Solomon admitted that no one is sinless and that Israel would certainly turn away from God in the future. Loosely following the structure of the curses from Deuteronomy 28:15–68,

---

[1] "Horeb" in verse ten is another name for Mount Sinai.

Solomon asked that when God had to carry out his promised punishments he would also be quick to forgive when Israel returned to him. The detailed history of Israel, as shown in 1 and 2 Kings and the prophets, proves that God repeatedly answered Solomon's honest prayer. Solomon closed his prayer asking that the priests would faithfully carry out their duties, that the people would remain faithful, and that God would fulfill his promises.

In response to Solomon's prayer, God's presence did enter and fill the Temple, and his fire burned the offering on the altar in complete acceptance of it (7:1–3). The people were filled with awe, celebrating and worshiping him. For fourteen days they offered sacrifices and celebrated God, his presence, and his faithfulness as shown in Solomon's reign (7:4–10). During this party, they offered so many sacrifices that they had to move to the Temple's front lawn because the altar was too small to hold them all! After the two weeks were over, Solomon sent the people home "HAPPY AND CONTENTED BECAUSE OF THE GOOD THE LORD HAD DONE FOR DAVID, SOLOMON, AND HIS PEOPLE ISRAEL."

One night, after he had completed building both the Temple and his palace, "THE LORD APPEARED TO SOLOMON AT NIGHT" again (7:12–22). In one of the most-misused verses in modern Christianity, God promised Solomon, "IF MY PEOPLE, WHO BELONG TO ME, HUMBLE THEMSELVES, PRAY, SEEK TO PLEASE ME, AND REPUDIATE THEIR SINFUL PRACTICES, THEN I WILL RESPOND FROM HEAVEN, FORGIVE THEIR SIN, AND HEAL THEIR LAND" (vs. 14). However much Church Age Christians want to claim this for their various national identities, this was God's promise to do exactly what Solomon had asked in his prayer: when the people sinned and God had to judge them, according to his promises in Deuteronomy 18, he would restore them upon their repentance.[2]

For the sixth time, the writer reviewed the Davidic Covenant, giving special focus on the need for Solomon to continue to obey God to retain his blessings. However, if they turned from him, God would send them into exile and the Temple, which stood before Solomon in beauty, would be destroyed. The rest of the book shows how God fulfilled that part of his promise because

---

[2] Jeremiah 18:7–10 is much more appropriate for today, since it speaks of any nation's response to God, rather than Israel's.

of Solomon's and Israel's unfaithfulness, and the original readers, having returned from Persia, were able to look from the page to the Temple which stood in ruins before them, about 500 years after it was built.

Chapter eight summarizes the work that Solomon accomplished. The Temple and palace projects took "TWENTY YEARS" (vs. 1–6). He also rebuilt cities throughout the land (including into Lebanon, which was King Huram's territory). In correlation with the account in Joshua and Judges, the writer noted that not all of the Canaanites were driven out of the land, so Solomon made them manual laborers on his work crews (vs. 7–10). The comment "AND THEY CONTINUE IN THAT ROLE TO THIS VERY DAY" refers to the writer's time, showing that the land of Israel remained occupied by Canaanites, not just during Joshua or Solomon's time, but for approximately 1,000 years. In reality, the occupation has never ended, even into the 21st century AD.

Verses 11–15 show Solomon's heart during this time. Solomon had married Pharaoh's daughter, but he refused to let her live in David's palace, because the ark had been there, and she was not an Israelite.[3] Following David's instructions, Solomon kept the worship commands of the Mosaic Law rigidly. Every feast, every sacrifice, every holy day was enforced in Israel without fail during this time. He also established the worship system that David had created for the Levites and the priests (see 1 Chronicles 23–27). After the construction work was finished, Solomon had his sailors begin to explore the world and bring back gold and other items they found (vs. 16–18).[4]

Chapter nine records the famous visit of "THE QUEEN OF SHEBA." Sheba seems to have been somewhere between Ethiopia and the far southern part of the Arabian Peninsula, modern-day Yemen, as much as 1,400 miles away from

---

[3] This may also imply that Solomon knew that she worshiped other gods. Instead of having her leave them for Yehovah, he offered a compromise that simply kept her out of the way of his worship of Yehovah.

[4] There have been several discoveries in both North and South America hinting that Solomon's explorers may have traveled even this far during his reign.

Jerusalem.⁵ She was close enough to have heard of Solomon yet far enough away to not have regular dealings with him, so she traveled to Jerusalem "WITH A GREAT DISPLAY OF POMP" and many gifts (vs. 1–12). She brought with her some of the greatest questions and riddles she had, and he solved them quickly and easily. The combination of his wisdom and wealth amazed and impressed her, with the exact result that it was supposed to have: she praised Yehovah, the God of Israel. She gave Solomon immense wealth, and he gave her many treasures in return.

The second part of the chapter summarizes Solomon's wealth and influence (vs. 13–28). He received the modern equivalent of nearly a billion dollars' worth of gold every year in taxes, tariffs, and tribute. This contributed to the artwork and detail in his palace. His throne was decorated with ivory and gold and had statues of lions in front and beside it. He was so wealthy that silver was almost worthless (it was "AS PLENTIFUL IN JERUSALEM AS STONES"), and he used gold for even his cups and flatware. People from all over the world came to Jerusalem to hear him lecture and to bring local items to him. He paid what amounted to pennies for both horses and chariots, the best of Egypt.⁶ This is a wonderful preview of what it will be like in the Millennial Kingdom.

The chapter concludes Solomon's reign by mentioning three more sources that the writer used to gather his information—"THE ANNALS OF NATHAN THE PROPHET, THE PROPHECY OF AHIJAH THE SHILONITE, AND THE VISION OF IDDO THE SEER PERTAINING TO JEROBOAM SON OF NEBAT" (vs. 29–31). Solomon reigned for forty years before he died and was replaced by his son, Rehoboam.

Chapter ten opens with the crowning of Rehoboam, Solomon's son, as king over Israel, in Shechem, which was in central Israel (vs. 1–5). Jeroboam, son of Nebat, was one of the people who gathered at this event. He had been in Egypt because Solomon knew that God had promised to give part of the

---

⁵ If this is the true location of ancient Sheba, it indicates how far the story of Solomon was known.

⁶ This was contrary to God's instructions on two counts. He was not to amass horses for himself and was not to purchase any horses from Egypt (Deuteronomy 17:16).

nation to Jeroboam because of Solomon's sin (1 Kings 11:9–13, 26–40). The people plead with Rehoboam to exercise leniency on them because Solomon's building projects caused the people to work hard for a long time. They wanted Rehoboam to lighten their load, so he told them to return in three days for his answer.

Rather than seeking wisdom from God, Rehoboam sought counsel from two groups—the old men who had served Solomon and the young men he had grown up with (vs. 6–15). The old men urged him to lighten the people's work, which would guarantee their voluntary allegiance. The young men said he should beat them into submission. Rehoboam took the advice of his friends and told the nation he would be harsher than his father. In a surprising mutiny, the nation turned against him and crowned Jeroboam as their king (vs. 16–19). The writer noted that "ISRAEL HAS BEEN IN REBELLION AGAINST THE DAVIDIC DYNASTY TO THIS VERY DAY." He also declared that this was the method God used to fulfill his threat against Solomon and promise to Jeroboam.

Chapters eleven and twelve begin to describe the aftermath of the division of Israel's kingdom. Rehoboam intended to attack the rebellious tribes with men from Judah and Benjamin, but God did not allow it (11:1–4). "JUDAH AND BENJAMIN BELONGED TO" Rehoboam, but the other ten tribes went with Jeroboam, so he built up cities throughout the region and made sure they all had stores of food and weapons (11:5–12). However, "THE PRIESTS AND LEVITES WHO LIVED THROUGHOUT ISRAEL SUPPORTED HIM, NO MATTER WHERE THEY RESIDED," and many moved back to Jerusalem or somewhere in Judah because Jeroboam did not let them carry out Yehovah's ministry in his kingdom; his was full of idolatry (11:13–17). In an explanation of why Israel (the ten northern tribes) degenerated much more quickly than Judah (the two southern tribes), the writer observed that the people in Israel who wanted to continue worshiping Yehovah faithfully moved out of Israel into Judah. Thus, not only did Israel have godless leadership, they hemorrhaged anyone who would have remained faithful, making Israel entirely godless.

The writer recorded that Rehoboam married two of his cousins, one of whom he loved the most, in addition to other unnamed wives and concubines

(11:18–21). In total, he had "EIGHTEEN WIVES AND SIXTY CONCUBINES" who gave him "TWENTY-EIGHT SONS AND SIXTY DAUGHTERS." He groomed Abijah, one of the sons of his favorite wife, to be his successor. He then spread out his other sons throughout his kingdom to rule over the cities so they would not vie for the throne (vs. 22–23). However, Rehoboam did not stay faithful to Yehovah, so God sent a coalition led by King Shishak of Egypt to attack Rehoboam in Jerusalem (12:1–4).

God sent the prophet, Shemaiah, to tell Rehoboam what was about to happen, and the king and his advisers immediately repented (12:5–11). Because of his character of perfect justice and his covenant promises to David, God accepted Rehoboam's repentance and did not have Shishak destroy them. However, he did allow Shishak to raid Jerusalem and seize all the treasures that Solomon had placed in the Temple and palace. The specific mention of the gold shields in 12:9 serves to reveal that Rehoboam was a cheap imitation of his father. He attempted a show of wealth and power by replacing the gold shields with bronze shields that were paraded around when he was present.

Although "JUDAH EXPERIENCED SOME GOOD THINGS" under Rehoboam's rule, he was not a faithful follower of Yehovah, and he reigned for only 17 years before he died and Abijah took his place (12:12–16).

Chapter thirteen records the reign of Rehoboam's son, Abijah. Constable notes,

> This is the only place in Chronicles where the writer linked the reigns of the southern and northern kings (vv. 1-2). ... This chapter is the only assessment in Chronicles of the Northern Kingdom's sin. From here on, the writer's attention focused on Judah primarily.[7]

Abijah's reign was short, only three years, and he remained at war with Jeroboam during that time (vs. 1–2). The writer chose to focus on only one instance between the two of them, a battle in which God gave a decisive

---

[7] Constable, *Notes on 2 Chronicles, 2016 Edition*, 23.

victory to Abijah (vs. 3–20). Although Abijah was not a godly man (1 Kings 15:3), he did attack Jeroboam's position and publicly accuse Israel of turning away from God and the Davidic dynasty. His theology was at least sound enough that he knew of God's covenant promises with David and that Israel was against God if they were against David. When he realized that Jeroboam had divided his army into two fronts and that one of them intended to ambush Abijah from behind, he quickly called out to God for help, and God allowed him to slaughter "500,000 WELL-TRAINED ISRAELITE MEN." Additionally, Abijah took back under his rule some cities from Jeroboam, and "JEROBOAM DID NOT REGAIN POWER DURING THE REIGN OF ABIJAH." When Abijah died, his son, Asa, succeeded him (13:21–14:1).

Chapter fourteen through sixteen tell of Asa's reign. He was a godly king, destroying the idols and commanding Judah to fully return to Yehovah (14:1–8). He also fortified all his cities and built an army of almost 600,000 soldiers from Judah and Benjamin. Under his rule, Judah had peace for at least the first ten years. However, about fifteen years into Asa's reign (15:10), "ZERAH THE CUSHITE" attacked Asa with a million soldiers (14:9–10). Asa prayed to God for help, asking him to deliver the Judahites from destruction (14:11–15). God answered, and Asa destroyed not only the Cushite army but also several other towns south of Judah and some of the nomads who had helped watch the Cushite livestock.

After Asa returned to Jerusalem, God sent "AZARIAH SON OF ODED" to him with this message: "THE LORD IS WITH YOU WHEN YOU ARE LOYAL TO HIM" (15:1–7). He promised Asa that as long as he stayed faithful to God, he would be blessed by God, "BUT IF YOU REJECT HIM, HE WILL REJECT YOU." Israel had been floundering without a truly faithful king since David, but Asa was reversing that. This encouraged Asa, and he continued cleaning up the land from the idols left by Solomon, Rehoboam, and Abijah (15:8–18). He also deposed his grandmother, Maacah, "FROM HER POSITION AS QUEEN MOTHER," because of her contributions to Judah's idolatry. Although he did not get rid of every high place of idol worship throughout the land, his faithfulness was obvious even into Israel, where many of them moved to Judah "WHEN THEY SAW THAT THE

LORD HIS GOD WAS WITH HIM." For the next twenty years, there was peace in Judah.

"IN THE THIRTY-SIXTH YEAR OF ASA'S REIGN, KING BAASHA OF ISRAEL ATTACKED JUDAH," and he stationed an outpost to make sure no one could enter or leave Asa's realm (16:1–10). Instead of relying solely on God, like he did when the Cushite attacked, Asa turned to Ben Hadad of Syria for help. He sent the Syrian king all the gold and silver that was left (what Shishak did not take to Egypt) in an attempt to have him break his treaty with Israel and ally with Judah instead; his plan worked. This caused God to be angry with Asa, and he sent Hanani to give Asa this message: "BECAUSE YOU RELIED ON THE KING OF SYRIA AND DID NOT RELY ON THE LORD YOUR GOD, THE ARMY OF THE KING OF SYRIA HAS ESCAPED FROM YOUR HAND." God would have given Asa the Syrian army like he did the Cushite army, but now he would not. Instead, Judah would continue to be at war and not have peace. This upset Asa, so he imprisoned Hanani and turned against his own people.

For the last three years of his life, Asa battled a foot disease and died after ruling for forty-one years (16:11–14). Sadly, his illness was another period during which "HE DID NOT SEEK THE LORD." So, Asa died as an unfaithful king, opposite of how he began.

Chapters seventeen through twenty are tied for the second-longest section in 2 Chronicles having to do with a single king.[8] This chapter summarizes Jehoshaphat's reign. In addition to fortifying the cities of Judah, he also built up military strength in the new cities that Asa had won during his war with Israel (vs. 1–2). The best thing about Jehoshaphat was that he was godly like David (vs. 3–6).[9] Not only did he not chase the pagan Baals, but he also tore down idols and shrines, even some that his father had left standing.

---

[8] Chapters 1–9 record Solomon's reign and chapters 29–32 tell of Hezekiah's.

[9] David was consistently the benchmark for Judah's kings. In both Kings and Chronicles they are described as godly like David, godly but not quite like David, or wicked not following David.

One of the things that made him unique was the teaching circuit he established (vs. 7–9). Early in his reign, he sent five men across his kingdom to work with the Levites to teach the people the Law. There were no synagogues yet,[10] so they probably met in homes or the public courtyards of the cities.[11] Because of this strong commitment to obedience and faithfulness, "THE LORD PUT FEAR INTO ALL THE KINGDOMS SURROUNDING JUDAH" (vs. 10–19). Not only did they not attack him, but even the Philistines paid him tribute! As his influence increased, Jehoshaphat continued to build up his cities and store food and supplies. He also kept a strong standing army in Jerusalem.

Chapter eighteen records one of Jehoshaphat's missteps, due to an alliance (by marriage) that he made with Ahab, king of Israel (vs. 1–8). After some time, Jehoshaphat visited Ahab, who proposed that they attack Syria together. All of Ahab's prophets said that they would win, but Jehoshaphat wanted to hear from one of Yehovah's prophets. Ahab knew of one, Micaiah, but did not like him, because he always prophesied against Ahab.[12]

Finally, Jehoshaphat convinced Ahab to let Micaiah come (vs. 9–13). The false prophets were still predicting the utter defeat of Syria, and Ahab's messengers "suggested" to Micaiah that he go along with the rest. He declared, "AS CERTAINLY AS THE LORD LIVES, I WILL SAY WHAT MY GOD TELLS ME TO SAY!" When he arrived and was asked for God's answer to the kings' question, he surprisingly agreed with the other prophets (vs. 14–27). However, when pressed to make sure he was telling the truth, he admitted that God's real message was that Israel would be defeated and scattered. The reason for the

---

[10] Synagogues did not come into existence until during the captivity, when the exiles gathered together to hear the Law in their own language. The word synagogue comes from the Greek word συναγωγή (sunagōgē), which means "a gathering place."

[11] Honestly, this was a brilliant idea. If the people knew the Law, they were less likely to disobey it, meaning that Judah would stay in favor with God, which would make Jehoshaphat's reign easier and more peaceful. From a Church Age perspective, it shows that teaching people in homes, where their lives intersect the Scriptures, is a powerful tool and wise principle.

[12] When God's spokesman can say nothing good about a person, it should tell us something about that person.

deception was that God was allowing an angelic messenger to deceive the king to lead him to his defeat.[13] Ahab ordered that Micaiah be put into prison until he returned from battle. Micaiah remarked, "IF YOU REALLY DO RETURN SAFELY, THEN THE **LORD** HAS NOT SPOKEN THROUGH ME!"

Ahab cunningly convinced Jehoshaphat to wear his royal robes into battle while Ahab disguised himself (vs. 28–34). Naturally, he thought that they would kill Jehoshaphat while he escaped. This almost happened until the Syrians discovered that it was not Ahab dressed in his royal attire. In what can only be attributed to God's direction, an anonymous Syrian archer randomly shot an arrow that pierced Ahab's armor, and he bled out in his chariot.

Chapter nineteen concludes the story of the battle from chapter eighteen. When Jehoshaphat returned home to Jerusalem, God had another message waiting for him (vs. 1–4). God sent the prophet, Jehu, to tell Jehoshaphat that his alliance with Ahab, and especially the attack on Syria, was unwise and displeasing to him. However, God was pleased with the work the king had done to remove the idols from Judah.

Jehoshaphat made it his business to go out of Jerusalem among his people and remind them to serve and worship God (vs. 5–11). He made sure that the judges remembered that the decisions they made needed to be strictly in line with the Law because they were representing God in their duties. Back in Jerusalem, he made sure that the Levites were attending to their responsibilities properly as well so that they would stay in favor with God. Concerning the Davidic Covenant, Jehoshaphat was one of the best kings Judah had.

Chapter twenty concludes Jehoshaphat's reign with a major victory and a few failures. At some point during his reign, a coalition of Moabites, Ammonites, and others marched up from southeast of the Dead Sea to attack Judah (vs. 1–4). When he heard about this, Jehoshaphat immediately went to

---

[13] This passage (and its parallel in 1 Kings 22) provides an insightful look into the inner workings of how God balances his sovereignty with the fact that angels have influence and control over national leaders in this world.

Yehovah for help. He had everyone in his kingdom fast and pray for God's favor and response. Standing in front of the Temple, Jehoshaphat invoked Solomon's prayer from chapter six and the promises God made to Israel in Deuteronomy 18, that if the people were in sin and repented, then God would deliver them from their enemies (vs. 5–12). He also remembered that God had not permitted Israel to conquer these nations when they were on their way into Canaan, but now they were being attacked by the same ones. He wanted to know how they should respond.

At that moment, the Holy Spirit came upon a Levite named Jachaziel (vs. 13–19). He said that Jehoshaphat should lead his army out to meet the enemy, but they would not fight; God would destroy their enemies for them. Because of this word, the people worshiped and celebrated loudly. "EARLY THE NEXT MORNING," the king did exactly what God had said (vs. 20–25). He took his army out to where they could see the enemy, but, instead of attacking, Jehoshaphat told them to break out in worship. Immediately, the Moabites and Ammonites turned against their allies, destroying them, then they turned against each other. It was over without a single Israelite lifting a weapon in battle. When the Israelites entered the enemy camp, they found so much plunder that it took three days to get it all back to Jerusalem. "ON THE FOURTH DAY THEY ASSEMBLED IN THE VALLEY OF BERACHAH, WHERE THEY PRAISED THE LORD" (vs. 26–30). The name "Berachah" means "to bless or praise," so it was "the valley of praise." The news of this victory went out to all the surrounding nations, making them even more afraid of Jehoshaphat and Yehovah.

Jehoshaphat died after ruling for twenty-five years (vs. 31–37). While most of those years were good, and he did many great things for God, he did not obey perfectly. Upon his death, there were still pagan shrines that stood in Judah. In addition to his unwise alliance with Ahab, he made one with Ahaziah of Israel as well, bringing God's judgment upon the ships that they built to carry cargo.

Chapter twenty-one tells of the reign of wicked Jehoram of Judah. Instead of following Jehoshaphat's godly path, Jehoram married Ahab of Israel's daughter and was more like wicked Ahab (vs. 1–7). Even though Jehoshaphat had sent Jehoram's brothers away to rule cities within the kingdom, Jehoram hunted them down and had them killed.

Under his reign, Edom broke free from Judah's rule and defeated him in battle; the people of Libnah broke away as well (vs. 8–11). Not only did he choose to not worship Yehovah, "HE ENCOURAGED THE RESIDENTS OF JERUSALEM TO BE UNFAITHFUL TO THE LORD AND LED JUDAH AWAY FROM THE LORD." Elijah the prophet sent him a letter informing him that, because of his wickedness, God was going to act against him (vs. 12–20). He did this by stirring up the Philistines against him. They attacked and killed or captured all his family, except his youngest son, Ahaziah. God also infected Jehoram with an intestinal disease, which eventually killed him after two years. However, God did not wipe out their dynasty as he often did in Israel, because they were still part of David's eternal dynasty.

Chapter twenty-two records the rise and fall of Jehoram's son, Ahaziah. He was also a wicked king because he was still from the family of Ahab and followed his mother's evil counsel (vs. 1–6). Ahaziah made an alliance with Joram of Israel to attack the Syrians, but they were defeated and ran back to Jezreel in Israel, where Ahaziah visited Joram. While they were there, God sent Jehu to kill Joram and his family (vs. 7–9). When he discovered that Ahaziah and his officials were there, he killed them, too.

Because there was no one in Ahaziah's family ready to take the throne, his mother seized control and determined to wipe out the Davidic line (vs. 10–12). However, Ahaziah's sister, Jehoshabeath, had married Jehoiada the priest. She took Ahaziah's infant son and his nurse and hid them in a closet in the Temple for six years until the son could assume the throne.

Chapter twenty-three picks up six years after Ahaziah's death. His mother, evil Athaliah, had been ruling during this period when Jehoiada decided it was time to reveal the true king (vs. 1–7). He brought together the commanders of the royal and Temple guards and made them swear an oath of allegiance to God and possibly to the king, which they all did. He then presented young Joash to them. Jehoiada knew that the boy would need constant protection until his enemies were defeated, so he set up a rotation of the guards so that there was always one unit protecting him in the Temple. The commanders did as Jehoiada instructed and continued to report to him (vs. 8–11). How long they did this is not recorded here, before Jehoiada brought the boy out and presented him to the people as Judah's true king.

When Athaliah heard the noise of the people celebrating their new king, she left the palace and joined the crowd to see what was happening (vs. 12–15). She immediately recognized what had taken place and tried to start a riot, calling it a conspiracy and treason by Jehoiada. However, the priest had the guards seize her, take her outside the Temple, and execute her. Anyone who followed them was to be executed as well. He also "DREW UP A COVENANT STIPULATING THAT HE, ALL THE PEOPLE, AND THE KING SHOULD BE LOYAL TO THE LORD." They kept their word immediately by destroying Baal's temple and altar and killing Baal's priest and reinstating the priests and Levites of Yehovah (vs. 16–21). The whole nation celebrated Athaliah's death and the peace that came with it.

Chapter twenty-four tells the story of Joash, another Davidic king who started well but ended badly. Because he "WAS SEVEN YEARS OLD WHEN HE BEGAN TO REIGN," the godly priest, Jehoiada, became his counselor and teacher (vs. 1–3). The key statement describing Joash's life was that he "DID WHAT THE LORD APPROVED THROUGHOUT THE LIFETIME OF JEHOIADA THE PRIEST." Ultimately, Jehoiada, not Joash, was the one faithful to God. Under Jehoiada's leadership, one of the actions Joash immediately authorized was the repair that the Temple badly needed (vs. 4–5). When the Levites balked at collecting the annual tax that Moses had commanded for the upkeep of the Tabernacle, Joash insisted that they begin immediately, so they built a chest and set it out where the people could give freely (vs. 6–14). When it was full, they emptied and counted it. Once they had enough, they hired craftsmen to do the work, and they completed it. The rest of the silver was used to fashion more utensils for use in the Temple.

The turning point for Joash was when Jehoiada died (vs. 15–22). Without his godly direction, Joash followed the path of his ancestor, Rehoboam, and listened to wicked counsel. They stopped supporting and worshiping at the Temple and reinstated the pagan shrines. God's prophets could not bring them back. Even when Jehoiada's son, Zechariah, stood up and called out their sin, Joash had him killed on the Temple grounds.[14]

In punishment for his sins, God brought the Syrian army against Joash and defeated him (vs. 23–27). Joash was badly wounded in the battle and ended up being killed by two of his own men, because of his sin against Zechariah. Joash reigned for forty years and did some good things, but only at the direction of Jehoiada. His son, Amaziah, succeeded him as king.

Chapter twenty-five tells of Judah's next king, Amaziah, son of Joash of Judah. He was not an evil king like some of the others, but not one we would call a godly king (vs. 1–4). "HE DID WHAT THE LORD APPROVED, BUT NOT WITH WHOLEHEARTED DEVOTION." He did follow the Law, executing only his father's murderers and not their entire families, as many rulers would do.

Planning to go into battle, Amaziah counted his troops to find only 300,000 men, so he hired another 100,000 from Israel (vs. 5–13). However, God sent a prophet to tell him not to use the Israelite soldiers because God could not bless an alliance between Judah and Israel. Amaziah asked about the money he had paid them already, and the prophet replied, "THE LORD IS CAPABLE OF GIVING YOU MORE THAN THAT." This satisfied the king, so he sent them home. They were angry at the dismissal, though, so when Amaziah fought with Edom, the Israelites raided Judah, killing 3,000 people and taking a lot of wealth.

Unfortunately, Amaziah returned from Edom with some of their gods, and he began to worship them instead of Yehovah (vs. 14–16). When the prophet tried to confront him about it, Amaziah told him to be quiet or be killed. The prophet stopped but only after saying that God would punish Amaziah for this.

After his successful war against Edom, Amaziah became overconfident and challenged Jehoash of Israel to battle as well (vs. 17–24). Not wishing a civil war, Jehoash refused, telling the young Amaziah to not become arrogant,

---

[14] This is the Zechariah mentioned by Jesus in Matthew 23:35 and Luke 11:51, who was killed as a prophet between the altar and the temple.

because Israel would easily defeat Judah. Amaziah would not listen, so Jehoash attacked and thoroughly defeated Judah, capturing Amaziah and breaking down part of Jerusalem's wall. Fifteen years after Jehoash of Israel's death, Amaziah was assassinated (vs. 25–28).

Chapter twenty-six introduces Amaziah's son, Uzziah.[15] Much more is written about him here than in 2 Kings 15. He "WAS SIXTEEN YEARS OLD" when his father died, and he became king (vs. 1–5). Uzziah reigned over Judah for fifty-two years, and he was much like his father in that he began by serving God well, but did not end well. As long as he served God, he maintained a strong military and kingdom, defeating the Philistines, Arabs, and Meunites (vs. 6-10). He fortified Judah's cities and extended his kingdom as far as the border of Egypt. He planted vineyards and built up his ranching operations. Judah lived well when Uzziah served God.

Uzziah was also famous for his military (vs. 11–15). In addition to more than 307,000 skilled warriors, he invented "WAR MACHINES," an early form of automatic weapons designed to shoot arrows and rocks from the top of his city walls. Unlike some of the kings under the Philistine occupation, who were not allowed to have metal weaponry, Uzziah outfitted his soldiers with "SHIELDS, SPEARS, HELMETS, BREASTPLATES, BOWS, AND SLINGSTONES FOR THE ENTIRE ARMY."

All this made him proud of his achievements, which also led to his downfall (vs. 16–21). At some point during his reign (unknown to us), he presumptuously went into the Temple and tried to offer incense to God, something that was limited only to the priests.[16] Azariah, the high priest, and eighty other priests tried to stop him, but he angrily refused. Immediately, God

---

[15] In 2 Kings 15, his name is listed as Azariah. Constable explains this by surmising that Uzziah was his "throne name," while Azariah was his "personal name." (Constable, *Notes on 2 Chronicles, 2016 Edition*, 36). The probable reason for using a different name is that the high priest was also named Azariah (vs. 20), but he was not mentioned in the 2 Kings account, so there was no confusion.

[16] Even Aaron's own sons, Nadab and Abihu, were killed instantly by God when they offered incense wrongly (Leviticus 10:1–2), and they were priests.

struck him with a skin disease that lasted the rest of his life, limiting his role in government and forcing his son, Jotham, to co-rule with him. When Uzziah finally died, he was buried near his royal ancestors but still on the outskirts because of his uncleanness before God, and Jotham succeeded him (vs. 22–23).

Chapter twenty-seven is only nine verses, a short account of Jotham's reign. He continued his father's work in strengthening Judah by fortifying the cities and building stronger walls. However, the secret to his success was the same as the previous three when they started—"HE WAS DETERMINED TO PLEASE THE LORD HIS GOD." The writer made a special point to mention that he did not enter the Temple as his father did. He defeated the Ammonites and gained tribute from them for at least three years, further strengthening his position. He reigned for a total of sixteen years before he died and his son, Ahaz, took the throne.[17]

Chapter twenty-eight is the story of Jotham's son, Ahaz. He was a wicked king in Judah who broke from the pattern of the previous four kings who at least tried to serve God (vs. 1–4).[18] Ahaz was blatant in his rejection of Yehovah, publicly worshiping pagan gods and even practicing the pagan ritual of sacrificing one of his sons in fire, intentionally undoing what several of his predecessors had done toward cleaning up the nation. Because of this rebellion, "THE LORD HIS GOD HANDED HIM OVER TO THE KING OF SYRIA" and to the king of Israel, both of whom defeated him soundly, killing more than 120,000 Judean warriors and taking many others captive (vs. 5–8).

In an interesting twist, God sent the prophet Oded to tell the Israelites to return their captives to Judah (vs. 9–15). Although God had allowed them to defeat Judah in punishment for Ahaz's sin, they would have been wrong to keep their brothers as captives. Wisely, they obeyed the prophet and sent the

---

[17] How many of Jotham's sixteen years overlapped with Uzziah's 52 years or whether they were all in addition to the coregency is not recorded.

[18] Notice, once again, the comparison, not just to immediately previous kings, but to David himself. See the note on chapter seventeen.

Judean captives back, even supplying them with clothing, medicine for their wounds, and transportation for those who could not walk themselves.

During this time, Judah was losing the ground it had gained under earlier kings (vs. 16–25). The Edomites took captives, and the Philistines took over cities they had lost. Rather than turning to Yehovah, Ahaz contacted the Assyrians to help him,[19] paying them with "RICHES FROM THE LORD'S TEMPLE, THE ROYAL PALACE, AND THE OFFICIALS," but they proved to be more trouble than help. Even still, Ahaz chose to worship the Assyrian gods, because he thought they were stronger than Yehovah (who had not helped him), and he shuttered the Temple, setting up pagan altars throughout Jerusalem. Because of his disloyalty, he was not buried with the other Judean kings when he died (vs. 26–27). His son, Hezekiah, replaced him.

Chapters twenty-nine and thirty begin the account of Hezekiah's reign.[20] He was compared to David as a godly king (29:1–2). As soon as he became king, he immediately went to work undoing the damage his father, Ahaz, had done (29:3–19).[21] In his first month, he reopened the Temple and began repairing it. He reestablished the priests and the Levites and ordered them to begin purifying the Temple and grounds. They started by removing anything ceremonially unclean and consecrated every square inch of the facility.[22] This took them about two weeks to clean thoroughly. The significance of "THE SIXTEENTH DAY OF THE FIRST MONTH" is that Passover was to begin on the

---

[19] It was this event that prompted the famous "Christmas" passage of Isaiah 7, where Isaiah said that Ahaz's sign from God would be a young woman giving birth to a son and calling him Emmanuel.

[20] Solomon, Jehoshaphat, and Hezekiah are the only kings to receive more than one chapter in 2 Chronicles about their reigns.

[21] One of the greatest differences between 2 Kings and 2 Chronicles is that the next three chapters detailing Hezekiah's changes are summed up in a single verse in 2 Kings 18:4.

[22] Verse 17 says that they started this "ON THE FIRST DAY OF THE FIRST MONTH." As will be shown in chapter 30, this referred to the Jewish calendar year, not the first day of Hezekiah's reign in verse three, because he hoped to have it done in time for Passover, but it was not.

fourteenth day of the first month and the Feast of Unleavened Bread on the fifteenth, but the altar was not ready (Leviticus 23:5–6).

"EARLY THE NEXT MORNING" (the seventeenth day of the first month), Hezekiah and the officials went to the Temple to sacrifice and worship (29:20–36). They offered a sin offering for the entire nation and to make the Temple usable again, and they followed the instructions for making the altar ready for the daily sacrifices. Once all this was done, he ordered the musicians to begin their worship and for the burnt sacrifices to begin. They sang the songs of David and Asaph while the burnt sacrifices were offered, then the people were released to bring their own offerings, totaling 670 bulls, 100 rams, 200 lambs, and 3,000 sheep.

Hezekiah wrote letters inviting all Israelites—in both Judah and Israel, on the west and east side of the Jordan River—to come to the Temple in Jerusalem and celebrate the Passover (30:1–9). Under Mosaic Law, the Passover could be postponed for some people who could not make it to the Temple at the correct time (Numbers 9:1–14). Because the Temple and priests were still not ready, they scheduled it for the second month for everyone as God had permitted. In his letter, Hezekiah pled with his Jewish brothers to turn back to Yehovah and worship him instead of the gods their kings had led them to serve.

As Hezekiah's messengers worked their way from city to city with his message, they met resistance and mocking from some but humility and acceptance from others (30:10–20). Jerusalem was crowded with people who wanted to genuinely worship Yehovah, and the priests were offering sacrifices for people as fast as the Levites could slaughter the animals. In an act of infinite grace, God even accepted those who were not ceremonially clean, because Hezekiah asked God's forgiveness, that he would overlook the ritual uncleanness and see the hearts of the true worshipers.

In addition to celebrating the Passover, they continued with the Feast of Unleavened Bread for the next week as prescribed in the Law (30:21–31:1). But they were not done, and they decided to celebrate for another seven days in pure voluntary worship. Thousands more bulls and sheep were sacrificed as freewill offerings, supplying the entire people with food for their feast. No one alive had seen anything like it. "THERE WAS A GREAT CELEBRATION IN JERUSALEM, UNLIKE ANYTHING THAT HAD OCCURRED IN JERUSALEM SINCE THE TIME OF KING SOLOMON SON OF DAVID OF ISRAEL." As the culminating event of the celebration, the men went throughout Judah, Benjamin, Ephraim, and Manasseh destroying the pagan shrines, idols, and sacrificial places set up for other gods.

Chapter thirty-one concludes the Chronicler's account of Hezekiah's spiritual reforms in Judah. Once the Passover celebration and after-feast had finished and the people returned home, he went about making sure that the priests and Levites were provided for, according to the Mosaic Law (vs. 2–8). After the pattern of his ancestor, David, who said, "I WILL NOT OFFER TO THE LORD MY GOD BURNT SACRIFICES THAT COST ME NOTHING" (2 Samuel 24:24), Hezekiah opened his personal fields to supply animals for the regular sacrifices. Then he gave the order for the people in Jerusalem to pay the tithe that the Law required so the priests and Levites had enough. Everyone in Judah freely and gladly paid their proper amount, and the piles kept growing for five months.

Asking about the amount collected, Hezekiah learned that the priests had received far more than enough, so it would last them for a long time (vs. 9–19). Hezekiah was glad and ordered that storerooms be added to the Temple structure. He also had them disburse the provisions among the priests and Levites throughout the land, even those who were not old enough to serve in the ministry yet.

In one of the greatest epitaphs in Scripture, God inspired this summary of Hezekiah's work: "HE DID WHAT THE LORD HIS GOD CONSIDERED GOOD AND RIGHT AND FAITHFUL. HE WHOLEHEARTEDLY AND SUCCESSFULLY REINSTITUTED SERVICE IN GOD'S TEMPLE AND OBEDIENCE TO THE LAW, IN ORDER TO FOLLOW HIS GOD" (vs. 20–21).

Chapter thirty-two concludes Hezekiah's story with a great victory and a few minor failures.[23] Judah came under attack by King Sennacherib of Assyria

---

[23] In this case, "minor" is relative. Because of the purpose of the Chronicles is to emphasize the Davidic Covenant, Hezekiah's mistakes are glossed over, not detailed

(vs. 1–5). Wisely, Hezekiah took steps to fortify his cities and even redirected the water supply to try to keep the Assyrians from having access to it. He also made sure to remind his army that God was fighting for them, so they should be encouraged and not afraid (vs. 6–8).

Sennacherib sent messengers to Jerusalem to announce that Yehovah was powerless before the Assyrian army (vs. 9–15). After all, Hezekiah himself had eliminated all the altars except for the one in the Temple in Jerusalem. That must have weakened Yehovah and made him upset with Hezekiah (a natural misunderstanding from a pagan worshiper). Not only that, but not one of the tribal gods that Assyria faced had been able to protect their nations. They even went so far as to yell in Hebrew to the guards on the wall, trying to convince them that Hezekiah was only deceiving them and that Yehovah could never protect them (vs. 16–19). "THEY TALKED ABOUT THE GOD OF JERUSALEM AS IF HE WERE ONE OF THE MAN-MADE GODS OF THE NATIONS OF THE EARTH."

Hezekiah and the famous prophet, Isaiah, prayed to God for help (vs. 20–23). Not only did he destroy Sennacherib's army, but when the king returned to Assyria, he was killed by his own sons, in utter humiliation. Thus, God protected Hezekiah and Judah from their enemies, bringing peace to their land and fear and respect from the surrounding nations.[24]

During the time of the Assyrian invasion, Hezekiah came down with a terminal illness (vs. 24–26). He prayed, asking God for healing and for a sign that he would be healed, and God gave him both. However, this sickness turned Hezekiah against God for a short time, but he repented, and God restored him.

The rest of the chapter tells of Hezekiah's great wealth and respect (vs. 27–33). No one did more for the spiritual life of Judah (and even Israel) after David than Hezekiah.[25] Upon his death, he was buried with great honor by his people, and his son, Manasseh, succeeded him.

---

out. The writer knew that his readers had access to the same sources he did, including the book of Kings, where the events are included in much more detail.

[24] This story is told in much more detail in 2 Kings 18–19 and Isaiah 36–37.

[25] The reference in verse 23 to "THE VISION OF THE PROPHET ISAIAH SON OF AMOZ" is known to us as the book of Isaiah in the Hebrew Scriptures / Old Testament. This is

Chapter thirty-three tells of the next two kings of Judah, Manasseh and Amon. Manasseh was twelve years old when Hezekiah died and he became king (vs. 1–9). In contrast to Hezekiah, Manasseh was one of the worst kings in Judah. Not only did he undo the reforms Hezekiah had made, but he also took Judah away from God further than any of the other wicked kings. In addition to setting up idols and altars to the pagan gods, Manasseh worshiped the sun, moon, and stars. He practiced human sacrifice, necromancy, and divination. Witches and sorcerers were common in his realm. Whereas other kings just closed down the Temple, Manasseh put an idol to a pagan god in it! God's estimation of Judah under Manasseh was that "THEY SINNED MORE THAN THE NATIONS WHOM THE LORD HAD DESTROYED AHEAD OF THE ISRAELITES."

What happened next is found only in Chronicles, not in 2 Kings 21. When Manasseh refused to listen to God's prophets, God sent Assyria to punish him (vs. 10–20). He was taken to Babylon where he "TRULY HUMBLED HIMSELF BEFORE THE GOD OF HIS ANCESTORS." God responded to his prayer for mercy and restored him to his throne in Judah. Manasseh proved his repentance was genuine by removing all of the wicked things he put in place, and he led the people back to worshiping Yehovah only. He also built up his cities around Judah, after Assyria had defeated them. After fifty-five years as king, Manasseh died, and his son, Amon, became king.

The chapter ends with a short account of Amon's reign (vs. 21–25). For two years, he was a wicked king like Manasseh before his repentance. He was assassinated, then his conspirators were killed as well. Josiah, Amon's son, became the next king.

Chapter thirty-four introduces Josiah's rule in Judah. He was only eight years old when Amon died and he took the throne. He was the last good king of Judah (vs. 1–2). The writer compared him to David and said that Josiah "DID NOT DEVIATE TO THE RIGHT OR THE LEFT."

---

great internal proof that Isaiah was written and known by the Jews before the time of the post-exilic return to Israel, when Chronicles was written.

Little is known about his early years (2 Kings 22 says that he was guided by a godly priest like Joash was), but as he began to seek to obey God, he found ways that he could lead the people back to worshiping Yehovah (vs. 3–7). This included tearing down the shrines, altars, and idols of the pagan gods throughout the land.

During his eighteenth year as king, he ordered the Temple to be repaired (vs. 8–21). During the renovation, "Hilkiah the priest found the law scroll the Lord had given to Moses." Shaphan the scribe took it to Josiah with a progress report on the Temple and read him the scroll. Josiah was devastated and insisted that they find a prophet who could give them a message from God. It was clear that the nation had not obeyed Yehovah, and the scroll said that they were to be judged. Josiah's men did find a prophetess who told them that the judgment must take place (vs. 22–28). However, because Josiah had humbled himself immediately when he read the law, God promised that the destruction would take place after his time and that he would die in peace.

Hearing this from the prophetess, Josiah gathered the people of Judah and reaffirmed the Mosaic Covenant between them and God (vs. 29–33). He went about tearing down all the idolatrous paraphernalia he could find and continually encouraged the people to worship Yehovah alone. "Throughout the rest of his reign they did not turn aside from following the Lord God of their ancestors."

Chapter thirty-five concludes Josiah's reign, beginning with the resumption of the Passover (vs. 1–19). In the eighteenth year of his reign, after the renewal of their covenant with God, the people of Judah celebrated a Passover that the writer described being unlike any "observed in Israel since the days of Samuel the prophet." This is not meant to discredit the Passover that Hezekiah reinstituted, but just the number of sacrifices offered under Josiah simply eclipsed Hezekiah's. This was probably because Josiah had much more time to prepare than Hezekiah did, so he and the people were ready both with their hearts and sacrifices.

Given his great heart for God and the major reforms he made in Judah on behalf of Yehovah, Josiah's death was unceremonious and anticlimactic (vs.

20–24). Pharaoh Necho of Egypt passed by Judah to do battle along the Euphrates River, but Josiah took his army out to meet Necho. The Pharaoh insisted that he was under orders from God to not engage with Judah and asked Josiah to leave him to his business. Unfortunately, Josiah did not listen. He disguised himself and attacked Necho. Much like Saul and Ahab, he was "accidentally" shot by an Egyptian archer. Seeing he was wounded, he had his aides take him back to Jerusalem, where he died.

Verse 25 points to another historical record from Judah that is no longer available to us today. It seems that Jeremiah wrote some laments regarding Josiah's death that the people were still singing in post-exilic Jerusalem. The Book of Laments should not be confused with our book of Lamentations (also written by Jeremiah) because that has to do with the fall of Jerusalem about 20 years later, not Josiah's death.

Chapter thirty-six concludes not only this book, but the Hebrew Bible,[26] and the history of pre-exilic Judah. Even though the next four kings were part of David's family, it is safe to say that the Davidic dynasty was paused with Josiah's death. David's descendants were technically on the throne, but they were only puppet kings for foreign governments.

Josiah's son, Jehoahaz, was king for three months before Pharaoh Necho deposed him and took him to Egypt (vs. 1–4). Necho installed Jehoahaz's brother, Eliakim, instead and gave him the name Jehoiakim.

Jehoiakim ruled for eleven years, but it was during his reign that Nebuchadnezzar invaded Jerusalem twice (605 and 598 BC) before finally taking Jehoiakim captive (vs. 5–8). Next was Jehoiachin, who ruled for only "THREE MONTHS AND TEN DAYS" before Nebuchadnezzar captured him as well and installed Zedekiah (vs. 9–10). Zedekiah ruled for eleven years under Nebuchadnezzar (vs. 11–14). It was under his leadership when Nebuchadnezzar finally took Jerusalem fully because of an attempted coup by Zedekiah in 586 BC.

---

[26] As noted in the Introduction, the book of Chronicles is the final book in the Hebrew Scriptures, which is not in the same order as our Old Testament.

Verses 15–21 contain the book of 2 Chronicles in a nutshell: the people and their kings rebelled and continually rejected God's warnings and messengers until he finally handed them over to the Babylonians, who killed and captured many of them. Just like Jeremiah prophesied, they would remain in Babylon for seventy years.

But the book could not end there because its original readers were no longer in Babylon. They were back in Jerusalem rebuilding the city and the Temple. Much like a short video after the credits of a blockbuster movie hints that the story is not over, verses 22–23 show that, even in the face of constant rejection, God is the consummate promise-keeper. Just like he said, he brought the people back to the land under the direction of Cyrus of Persia. Even this pagan king recognized that he was under the direction of Israel's God. How much more should his own people worship and serve him faithfully. *To God be the glory!*

Ezra

Ezra and Nehemiah were originally one book in the Hebrew text because they tell the three-part story of Israel's return from captivity in Babylon/Persia. When the Hebrew text was translated into Greek (the Septuagint), this was retained as one book, called Esdras B (or 2 Esdras).[1] It was not until Origen (*c.* 184–253) and, later, Jerome in the 4th century that the book was finally split into two, each carrying the name of the respective writers.

In a similar manner to how Babylon took Israel captive in three sets (605, 597, 586 BC), Israel returned to her land with Persian permission in three sets as well (539, 458, 445 BC), each with a major person leading them—Zerubbabel, Ezra, and Nehemiah. Because of this major Persian influence and context, it is not surprising that Ezra is second only to Daniel in the amount of its text being written in Aramaic instead of Hebrew (Ezra 4:8–6:18; 7:12–26; Daniel 2:4b–7:28).

The book of Ezra spans approximately 80 years, from Cyrus' first pronouncement in 539 BC to Ezra's arrival under Artaxerxes I in 458 BC. Chapters 1–6 tell of Zerbbabel's work to restore the Temple. Chapters 7–10 tell of Ezra's work to finish the Temple and get it running again. Between chapters six and seven falls Ezra and Nehemiah's births and the story of Mordechai and Esther. The prophets Haggai and Zechariah played a major role in keeping the people on track during Zerubbabel's leadership.

---

[1] "Esdras" is the Greek version of the name Ezra. Esdras A (1 Esdras), 3 and 4 Esdras are apocryphal books and are not part of the biblical canon.

The theme of Ezra is the spiritual restoration of Israel. Ezra was a scribe and priest, so he focused on restarting the sacrifices in the Temple and the spiritual purification of God's people.

Chapter one is dated to 539 BC, "THE FIRST YEAR OF KING CYRUS OF PERSIA," after he had overthrown Babylon (vs. 1). It seems unlikely that God spoke directly to Cyrus, instructing him to have the Temple in Jerusalem rebuilt (although it is not impossible). It is more likely that he knew that he had been named more than 150 years earlier by Isaiah (44:28) as the one who would do this.[2] In 2 Chronicles 36:22–23, this action was said to have fulfilled Jeremiah's prophecy as well (Jeremiah 29:10). Cyrus proclaimed that all Jews throughout his kingdom were allowed to return to their homeland and rebuild the Temple (vs. 2–4). Additionally, he commanded that their neighbors help by providing "SILVER, GOLD, EQUIPMENT, AND ANIMALS, ALONG WITH VOLUNTARY OFFERINGS FOR THE TEMPLE OF GOD WHICH IS IN JERUSALEM." This meant that the exile was over; they could all go home. However, as the stories of Ezra, Nehemiah, and Esther record, 60 years later there were still many Jews in Persia. The only explanation is that they had become settled there and were spiritually apathetic, with no urgency to return.[3]

"JUDAH AND BENJAMIN" were named specifically because they constituted the southern kingdom captured by Babylon (vs. 5–11). Since Babylon had overthrown Assyria, which had captured the ten northern tribes, all the tribes were represented in the return (see the reference to "Israelites" in 2:2). The "PRIESTS AND LEVITES" returned as well, leaving little or no godly influence at all for the Jews who chose to remain in Persia. In addition to the money given by the people, Cyrus ordered that the Temple vessels and utensils that Nebuchadnezzar had taken (see Daniel 1:1–2) be returned to Jerusalem.

---

[2] Daniel was reading a copy of Jeremiah's prophecy just prior to this (Daniel 9:1–2), so it is not impossible that he may have had a copy of the much older Isaiah as well.

[3] Constable cites Josephus to support this view: "Yet did many of them stay at Babylon, as not willing to leave their possessions" (*Antiquities*, 11:1:3). This may explain the complete lack of reference to God in Esther. The true worshipers had returned, leaving behind the comfortable, unbelieving Jews.

There is a noticeable discrepancy between the number of items listed and the total number given. Two options have been offered for this. First, the actual numbers may have been lost as the text was copied. However, it is more likely that the list was not intended to be a detailed itemization of everything. Instead, the Persian royal treasurer probably counted out only the larger pieces and simply totaled the rest. Both options seem possible since none of the various counts (whether in the Hebrew text, the Greek Septuagint, or Josephus' account) add up to 5,400. All of the pieces were entrusted to Sheshbazzar,[4] who took them back to Jerusalem.

Chapter two gives the general list of nearly 50,000 men and women who returned to Jerusalem under Cyrus' program. Because the land of Israel was divided by tribe and family/clan, and those properties were required to stay within their families (Leviticus 25), knowing one's genealogy was essential, so Ezra grouped the returning exiles into nine broad categories, based on their family lines:

1) "THE DESCENDANTS OF" certain men who could be used to trace family lines (vs. 3–20, 29–32, 35)
2) "THE MEN OF" specific cities in Israel (vs. 21–28, 33–34)
3) "THE PRIESTS" from specific families (vs. 36–39)
4) "THE LEVITES" from two families (vs. 40)
5) "THE SINGERS"; also called "THE DESCENDANTS OF ASAPH" (vs. 41)
6) "THE GATEKEEPERS" from their families (vs. 42)
7) "THE TEMPLE SERVANTS" and 8) "THE DESCENDANTS OF THE SERVANTS OF SOLOMON" were counted together, although listed separately (vs. 43–58)

---

[4] The identification of Sheshbazzar is unclear. Some think this was the Babylonian name for Zerubbabel, but he is mentioned only four times in Scripture (1:8, 11; 5:14, 16), so this seems unlikely. Since he was appointed by Cyrus as the first governor of Judah (5:14), and since he was not named in chapter two in the list of Jewish captives who returned, it is possible he was a trusted Persian. If Shenazzar is an alternate spelling, then he may have been Zerubbabel's uncle (1 Chronicles 3:17–19).

9) those "UNABLE TO CERTIFY THEIR FAMILY CONNECTION OR THEIR ANCESTRY" (vs. 59–63)

These were all who obeyed God's word through Isaiah (48:20) and Jeremiah (50:8). When they finally reached Israel, they all reestablished and "LIVED IN THEIR TOWNS" (vs. 70).

Chapter three begins to record the long process of rebuilding the Jerusalem Temple. Although no exact date is given for when the Israelites arrived in Jerusalem, they erected the altar on "THE FIRST DAY OF THE SEVENTH MONTH," so they could offer sacrifices (vs. 1–6). By this time, the Jews used two calendars, the sacred and the civil, which were six months off from each other. On the sacred calendar, the seventh month (the first month of the civil calendar) contained the Feast of Trumpets (Rosh Hashanah, New Year) on the first, the Day of Atonement (Yom Kippur) on the tenth, and the week-long Feast of Tabernacles starting the fifteenth, so this was a very important month for them. Essentially, they were able to begin their new year with worship by sacrificing on the altar, which they greatly celebrated. However, the Temple itself still was in ruins.

To build the Temple, they needed supplies, so they contracted with some of the same people with whom Solomon originally worked (Sidon, Tyre, and Lebanon) and put the Levites and others to work as well (vs. 7–9). Some of the older exiles, who remembered Solomon's Temple, must have anticipated returning it to its former glory.[5] Seven months after the altar was put to use, under the leadership of Zerubbabel and Jeshua the priest (also called Joshua), they finished laying the foundation of the Temple, marking out its footprint. It was a day of grand celebration. The priests and the Levites dressed in their ceremonial robes and sang the songs of David in the presence of the people

---

[5] Nebuchadnezzar finally destroyed Jerusalem and the Temple in 586 BC, fewer than 50 years earlier, so it is likely that some of the Jews would have remembered it, although even then it had been stripped of much of its original beauty and detail. It was still better than what they were going to be able to create. God makes this same point in Haggai 2:3.

(vs. 10–13). Ezra said that "ALL THE PEOPLE GAVE A LOUD SHOUT AS THEY PRAISED THE LORD" which, combined with the weeping from the older generation, could be heard throughout the region.

Chapter four introduces a new problem that the Israelites had to face. When the leaders of the surrounding regions heard that the Temple was being rebuilt, they attempted to stop the progress by two different methods. The first attempt was sabotage (vs. 1–3). They approached Zerubbabel and Joshua, asking if they could help build the Temple. Since they are described as "enemies," they certainly would have tried to destroy it from the inside. Their offer was rejected, though, so they had to try something else. Their second attempt was a discouragement campaign (vs. 4–5). They worked through the people, spreading rumors and lies, trying to kill the morale of the workers. They worked their campaign for more than 15 years.[6]

Beginning with verse six and extending to all but the last verse of the chapter, Ezra jumped ahead 50–80 years, showing their enemies continued to work against them (vs. 6–23). Both "AT THE BEGINNING OF THE REIGN OF AHASUERUS" (also called Xerxes I, 486–465 BC; see Esther 1:1) "AND DURING THE REIGN OF ARTAXERXES" (465–425 BC), while Nehemiah was working on building the city walls, they asked the Persian king to help them stop the progress. They claimed that, once the city was rebuilt[7], the Jews would revolt and stop paying taxes. The king agreed, saying that the Jews have "CONTINUALLY ENGAGED IN REBELLION AND REVOLT," so he permitted them to forcibly stop the Jews' work. This is where the story of Nehemiah will continue.

Jumping back to Zerubbabel's day from the beginning of the chapter, the demoralization campaign succeeded, and "THE WORK ON THE TEMPLE OF GOD IN JERUSALEM CAME TO A HALT" (vs. 24). The foundation lay bare "UNTIL THE SECOND YEAR OF THE REIGN OF KING DARIUS OF PERSIA" or 520 BC.

---

[6] The next generation of enemies used these same tactics almost 100 years later during Nehemiah's building project (see Nehemiah 4 and 6, for example).

[7] Notice this is about "the city" not the Temple, showing that it is during a later phase of construction.

Chapter five introduces Haggai[8] and Zechariah[9], the prophets who worked to counteract the demoralization campaign against the Jews (vs. 1–2). As God's spokesmen, they encouraged the people to get back to work after more than fifteen years of living with only an altar. This brought another attack from their enemies. They asked who permitted them to build the Temple (vs. 3–17). The Jews claimed that Cyrus had given them permission, so the accusers wrote a letter, asking Darius to verify this in the royal archives. In this letter was the Jews' full admission of why this disaster took place: their sin against God. They recognized that their exile by Nebuchadnezzar was punishment and that Cyrus' order was the fulfillment of God's promise to return them to their land.

Chapter six continues immediately from chapter five. Darius received the letter from the Jews' accusers with great interest (vs. 1–2). After a search through the Persian archives, they did find a scroll with Cyrus' orders on it. Not only did Cyrus give permission to build the Temple, but he also specified how large it should be, and he had promised that the royal treasury would finance the project (vs. 3–5). Upon this discovery, Darius wrote a letter to the regional leaders who were trying to stop the Temple project: "ALL OF YOU STAY FAR AWAY FROM THERE! LEAVE THE WORK ON THIS TEMPLE OF GOD ALONE" (vs. 6–12). He also ordered that they provide the Jews everything they needed to finance it and the animals to sacrifice daily to God. (Of course, in their prayers, he expected them to ask "FOR THE GOOD FORTUNE OF THE KING AND HIS FAMILY"). If anyone refused to obey these commands, the punishment would be severe. Darius ordered that a support beam would be pulled out of the rebel's house, and the criminal was to be executed by being impaled on it. Finally, his house was to be knocked down and turned into a dunghill, where local waste and excrement were piled.

With everything laid out before them, and their opponents shut down, the Jews got back to work on the Temple, completing it four years later (vs. 13–15). "THE MONTH OF ADAR" is the twelfth month of the sacred calendar, so the

---

[8] Haggai 1:1; 2:1, 10, 20
[9] Zechariah 1:1, 7; 7:1

Temple was completed, and the Jews were able to dedicate it in time to celebrate the Passover and the Feast of Unleavened Bread the following month (vs. 16–22). They re-established the priesthood and the entire Levitical system. Following the pattern of Solomon (although not nearly as elaborate), they sacrificed hundreds of animals, enough for everyone to eat and celebrate. They also made sacrifices for the sins of all the people, purifying themselves before God.

Chapter seven begins the second half of the book, moving forward in time about 60 years to "THE SEVENTH YEAR OF KING ARTAXERXES" (458 BC). During the period between chapters six and seven (520–458 BC), the story of Esther took place (c. 483–472 BC), and both Ezra and Nehemiah were born in Persia.[10] In the first six chapters, Ezra recorded Zerubbabel's story, but here he picked up his own.

Ezra was a priest who could trace his lineage back to Aaron (unlike some of the others in 2:61–63). He was also "A SCRIBE WHO WAS SKILLED IN THE LAW OF MOSES" (vs. 1–6). He had asked Artaxerxes for permission to return to Israel with more people and possessions for the Temple service, which he received. There are two points he specifically mentioned about his journey. First, it took nearly four months, which must have been good time, "FOR THE GOOD HAND OF HIS GOD WAS ON HIM" (vs. 7–10). Second, his devotion to the Scriptures was three-fold: study it, obey it, and teach it. This is a model for all believers.

The rest of the chapter contains the letter which Artaxerxes gave to Ezra (vs. 11–26). It was much like Cyrus' decree 80 years earlier. Artaxerxes allowed all the Jews in his kingdom to return to Israel with Ezra. Not only did the king send animals and money, but Ezra was also encouraged to receive a collection from others in Persia to take to the Temple with him. If they received any money that they did not spend on animals for sacrifice, it was left to their discretion how to use it. If they needed any more, it was to come from the

---

[10] Since Nehemiah was already serving as cupbearer to the king in 445 BC and Ezra returned to Jerusalem in 458 BC, it is likely that they were both born during the time of Esther.

royal treasury. To avoid the issues that had come up before from the other regional leaders, Artaxerxes specifically directed that they were to assist Ezra in whatever he needed, even from their treasuries. Finally, the king told Ezra to "APPOINT JUDGES AND COURT OFFICIALS WHO CAN ARBITRATE CASES ON BEHALF OF ALL THE PEOPLE" and train those who did not know the Mosaic Law. Whatever the judges decided was the law of the land. The last two verses record Ezra's personal praise to God for his favor and hand in guiding the king in this way (vs. 27–28).

Chapter eight opens with a summary of the people who accompanied Ezra back to Israel in this second big return (vs. 1–14). Unlike Zerubbabel's nearly 50,000 exiles in chapter two (probably plus families), fewer than 1,500 signed up to go with Ezra. Ezra's plans required Levites as well as priests, but none volunteered so he sent recruiters to persuade the Levites to come, gaining another 260 men and their families (vs. 15–20).

With his group of about 1,700 men, Ezra "CALLED FOR A FAST" before taking one step of this journey (vs. 21–36). In a moment of inspired transparency, Ezra admitted that he was too embarrassed to ask the king for protection, even though there were women and children and a lot of money at stake. The reason for his embarrassment was that he had confidently said that God would protect them, so they pled with God to honor that faith. The journey took three-and-a-half months (compare vs. 31 with 7:8), and God protected them the entire way. After settling in for three days' rest, they got to work, taking inventory of everything they had brought with them and handing it over to the priests and Levites already working in the Temple.

Chapters nine and ten are difficult for many modern believers because of the harsh action that Ezra took against the Jews in Jerusalem. Once everything was settled both in Jerusalem and with the regional leaders outside of Israel, some of the Jewish leaders approached Ezra with troubling news: since Zerubbabel's time, many of the Jewish men had married foreign wives who did not worship Yehovah (vs. 1–2). "WORSE STILL, THE LEADERS AND THE OFFICIALS HAVE BEEN AT THE FOREFRONT OF ALL THIS UNFAITHFULNESS!" Ezra was devastated (vs.

3–4). They had been taken captive for this very reason, because they had turned away from God to idols, often at the request of their Canaanite wives.[11]

After hours of quiet contemplation and private prayer, Ezra finally rose to his knees before God and prayed for the forgiveness of this great wickedness in Israel (vs. 5–15). He openly acknowledged their sin and the exile from which they had just returned. He praised God for his mercy on preserving the remnant that the ancient prophets had extolled him for. Yet in the face of all of this mercy, God's people were blatantly sinning again. Fluent in the Mosaic Law, he quoted God's command, that they were not to have anything to do with the inhabitants of the land, yet here they were intermarrying with them again. Ezra wondered if God could even let a remnant survive this time. He begged for God's mercy once again.

Chapter ten ends this story abruptly. "WHILE EZRA WAS PRAYING AND CONFESSING, WEEPING AND THROWING HIMSELF TO THE GROUND BEFORE THE TEMPLE OF GOD," the Jews had begun to gather around, watching and listening to his prayer (vs. 1–4). In response, they, too, began to weep loudly for their sin. Acknowledging their position, they told Ezra to help them make a covenant with God that they would send away these women and children if God would spare them.

Ezra called for a meeting of all of the Jews in the land three days from then. Anyone who refused to appear would forfeit all property in the land and become an outsider, unable to access the Temple and God (vs. 5–9). When the day came for the meeting, all the people came and sat in the Temple before God, shivering in the rain. Constable points out that "God sent rain (v. 9; fertility) when His people got right with Him. He had promised to do this in Deuteronomy 11:10–17."[12]

---

[11] This was Solomon's downfall (1 Kings 11:1–10), which led to the divided kingdom and centuries of deep idolatry.

[12] Constable, *Notes on Ezra, 2016 edition*, 44.

Ezra commanded that every man who had married a foreign wife was to divorce her (vs. 10-17).[13] Because this required legal action and a certificate for each woman to take with her, the men said that it could not happen quickly, so they suggested that Ezra and the leadership examine the men by family groups until they were able to process everyone. Ezra agreed with this plan and noted that it took two months to work everyone through the process. Verses 18–44 list 17 priests, 10 Levites, and 84 others who needed to divorce their foreign wives and went through the proper legal process to do so.

The book of Ezra-Nehemiah will pick up twelve years later with the third and final major return of exiles to the land under the leadership of Nehemiah. In the meantime, Ezra continued to work at the purification of Jerusalem, the Temple, and the ancient people of God. As Nehemiah noted, Ezra's work was not as successful as they expected.

---

[13] Those who believe that divorce is sin have difficulty with this passage. They miss two key points. First, God never calls divorce a "sin," although Malachi 2:16 does say that God hates it because it is always the result of sin. Second, rather than outlawing divorce, God regulated it in the Mosaic Law (Deuteronomy 24:1–4) and gave additional revelation for Christians in 1 Corinthians 7. See my book, *Marriage, Divorce, and Remarriage*, for a detailed explanation of the biblical teaching on this topic.

Nehemiah

Nehemiah is the last of the historical books of the Old Testament (for more information about the chronology of the books, see "Introduction to the Old Testament," page 2). It was originally combined with Ezra as part of the same story (see also the introduction to Ezra). Whereas the book of Ezra addresses the spiritual restoration of Israel—the initial return from captivity and the rebuilding of the Temple—Nehemiah focuses more on the political restoration, reestablishing Israel as a nation.

The dating of Nehemiah is important for at least a couple of reasons. First, there has been some dispute regarding which Persian king Nehemiah served. He should be understood as Artaxerxes I, the same man as in Ezra 7. Second, this helps interpret the 70 weeks of Daniel 9:24–27. Of all of the commands and allowances for the Jews to return to Israel after their captivity, only the command in Nehemiah 2 fits the Daniel 9:25 description "TO RESTORE AND REBUILD JERUSALEM... WITH PLAZA AND MOAT, BUT IN DISTRESSFUL TIMES." This took place in 444 BC The rest of Daniel's prophecy (e.g., the cutting off of Messiah) occurred in AD 33, just as promised.

Most of Nehemiah was written in the first person, that is, Nehemiah used the pronouns *I, me,* and *my* as he wrote of his experiences. He provided a firsthand account of the balance between his leadership skills and personality and God's grace at work in and through him as he led the Israelites in obedience to God, along with godly men like Ezra and Malachi.

Chapter one opens with a specific date, "IN THE MONTH OF KISLEV, IN THE TWENTIETH YEAR" (vs. 1). This would have been 445–444 BC, about 13 years after Ezra had gone to Jerusalem (Ezra 7:7). When his brother, Hanani, and some others made their way back from Jerusalem to Susa, Nehemiah naturally inquired about the status of his people and the holy city. Zerubbabel had gone there in 539 BC, almost a hundred years earlier (Ezra 1:1), to begin the restoration, but there was considerable trouble and distraction, and they did not accomplish much beyond building the Temple.[1] Ezra brought another group back to Jerusalem in 458 BC (Ezra 7:7), but his time was spent purifying the people again and restoring the proper worship in the Temple.

Nehemiah was crushed at the news that "THE WALL OF JERUSALEM LIES BREACHED, AND ITS GATES HAVE BEEN BURNED DOWN" (vs. 3). After nearly 100 years since Zerubbabel, he expected that Jerusalem would have been a strong, fully functioning city again. Like Daniel so many years before and Ezra just a dozen years earlier, Nehemiah fell before God in prayer, confessing sin on behalf of his nation (vs. 4–7). In addition to his confession, his prayer included two other key points. First, he quoted from the Land Covenant God made with Israel in Deuteronomy 30, knowing that God had obligated himself to fulfill those promises (vs. 8–10). Second, Nehemiah already had a plan to confront the king, so he asked God for success in that meeting (vs. 11). He was not afraid to use the secular connections he had to accomplish God's work.

Chapter two places Nehemiah's conversation with the king in the month of Nisan, which was the first month on the Jewish calendar. Kislev (1:1) was the ninth month of the previous Jewish year, meaning that Nehemiah prayed on this issue and formulated his plan for about three or four months before approaching Artaxerxes with it. As the king's cupbearer (1:11), Nehemiah had close access and a good relationship with the king, so he planned to use that carefully. One day, as he began to look for the right opportunity, the king noticed that Nehemiah was not his normal self; he seemed depressed (vs. 1–2). Nehemiah used this to approach his topic. The Persians were proud of the way they took care of their dead, so Nehemiah mentioned how the graves of his ancestors were desolate and the gates of his city had been burned (vs. 3).

---

[1] The books of Ezra and Haggai recount some of the issues they had to deal with when helping the people build the Temple.

The king knew that Nehemiah was about to make a request, so he asked him to be honest (vs. 4–9). Even though he had prayed for this very situation for months, Nehemiah "QUICKLY PRAYED" again and made the ask. He wanted permission to leave the king's service to re-establish Jerusalem and make it inhabitable again. Naturally, the king wanted to know how much time this would take, so Nehemiah "GAVE HIM A TIME," though he did not record it here. Secondly, he asked that the king would give him letters to secure resources and materials for this project. Cyrus had originally promised to fund the entire Temple project (Ezra 3:7; 6:4, 8–9), and Artaxerxes had done the same earlier (Ezra 7:21–24), so Nehemiah asked that he would do something similar, at least the wood for the city walls and gates, and the king agreed.

After staying in Jerusalem for three days, Nehemiah took off one night to examine the situation without a lot of questions (vs. 11–16). Although there were a few men with him, he did not tell anyone what he was doing. Throughout the night he walked around the entire wall, looking at what needed to be done. Upon returning (presumably the next morning), Nehemiah met with the elders and leaders, explaining his purpose and goals to rebuild Jerusalem (vs. 17–18). He also told them about his deal with the king. This news cheered them, and they began to make preparations for the work.

The chief enemies of this project were the local Gentile officials Sanballat and Tobiah, who are named only in Nehemiah. They had already become wary when Nehemiah arrived from Susa (vs. 10). Now they began their active campaign to disrupt the project, but Nehemiah stood against them, declaring that God was at the helm of the work (vs. 19–20).[2]

Chapter three shows the men getting to work based on Nehemiah's plan and encouragement from chapter two. Nehemiah named ten gates—Sheep, Fish, Jeshanah, Valley, Dung, Fountain, Water, Horse, East, Inspection—and three towers (probably guard towers)—Tower of the Hundred, Tower of

---

[2] If only Nehemiah's argument against Israel's enemies then was reaffirmed by Israel's allies today: "YOU HAVE NO JUST OR ANCIENT RIGHT IN JERUSALEM" (vs. 20).

Hananel, Tower of the Fire Pots—that needed to be rebuilt. The genius of his plan was two-fold as shown in repeated phrases throughout the chapter.

First, he had friends working alongside each other on sections of the wall "ADJACENT" to each other. This helped keep the morale up, which was going to be necessary in the face of opposition. Secondly, Nehemiah had people work on sections of the wall "OPPOSITE THEIR HOUSE." Naturally, those who lived in Jerusalem had a vested interest in the walls by their homes being secure, so Nehemiah let them work on those sections. By verse thirty-two they had come full circle to the Sheep Gate where they began in verse one.

Chapter four introduces the opposition that Nehemiah and his crew faced during the rebuilding project. This was not new. Both Zerubbabel and Ezra were attacked for trying to rebuild the Temple earlier (Ezra just a dozen years earlier), and Nehemiah knew that he would not be able to do his work easily.

Sanballat and Tobiah (along with Geshem the Arab) were first mentioned at the end of chapter two, but here their plan is put into action. Their opposition campaign began in their own countries by insulting the Jews and their project. Sanballat simply rejected the idea that they could accomplish it, while Tobiah (like a five-year-old) laughed, "A fox could knock it down!" Yet, none of this dissuaded the Jews. Nehemiah prayed for strength and confidence, and the people enthusiastically got the wall built halfway (vs. 4–6).

Their second attempt was a military strike against Jerusalem (vs. 7–12). They promised to infiltrate the work crew and slaughter them, but people living outside the city heard of the plan and warned Nehemiah. He was a man of both prayer and action, so not only did he ask God for protection, he stationed guards around the workers (vs. 13–23). In fact, he had the same people (who already had taken ownership of the project) take turns building and guarding. However, even the builders kept their swords on them in case the battle alarm was sounded. Nehemiah did not even allow them to put their swords or spears down to change clothes. They were always on alert.

Chapter five introduces new trouble that Nehemiah had to address. Before he arrived in Jerusalem, there had been famine, and the people had to sell their property to buy grain (vs. 1–6). However, the taxes were so high that they also sold themselves and their children into slavery just to eat. If this had been the work of another nation, Nehemiah would have had little say. However, when he learned that these acts were done by "THEIR FELLOW JEWS," he was furious. The Mosaic Law was clear that the Jews could borrow from and lend to each other, but there was to be no interest and slaves were to be released at the Jubilee year (Leviticus 25:35–46).

When Nehemiah gathered the leaders together, he charged them with this unspeakable act, pointing out the irony that many Jews had just been released from captivity, only to find themselves in the same situation in their own land (vs. 7–8). He admitted that his family was also loaning money and grain, but they did not demand collateral or charge interest (vs. 9–13). The leaders agreed that they were wrong and promised to return everything they had unjustly taken and stop charging interest. Because of this (and probably other obvious leadership traits), Nehemiah became the governor of Judah for twelve years (vs. 14–19). Not only did he not treat the people harshly like the previous leaders had, he took nothing from the people but instead shared with them from his own wealth.

Chapter six records the third and fourth attempts to dissuade Nehemiah and prevent the city wall from being completed. Once the wall was finished (except for the doors on the gates), Sanballat and Tobiah called for a meeting with Nehemiah. Their previous attempts to lower the morale and their threats of military opposition had not worked, so they intended to assassinate Nehemiah to stop the work (vs. 1–4). Four times they asked for a meeting and four times Nehemiah responded saying his work was too important to stop for a meeting.

The fifth time they contacted him, they tried yet another tactic (vs. 5–9). In addition to the request for a meeting, they accused Nehemiah of setting up a kingdom with plans to revolt against Persia. This was not true, of course, so Nehemiah simply rejected it and kept working. He did not let their words or actions keep him from doing what God had called him to do. Instead, he continually asked God to strengthen him and keep him focused.

Their final attempt was to use Nehemiah's faith against him (vs. 10–14). Several "prophets" and "prophetesses" had joined Tobiah's payroll and tried to use their position to speak against Nehemiah as if from God. One tried to convince Nehemiah to go into hiding, but he discerned that these people were not really from God, so he prayed for wisdom for himself and God's judgment on these liars.

Finally, the wall was completed, "IN JUST FIFTY-TWO DAYS" (vs. 15–19). This frightened Nehemiah's enemies because they knew that God was with the Israelites. At this point, Nehemiah added the note that many of the wealthy Jews had ties to Tobiah, which had probably slowed down the work.

Chapter seven is similar to Ezra 2 in that it provides a list of some of the people who had returned to Israel, by name, during the first return. The goal was not to name precisely every person or even every family or clan. Those who insist that this was the purpose conclude that there are errors or contradictions because the numbers do not add up to the total given. Rather, both Ezra and Nehemiah gave a sample list of names and counts as a subset of the whole. The point is that it was not just a nameless, faceless number that returned; these were real people, with real families living out this very real situation. Wiersbe likened it to the Old Testament version of Hebrews 11.[3]

Once the doors were inserted into the gates, the wall was completed (vs. 1–4). At this point, Nehemiah made the necessary appointments to put people at the right places for both security and worship. Jerusalem needed both guards and singers. As he did with the builders in chapter three, Nehemiah stationed some of the guards near their own homes because they had a vested interest in keeping those particular parts of the wall secure.

Chapter eight probably took place either just a couple of months after the wall was finished or a full year-and-a-half after they had begun. Chapter two

---

[3] Warren Wiersbe quoted in Constable, *Notes on Nehemiah, 2016 Edition*, 25.

states that Nehemiah approached the king about the wall in Nisan (the first month of the Jewish calendar). Assuming this was the beginning of the month and no preparations were needed so that Nehemiah could leave immediately, he would have arrived about the beginning of the third month, after a trip of 50 days or more. He spent three days examining the situation and deciding on his course of action before talking with the local leaders and making preparation for the project (2:11–18). The project itself took fifty-two days (6:15), putting them halfway into the fifth month. This leaves about one-and-a-half months before the first day of the seventh month on this very conservative timeline. The question is how much additional time passed that Nehemiah did not record. The beginning of this chapter states that "THE ISRAELITES WERE SETTLED IN THEIR TOWNS," which was not the case when Nehemiah first arrived. It does seem that Nehemiah would want the events in the following chapters to occur as soon as possible, rather than waiting for an entire year.

The first day of the seventh month was a special day of rest established by God (Leviticus 23:23–25). Ultimately, when the civil calendar separated from the sacred calendar in Israel, this day became *Rosh Hashannah*, the first day of the new civil year. Additionally, every seven years at the Feast of Tabernacles (the fifteenth through twenty-first of the seventh month), the entire Law was to be read to the nation (Deuteronomy 31:10–13). Nehemiah appointed Ezra to read the Law to them (vs. 1–8). (This is the first time Ezra appears in Nehemiah's account.) All the people "WHO COULD UNDERSTAND" the Law stood quietly and listened to Ezra read "FROM DAWN TILL NOON."[4] He did this from a raised wooden platform, so the people could hear him. Additionally, the Levites taught and explained it to the people so they understood it clearly.

---

[4] There are two possible meanings of this statement. First, it is possible that younger children were not required to attend this meeting. Without making too broad of an application, this could support the concept of the importance of age-appropriate environments in church (e.g., Sunday School, children's programs, etc.). Second, it is possible that this referred to some who no longer understood Hebrew. In this case, the Levites may have translated for them apart from the main group.

When they understood how far from God's law they had gone, it brought a revival to the nation, (vs. 9–12). As they stood before Yehovah and wept, Ezra, Nehemiah, and the Levites encouraged them to stop weeping and rejoice because this was a special day to celebrate. They were to rest and eat together, which they did. On the second day, when they gathered again "TO CONSIDER THE WORDS OF THE LAW" (because they were so hungry to hear from God), they discovered the command to celebrate the Feast of Tabernacles, so they went out to gather the branches necessary to obey and participated happily (vs. 13–18). This is something they had not done for nearly 1,000 years, "FROM THE DAYS OF JOSHUA SON OF NUN." Each day they heard Ezra read to them the Law, over and over again, and "EVERYONE EXPERIENCED VERY GREAT JOY."

Chapter nine jumps forward a few weeks to "THE TWENTY-FOURTH DAY OF THIS SAME MONTH" (vs. 1). The Israelites had gathered once again to listen to the Law, to confess their sins, and to pray. During this time the Levites recited the history of their nation, going back to God's initial call of Abram (Genesis 11:31; Acts 7:2–4). The purpose of this recitation was not to focus on Israel's journey but rather God's provision for them on that journey. From verse five to thirty-seven, the NET Bible includes 86 uses of the singular pronouns *you* or *your* in the Levites' prayer to God. Throughout the story, they emphasized God's goodness and the Israelites' repeated rebellion and disobedience. No matter how many times they turned away and he judged them, "DUE TO YOUR ABUNDANT MERCY YOU DID NOT DO AWAY WITH THEM ALTOGETHER; YOU DID NOT ABANDON THEM. FOR YOU ARE A MERCIFUL AND COMPASSIONATE GOD" (vs. 31).

They concluded their prayer with a petition that God would remember them one more time as they turned back to him in this time of poverty and adversity (vs. 32–37). In keeping with the pattern of their ancestors, they drafted a legal document stating their promise to uphold the covenant Law (vs. 38; this is 10:1 in the Hebrew text).

Chapter ten lists the names of the men who signed the covenant (chapter nine) before God. Much like the U.S. Declaration of Independence formalized the break with Britain, this was Israel's formal declaration of dependence on Yehovah.

In verses one through twenty-seven, Nehemiah is named alongside twenty-two priests, seventeen Levites, and thirty-eight other leaders. The remainder of the people entered "INTO A CURSE AND AN OATH" to obey the Law as God had given it to Moses. The specific oath they took is outlined in verses thirty through thirty-nine. It included specific mention of not marrying foreign people, observing the Sabbath, and giving offerings for the priests and Levites. They also acknowledged their responsibility to bring the firstfruits of their land and redeem their firstborn sons as God had directed. Finally, they promised, "WE WILL NOT NEGLECT THE TEMPLE OF OUR GOD."

Chapter eleven and the first half of chapter twelve recount the issue of who was going to live in Jerusalem. When the rebuilding project started, there were only a few homes in Jerusalem, probably owned mostly by priests and Levites who attended the Temple. With the city newly functional, people needed to move in so that it would not fall again to an enemy attack.

However, moving to Jerusalem meant leaving whatever homes they had already established, so there were two ways that Jerusalem got its new inhabitants. First, some people volunteered (vs. 2). Second, the rest were divided into groups of ten men (families), and they cast lots to determine which one would move. Thus, a little more than ten percent of the Israelites moved into Jerusalem. Most of these were from the tribes of the surrounding region, Benjamin and Judah, along with priests and Levites. The rest of the people continued settling back in their original tribal lands from which they had been expelled in the captivities.

Chapter twelve begins with a list of names of Levites and priests, making it easy to overlook, but its importance should not be missed. Because the priests and temple servants were all required to come from the tribe of Levi, the leaders needed to know who could serve and who could not; correct genealogical identification was essential. Even more important was identifying which of the Levites were from Aaron's family and could serve as priests and as the high priest. Because God established these rules in Exodus, the resumption of Temple worship would be futile—and even fatal—if the wrong people attempted to participate. In 3:1 and 3:20 the high priest at this time was identified as Eliashib, so the list in verses ten and eleven names the succession of five high priests.[5] The line of Levites is traced back to those who returned with Zerubbabel nearly one hundred years earlier and whose descendants were still serving in Nehemiah's time. The "BOOK OF CHRONICLES" (vs. 23) should not be confused with the biblical books of "Chronicles." This was a generic term meaning "the official record books."

The rest of the chapter describes "THE DEDICATION OF THE WALL OF JERUSALEM" (vs. 27–47). After "THE PRIESTS AND LEVITES HAD PURIFIED THEMSELVES, THEY PURIFIED THE PEOPLE, THE GATES, AND THE WALL." Then the people sang and played instrumental music and danced in celebration of Yehovah. There were "TWO LARGE CHOIRS" who stood opposite each other in the Temple and "SANG LOUDLY." Men, women, and children all joined in, offering praise and sacrifice at the Temple. "THE REJOICING IN JERUSALEM COULD BE HEARD FROM FAR AWAY." In an attempt to keep their oath from chapter ten, they appointed men to oversee the reception of offerings for the Temple storehouse so that the priests and Levites would be taken care of.[6] It was probably the happiest day anyone in Jerusalem had ever seen or would see in their lives.

Chapter thirteen is a compendium of issues that Nehemiah had to correct as he concluded the story of the Old Testament. Verse thirty is a good summary of the whole chapter: "I PURIFIED THEM OF EVERYTHING FOREIGN, AND I ASSIGNED SPECIFIC DUTIES TO THE PRIESTS AND THE LEVITES." There were four main areas of Jewish life that Nehemiah had to purify. Verse six reveals that Nehemiah had returned to his work in Persia for a while after residing in Israel

---

[5] Some of these names may have been added or appended later to show that the line was established even after the captivities.

[6] This is the context for Malachi 3:10. It is not about bringing a tithe to church; it was about the people fulfilling their promise to financially support the priests and Temple workers.

for twelve years (compare to 2:1).[7] "AFTER SOME TIME" he returned to Israel to find several issues that needed to be corrected, which he did.[8]

First, although the Israelites had excluded the Moabites and Ammonites from entering the Temple (as God had instructed Moses to do), Eliashib had set aside one of the Temple storerooms for Tobiah's (the Ammonite; 2:10) personal possessions, because he was Eliashib's relative (vs. 1–9). When Nehemiah discovered this, he "cleaned house," throwing out all of Tobiah's belongings and having the Temple storerooms purified and filled with their proper items.

Second, the people had broken their oath to bring offerings to supply the Levites with food, so the Levites had to go work in the fields to provide their food instead of being able to serve full-time in the Temple (vs. 10–14). Nehemiah reinstated the offerings and appointed new, trustworthy, men over the storerooms.

Third, Nehemiah discovered that the people were no longer observing the weekly Sabbath (vs. 15–22). Not only were they working in their fields, but they were also transporting goods to buy and sell from each other and foreigners in Jerusalem under the shadow of the Temple on the Sabbath days. Since the local leaders were not doing anything to stop this, Nehemiah ordered the city gates to be closed for the Sabbath and not reopened until the Sabbath was completely over. Some merchants thought this was just a temporary thing or a mistake, so they camped outside the gates for a few weeks. Finally, they realized that Nehemiah meant business.

Finally, Nehemiah discovered that the men had begun to marry foreign wives again (vs. 23–31). This was the same thing that had led Solomon into idolatry along with many of their former generations of ancestors. Ezra had already dealt with this about twenty-five years earlier (Ezra 10), but the people

---

[7] It was not a mistake for Nehemiah to refer to Artaxerxes as "KING OF BABYLON" instead of king of Persia, because Persia had overthrown Babylon, which was included in the Persian empire at this time. Constable notes that he may have used this term if Artaxerxes was in the city of Babylon during this time.

[8] Since many of the issues that Nehemiah outlined in this chapter were also addressed by Malachi, it is probable that they worked together on them.

had gone back to it. Even worse, one of the high priest's sons "WAS A SON-IN-LAW OF SANBALLAT THE HORONITE," so Nehemiah excommunicated him from Israel.

This, along with the parallel messages of Malachi, is the chapter that closes the story of the Old Testament. For the next four hundred years, the people obeyed and disobeyed variously while suffering the "FAMINE...[OF] AN END TO DIVINE REVELATION" that Amos prophesied (8:11). During these centuries, God was silent until he spoke again through the angel Gabriel to an old priest in the very Temple that Ezra and Nehemiah worked tirelessly to rebuild and purify (Luke 1).

Esther

The book of Esther stands apart in the Scriptures in several ways. First, it is one of only two books named after a woman, the other being Ruth. Second (and often overlooked), is the realization that, unlike Ruth, the heroine of this story was never portrayed as a faithful servant of God. Instead, Esther committed several violations of the Mosaic Law just in this short account, yet God used her in a great way, despite her blatant sin. Third, and probably the most important, there is no mention of God anywhere in the book. Several explanations have been given for this, but it is evident that the lack of reference to God does not mean the absence of God himself. His hand is certainly visible throughout the story, as shown in the constant preservation of his people. However, the fact that none of the primary Jewish characters in the narrative ever pray to or acknowledge God in any way gives a sad insight into the spiritual apathy of the Jews still living in Persia at that time.

The writer of this book never gave his name, but it is usually attributed to Mordecai himself. The book of Esther covers about ten years (483–472 BC) and fits between chapters six and seven of Ezra, about 55 years after the end of Daniel.

Chapter one essentially sets the scene for the "real" story found in the rest of the book. History has definitively proven Esther's Ahasuerus (vs. 1) to be the famous Xerxes (his more well-known Greek name), who ruled Persia from 486–464 BC. He was a volatile man, whose moods swung from overly generous to unspeakably brutal. The banquet he gave "IN THE THIRD YEAR OF HIS REIGN" (vs. 3) came at the culmination of a long time planning an attack on Greece. It was a premature celebration of his presumed victory, following a six-month showing off of "HIS ROYAL GLORY AND THE SPLENDOR OF HIS MAJESTIC GREATNESS" (vs. 4).

On the seventh day of the banquet, during which "THERE WERE NO RESTRICTIONS ON THE DRINKING" (vs. 8),[1] the king commanded his queen, Vashti, to make an appearance at the men's banquet (vs. 9–12). There is a lot of speculation as to why she refused to appear, often based on the assumption that he expected her to appear nude; however, the writer did not say, so the reason she refused is less important than the fact that she did.[2]

The drunken king sobered immediately, thoroughly humiliated in front of his court and enraged at his queen (vs. 13–22). He met with his Cabinet, the Persian "Council of Seven," for advice. They feared that the queen's display would incite a women's liberation movement, leading to all the women in the kingdom openly disobeying their husbands. They recommended that the queen be stripped of her title and a new queen chosen in her place. (Vashti was not executed, though, and exerted incredible influence years later as the queen mother in her son's kingdom.) Additionally, the king wrote an open edict that all men should rule their own families, which was ironic since he failed so publicly.

Some estimate that the Persian Empire included 60 different nationalities at this time, but it was intentionally not a "melting pot." Rather than one cohesive population with one language, the Persians insisted that ethnicities and cultures remained distinct, demonstrated by the command to speak their various languages at home, possibly so that any uprising would be limited to a local area or group.

---

[1] The Hebrew text says that no one was compelled to drink wine, which seems to mean the opposite of the NET translation here. However, although drinking was not required, there were also no limitations on it, since the stewards were to serve "according to the desires of each person" (NASB). Thus, even if some did not drink, the level of intoxication of others, including the king himself, must have been tremendous.

[2] History notes that she was probably pregnant with Xerxes' son, Artaxerxes I, at the time. Artaxerxes was the king Nehemiah served under 40 years later.

Chapter two takes place 3–4 years after chapter one (compare 1:3 with 2:12, 16). During this time, Xerxes did attack Greece and was soundly beaten. He returned home dejected and looking for comfort, only to remember what he had done to Vashti before he left (vs. 1). Someone suggested that a new, younger queen is what he needed and that he should make his selection from all of the beautiful young virgins throughout his kingdom (vs. 2–4). The process would be overseen by the manager of the king's harem.

Living in Susa (Persia's capital) at the time was Mordecai, a Jew whose great-grandfather had been taken captive to Babylon about 120 years earlier, at the same time as Ezekiel. This would make the family of Mordecai and his cousin, Esther, upper class or royalty of Jerusalem. When Esther's parents died, Mordecai took her into his home to care for her as his daughter (vs. 5–7).

Esther[3] was very beautiful and seems to have had a warm and personable attitude, so when she was taken into the harem, she gained favor very quickly, much like Daniel. Unfortunately, unlike Daniel, who determined that he would follow the Mosaic Law no matter the cost (Daniel 1:8), Esther did not hold that conviction. Instead, it seems she willingly did whatever was necessary to fit in, even to the point of having sex with the king outside of marriage, then marrying the non-Jewish king, all with Mordecai's approval (vs. 8–14).[4] We can also assume that, unlike Daniel, she did partake of food and drink forbidden by God's Law. The only thing Mordecai did insist was probably the most devastating: that she must not disclose that she was Jewish (vs. 10).

It is important to note that the Jews still in Persia at this time were there by choice. They or their families had decided to not return to Israel with Zerubbabel sixty years earlier. They found themselves comfortable in Persia, and this may account for the lack of concern for God's Law, even among the "heroes" of this story.

---

[3] "Esther" was the young woman's Persian name, meaning "star." It is related to the name Ishtar, the pagan goddess of love. Her Hebrew name, Hadassah, means "myrtle."

[4] Had she not been chosen as the queen, Esther would have remained in the harem as a concubine, a women kept solely for sex with the king but not truly a wife.

Through God's silent leading, Xerxes did choose Esther as his queen in Vashti's place (vs. 15–18). The comment that "MORDECAI WAS SITTING AT THE KING'S GATE" (vs. 19) implies that he had a position in the government at that time. Whether that was because of Esther's influence is unknown. However, because of that position, God allowed Mordecai to overhear an assassination plot against Xerxes and warn Esther in time to stop it (vs. 21–23). This event would come up again at just the right time.

Chapter three introduces the story's villain, Haman, who was from the nation of Agag, part of the Persian Empire (vs. 1). For a reason never given, Ahasuerus/Xerxes had promoted Haman to be one of his closest counselors. This took place about four years after chapter two (compare 2:16 and 3:7). Haman's new position required the honor and respect of the people, but Mordecai refused (vs. 2–3). It seems that he gave his Jewish ancestry as an explanation, exactly the opposite of his instructions to Esther. However, if he was not a particularly religious Jew, one wonders why Mordecai would not bow in respect to Haman, and he was even asked that question (vs. 4–5).

One reason that is worth exploring, but can only be speculated, comes from clues sprinkled throughout the story that Jews would find significant. Consider these parallels. Mordecai was the great-grandson of Kish, from the tribe of Benjamin (2:5). Six hundred years earlier, King Saul was the son of another Kish, also from the tribe of Benjamin (1 Samuel 9:1). Saul failed to destroy the Amalekites at God's command. Instead, he spared the king, whose name was Agag (1 Samuel 15:1–3, 7–9). Mordecai opposed a man from the nation of Agag. It is apparent from Haman's response to Mordecai's insult that he already harbored a hatred for the Jewish people at large, not just Mordecai (vs. 5–6, 10). Eradicating an entire ethnicity for the actions of one man hints at a deeper issue.

The rest of the chapter outlines Haman's plan for this execution of all Jews within the borders of Persia (which extended from "INDIA TO ETHIOPIA" at this time, including the land of Israel; see 1:1). Without giving any detail, he asked the king if he could wipe out "A PARTICULAR PEOPLE" throughout the kingdom (vs. 8-11). He explained that, because they followed different laws, it was "NOT

APPROPRIATE FOR THE KING TO PROVIDE A HAVEN FOR THEM." To sweeten the deal, Haman promised to pay back the royal treasury for the cost of using the king's army for this purpose (probably from the assets he would accumulate from the Jews he had killed). The "10,000 TALENTS OF SILVER" would be close to 200 million dollars in today's money, a generous amount even for a mission that large. The plan worked, and the king agreed, going so far as to tell Haman to keep his money. The king would finance the eradication of an entire people group without even knowing who they were.

By the casting of lots (called a *pur* in Akkadian), Haman determined that the day of this genocide would be eleven months later (vs. 8). With the king's approval and signature stamp, Haman wrote the decree that exactly eleven months from that date, every Jew in the empire was to die, regardless of age or gender (vs. 12–15). With a flair for the dramatic (and possibly an evil laugh), he wrote "THAT THEY SHOULD DESTROY, KILL, AND ANNIHILATE ALL THE JEWS" in one day. It was going to be a massacre. The final verse shows the intensity of the evil in Haman and the total apathy in the king: "THE EDICT WAS ISSUED IN SUSA THE CITADEL. WHILE THE KING AND HAMAN SAT DOWN TO DRINK, THE CITY OF SUSA WAS IN AN UPROAR."

Chapter four is a key chapter in this story. Although it seems to be nothing more than a conversation while the reader waits for the "real" action to start, this conversation is essential. While Jews throughout the whole empire were in loud, public mourning because of the new law, Esther knew nothing about it (vs. 1–9). The only reason she found out when she did was because of Mordecai's actions right outside the palace. When she heard about him, she did everything she could to stop his mourning but to no avail. Mordecai relayed to Esther all of the details of the law, including a copy of it, and "GAVE INSTRUCTIONS" for her to talk to the king about it.

Her response was not what he wanted to hear (vs. 10–11). The Persians had a law, which Mordecai must have known well, that no one—including the queen—was allowed to approach the king without first being summoned. Additionally, if anyone did approach him and he did not extend his scepter to receive him, that person was killed on the spot. Esther was especially concerned because she had not seen him for any reason for about a month.

Mordecai's response is a template for every great inspirational speech ever given (vs. 12–14). First, he stated the danger: "DON'T IMAGINE THAT BECAUSE YOU ARE PART OF THE KING'S HOUSEHOLD YOU WILL BE THE ONE JEW WHO WILL ESCAPE." Second, he warned of the consequences of inaction: "IF YOU KEEP QUIET AT THIS TIME, LIBERATION AND PROTECTION FOR THE JEWS WILL APPEAR FROM ANOTHER SOURCE." Third, he cast his vision: "IT MAY VERY WELL BE THAT YOU HAVE ACHIEVED ROYAL STATUS FOR SUCH A TIME AS THIS!"

Esther responded once more, agreeing to do it (vs. 15–17). She asked Mordecai for only one thing: get every Jew in the area to fast for three days for her. Most scholars assume that this included prayer to God, even though it is not explicitly mentioned. At the end of three days, she would approach the king, regardless of the outcome. The chapter ends with Mordecai no longer giving her instructions but following hers.

Chapter five picks up the story three days later. We assume she and her people had fasted and prayed for three days, so she put on her royal robes and crown and approached the throne room (vs. 1–2). Seeing her standing in the hallway, the king extended his scepter, inviting her in. This must have given her a little bit of hope.

It was one of his generous days, and Ahasuerus was still in love with Esther. He knew there was a reason she came to see him without an invitation, so he asked what was on her mind. He promised he would give up to half of the kingdom to her if that was what she wanted (vs. 4–8). Wisely, she requested a private audience, with only the king and Haman, at a banquet. The king agreed. At the banquet, he asked again what she wanted. In what was probably similar to Gideon's fleece (Judges 6:36–40), testing God, Esther waited one more day. If the king and Haman would come back the next day for another banquet, she would finally ask what she wanted. Again, the king agreed.

Haman went home exceptionally delighted at the special treatment he had received—a private banquet with the king and queen two days in a row! He threw a party of his own to brag to his wife and friends (vs. 9–14). Nothing could spoil the day—except Mordecai. He continued to ignore Haman, which infuriated him, but Haman brushed it off for one more day. During his party, he groused about Mordecai to his guests, and one suggested that he kill Mordecai now, instead of waiting for the massacre later that year.

The "gallows" mentioned should not be confused with a platform where someone is hung with a rope. A better translation may be a "pole." History shows that, whereas the Babylonians regularly threw people alive into fire (see Daniel 3), the Persians often impaled their enemies on a sharp pole, where they would hang, possibly for days, bleeding out in the hot Middle Eastern sun. Of all things, this brought a smile to Haman's face, cheering his mood, and he went about having it built in his own backyard, looking forward to seeing Mordecai on it.

Chapter six contains the plot twist of the story. At this point, the reader might assume that the Jews may have to fight for their survival, and some of them would probably make it, but Mordecai was certainly doomed. The only way for Mordecai to be saved would be for something to happen to Haman, which seemed unlikely, given how close he was to the king.

Again, although God was silent, he was not absent. In Daniel, he gave Nebuchadnezzar dreams to grab his attention; in Esther, he simply kept the king from sleeping, so he had to find another way to spend his time (vs. 1–5). Being the narcissist he was, Xerxes asked to have the chronicles of his reign (his greatest achievements) read to him. During the reading, he discovered that Mordecai had saved him from an assassination attempt four years earlier, and nothing was ever done to reward him for that. Even for the volatile king that was unheard of. Although it was early in the morning, Haman was already in the hallway hoping for a meeting with the king to discuss what to do with Mordecai. Little did he know the king also wanted to talk about Mordecai. Xerxes saw him and called him in.

As Haman walked into the room, the king waved him over and asked, "WHAT SHOULD BE DONE FOR THE MAN WHOM THE KING WISHES TO HONOR?" (vs. 6–11). What was Haman to think? Surely, he was the man to be honored, so he greedily suggested everything he wanted—royal clothes, royal authority, and the abject humiliation of all who opposed him through public exaltation. The king thought this was a brilliant idea and commissioned Haman to do all of this personally for Mordecai. Haman went through dejection and despair rapidly into depression. How could this have happened to him? Gathering with his wife and the same friends who gave him the idea of murdering Mordecai (5:14), Haman was finally faced with the truth: "IF INDEED THIS MORDECAI ... IS JEWISH, YOU WILL NOT PREVAIL AGAINST HIM. NO, YOU WILL SURELY FALL BEFORE HIM!" (vs. 13). Without even the time to process this thought, Haman was called to Esther's second banquet with the king.

Chapter seven begins with Haman having just faced the truth of his fall before Mordecai and ends with the reality of it. At Esther's second banquet, the king asked again what it was she really wanted (vs. 1–4). As she had promised, she finally spoke her mind. There was a great evil in the kingdom, unbeknownst to the king, that had threatened her life and her entire people. What was it she wanted? She asked for her life.

The king was shocked (vs. 5–7) How could this be? Who in his kingdom could have pulled off this treachery right under his nose? When Esther revealed that it was Haman, he was terrified, and the king was enraged. He stormed out of the room to walk around his garden to think. Meanwhile, Haman had thrown himself at Esther to beg for mercy, but Xerxes came back into the room only to see him lying on the couch with her (vs. 8–10). Having lost all trust in Haman, the king wondered aloud if he would dare assault her with him right there. What irony that the man who intended to exterminate all Jews was begging this Jewish woman for his own life!

The writer noted that Harbona (one of the king's trusted eunuchs named in 1:10) covered Haman's face before leading him out of the palace. To have one's face covered before the king was a sign that he was no longer welcome. Minutes ago he was second-in-command over the entire empire. Now he was the first most-wanted criminal, not worthy even to be in the king's presence. As the final nail in his coffin, Haman's plan to murder Mordecai was also revealed to the king. On the same day that the king had Mordecai rewarded for saving his own life, he discovered that Haman intended to kill Mordecai.

How much more insult could he accomplish in one day? Harbona noted that Haman planned to impale Mordecai in Haman's backyard. The king thought that was a fitting end for Haman's treachery, and he was executed that very day.

Chapter eight begins with yet another revelation for the king. Not only had Mordecai saved his life, but he was also Esther's cousin, part of the group Haman wanted to exterminate (vs. 1–8). It seems that the king took over Haman's estate, since he officially committed treason, and gave it to Esther. To Mordecai, he gave Haman's old job, Prime Minister over the empire. Although that was a wonderful turn of events, it did not solve the problem. In nine months (vs. 9), the Jewish people were still scheduled to be annihilated, so Esther once again begged for her life and the lives of her people. The problem was that Persian law could not be rescinded (vs. 8; see Daniel 6:8, 15, 17), so the king told Mordecai to write a new law, anything he wanted, to offset the previous law.

Following the same pattern as Haman, Mordecai called the official scribes to have a new law written (vs. 9–14). The wisdom of this law is astounding. Mordecai could have done anything, but all he did was give the Jews the ability to fight back and protect themselves on the day of the attack, even the women and children, who were supposed to be victims of the genocide. Using identical language as in Haman's original law (3:13), Mordecai decreed that the Jews were allowed "TO DESTROY, TO KILL, AND TO ANNIHILATE" anyone who came against them.

For the next nine months, Jews throughout the empire celebrated the new law and made preparations for their defense (vs. 15–17). The writer included an interesting note that some people even pretended to be Jews after this, apparently because they were fearful that the Jews would arbitrarily kill people when the time came.

Chapter nine is the true climax of this story; everything else simply laid the foundation for the great day of the attack. On the appointed day, there was a great war, and everyone expected that the Jews would be no match for the king's army, even though they were allowed to defend themselves (vs. 1–10). However, the greatest plot twist of them all was that the Jews were winning! Part of the reason for this was that many of the king's own men had begun to help the Jews out of fear of Mordecai. In the capital alone, the Jews killed 500 men, including Haman's ten sons.

Naturally, the king was interested in the results of the day (vs. 11–17). Upon hearing about the 500 killed in Susa and Haman's sons, he asked Esther if she had any further requests. She asked for two more things. First, she requested that the law be extended one more day, just inside the capital city. This would definitively remove any anti-Semites from the king's presence, so nothing like this could happen again. Second, she asked that Haman's sons be hung on poles for all to see and remember his treachery. The king agreed, and on the second day, the Jews killed another 300 men. Across the empire, 75,000 enemies were killed on the first day, and the Jews outside of Susa rested on the second day. The writer noted three times that, although the law allowed them to do so, the Jews did not confiscate the property of the people they killed (vs. 10, 15, 16). This was an act of grace on their part.

From this would-be genocide came a great Jewish holiday (vs. 18–32). Named after the *pur* that Haman used to decide the day of their deaths, *Purim* (the plural of *pur*) was commanded by Esther and Mordecai to be celebrated annually on the anniversary of the Jews' deliverance. For two days each year, Jewish people around the world remember their potential annihilation and subsequent rescue. This usually takes place in March, on the fourteenth and fifteenth days of Adar on the Jewish calendar (vs. 21). Celebration is to include **"BANQUETING, HAPPINESS, SENDING GIFTS TO ONE ANOTHER, AND PROVIDING FOR THE POOR"** (vs. 22). Even today, the book of Esther is read in the synagogues during Purim, with Mordecai's name often eliciting loud cheers and Haman's name being drowned out each time with booing, hissing, and other loud noises.

Chapter ten contains only three verses, a short ending to the story. King Ahasuerus reigned for another eight years (for a total of twenty years) and accomplished many great things for the Persian Empire and people, including some major construction projects. As for Mordecai, he continued to be a great ruler under Ahasuerus. Although nothing else is definitively known about him, Persian records tell of a man named *Marduka* who served this king. Since the king was assassinated, it stands to reason that Mordecai either died by that time or was also deposed in the *coup*.

Thus, the story comes to an end with the Jewish people held in high regard and free of fear, to the point that another Jew, Nehemiah, held a trusted position close to Ahasuerus' son even twenty years later (Nehemiah 1:11). Ezra 7:1 picks up the narrative only seven years after Ahasuerus' death with the second major Jewish return to Jerusalem (Ezra 7:7–8).

www.ingramcontent.com/pod-product-compliance
Lightning Source LLC
Chambersburg PA
CBHW070043080526
44586CB00013B/893

NOTES:

NOTES:

www.ingramcontent.com/pod-product-compliance
Lightning Source LLC
Chambersburg PA
CBHW070042080526
44586CB00013B/877